Introduction to the Foundations of American Education

Fourth Edition

JAMES A. JOHNSON
Northern Illinois University

HAROLD W. COLLINS
Northern Illinois University

VICTOR L. DUPUIS
Pennsylvania State University

JOHN H. JOHANSEN
Northern Illinois University

Allyn and Bacon, Inc.
Boston   London   Sydney   Toronto

PRODUCTION EDITOR: *Judith Leet*
INTERIOR DESIGNER: *Ron Kosciak*
MANUFACTURING BUYER: *Karen Mason*

Printing number and year (last digits):
10 9 8 7 6 5 4 3   85 84 83 82 81 80

Library of Congress Cataloging in Publication Data

Main entry under title:

Introduction to the foundations of American education.

  Companion vol. to Foundations of American education, readings.
  Includes bibliographies and index.
   1. Education—United States.   2. Educational sociology—United States.
3. Education—Philosophy.   4. Educational law and legislation—United States.
I. Johnson, James Allen, date–   II. Title.
Foundations of American education.
LA212.157 1979   370'.973   78-26582
ISBN 0-205-06566-X

Printed in the United States of America.

Contents

11   ORGANIZATION AND ADMINISTRATION OF PUBLIC EDUCATION 193

12   FINANCING PUBLIC EDUCATION 222

PART IV   HISTORICAL FOUNDATIONS OF EDUCATION 243

13   ANTECEDENTS TO AMERICAN EDUCATION 245

Preface

THE FOUNDATIONS OF AMERICAN EDUCATION CONSTITUTE THE very basis of professional teacher education. It is through a study of the foundations of American education that the future teacher develops an understanding of the administration of present-day schools; becomes aware of the school's role in society and of its responsibility for helping to solve our social problems; comes to appreciate the proud heritage of the teaching profession; begins to formulate a personal eduational philosophy; and develops an understanding of curricula.

This new fourth edition is divided into seven parts:

Professional Aspects of Teaching
School and Society
Control, Organization, and Support of American Education
Historical Foundations of Education
Philosophical Bases of Education
The Structuring of Educational Programs
American Education and the Future

The last part, American Education and the Future, is a recent addition to the book.

This textbook endeavors to present each foundational area factually. Each area is also documented by the views of selected authorities in the field. Convenient supplemental enrichment reading is provided in a companion volume—*Foundations of American Education: Readings, Fourth Edition*. Furthermore, the authors have constructed a teaching aid for the instructor of foundations courses in the form of a *Resource Booklet and Overhead Transparency Masters*, which is correlated with this book. In addition, three hours of audio-cassette tapes, which have been coordinated with each part of the text, are available as a teaching aid.

In creating these three volumes and the tapes, the authors have kept in mind the problems encountered by instructors of foundations of education courses and have attempted to construct a set of instructional material that is comprehensive, interesting, and timesaving for both the student and the instructor.

This book and its companion volume of readings are intended to serve as basic material for courses in the foundations of education. The correlated booklet of teaching aids should enrich such courses and allow the instructor many options.

The authors have made a deliberate attempt to make the contents of this book as direct and as easy to understand as possible. Furthermore, they have attempted to remove the foundations from the realm of theory and to present them as useful tools for the practicing educator.

The authors are indebted to the many people throughout the United States who have used the previous editions of this book and have provided valuable suggestions for this fourth edition.

JAJ
HWC
VLD
JHJ

Major Educational Issues Discussed in This Book

1. How much academic freedom and academic responsibility should teachers have?
2. What are the nature and the extent of the teacher surplus?
3. What are some of the reasons for the surplus of teachers?
4. How do the average starting salaries of public school teachers compare with the average starting salaries in private industry?
5. How do teacher salaries compare throughout the United States?
6. How has the increased recognition of student rights and responsibilities affected the work of teachers?
7. What are the rights of teachers to bargain collectively? What are the rights of teachers to strike?
8. What impact will the so-called Buckley Amendment (the law regarding the privacy of student records) have on the practices of classroom teachers?
9. Does the trend toward concentrated teacher efforts for political action represent a prudent move for teacher organizations?
10. What advantages would the merger of the NEA and AFT bring to the members of the larger organization?
11. To what extent is teaching regarded as a profession?
12. What values should public schools attempt to transmit?
13. What role should the public schools play in America's race relations problem?
14. What role should the public schools play in America's poverty problem?
15. What should the public schools do about school dropouts?
16. What responsibility does the public school have in combating crime and delinquency?

17. What role should the public schools play in combating sexism in our society?
18. To what extent should American public schools educate for international understanding and cooperation?
19. In what ways can the schools deal with drug abuse and environmental problems?
20. Who should control American public education?
21. What should be the relationship between religion and the public schools?
22. What are the rights of parents and pupils in the public schools?
23. Should state boards of education be elected or appointed?
24. Is busing a feasible way to bring about integration? Why?
25. How should public schools be organized and administered?
26. How should public schools be financed?
27. Can equality of opportunity be achieved?
28. Of what value is the study of the history of education?
29. To what extent can contemporary American educators learn from schools of the past?
30. What are the colonial antecedents for the education of American blacks?
31. How did private education in the United States begin?
32. What are the highlights of the history of black education in America?
33. What story does the history of the education of women tell us?
34. What kinds of teacher needs are related to the study of educational philosophy?
35. Which educational philosophy has the most to offer contemporary American public education?
36. What does *existentialism* offer as an educational philosophy?
37. What are the limitations of *experimentalism* as an educational philosophy?
38. What are the distinctions between traditional and progressive educational philosophy? Between a traditional and a progressive classroom?
39. How does mainstreaming legislation create *due process* concerns for all types of learners in the school?
40. How do societal values affect the role of today's school?
41. What is the subculture of the school, and how does the teacher cope with it?
42. What changes in values have taken place in American society during the last three decades?
43. How has career education increased significantly in American schools?
44. What are the major areas of social need that the federal government has supported financially by the establishment of nationwide educational programs?

45. How has the *back-to-basics* movement affected the schools' program?
46. How are patterns of curriculum organization affected by social desires and national goals?
47. How does a particular school district determine which innovative practices to incorporate within its program?
48. What will be the impact of the increase in early childhood programs on the school curriculum?
49. How do both norm-referenced and criterion-referenced data collection assist in program evaluation?
50. How are minimal competency standards in the curriculum related to accountability?
51. Can the people of the world determine a preferable future?
52. What role is education likely to play in the future?
53. What family life-styles are likely to prevail in the future?
54. How will education be financed in the future?

PART I

Professional Aspects of Teaching

Considerable data support the contention that education is the largest enterprise in the United States. Of the 214 million people in our population, more than three out of every ten are directly involved in the educational process. Formal education was recently reported as a full-time activity involving about 63 million people as either students or teachers and administrators— more than one person in four. Educational opportunities are offered by more than 100,-000 elementary and secondary schools, more than 3,000 colleges and universities, 8,000 noncollegiate and technical schools, as well as numerous sponsors of adult education activities.[1]

The magnitude of the educational enterprise may be further expanded if the millions of people who are indirectly involved in education-related occupations are included. Consider alone, for example, the many people employed by the automotive industry who manufacture the various vehicles needed by the schools. Consider those

employed in the construction and related trades involved in the construction and maintenance of school buildings and grounds. Various research and development employees work at education-related tasks. In addition, employees of paper manufacturers, printing concerns, and publishing companies, as well as manufacturers of various other instructional and material resources used by the schools, swell the ranks of those indirectly involved in the educational enterprise.

Some recent trends, however, indicate that an overall reduction in the magnitude of education may be under way. Declining birth rates suggest that zero population growth is close at hand. These declining birth rates have prompted most school districts to engage in careful examinations of their local growth projections. Enrollment data from 1965, projected through 1985 for the entire United States, illustrate the decline in public school pupil population for both the elementary schools and the high schools. In the public elementary schools, enrollments increased sharply from approximately 30,500,000 pupils in 1965 to

1. Mary A. Golladay, *The Condition of Education* (Washington, D.C.: U.S. Government Printing Office, 1977), p. 2.

a peak enrollment of approximately 32,-500,000 pupils in 1969—a 6 percent gain. Elementary enrollments have declined sharply since 1969 to approximately 30,-500,000 pupils in 1975 (the same as the 1965 level—or a 6 percent loss), and are projected to decline further to approximately 28,800,000 by 1985—another 6 percent loss.

During this same period, enrollments in the public high schools increased steadily from approximately 11,600,000 pupils in 1965 to a peak enrollment of approximately 14,300,000 pupils in 1976—a 19 percent gain. Public high school enrollments are now declining, with enrollments projected to be approximately 11,900,000 by 1985 (close to the 1965 enrollment level—a 17 percent loss). In addition to the apparent stabilization of public school enrollments, many educational planners are also projecting an eventual stabilization of school expenditures. While the growth rate is stabilizing for the public schools, the entire field of education will continue to be one of the largest employment fields in our nation.

Teachers represent the foundation of the educational system. While the total number of persons qualified to teach continues to increase, the rate of increase has declined. Increasing percentages of teachers holding advanced degrees indicate that teachers of today are better prepared academically than were their predecessors. At the same time, teacher concerns have broadened to an unprecedented degree: topics such as teacher supply and demand, teacher salaries, academic freedom, student rights, tenure, professional liability, professional organizations for educators, and teacher unions are typical present-day concerns that were probably not included in former teacher-preparation programs. These concerns have contributed greatly to the complexity of the teaching profession.

Teachers have increased opportunities for changes in career direction—to move from regular classroom matters to such specialty areas as supervision of instruction, school administration, guidance and counseling, business management, special education, and so forth. This kind of change in an educator's career often requires additional training or advanced degrees, coupled with additional certification requirements.

These and other aspects of the teaching profession warrant early discussion in a book of this kind, designed to discuss the foundations of American education. It is hoped that Part I will provide the prospective teacher with an awareness of some of the professional aspects of teaching.

CHAPTER 1

Teaching as a Career

AFTER ONE HAS SPENT SEVERAL YEARS—AS EACH OF THE AUTHORS has—enjoying the rewards and pleasures associated with a chosen professional career, it is tempting to write only about the positive qualities of that career—in this case, teaching. Given satisfaction with one's chosen career, it also becomes easy to dwell on the positive to the extent that a Pollyannaish tone emerges. In fact, certain critics of teacher-preparation programs have clamored for a more hard-nosed "tell it as it is" approach, which would give equal attention to the frustrations, problems, and traumas associated with a teaching career. It is not the purpose of this introductory chapter to cover all possible positive and negative aspects of teaching. Rather, the purpose is to present selected, significant dimensions of teaching as a career. It will come as no surprise to the reader that the biases of the authors tend to support the career choice of teaching as an excellent choice.

Profile of the Public School Teacher

Although there is no single set of average statistics to which a beginning teacher can attach major significance, average statistics for currently practicing teachers are helpful in building a profile of the public school teacher. Such a profile becomes helpful in viewing the middle-ground characteristics of teacher groups such as those the beginner will eventually be joining.

During the 1976–77 school year, the average public school teacher had taught for twelve years, nine of which were in the same school system. The elementary school teacher taught an average of 25 pupils during the day. The secondary school teacher taught a total of 131 pupils daily in five class periods. All but .7 percent of the classroom teachers had at least a bachelor's degree. Table 1–1 gives the characteristics that describe the average public school teacher in the 1976–77 school year.

Table 1–1. The average public school teacher, school year 1976–77.

Item	All Teachers	Elementary		Secondary		
		Total	Women	Total	Men	Women
1	2	3	4	5	6	7
Years of experience	12	13	13	11	12	10
Years in system of present employment	9	9	9	8	9	7
Average number of pupils taught per day		25	25	131	131	132
Classes per day—departmentalized	5	6	6	5	5	5
Salary	$13,016	$12,759	$12,569	$13,289	$14,278	$12,198
Highest degree held						
None	0.7%	0.7%	0.8%	0.8%	1.1%	0.4%
Bachelor's	56.6	61.1	64.0	51.6	43.1	61.0
Master's & Ed.S.	42.5	38.0	35.2	47.5	55.4	38.7
Doctor's	0.2	0.2	—	0.2	0.4	—

Source: Annual Survey of Teacher Members, 1976–77. Research Report. National Education Association, Washington, D.C. Reprinted by permission.

In addition to the data in Table 1–1, another National Education Association (NEA) survey of its members reported that today's teacher is younger, better educated, better paid—and more fed up with the job—than ever before. The average teacher is now thirty-three years old, compared to forty-one in 1961, and has ten years of experience. The percentage of teachers with twenty or more years of experience is half what it was fifteen years ago (down from 28 percent in 1961 to 14 percent in 1976).[1]

Educators in the Schools

Teachers.   Obviously most of today's schools are complex organizations in which the expertise of various specialized educators is utilized to serve the pupils' educational needs during the school day. Of central importance to the daily operations of our schools is the classroom teacher. The following statement, although formulated in the late sixties, expresses eloquently the nature of the teacher's function.

> The stereotype of the public school teacher as a patient, overworked, and unsophisticated maiden lady is laughably unrealistic, and no new stereotype can be invented to take its place. Many generalizations about the nature of teaching also are quickly becoming outdated. It is no longer necessarily true that a teacher is badly paid, has a three-month vacation every year, is solely responsible for a roomful of students all day or every hour, refrains from political activity, or can advance only by becoming an administrator. Each of these conditions still exists in many school systems, but each has been replaced in many others because of the changes in the concepts of the function of education and the best ways to fulfill that function. Professional negotiation between school boards and staff organizations, an 11- or 12-month school year, team teaching and role differentiation, and assumption of social responsibility have already exploded the boundaries of the self-contained classroom and self-contained school. The range of functions, salaries, and working conditions in regular nonpublic day schools . . . is even greater than in the public schools.
>
> The public school teacher today has many roles, some of them newly emphasized. In his classes, he serves as counselor and guide to his students. He is a bearer of the culture, passing on to his students what he has received from his background and education and learning from them in turn. He administers the educational program of the school in his classes and contributes to it his own expertise. He represents and explains the school to the community and promotes the relevance of the school to its students and to society. He maintains his professional ability at a high level and contributes to the advancement of the teaching profession.
>
> The major function of the teacher, however, is still to confront students face-to-face and use his intelligence, perceptiveness, and professional skill to develop in them the ability to reason, the habit of using that ability, and the knowledge necessary to relate that ability to the requirements of their lives. The ways in which he does this vary from level to level of education,

1. National School Public Relations Association, *Education U.S.A.,* 11 July 1977, p. 335.

from system to system, from school to school, and from teacher to teacher—and they are constantly changing. . . .

The changes teachers are working for are far from universally accomplished. Whether a teacher is satisfied with his role depends on his own conception of that role and on the degree to which that conception is shared by the school administration, the school board, and the local community. The teacher may be considered a responsible, intelligent, highly educated, and well-informed individual capable of creating, in cooperation with other staff members, a design for educating the children assigned him, as well as of carrying out such a design. He may be considered a dependent, unimaginative, and minimally educated employee whose work and welfare must be cared for by a benevolent administration—a babysitter with a bachelor's degree. He may be considered a radical on his own behalf, whose involvement with others, including students, is incidental. There are many broad conceptions of who the teacher is and many gradations within each conception. The teacher's idea of himself may differ greatly from the ideas of the administration and the community, but he is increasingly able, by his professional behavior and through professional organizations, to influence the views of others.[2]

Educational Specialists.   As the public schools have become more complex, many new specialized positions have developed for educators in the schools. The range of specialized occupations in the schools present opportunities for both prospective and regular classroom teachers to further their careers by obtaining additional preparation in a specialized area. Certificated educational specialists work with the handicapped to overcome hearing, seeing, and speaking problems—or with students who have other physical, mental, or emotional handicaps. Specialists work as academic and vocational counselors, as librarians and learning resource directors, as teachers of students who have learning difficulties, and as teachers of bilingual students. Some schools are fortunate enough to have specialists assist with music, fine arts, and athletics—and to develop programs for the gifted students. While many of these specialists work for the most part as classroom teachers, each has had additional preparation to qualify for the specific and specialized teaching assignment.

Auxiliary Personnel.   The use of auxiliary personnel, generally known as teacher aides, is increasing in the schools. Nonprofessional workers may supervise lunchrooms and playgrounds, or they may assist with homework, seat work, record keeping, bulletin board displays, small group work, and assorted related tasks. The education and experience required of auxiliary personnel vary with the tasks they perform. The number of auxiliary personnel is determined, for the most part, by the financial resources of the school system. When particular school

2.   National Commission on Teacher Education and Professional Standards. *Careers in Education* (Washington, D.C.: NEA, 1968) pp. 3–5. Reprinted by permission.

Teaching as a career can be very rewarding. (*Photograph courtesty of HUD*)

systems face financial difficulties, the ranks of auxiliary personnel are usually the first to be reduced.

Supervision and Administration.   The management of complex educational organizations requires supervisory and administrative personnel. The primary responsibility for supervisors in the schools is to ensure the maintenance of high-quality instruction. To this end, supervisors are usually responsible for providing inservice programs to keep teachers informed about new methods and innovative materials associated with successful teaching.

The principalship and the superintendency are among the more familiar careers in educational administration; other administrator careers are related to business management, school personnel, pupil personnel services, curriculum, and buildings and grounds. The various positions in educational administration usually provide the greatest opportunity for twelve-month employment—thus the greatest opportunity for higher salaries.

This simplistic overview of the job opportunities in teaching at least provides the prospective teacher with the conceptual notion that teaching can be expanded in several ways. Career adjustments and mobility can be planned and carried out at many stages of a teaching career. One hopes that much-needed bright, young students will continue to aspire to become teachers.

Teaching: A Profession or a Semiprofession?

Although it seems unlikely that prospective teachers would be greatly concerned about whether teaching is regarded as a profession or a semiprofession, occupational status is of some importance to most people. The report of the Bicentennial Commission on Education for the Profession of Teaching of the American Association of Colleges for Teacher Education provides the following discussion:

> In the hierarchical structuring of occupations within our society, the professions occupy the top position. Quite naturally, occupations strive to as high a position within the hierarchy as they can possibly achieve. The word *profession* has been self-applied to many occupations, especially in modern times. Opting to use the name does not, however, insure that the status of profession will thereby be achieved.[3]

CHARACTERISTICS OF A PROFESSION

As is often the case in societal matters, criteria used by the society in determining occupational status tend to be obscure and imprecise. Students of occupations—notably sociologists—have devoted their attention to discerning and stating the criteria, however. The list of characteristics which follows is a composite drawn from a variety of authoritative sources.[4]

1. Professions are occupationally related social institutions established and maintained as a means of providing essential services to the individual and the society.

2. Each profession is concerned with an identified area of need or function (e.g., maintenance of physical and emotional health, preservation of rights and freedom, enhancing the opportunity to learn).

3. The profession collectively, and the professional individually, possesses a body of knowledge and a repertoire of behaviors and skills (professional culture) needed in the practice of the profession; such knowledge, behavior, and skills normally are not possessed by the nonprofessional.

4. The members of the profession are involved in decision making in the service of the client, the decisions being made in accordance with the most valid knowledge available, against a background of principles and theories, and within the context of possible impact on other related conditions or decisions.

5. The profession is based on one or more undergirding disciplines from which it draws basic insights and upon which it builds its own applied knowledge and skills.

6. The profession is organized into one or more professional associations which, within broad limits of social accountability, are granted autonomy in control of the actual work of the profession and the conditions

3. Robert Howsam, Dean C. Corrigan, George W. Denemark, and Robert J. Nash, *Educating a Profession* (Washington, D.C.: American Association of Colleges for Teacher Education, 1976), pp. 6–9.
4. C. Argyris and D. A. Schon, *Theory in Practice* (San Francisco: Jossey-Bass, 1974); E. H. Schein, *Professional Education* (New York: McGraw-Hill, 1972).

which surround it (admissions, educational standards, examination and licensing, career line, ethical and performance standards, professional discipline).

7. The profession has agreed-upon performance standards for admission to the profession and for continuance within it.

8. Preparation for and induction to the profession is provided through a protracted preparation program, usually in a professional school on a college or university campus.

9. There is a high level of public trust and confidence in the profession and in individual practitioners, based upon the profession's demonstrated capacity to provide service markedly beyond that which would otherwise be available.

10. Individual practitioners are characterized by a strong service motivation and lifetime commitment to competence.

11. Authority to practice in any individual case derives from the client or the employing organization; accountability for the competence of professional practice within the particular case is to the profession itself.

12. There is relative freedom from direct on-the-job supervision and from direct public evaluation of the individual practitioner. The professional accepts responsibility in the name of his or her profession and is accountable through his or her profession to the society.

CHARACTERISTICS OF SEMIPROFESSIONS

In addition to the classic professions of law, medicine, theology, and university teaching and to newer professions such as architecture, engineering, and optometry, there is a much longer list of occupations which aspire to professional status. Some of these can be dismissed as pretenders. Others are somewhere near the periphery of professional status on the basis of the criteria specified earlier. Because they are dynamically developing and approaching societal and professional acceptance, these may be described *as emergent professions.* (Figure 1 indicates the categories or levels of professions to which reference is made.) They are about to become professions. . . .

The semiprofessions are occupations which sociologists have chosen to define as meeting some of the criteria of professions, but not others. . . .

These characteristics, supplemented by others drawn from different sources, constitute a list of 12 characteristics of semiprofessions. In most cases, the characteristic is expressed in terms of the degree to which semiprofessions meet the criteria of mature professions as listed earlier.

1. Lower in occupational status.
2. Shorter training periods.
3. Lack of societal acceptance that the nature of the service and/or the level of expertise justifies the autonomy which is granted to the professions.
4. A less specialized and less highly developed body of knowledge and skills.
5. Markedly less emphasis on theoretical and conceptual bases for practice.

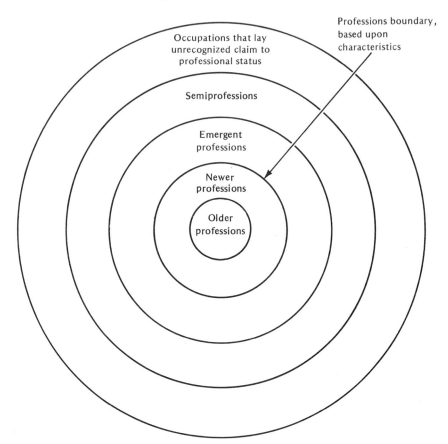

Figure 1.   Levels of professions

6. A tendency for the professional to identify with the employment institution more and with the profession less. (Note that it is not the condition of employment rather than private practice which makes the difference. Rather it is the identity relationship.)
7. More subject to administrative and supervisory surveillance and control.
8. Less autonomy in professional decision making with accountability to superiors rather than to the profession.
9. Management of organizations within which semiprofessionals are employed by persons who have themselves been prepared and served in that semiprofession.
10. A preponderance of women.
11. Absence of the right of privileged communication between client and professional.
12. Little or no involvement in matters of life and death.

It should be pointed out that the classification of professions into "full" and "semi" categories is primarily an analytic exercise which, however, does appear to represent reality rather closely. In this sense it has great utility. On the other hand, the distinctions do not appear as clearly in practice. The semiprofessions as categorized by sociologists often are recognized in state law as professions and granted licensure and even professional practices privileges.

It seems apparent from the previous discussion that teaching might best be viewed as an emergent profession. A significant characteristic of teaching, which might contribute to its semiprofessional designation, is the relatively short training period required before a beginner enters the teaching ranks. However, most teachers now continue formal schooling in advanced degree programs; and during their careers many teachers often spend as much time in formal training activities as members of the more mature professions.

Summary and Implications

From the outset, the authors wish to stress their belief that teaching is not an appropriate career choice for everyone. For those who possess the prerequisites of commitment to education, the adequate personal and social skills, and the basic ability to develop the technical skills, a teaching career would be an excellent choice. Teaching provides opportunities for one to work with other college-trained individuals, each committed to the education of young people. Within the career frame-

A teacher has the opportunity to stimulate and challenge the young student. (*Photograph by Talbot Lovering*)

work, many avenues are available for teachers to specialize, to modify their career orientation, or to seek well-paying supervisory or administrative positions.

In addition, teaching is for the most part an emergent profession—with the potential for developing into a full profession. Perhaps one of the greatest challenges remaining for contemporary educators is to develop a body of recognized professional standards. Thus far, there has not been a consensus among educators on the development of appropriate technical skills that all teachers should master. As prospective teachers join in the development of these professional and technical skills, the career of teaching will further develop toward becoming a full profession.

Discussion Questions

1. Of the teachers you have had, what characteristics appear most important for being a successful teacher? Are there differences between elementary and secondary teachers? Secondary and college teachers?

2. What work aspects make teaching a good career choice? A poor career choice?

3. Many college students consider heavily future job availability in making career choices. Why would this be a poor criterion for selecting a teaching career? How would you defend this criterion for selecting a teaching career?

4. Over the years it has been commonly suggested that teaching offers job security. Does this belief have merit today? Why is job security a worthy consideration for making a career choice?

5. Since the average starting salaries of classroom teachers are less than the average starting salaries of graduates with bachelors' degrees who are employed in industry, there must be other advantages for selecting teaching as a career. What are some of these advantages? How would you make up for the economic limitations associated with teaching? Or are the alleged economic limitations for teachers exaggerated? Discuss.

Supplemental Activities

1. Invite a career counselor to your class to discuss the pros and cons of teaching as a career.

2. Poll a group of retired teachers regarding the advice they would have for prospective teachers.

3. Write to your state teachers' association for materials about the career of teaching. Ask about employment opportunities, working conditions, retirement benefits, and the like.

4. Arrange for a panel of teachers (elementary, secondary, college) to discuss with your class the working life of today's teachers. Discuss problems encountered with school administrators.

5. Arrange for a panel of school administrators (elementary, secondary, college) to discuss with your class the working life of today's teachers. Discuss problems encountered with classroom teachers.

Bibliography

Carnoy, Martin. "The Role of Education in a Strategy for Social Change." *Comparative Education Review* (October 1975): 393–402.

Corkhuff, Robert R., and Pierce, Richard M. *Teacher as Person.* Washington, D.C.: National Education Association, 1976.

"Experienced Teachers Giving Up." *Education U.S.A.,* July 1977, pp. 335, 340.

Gallup, George H. "Tenth Annual Gallup Poll of the Public Attitudes Toward the Public Schools." *Phi Delta Kappan* (September 1978): 33–45.

Lopate, Phillip. *Being With Children.* New York: Doubleday, 1975.

Murphy, Mary Kay. "Getting a Jump on Career Choices." *American Education* (June 1973): 18–23.

National Education Association. *Financial Status of the Public Schools, 1977.* Washington, D.C.: NEA, 1977.

Teaching as a Career. Washington, D.C.: American Federation of Teachers, AFL-CIO, n.d.

Toombs, William. "Developing Today's Faculty for Tomorrow's Students." *The Educational Forum* (March 1977): 365–372.

Weigland, James E. *Developing Teacher Competencies.* Englewood Cliffs, N.J.: Prentice-Hall, 1971.

CHAPTER 2

Teacher Supply and Demand

THE POPULATION OF STUDENTS IN THE PUBLIC SCHOOLS GREW steadily for twenty-seven consecutive years before reaching an all-time high of 59.7 million students in the fall of 1971. At roughly the same time, annual decreases at the elementary level became apparent by 1970, with the decreases beginning at the high school level in 1976. However, the number of new teachers graduating from college, as well as the number of former teachers ready to reenter the teaching profession, continued to increase. In a very short time, the teacher shortage in the sixties changed to a general teacher surplus in the seventies. While enrollment declines are projected to continue into the early eighties, corresponding decreases in pupil-teacher ratios are expected to offset the enrollment decreases and to stabilize the teacher surplus problem. The stabilization of the educational enterprise projected for the eighties will enable prospective teachers to make more dependable plans for entering the profession. In addition, the dramatic reduction in teacher-preparation programs over the last few years indicates that those who persist in their desire to become teachers will be among a select group of prospective employees.

Nature and Extent of the Teacher Surplus

There is considerable debate in education circles about the exact nature and extent of the oversupply of teachers. Although the supply of beginning teachers has been declining dramatically, other factors related to teacher demand need to be analyzed. Increasing overall school costs, which limit the amount that pupil-teacher ratios can be lowered, are another factor that impinges upon the availability of teacher positions. Since alternative employment opportunities for teachers have also decreased, the rate of teacher turnover has decreased and thus the number of openings for new teachers has been reduced. The nature and extent of the teacher surplus for the years ahead will continue to be related to pupil-teacher ratios, teacher turnover, student enrollment, availability of new teachers, and general economic conditions. In addition, continued development of early retirement incentive programs, coupled with predicted increases in birthrates for the mid-eighties, could conceivably turn the mid-seventies teacher surplus to a mid-eighties teacher shortage.

In a report issued by the U.S. Department of Health, Education, and Welfare, entitled *Projections of Teacher Supply and Demand to 1980–81*, the effects of high, intermediate, and low teacher turnover were considered in relation to the demand for new teachers. As shown in Figure 2–1, the projections for 1980–81 of the excess supply in relation to the demand for new teachers range from 80,400 (based on a high rate of teacher turnover) to 149,400 (based on a low rate of teacher turnover), with an intermediate projection of 123,400 (based on an intermediate rate of teacher turnover).

The supply of new teachers is usually derived from the number of graduates who have recently received a degree qualifying them to teach. There will continue to be a steady increase in the number of graduates with bachelors' degrees into the eighties. However, when all the fields of study are compared, education will probably be one of the fields with a most noteworthy decline. The number of degrees granted in education is expected to decrease from approximately 300,000 in 1971–72 to 162,050 in 1975–76 to 136,770 in 1985–86. Other fields that will probably show nearly continuous decreases during the next ten years will be social sciences, foreign languages, and humanities. Of all the fields of study, the number of bachelors' degrees granted in the health professions has made the most notable increase in the past ten years.

Classroom Teachers and Pupil-Teacher Ratios

Figure 2–2 and Table 2–1 show the number of classroom teachers in regular elementary and secondary day schools by institutional control and organizational level in the United States from 1965 to 1975—with projections through 1985.

Table 2–2 shows the decrease in pupil-teacher ratios from 1965 through 1975. The projected pupil-teacher ratios are based on the assumption that the ratio of enrollment to the number of teachers will follow the 1965–1975 trend right up to 1985.

The number of classroom teachers in public elementary schools increased from 965,000 in 1965 to 1,183,000 in 1975 primarily as a result of decreased pupil-teacher ratios (from 27.6 in 1965 to 21.7 in 1974). Although enrollments in public elementary schools are expected to decrease by nearly 1.8 million students by 1980, corresponding decreases in pupil-teacher ratios are expected to offset the enrollment decreases, resulting in a level of about 1,125,000 teachers through 1980. By 1985, the pupil-teacher ratio is expected to have decreased to 19.4,

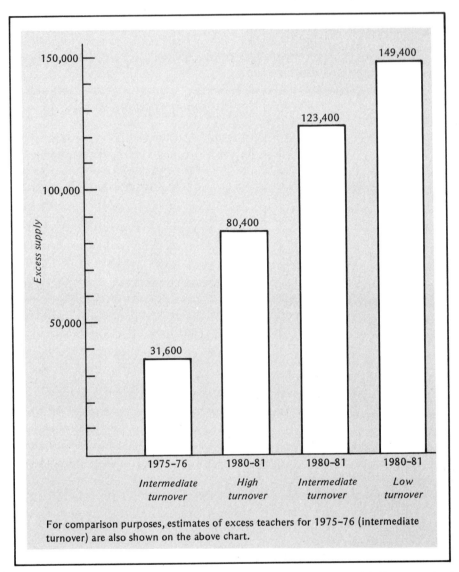

Figure 2–1. Range of excess teacher supply projections.

For comparison purposes, estimates of excess teachers for 1975–76 (intermediate turnover) are also shown on the above chart.

Source: Projections of Teacher Supply and Demand to 1980–81. U.S. Department of Health, Education, and Welfare.

which, along with increased enrollments, will account for an increase to 1,299,000 classroom teachers in public elementary schools.

The number of classroom teachers in public secondary schools increased from 748,000 in 1965 to 1,019,000 in 1975 as a result of large enrollment increases (15.5 million in 1965 to 18.7 million in 1974) and significant reductions in the pupil-teacher ratio (from 20.3 in 1965 to 18.8 in 1975). For the next few years, the number of teachers in public secondary schools is expected to increase slightly as enrollment remains

Figure 2–2. Classroom teachers in regular elementary and secondary day schools, by institutional control and organizational level: United States, fall 1965 to 1985.

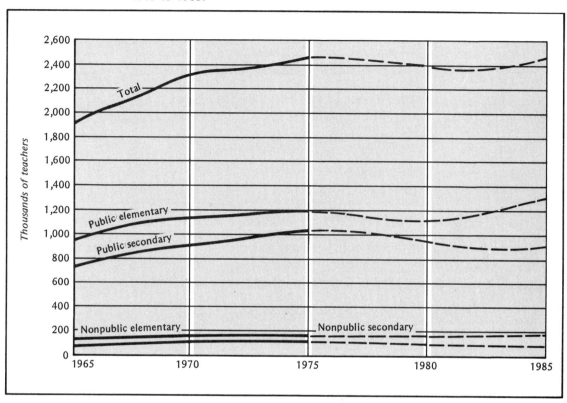

Source: National Center for Education Statistics, Washington, D.C., 1977.

Table 2–1. Classroom teachers in regular elementary and secondary day schools, by institutional control and organizational level: United States, fall 1965 to 1985 (in thousands).

Year (fall)	Total Public and Nonpublic			Public			Nonpublic (estimated)		
	K-12	Elementary	Secondary	K-12	Elementary	Secondary	K-12	Elementary	Secondary
1965	1,933	1,112	822	1,710	965	746	223	147	76
1970	2,288	1,281	1,007	2,055	1,128	927	233	153	80
1975	2,463	1,354	1,109	2,203	1,183	1,019	261	171	90
Projected									
1980	2,405	1,362	1,043	2,122	1,174	948	283	188	95
1985	2,484	1,498	986	2,188	1,299	889	296	199	97

Source: National Center for Education Statistics, Washington, D.C., 1977.

Table 2–2. Pupil-teacher ratios in regular elementary and secondary day schools, by institutional control and organizational level: United States, fall 1965 to 1985.

Year (fall)	Public		Nonpublic (estimated)	
	Elementary	Secondary	Elementary	Secondary
1965	27.6	20.8	33.5	18.1
1970	24.4	19.8	26.5	16.4
1975	21.7	18.8	22.8	15.5
Projected				
1980	20.4	18.1	20.7	14.8
1985	19.4	17.5	19.6	14.5

Source: National Center for Education Statistics, Washington, D.C., 1977.

fairly stable and pupil-teacher ratios continue to decrease. However, sharp enrollment drops expected in the early 1980s will be too large to be offset by decreasing pupil-teacher ratios, and, as a result, the number of teachers in public secondary schools for 1985 is expected to be 889,000 (130,000 fewer than in 1975).

The number of classroom teachers in nonpublic elementary schools

The demand for minority teachers will exceed the supply. (*Photograph by Frank Siteman, Stock, Boston*)

increased from 147,000 in 1965 to 171,000 in 1975, even though enrollment in these schools has decreased by an estimated one million students. The increase in the number of teachers occurred because the large decreases in enrollment were more than offset by a sharp reduction in pupil-teacher ratios—from 33.5 in 1965 to 22.8 in 1975. It is estimated that all of the decreases in enrollment and corresponding reductions in the pupil-teacher ratios occurred in Catholic elementary schools, which made up 89 percent of nonpublic elementary enrollment in 1965 and 65 percent in 1975. It is expected that pupil-teacher ratios will continue to decrease while enrollments remain the same, resulting in an increase in the number of teachers in nonpublic elementary schools from 171,000 in 1975 to 199,000 in 1985.

The number of teachers in nonpublic secondary schools increased from 76,000 in 1965 to 90,000 in 1975 and is expected to be 97,000 in 1985. All of the past and present increases in the number of these teachers is attributable to reductions in pupil-teacher ratios, since enrollment in nonpublic secondary schools has remained at about 1,400,000 students from 1965 to 1975 and is expected to remain at this level through 1985.

Teacher Demand   Although there are undoubtedly additional factors that help account for the current oversupply of teachers, three major factors—new teachers entering the job market, restricted school budgets, and lower birth rates—probably account for the bulk of the current teacher surplus. Obviously lower birth rates result in a decline of the school-age populations. Figure 2–3 illustrates the resulting decline in the elementary school-age population through at least 1980, with the possibility of slight increases by 1985. The high-school-age population has now started to decrease; this decrease is projected to continue through 1985. The young adult population (18 to 21 years) will continue to grow through 1980, then decline slightly by 1985.

Although declining enrollments obviously work to reduce the demand for new teachers, additional new teachers will continue to be needed to accommodate lower pupil-teacher ratios and to offset teacher turnover. Table 2–3 shows the total demand for additional public elementary and secondary school teachers (not employed in the public schools the previous year) including those needed to allow for enrollment changes, for lowering pupil-teacher ratios, and for replacement of teachers leaving the profession. During the period 1971 to 1975, the cumulative demand for additional public school teachers (including returnees to the profession) was estimated at 778,000. After decreasing to 574,000 from 1976 to 1980, the cumulative demand is expected to increase to 702,000 from 1981 to 1985. Therefore, about 1.3 million new teachers or returnees to the profession are expected to be employed by the public schools from 1976 to 1985.

Figure 2–3. School- and college-age population, with alternatives: United States, October 1965 to 1985.

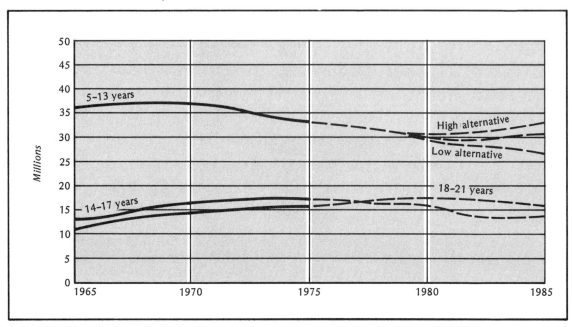

Source: National Center for Education Statistics, Washington, D.C., 1977.

The projected demand for additional public school teachers is shown in Table 2–3. The number of teachers necessary to take care of enrollment changes and pupil-teacher ratio changes was computed for each year as the difference between the total employed for the current year and the total employed for the previous year. The number for turnover was based on the assumption that 6 percent of the total classroom teachers will leave the profession temporarily or permanently each year.

Studies made by the U.S. Commissioner of Labor Statistics suggest that supply and demand predictions are always tenuous in our rapidly changing society and that the supply-demand relationship is likely to be affected by a number of unpredictable adjustments. With labor supply constraints lifted, more communities may introduce or expand kindergartens, nursery schools, and curricula for the handicapped and for the gifted. In addition, as the supply of teachers improves, local school officials may feel they can improve the quality of education by hiring additional teachers to reduce class size. The resulting effect on requirements for teachers could be very significant.

Yet another prediction of the future teacher supply and demand, made by William S. Graybeal of the Research Division of the National Education Association, is presented in Figure 2–4. This figure shows that

Table 2–3. Estimated demand for classroom teachers in regular public elementary and secondary day schools: United States, fall 1970 to 1985 (in thousands).

| Year (fall) | Total Teacher Demand | Demand for Additional Certificated Teachers | | | |
		Total	For Enrollment Changes	For Pupil-Teacher Ratio Changes	For Teacher Turnover
(1)	(2)	(3)	(4)	(5)	(6)
1970	2,055	. . .	. . .	. . .	. . .
1971	2,063	131	9	−1	123
1972	2,103	164	−12	52	124
1973	2,138	161	−7	42	126
1974	2,165	155	−19	46	128
1975	2,203	167	−4	41	130
1971–75	. . .	778	−33	180	631
Projected					
1976	2,208	138	−22	28	132
1977	2,197	121	−33	22	132
1978	2,175	109	−44	22	131
1979	2,149	104	−48	22	130
1980	2,122	102	−44	17	129
1976–80	. . .	574	−191	111	654
1981	2,111	116	−32	21	127
1982	2,106	122	−22	17	127
1983	2,120	140	−4	18	126
1984	2,149	156	11	18	127
1985	2,188	168	21	18	129
1981–85	. . .	702	−26	92	636

Source: National Center for Education Statistics, Washington, D.C., 1977.

there were varying degrees of a teacher shortage during the 1950s and 1960s and predicts a growing oversupply of teachers throughout the 1970s to a point at which there will be approximately 275 percent more beginning teachers than jobs available by the end of this decade.

The NEA quickly goes on to point out, however, that the teacher surplus would disappear quickly if our society wanted high-quality education badly enough to pay the taxes necessary to support it. In other words, if the pupil-teacher ratio were to be lowered significantly, all the surplus teachers would be absorbed quickly into the schools. It is even conceivable that, if such a trend were to become pronounced,

Figure 2–4. Supply of beginning teachers as percent of normal demand, 1952 to 1979, according to present trends.

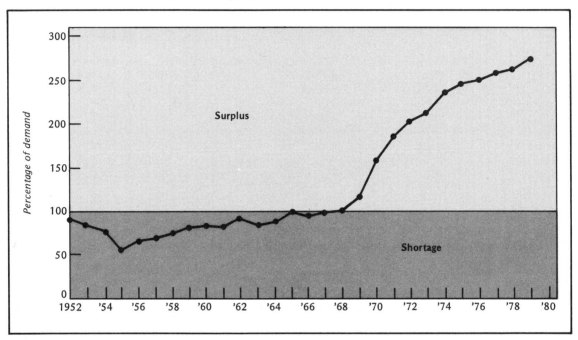

Source: William S. Graybeal, "Teacher Surplus and Teacher Shortage," *Phi Delta Kappan* (October 1971): p. 83. Used by permission.

there might be a significant shortage of teachers in the next decade. Unfortunately most authorities do not believe that the average taxpayer is willing to pay for such an improved public school system.

Teacher Surplus— Good or Bad?

Depending upon one's viewpoint, there are a number of good things and a number of bad things about the current teacher surplus.

If you are a recent college graduate looking for a teaching position, you would naturally view the surplus as bad if you could not find a job. Many people also feel that the teacher surplus is at least partially brought about by the shortage of funds made available to the school districts. There is little doubt that the surplus teachers in this country could substantially improve American education if the school districts could afford to hire them. Some teachers who have lost their jobs, after acquiring a year or two of experience, feel that the teacher surplus is bad because school districts tend to hire beginning, less well-paid teachers to fill vacancies.

On the other hand, there are a number of good things about the teacher surplus. During the 1950s and 1960s, school districts had to hire many poorly prepared teachers because of the shortage of fully certified

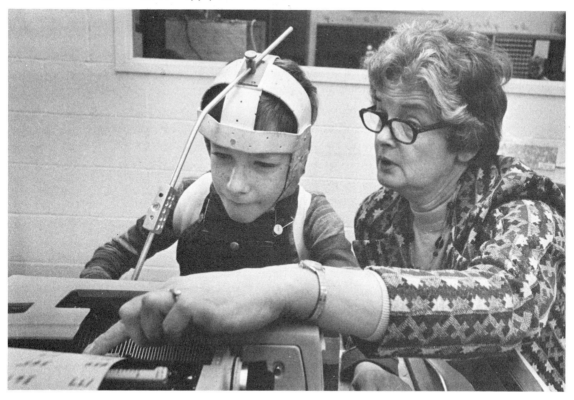

Handicapped children are given specialized attention by trained personnel. (*Photograph by George Bellerose, Stock, Boston*)

teachers. The current surplus will make it possible for districts not only to hire fully certified teachers but also to be selective from among such teachers. The current oversupply of well-qualified teachers should also make it possible for school districts to replace substandard and provisionally certified teachers they may have employed. Yet another good thing about the teacher surplus is that it should provide some relief for colleges and universities that have been struggling during the years of teacher shortage to turn out enough teachers for the nation's classrooms. Many teacher educators are hopeful that the end of the teacher shortage will now permit colleges and universities to concentrate on producing fewer teachers of higher quality—rather than simply turning out large numbers.

Minority Teachers— Equity and Parity   Recent attempts of teacher organizations to lower the pupil-teacher ratio appear to be concentrated on "equity and parity" for minority teachers. A recent issue of *Education Daily* quoted an NEA official as follows:

> To reach the national student-teacher ratio of 22.5 to 1, schools would have to hire about 116,000 more blacks, 84,500 more Spanish-speaking, 7,400

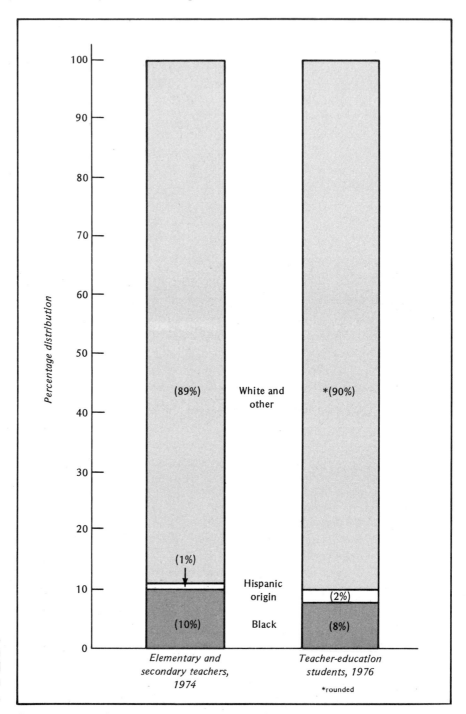

Source: National Center for Education Statistics, Washington, D.C., 1977.

Figure 2–5.
Racial composition
of teachers and
teacher-education
students.

more American Indians, and 3,000 more Asians, according to NEA Teachers' Rights Program Director Samuel Ethridge. And the biggest problems, Ethridge told a recent Association for the Study of Afro-American Life and History convention in New York, are in the North.

Although it may be simple for teacher organization officials to make blanket statements regarding equity and parity for minority teachers, Figure 2–5 highlights a significant fact that precludes accomplishing this task immediately. It appears that a somewhat smaller percentage of teacher-education students than teachers generally are from minority groups and that the minority pool of teacher-education students is not adequate for projected needs. Teacher organizations should increase efforts to encourage ethnic minority students to pursue teaching as a career choice.

Special Education Personnel   The development of programs designed for training teachers to meet special education needs will be helped somewhat by the surplus of teachers. The 12 April 1974 *Education Funding News* outlined a particular Office of Education $3-million program for training teachers to meet the special needs of exceptional children in a regular classroom setting:

> The thrust of the one-shot fiscal 1974 program is on training regular classroom teachers, rather than "special education" personnel, and on working with exceptional children in the regular classroom. Exceptional children include mentally, physically, and emotionally handicapped children as well as intellectually gifted children.

Figure 2–6 reflects the impact of this federal funding for training special education teachers; it also illustrates the decrease in the number of all bachelor's degree graduates qualified to teach during the mid-seventies.

Summary and Implications   Obviously, in this chapter we have discussed only a few of the facets of teacher supply and demand. The current teacher surplus seems likely to continue for some time. Until such time as supply and demand reach an equilibrium level, teacher-education institutions and the various other education agencies will need imaginative and bold programs for examining new role models for teachers and for reassessing existing teacher-education programs. Students considering a teaching career will need much new information about alternative formats or institutions for their education. Teacher educators must rethink recruitment policies, criteria for admission, and credentialing policies. While the brief mention of some of the effects of a teacher surplus seems to portray a rocky road to entry in teaching, the overall, long-term view suggests a stronger profession with better-trained, better-qualified, and better-paid teachers.

Figure 2–6.   Supply of beginning teachers by area.

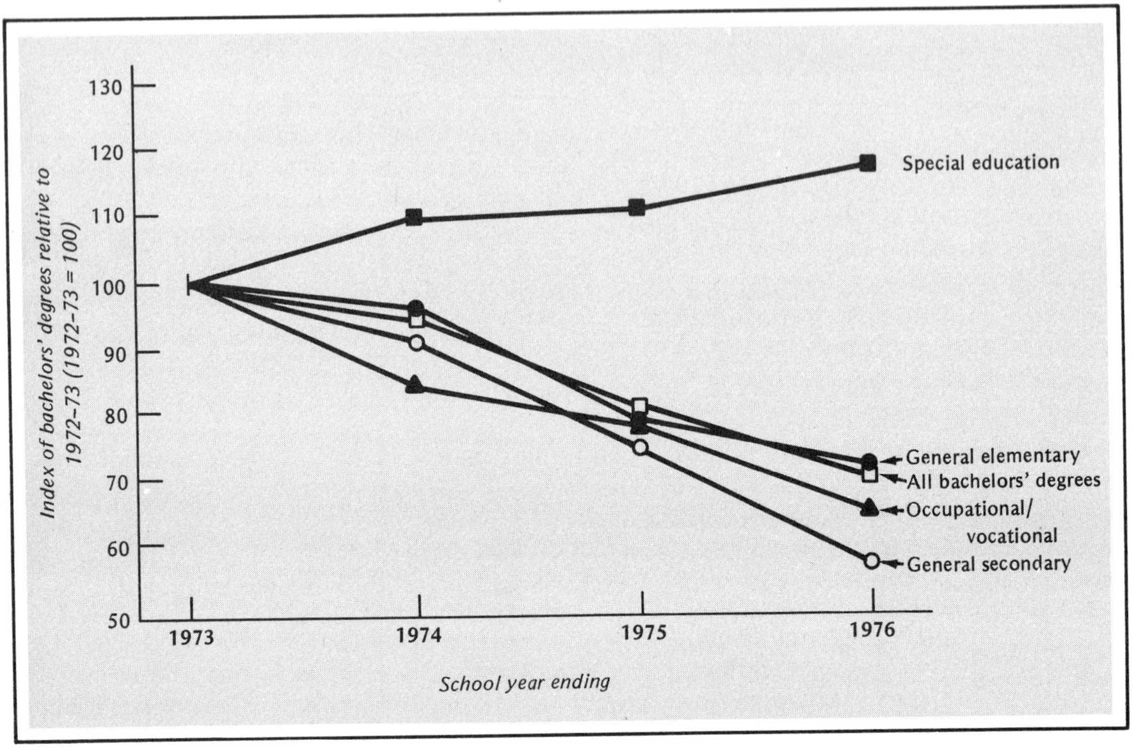

Source: National Center for Education Statistics, Washington, D.C., 1977.

Discussion Questions

1. In our larger school systems, the boards of education have formulated plans for the involuntary transfer of teachers to implement integration. What is your opinion of such teacher transfer plans?

2. What effect would a prolonged teacher surplus have on the attitudes of college students who are contemplating a teaching career? Would more highly qualified students be admitted to teacher-education programs?

3. Although some industries offer incentives for early retirement in order to hire newly trained people, other groups exist to advocate the elimination of mandatory retirement rules.

What are your views on the pros and cons of early retirement incentives versus mandatory retirement rules as related to public school teachers?

4. The declining birth has contributed to the teacher surplus, since fewer students are being enrolled. What are some of the ways in which fewer students per teacher could improve the quality of education?

5. How can the colleges and departments of education do a better job of preparing beginning teachers in order to enhance their chances of employment in a tight job market?

Supplemental Activities

1. Invite a member of your school's placement office to class to discuss application procedures, credentials, and teacher supply and demand.

2. Invite hiring officials from nearby school districts to your class to discuss teacher supply and demand. Compare this discussion to the earlier discussion with the placement officer.

3. Invite representatives of the teachers' organizations to your class to discuss teacher supply and demand. Compare this discussion to the two previous questions.

4. Write to the Chamber of Commerce in several states requesting information on job opportunities for teachers. Compare the responses. Discuss the implications as related to beginning teacher salaries, living conditions, cost of living, and other economic factors.

5. Review a major newspaper for at least one week to obtain a selection of current discussions about education-related topics. Present a report on your findings. Also present your judgment on trends indicated by your findings.

Bibliography

Alford, Albert L. "The Education Amendments of 1976." *American Education* (January–February 1977): 6–11.

American Federation of Teachers, AFL-CIO. *AFT Legislative Program*. Washington, D.C.: American Federation of Teachers, AFL-CIO, n.d.

Cronin, Joseph. *Illinois Education in 1975—Progress and Problems*. Illinois Office of Education, 1975.

Curtis, S. J., and Boultwood, M. E. A. *A Short History of Educational Ideas*, 4th ed. Great Britain: University Tutorial Press, 1975.

Mann, Dale. "Education in the Carter Administration." *Phi Delta Kappan* (September 1977): 27–30.

Morris, Van Cleve, and Pai, Young. *Philosophy and the American School*, 2nd ed. Boston: Houghton Mifflin, 1976.

National Education Association. *The Affirmative Action Plan for the NEA*. Washington, D.C.: NEA, 1975.

National Center for Education Statistics. *Projections of Education Statistics to 1985–86*. Washington, D.C.: NEA, 1977.

"A Teachers' War That's Costing Millions." *U.S. News and World Report*, April 1976, pp. 90–91.

Toombs, William. "Developing Today's Faculty for Tomorrow's Schools." *The Educational Forum* (March 1977): 365–372.

CHAPTER 3

Salaries

IN 1976, THERE WERE 7,541,000 PEOPLE EMPLOYED IN EDUCATION services—or 8 percent of the total civilian labor force of 94,773,000, according to the U.S. Bureau of Labor Statistics. Of this number, 2,208,-000 were teachers employed in the public and private elementary and secondary schools.

For many years, teachers have been considered poorly paid for their efforts in relation to the college preparation required for certification. Such intangible rewards as the opportunity to work with children and professional status in the community were assumed to be attractive fringe benefits. As teacher organizations became increasingly powerful and more militant, particularly during the decade of the sixties, teachers began to demand increased salaries and other fringe benefits. Consequently boards of education have approved substantial increases in salaries and benefits over the past few years. Teaching as a career now may be considered economically attractive.

The average salary of $13,830 paid the instructional staff (including principals, supervisors, teachers, librarians, and related instructional workers) in 1976–77 is 94 percent greater than the 1966–67 salary of $7,129.

Are Teachers Overpaid? Increases in teacher salaries over the past decade have not been unanimously supported by the taxpayers who support the schools. Many feel that teachers work only a small number of hours a day and have all the school holidays as paid vacations. As long ago as 1969, an article in *True* magazine expressed the notion that teachers were overpaid. The article began with the following want ad:

> WANTED: Men, women, age 22 to 60. Any reasonable degree of brightness; C-average college students and drop-outs from harder professions

Salaries of men and women compare favorably. (*Photograph by Talbot Lovering*)

perfectly acceptable. Interesting work; prestige positions; high starting pay and guaranteed raises, not dependent on competence. Promotions assured; no ambition or initiative required. Ironbound security; our employees cannot be fired. Ridiculously generous pension plan. Minimum 10 weeks vacation a year. . . .[1]

The author developed his thesis further by quoting statistics showing that, during the fourteen-year period from 1951 to 1965, the pay of American classroom teachers rose by an average of 105 percent, whereas the pay of other professions did not fare as well. The other professions used in contrast to teachers were factory production workers whose pay in the same period rose 69 percent, federal employees whose pay rose 90 percent, and police and firemen in large cities whose pay rose 86 percent.

Apparently the taxpaying public continues to object to the increasing costs for education. The increasing number of defeated local school tax referenda is evidence that taxpayers throughout the nation are no longer willing to pay additional taxes that could be used to provide higher teacher salaries. Also current legislative cutbacks at the state level re-

1. C. C. Chance, ''Let's Stop Overpaying Teachers,'' *True*, September 1969, p. 10.

flect a general feeling that the return on dollars spent for education—spent mostly for salaries—is minimal indeed.

Whether or not teachers are adequately paid will continue to be discussed by members of the taxpaying public. Teachers working through their powerful organizations will continue their efforts to upgrade salaries and other economic aspects of teaching. Taxpayers, governmental agencies that support schools, and others not in direct contact with the schools will probably continue to regard teacher salaries as adequate at present levels. The remainder of this chapter attempts to survey the current status of teachers' salaries.

General Salary Information   Most of the salary data reported here were compiled from various studies conducted under the auspices of the Research Division of the NEA. Salary schedules typically contain increments recognizing years of experience and advanced preparation. Caution should therefore be exercised when reviewing salary data, since they may reflect the high proportion of men with masters' degrees and the high proportion of women and older teachers in the elementary schools.

Public school teacher salaries have greatly improved during the past few years. Table 3–1 shows the rise in average annual salaries of public school instructional staff from 1966–67 up to 1976–77. As general economic conditions surged upward, teachers' salaries rose accordingly. The percentage of change in instructional salaries from 1967 to 1977 exceeded 100 percent in seventeen states. Alaska (140 percent), Michigan (120 percent), New Mexico (117 percent), and South Dakota (115 percent) showed the greatest change in instructional salaries—with Florida (60 percent) and Louisiana (62 percent) showing the least change.

Table 3–2 compares per capita income and instructional staff salaries from 1966–67 to 1976–77. While instructional salaries were 2.147 times the per capita income for 1976–77, instructional salaries were 2.376 times the per capita income in 1966–67. This comparison tends to offset claims that increases in instructional salaries during the last decade have been excessive. In terms of the economic variables associated with rises in the per capita income, increases in instructional salaries during the seventies have not kept pace with similar increases in the sixties.

The mean household income of teachers for 1976 was approximately $20,000, while the mean teacher's salary for 1976 was approximately $12,000. This finding suggests that many teachers either have a second income job or have a second family member providing income.

In comparing increases in salaries for different subgroups, the percentage of increase as well as the dollar amount is important. Table 3–3 compares the percentage of salary increase for the periods 1966–1971, 1971–1976, and 1966–1976 for all teachers and then for subgroups according to sex, level (elementary or secondary), degrees held, age, size of system, and geographic region.

Table 3–1.   Average salaries of instructional staff, 1966–67 and 1976–77.

State	1966–67			1976–77			Percent Change 1967 to 1977
	Amount	Rank	Percent of U.S. Average	Amount	Rank	Percent of U.S. Average	
1	2	3	4	5	6	7	8
U.S. Average	$7,129	. . .	100.0	$13,830	. . .	100.0	94.0
Alabama	5,800	42	81.4	10,805	48	78.1	86.3
Alaska	9,392	1	131.7	22,574	1	163.2	140.4
Arizona	7,430	15	104.2	15,000	10	108.5	101.9
Arkansas	5,113	48	71.7	10,100	49	73.0	97.5
California	9,000	2	126.2	17,000[a]	3	122.9	88.9
Colorado	6,824	22	95.7	13,300	21	96.2	94.9
Connecticut	7,959	4	111.6	14,264	12	103.1	79.2
Delaware	7,804	6	109.5	13,757	18	99.5	76.3
Florida	7,085	18	99.4	11,319	38	81.8	59.8
Georgia	6,075	36	85.2	11,945[a]	32	86.4	96.6
Hawaii	7,910	5	111.0	16,416[a]	5	118.7	107.5
Idaho	6,012	38	84.3	11,381	37	82.3	89.3
Illinois	7,525	14	105.6	15,136	9	109.4	101.1
Indiana	7,663	8	107.5	13,256	22	95.8	73.0
Iowa	6,531	28	91.6	12,799	26	92.5	96.0
Kansas	6,270	32	88.0	12,273	30	88.7	95.7
Kentucky	5,680	45	79.7	11,648	36	84.2	105.1
Louisiana	6,598	27	92.6	10,668[a]	47	77.1	61.7
Maine	5,950	39	83.5	11,099	41	80.3	86.5
Maryland	7,547	13	105.9	15,432	7	111.6	104.5
Massachusetts	7,550	12	105.9	12,970	24	93.8	71.8
Michigan	7,650	9	107.3	16,848	4	121.8	120.2
Minnesota	7,050	19	98.9	14,225	13	102.9	101.8
Mississippi	4,707	50	66.0	9,741	50	70.4	106.9
Missouri	6,307	30	88.5	11,868	33	85.8	88.2
Montana	6,300[a]	31	88.4	12,394	28	89.6	96.7
Nebraska	5,800	42	81.4	11,763	35	85.1	102.8
Nevada	7,786	7	109.2	14,195	14	102.6	82.3
New Hampshire	6,207	33	87.1	11,061	42	80.0	78.2
New Jersey	7,647	10	107.3	15,252	8	110.3	99.5
New Mexico	6,740	25	94.5	14,600	11	105.6	116.6
New York	8,500	3	119.2	17,600[b]	2	127.3	107.1
North Carolina	5,869	41	82.3	12,337	29	89.2	110.2

Table 3–1. (*continued*)

State	1966–67			1976–77			Percent Change 1967 to 1977
	Amount	Rank	Percent of U.S. Average	Amount	Rank	Percent of U.S. Average	
1	2	3	4	5	6	7	8
North Dakota	5,515	46	77.4	10,775	44	77.9	95.4
Ohio	6,782	23	95.1	13,050	23	94.4	92.4
Oklahoma	6,103	35	85.6	10,750	45	77.7	76.1
Oregon	7,274	16	102.0	14,050	16	101.6	93.2
Pennsylvania	7,181	17	100.7	14,100	15	102.0	96.4
Rhode Island	6,975	20	97.8	13,381[a]	17	96.8	91.8
South Carolina	5,421	47	76.0	10,936	43	79.1	101.7
South Dakota	5,000	49	70.1	10,740	46	77.7	114.8
Tennessee	5,755	44	80.7	11,277	39	81.5	96.0
Texas	6,075	36	85.2	11,971	31	86.6	97.1
Utah	6,780	24	95.1	12,724	25	92.0	87.7
Vermont	6,200	34	87.0	11,114	40	80.4	79.3
Virginia	6,342	29	89.0	12,440	27	89.9	96.2
Washington	7,597	11	106.6	15,679	6	113.4	106.4
West Virginia	5,917	40	83.0	11,771	34	85.1	98.9
Wisconsin	6,954	21	97.5	13,465	19	97.4	93.6
Wyoming	6,635	26	93.1	13,329	20	96.4	100.9

Source: National Education Association, Research Division. *Estimates of School Statistics, 1967–68* Research Report 1967–R19. Washington, D.C.: NEA, 1967, p. 30. Reprinted by permission.
[a] Estimated by NEA Research.
[b] Median salary.

Salaries for Men and Women: Elementary and Secondary

Men and secondary teachers continue to have higher average salaries than women and elementary teachers.

	1966	1971	1976
Elementary	$6,119	$9,092	$11,803
Secondary	6,339	9,449	12,196
Men	6,639	9,854	12,838
Women	6,077	8,500	11,578

The percentage increase in mean salary is greater for men than for women, and the dollar amount of salary difference between men and women has increased since 1966. Elementary teachers, however, show a higher percentage increase for the decade than secondary ones. The dollar amount of difference between the mean salary of elementary and secondary

Table 3–2.   Comparison of per capita income and instructional staff salaries, 1966–67 to 1976–77.

Year	Per Capita Income	Average Instructional Staff Salaries	Ratio of Salaries to Income
1	2	3	4
1966–67	$3,001	$ 7,129	2.376
1967–68	3,188	7,630	2.393
1968–69	3,457	8,272	2.393
1969–70	3,733	9,047	2.424
1970–71	3,966	9,689	2.443
1971–72	4,195	10,213	2.435
1972–73	4,537	10,633	2.344
1973–74	5,049	11,253	2.229
1974–75	5,486	12,115	2.178
1975–76	5,903	13,094	2.218
1976–77	6,441	13,830	2.147

Source: U.S. Department of Commerce, Bureau of Economic Analysis. *Survey of Current Business* 57 (April 1977): 20; National Education Association, Research. *Estimates of School Statistics, 1976–77.* Washington, D.C.: NEA, 1977, p. 28. Reprinted by permission.

teachers in 1976 is similar to that in 1966. A greater proportion of men than women are in the highest salary bracket ($15,000 or more), 29.5 percent as compared with 15.6 percent. Although among both men and women, 23 percent earn in the range of $10,000 to $11,999, 52 percent of men as compared with 38 percent of women have salaries of $12,000 or more. The proportion of secondary teachers who earn $10,000 or more per year is not significantly different from the proportion of elementary teachers earning that amount.[2]

Salaries by Degree Held   Over the decade, the percent increase in mean salary of teachers with a bachelor's degree or less has been smaller than for those with a master's degree or higher, resulting in a significant increase in the proportion of high salaries among teachers with master's degrees. In 1966, only 1 teacher in 10 with a master's degree had a salary as high as $10,000, while five years later 6 teachers in 10 with a master's degree had a salary of at least $10,000. By 1976 more than 8 teachers in 10 with a master's degree earn at least

2. *Status of the American Public School Teacher, 1975–76.* (Washington, D.C.: National Education Association Research, 1977) pp. 44–45. Reprinted by permission.

Table 3–3. Comparison of percentage of salary increases for all teachers and for subgroups, 1966–1971, 1971–1976, and 1966–1976.

	1966–1971	1971–1976	1966–1976
All teachers	48.1	29.6	91.9
Men	48.4	30.3	93.4
Women	47.3	29.3	90.1
Elementary	48.6	29.8	92.9
Secondary	47.7	29.1	90.6
Bachelor's or less	44.9	27.6	80.1
Master's or higher	46.4	24.6	82.4
Under age 30	46.7	24.6	82.8
Age 30–39	48.0	29.1	91.1
Age 40–49	51.9	33.3	102.5
Age 50 or more	51.4	37.7	108.6
Large system	41.2	36.2	92.3
Medium system	49.8	27.8	91.5
Small system	47.3	27.9	88.5
Northeast	50.7	29.5	95.1
Southeast	50.2	29.5	94.5
Middle	50.5	26.5	90.1
West	40.9	35.4	90.8

Source: Status of the American Public School Teachers, 1975–76. National Education Association Research, 1977, p. 44. Reprinted by permission.

$10,000. The distribution below shows the salaries of 1976 teachers with bachelor's and master's degrees.[3]

	Bachelor's	Master's
Less than $10,000	45.2	14.4
$10,000–10,999	12.9	9.2
$11,000–11,999	12.6	12.2
$12,000–12,999	8.4	8.7
$13,000–13,999	6.4	10.8
$14,000–14,999	3.8	8.7
$15,000 or more	10.6	36.1

Salaries by System Size, Geographic Region   It has often been said that small school systems serve teachers as stepping stones to higher-salaried positions in larger school systems. The experiences of many teachers and much evidence could be gathered to illustrate this commonly held attitude:

3. Ibid.

Salaries in large and medium systems continue to be higher than those in small ones. Although medium and small systems had a greater percentage increase in mean salary between 1966 and 1971, by 1976 large and medium systems show a greater percentage increase in mean salary over the ten-year period since 1966 than do small systems. In dollar amounts, the difference between mean salary in large systems as compared with medium and small ones has increased over the past five years. Similarly, the dollar difference in mean salaries between teachers in medium and small systems is now greater than five years ago.[4]

	1966	1971	1976
Large system	$6,970	$9,843	$13,404
Medium system	6,304	9,444	12,072
Small system	5,666	8,347	10,678

Many factors of geographic area directly affect the financing of the public schools. Such factors as density of population, industrial complexity, and the strength of teacher associations are closely related to the average minimum salary for teachers.

Northeast teachers continue to have the highest average salary; Southeast teachers, the lowest.

	1966	1971	1976
Northeast	$6,860	$10,337	$13,387
Southeast	5,183	7,783	10,081
Middle	6,178	9,295	11,765
West	5,683	9,418	12,748

About 43 percent of Southeast teachers (1 teacher in 10 in 1971) has a salary in excess of $10,000, compared with at least 75 percent of teachers in the Northeast and West and 66 percent of teachers in the Middle states. Percent increase since 1966 in mean salary is greater in the Northeast and Southeast and less in the Middle and West. In dollar amounts, the difference between mean salary in the West and the Middle region has increased since 1971, while the difference between the West and Northeast has decreased. The dollar difference between the Southeast and other regions in mean salary has also increased.[5]

Beginning Salaries— Teachers versus Private Industry

The beginning salary of a teacher with a bachelor's degree is still considerably lower than the average salary paid to a beginner with a bachelor's degree in most other professional areas.

In the academic year 1976–77, the average salary for a beginning teacher with a bachelor's degree was $9,200; for other professions, the average for a beginner with a bachelor's degree was $11,921—a salary 29.5 percent higher than a teacher's. Table 3–4 compares the average starting salaries of public school teachers with starting salaries in private industry for 1970–71 and for 1976–77.

4. Ibid.
5. Ibid.

Table 3–4. Average starting salaries of public school teachers compared with those in private industry, 1970–71 and 1976–77.

Position or Subject Field	Average Starting Salaries	
	1970–71	1976–77
Beginning teachers with bachelors' degrees	$ 6,850	$ 9,200
College graduates with bachelors' degrees		
Engineering	10,476	13,980
Accounting	10,080	12,396
Sales—Marketing	8,580	11,316
Business Administration	8,124	10,224
Liberal Arts	8,184	10,020
Production Management	9,048	No data available
Chemistry	9,708	12,384
Physics	10,080	No data available
Mathematics—Statistics	9,468	11,928
Economics—Finance	8,880	10,644
Other fields	9,264	11,820
TOTAL—all fields (weighted average)	9,361	11,921

Source: Adapted from annual reports of Frank S. Endicott, Director of Placement, Emeritus, Northwestern University.

Salary Schedules and Yearly Increments

Each board of education is an agent of the state and is therefore empowered to set salary levels for employees of the school district that it governs. Each school system usually has a salary schedule that outlines the minimum and maximum salary for each level of study beyond the bachelor's degree and for each year of teaching experience. Table 3–5 is a typical salary schedule for teachers. On this salary schedule, a beginning teacher with a bachelor's degree (B.A. column) is paid $9,147; a beginning teacher with a master's degree (M.A. column) is paid $11,349; and a beginning teacher with a master's degree and 30 additional semester hours of graduate study (M.A. + 30 column) is paid $13,108. The other columns show the increases in starting salary for additional semester hours of preparation beyond the bachelor's degree and beyond the master's degree.

The first column in the salary schedule shows the teaching year for a typical teacher. It is important to note that teachers with less than a master's degree will be granted year-to-year increases for eleven years, whereas teachers with preparation beyond a master's degree are granted increments for up to fifteen years. Therefore teachers are rewarded both for a maximum number of years of experience and for additional education beyond the bachelor's degree. Salary schedules for school systems usually are renegotiated each year. Teachers who have reached the maximum experience level for their particular education do

Table 3–5.   Typical salary schedule for teachers.

Years of Experience	B.A.	Additional Semester Hours			M.A.	Additional Semester Hours			
		+8	+16	+24		+8	+16	+24	+30
0	9,147	9,589	10,028	10,468	11,349	11,788	12,228	12,668	13,108
1	9,589	10,028	10,468	10,907	11,788	12,228	12,668	13,108	13,549
2	10,028	10,468	10,907	11,349	12,228	12,668	13,108	13,549	13,988
3	10,468	10,907	11,349	11,788	12,668	13,108	13,549	13,988	14,429
4	10,907	11,349	11,788	12,228	13,108	13,549	13,988	14,429	14,869
5	11,349	11,788	12,228	12,668	13,549	13,988	14,429	14,869	15,308
6	11,788	12,228	12,668	13,108	13,988	14,429	14,869	15,308	15,748
7	12,228	12,668	13,108	13,549	14,429	14,869	15,308	15,748	16,189
8	12,668	13,108	13,549	13,988	14,869	15,308	15,748	16,189	16,628
9	13,108	13,549	13,988	14,429	15,308	15,748	16,189	16,628	17,069
10	13,549	13,988	14,429	14,869	15,748	16,189	16,628	17,069	17,507
11	13,988	14,429	14,869	15,308	16,189	16,628	17,069	17,507	17,949
12					16,628	17,069	17,507	17,949	18,390
13						17,507	17,949	18,390	18,828
14							18,390	18,828	19,269
15								19,269	19,709

not receive additional raises except when the salaries listed in the salary schedule are revised upward.

Fringe Benefits, Extra Pay, Moonlighting   In addition to the salary schedule amounts, various economic fringe benefits may be provided by the school system, including such benefits as sick leave, leaves with pay, leaves without pay, insurance, payroll deduction privileges, payments for tuition fees for advanced study, office space, separate lunchrooms, released time periods for lunch, and released time periods for preparation.

Most school systems pay teachers, in addition to their scheduled salary, for coaching athletic teams, coaching speech teams, production of musicals and plays, yearbook and newspaper assignments, sponsoring clubs, and extra duties of various kinds. In some cases, teachers also are paid for teaching an extra class beyond the regular teaching load.

Young married teachers, in particular, work at second jobs to supplement their teaching salary. The nature of these moonlighting jobs varies from working in gas stations to selling insurance to being employed part-time by other local agencies, such as park boards. The summer vacation period offers teachers many opportunities for second jobs. An advertisement that appears each week in a large city newspaper and that illustrates one type of summer job for teachers is shown above.

The environment of the classroom varies with a teacher's skill and creativity. (*Photograph by Talbot Lovering*)

Faculty Salaries in Two-Year and Four-Year Colleges and in Universities

After acquiring a graduate education—and usually advanced degrees—both beginning and experienced teachers may seek employment in colleges or universities. Faculty salaries in public two-year institutions are given in Table 3–6 with mean scheduled minimum and maximum salaries by academic rank shown for 1969–70 and 1976–77. Increases reported for 1976–77 ranged from 4 to 6 percent—with the greatest gain shown for the professor category.

Academic salaries of full-time teaching faculty in public four-year colleges and universities for 1969–70 and 1976–77 are shown in Table 3–7. The percentage of increase in 1976–77 ranged from 2.5 to 4 percent in the reporting institutions. Although the increase in 1976–77 was generally slight, the greatest gain appeared in the professor category.

Summary and Implications

The adequacy of teacher salaries will continue to be a topic of discussion among teachers and members of the taxpaying public. Prior to embarking on a teaching career, prospective teachers are advised to become familiar with the anticipated general level of teacher salaries and the broad social and political problems associated with the funding of

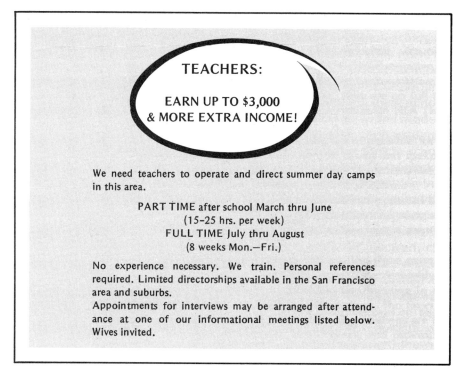

Figure 3–1. Newspaper advertisement.

Table 3–6. Mean schedule minimum and maximum salaries in public two-year institutions by faculty rank, 1969–70 and 1976–77.

Faculty Rank by Academic Year	Mean of Scheduled Minimum Salaries	Mean of Scheduled Maximum Salaries
Instructor		
1969–70	$ 7,571	$10,551
1976–77	10,487	15,379
Assistant professor		
1969–70	8,921	12,529
1976–77	12,092	17,888
Associate professor		
1969–70	10,531	14,771
1976–77	14,293	20,835
Professor		
1969–70	12,434	17,363
1976–77	16,810	24,344

Source: Adapted from National Education Association, Research. *Salaries Scheduled for Faculty in Higher Education, 1976–77.* Washington, D.C.: NEA, February 1978. Reprinted by permission.

Table 3–7. Mean scheduled minimum and maximum salaries in public four-year degree-granting institutions by faculty rank, 1969–70 and 1976–77.

Faculty Rank by Academic Year	Mean of Scheduled Minimum Salaries	Mean of Scheduled Maximum Salaries
Instructor		
1969–70	$ 7,397	$10,407
1976–77	10,453	14,598
Assistant professor		
1969–70	8,727	12,815
1976–77	12,411	18,053
Associate professor		
1969–70	10,676	15,653
1976–77	15,076	21,855
Professor		
1969–70	12,999	19,015
1976–77	18,357	26,713

Source: Adapted from National Education Association, Research. *Salaries Scheduled for Faculty in Higher Education, 1976–77.* Washington, D.C.: NEA, February 1978. Reprinted by permission.

the total educational venture. A continuing task of teacher organizations will be to argue convincingly for increased support of the schools—while at the same time maintaining the dignity of the profession.

Salaries paid to members of employee groups are typically affected by supply and demand. Although a somewhat somber forecast of the short-range demand for teachers was presented earlier, a longer-range view was more optimistic. With birth rates projected upward in the near future, enrollments are projected slightly upward, beginning in the mid-eighties. If the outcome is a shortage of teachers once again, teacher salaries will rise competitively with salaries for other occupations.

Discussion Questions

1. Many people believe that teachers are overpaid. As a prospective teacher, how would you respond to this charge?

2. Mean starting salaries of teachers and other graduates with bachelors' degrees were compared in Chapter 3. How would teachers' salaries compare with those of other professionals if teachers were paid for twelve rather than nine months of work?

3. Many young teachers work at a second job to increase their yearly income. What is your feeling about teachers holding an additional job?

4. What has the teaching profession gained and lost through collective bargaining and strikes?

5. Some experienced teachers would be willing to teach larger classes if they were paid more to do so. How do you feel about the notion of more pay for more students taught?

Supplemental Activities

1. Have each member of the class write to the board of education for the salary schedule of his or her local public schools. Compare the salary data obtained with the reported average data for the United States.

2. Identify several school districts that have had recent teacher strikes. Write to the teacher organizations in these districts requesting information on the strike issues. Summarize the data obtained.

3. Invite to your class a professional negotiator who has previously worked for a board of education to discuss contract negotiations from the board of education's point of view.

4. Research the literature and write a position paper comparing teacher salaries to the salaries of those with similar levels of training who work for business and industry.

5. Interview your state representative or state senator to determine his or her thinking on matters of teacher salaries. Report to your class on the interview.

Bibliography

Chance, C. C. "Let's Stop Overpaying Teachers." *True,* September 1969.

Gibbons, Russell W. "Union Muscle in Public Schools." *Commonweal,* 23 April 1976.

Golladay, Mary A. *The Condition of Education.* Washington, D.C.: National Center for Educational Statistics, 1977.

Illinois Education Association. *Illinois Teacher Salary Schedule and Policy Study, 1974–75.* Springfield, Ill.: Illinois Education Association, 1975.

Joffe, Carol. "Federal Funds." *American Education* (January-February 1977).

Munse, Albert. "Comparing School Expenditures." *American Education* (January-February 1975).

National Education Association. *Financial Status of the Public Schools, 1977.* Washington, D.C.: NEA, 1977.

National Education Association. *Status of the American Public School Teacher, 1975–76.* Washington, D.C.: NEA, 1976.

Projections of Teacher Supply and Demand to 1980–81. Washington, D.C.: U.S. Department of Health, Education, and Welfare, 1975.

Strong James. "Teachers' Union Ends Own Strike." *Chicago Tribune,* 25 August 1977, p. 7.

CHAPTER 4

Legal Aspects of Teaching

IN PRACTICING THEIR PROFESSION AND IN THEIR INTERACTIONS with pupils, parents, colleagues, and employers, teachers are subject to and protected by the United States Constitution, state constitutions, and statutory law. The effective practice of their profession requires not only that they be cognizant of their own rights but also that they be cognizant of the rights of others.

In the last few years there has been a substantial increase in the number of federal court cases dealing with education. Each year between 125 and 200 cases dealing with education are brought before the federal courts. Federal courts recently have abandoned their traditional hands-off policy in cases involving the judgment or discretion of local school boards. In the last several years, these cases have increasingly focused on questions of the constitutional rights of individuals. School-related court cases deal with such varied topics as a student's claim that he was not properly educated, a school board's right to fire teachers who strike illegally, the new privacy act relating to student records, school liability for punitive damages, suspensions, busing, corporal punishment, affirmative action procedures related to hiring teachers, and Title IX enforcement that outlaws sex discrimination practices in the schools.

This chapter deals with the relatively new topic of student rights and explains the rights and responsibilities of teachers in relation to teacher certification, loyalty oaths, corporal punishment, tenure, academic freedom, collective bargaining, strikes, and liability.

**Student Rights
and
Responsibilities**

Since the mid-sixties, much progress has been made toward a more active role for students than ever before and toward increased recognition of student rights and responsibilities. Many educators and lay citizens tend to bemoan progress toward student rights and responsibilities as legal trespass on the power of control over students in the school setting. Some claim little is ever decided to determine what constitutes student responsibility. Yet examination of various surveys and reports on student rights and responsibilities acknowledges the dual dimension of the trend. For example, the National School Public Relations Association cites the preamble to the Baltimore County Board of Education policy statement on student rights and responsibilities: "Students have responsibilities that are inseparable from and inherent in their rights. One of the most important is the responsibility to obey a school rule or policy until such a rule is revoked. Citizens in an orderly society must accept responsibilities commensurate with their rights."[1] Many court decisions are decided against students who are so nonconforming as to be considered beyond a reasonable norm. Often the courts support the local school authorities' right to exercise considerable control over matters that affect students. What occurs in many instances is that emotionalism becomes so great that the task of re-examining student rights and responsibilities becomes a moot part of the question.

American children have a basic right to an education; this right is assured in many state constitutions. It has been defined further by court decisions to the point where it is currently interpreted as meaning that each child in the United States shall have an equal opportunity to pursue education. In the words of one federal court decision:

> If sufficient funds are not available to finance all of the services and programs that are needed and desirable in the system, then the available funds must be expended equitably in such a manner that no child is entirely excluded from a publicly supported education consistent with his needs and ability to benefit therefrom.[2]

The right to an education, however, is not without certain prerequisites. Citizenship alone does not guarantee a free education. Statutes that establish public school systems for the most part also establish a means of meeting the operating costs of the system, largely through real estate taxes. This reasoning has given rise to the residence requirement necessary for school attendance without tuition payments. It should be made clear that residence does not mean that a student or his parents or guardians must pay real estate taxes; rather it means that the student must reside in the school district in which he or she de-

1. National School Public Relations Association, *Student Rights and Responsibilities* (Arlington, Va.: National School Public Relations Association, 1972), p. 2.
2. *Mills* v. *Board of Education of the District of Columbia*, 348 F. Supp. 866 (D.D.C. 1972).

sires to attend school. Residence is a prerequisite to the right to a free public education within a specific school district.

The right or privilege of a child to attend school is also dependent. upon his compliance with rules and regulations prescribed by the school. To facilitate the day-to-day orderly operation of schools, boards of education have been given the right to establish reasonable rules and regulations regarding pupil control and conduct. However, their actions in a number of instances have been challenged. The more common'challenges have been in the areas of corporal punishment, rights of married students to an education, dress codes, and freedom of expression.

Goss v. *Lopez* (U.S. Supreme Court, 1975), which dealt with the suspension of high school students in Mena, Arkansas, has become known as the "spiked punch case." In this case, certain students admitted adding beer to the punch at a school party, although school rules prohibited use of intoxicating beverages. However, two students who were suspended for a semester brought suit charging their due process rights were denied—because they were not present at the board meeting when the suspensions were handed out. In ruling that students cannot be suspended without some form of hearing, the Court said:

> The prospect of imposing elaborate hearing requirements in every suspension case is viewed wtih great concern, and many school authorities may well prefer the untrammeled power to act unilaterally, unhampered by rules about notice and hearing. But it would be a strange disciplinary system in an educational institution if no communication was sought by the disciplinarian with the student in an effort to inform him of his defalcation and to let him tell his side of the story in order to make sure that an injustice is not done. Fairness can rarely be obtained by secret, one-sided determination of the facts decisive of rights . . . Secrecy is not congenial to truth-seeking and self-righteousness gives too slender an assurance of rightness. No better instrument has been devised for arriving at truth than to give a person in jeopardy of serious loss notice of the case against him and opportunity to meet it.

Just a month after the *Goss* v. *Lopez* decision, the U.S. Supreme Court handed down a more significant decision related to the "spiked punch case," which affirmed that students may sue school board members who are guilty of intentionally depriving students of their constitutional rights. In *Wood* v. *Strickland* (95, S. Ct. 992, 1975) the Supreme Court held that school officials who discipline students unfairly cannot defend themselves against civil rights suits by claiming ignorance of pupils' basic constitutional rights. As a result of this decision, Judge Paul Williams, a federal judge in Arkansas, ordered that the girls who had been suspended could seek damages from individual school board members—although not from school district officials. The judge also ruled that the school records of the pupils must be cleared of the suspension incident. From these decisions, it is apparent that the U.S. Supreme Court is taking into account the rights of students.

Students' Bill of Rights

In light of the many decisions rendered by the courts each year, and the subsequent direction the schools must take from the precedents of such cases, what kind of guidelines are there for the practicing educator, the classroom teacher? There are many publications that ought to be read by, or at least made available to, all beginning and experienced teachers.

Study of such documents can provide specific information about the gamut of problems that affect teachers and students and about recent decisions by the courts. Perhaps a sounder basis for rational thinking by teachers would be provided by a broad bill of student rights under which educators could focus their thinking on any problems that might develop. The American Civil Liberties Union of Maryland has developed the following Bill of Rights for High School Students:

A BILL OF RIGHTS FOR HIGH SCHOOL STUDENTS[3]

"Neither students nor teachers shed their constitutional rights to freedom of speech or expression at the schoolhouse gate. That has been the unmistakable holding of the Supreme Court for almost fifty years." (*Tinker* v. *Des Moines*, 1969)

The following statement of student rights is intended as a guide to students, parents, teachers, and administrators who are interested in developing proper safeguards for student liberties. IT IS NOT A SUMMARY OF THE LAW, BUT SETS FORTH IN A GENERAL WAY WHAT THE ACLU THINKS *SHOULD* BE ADOPTED. . . .

ARTICLE I.   Expression
  A. Students shall be free to express themselves and disseminate their views without prior restraints through speech, essays, publications, pictures, armbands, badges, and all other media of communication. Student expression may be subject to disciplinary action only in the event that such expression creates a significant physical disruption of school activities.
  B. No reporter for a student publication may be required to reveal a source of information.
  C. Students shall have the right to hear speakers and presentations representing a wide range of views and subjects in classes, clubs, and assemblies. Outside speakers and presentations may be limited only by considerations of time, space, and expense.
  D. Students shall be free to assemble, demonstrate, and picket peacefully, to petition and to organize on school grounds or in school buildings subject only to reasonable limitations on time, place, and

3.   American Civil Liberties Union of Maryland, Baltimore, Md. Revised, March 1974. Reprinted by permission.

manner designed to avoid significant physical obstruction of traffic or significant physical disruption of school activities.

E. Students shall be free to determine their dress and grooming as they see fit, subject only to reasonable limitations designed to protect student safety or prevent significant ongoing disruption of school activities.

F. No student shall be required to participate in any way in patriotic exercises or be penalized for refusing to participate.

ARTICLE II. Religion

A. Students shall be free to practice their own religion or no religion.

B. There shall be no school-sanctioned religious exercises or events.

C. Religious history, ideas, institutions, and literature may be studied in the same fashion as any other academic subject.

ARTICLE III. Privacy

A. Students should be free from undercover surveillance through the use of mechanical, electronic, or other secret methods, including undercover agents, without issuance of a warrant.

B. Students should be free from warrantless searches and seizures by school officials in their personal effects, lockers, or any other facilities assigned to their personal use. General housekeeping inspections of lockers and desks shall not occur without reasonable notice.

C. Student record files:

1. A student's permanent record file shall include only information about academic competence and notation of the fact of participation in school clubs, sports, and other such school extracurricular activities. This file shall not be disclosed to any person or agency outside the school, except to the student's parents or guardian, without the student's permission.

2. Any other records (e.g., medical or psychological evaluations) shall be available only to the student, the student's parents or guardian, and the school staff. Such other records shall be governed by strict safeguards for confidentiality and shall not be available to others in or outside of the school even upon consent of the student.

3. A record shall be kept, and shall be available to the student, of any consultation of the student's files, noting the date and purpose of the consultation and the name of the person who consulted the files.

4. All records shall be open to challenge and correction by the student.

5. A student's opinions shall not be disclosed to any outside person or agency.

ARTICLE IV. Equality

A. No organization that officially represents the school in any capacity and no curricular or extracurricular activity organized by school authorities may deny or segregate participation or award or withhold privileges on the basis of race, color, national origin, sex, religion, creed, or opinions.

ARTICLE V.   Government

A. All students may hold office and may vote in student elections. These rights shall not be denied for any reason.

B. Student government organizations and their operation, scope, and amendment procedures shall be established in a written constitution formulated with full and effective student participation.

ARTICLE VI.   Due Process

A. Regulations concerning student behavior shall be formulated with full and effective student participation. Such regulations shall be published and made available to all students. Regulations shall be fully, clearly, and precisely written.

B. No student shall be held accountable by school authorities for any behavior occurring outside the organized school day or off school property (except during school sponsored events) unless such behavior presents a clear, present, and substantial ongoing danger to persons and property in the school.

C. There shall be no cruel, unusual, demeaning, or excessive punishments. There shall be no corporal punishment.

D. No student shall be compelled by school officials to undergo psychological therapy or use medication without that student's consent. No student may be required to participate in any psychological or personality testing, research project, or experiment without that student's written, informed, and willing consent. The nature, purposes, and possible adverse consequences of the testing, project, or experiment shall be fully explained to the student.

E. A student shall have the right to due process in disciplinary and investigative proceedings. In cases that may involve serious penalties, such as suspension for more than three days, expulsion, transfer to another school, a notation on the student's record, or long-term loss of privileges:

1. A student shall be guaranteed a formal hearing before an impartial board. That student shall have the right to appeal hearing results.

2. Rules for hearings and appeals shall be written and published, and there shall be full and effective student participation in their formulation.

3. The student shall be advised in writing of any charges brought against that student.

4. The student shall have the right to present evidence and witnesses and to cross-examine adverse witnesses. The student shall have the right to have an advisor of his or her own choosing present.

5. The hearing shall be open or private as the student chooses.

6. The student shall have a reasonable time to prepare a defense.

7. A student may not be compelled to incriminate himself or herself.

8. The burden of proof, beyond a reasonable doubt, shall be upon the school.

9. A written record of all hearings and appeals shall be made available to the student, at the school's expense.

10. A student shall be free from double jeopardy.

In Loco Parentis   Historically schools have functioned under the doctrine of *in loco parentis* (in place of a parent). This doctrine was interpreted to mean that schools could exercise almost complete control over students because they acted as parent substitutes. Under the doctrine of *in loco parentis*, the rules and regulations of local boards of education, particularly in respect to pupil conduct, usually were upheld by the courts. Recent years have seen a change toward an increased regard for the constitutional rights of pupils. The *Tinker* case (*Tinker* v. *Des Moines Independent Community School District,* 1969) was seen as a landmark case in the changing philosophy. The case involved a school board's attempt to prevent the wearing of black armbands by students protesting the hostilities in Vietnam. In 1969, the United States Supreme Court ruled against the Des Moines school board by a vote of seven to two. The Court in its majority opinion stated:

> the wearing of armbands in the circumstances of this case was entirely divorced from actually or potentially disruptive conduct by those participating in it. It was closely akin to "pure speech" which, we have repeatedly held, is entitled to comprehensive protection, under the First Amendment . . .
>
> First Amendment rights, applied in the light of the special characteristics of the school environment, are available to teachers and students. It can hardly be argued that either students or teachers shed their constitutional rights to freedom at the schoolhouse gate.

However, the Court also said:

> On the other hand, the Court has repeatedly emphasized the need for affirming the comprehensive authority of the States and of school officials, consistent with fundamental constitutional safeguards, to prescribe and control conduct in the schools. . . . Our problem lies in the area where students in the exercise of First Amendment rights collide with the rules of the school authorities.

It is important to note that the Court clearly designated in the *Tinker* opinion what they were *not* deciding.

> The problem posed by the present case does not relate to regulation of the length of skirts or the type of clothing, to hair styles, or deportment. . . . It does not concern aggressive, disruptive action or even group demonstrations. Our problem involves direct, primary First Amendment rights akin to "pure speech."

Justice Black, in dissenting, wrote:

> The Court's holding in this case ushers in what I deem to be an entirely new era in which the power to control pupils by the elected "officials of state supported public schools . . ." in the United States is in ultimate effect transferred to the Supreme Court.

Undoubtedly the Court's opinion in the *Tinker* case will have a long-lasting and widespread effect on the operation of schools in the United

States. It clearly delineated that students have constitutional rights whatever their age.

Much of the involvement of the courts in recent years, in dealing with student rights, has concerned pupils being accorded due process of law. Due process has two connotations—procedural and substantive. Procedural due process has to do with whether or not the procedures used in discipline cases are fair; substantive due process is concerned with whether or not the school authorities have deprived a student of basic substantive constitutional rights such as freedom of speech or personal liberty.[4]

Procedural due process frequently comes under scrutiny in cases of suspension and expulsion; these most often result from disciplinary action taken by the schools, which may or may not have violated a pupil's substantive constitutional right. In the *Tinker* case, in which students were suspended, the decision was made primarily on the violation of the substantive right of freedom of speech or expression.

Procedural due process cases generally involve alleged violations of the Fourteenth Amendment. They may also involve alleged violations of state constitutions or statutory law that call for specific procedures to be followed. Many states have specific procedures to be followed in cases of expulsion or suspension. Expulsion procedures usually involve notification of parents or guardians in a specific way, such as by registered mail, and a hearing before the board of education or a designated hearing officer. Suspension procedures are also usually quite specifically detailed, designating who has the authority to suspend, and the length of time that a suspension may be given. It behooves teachers and administrators alike to be cognizant of due process regulations. They should know the specific regulations in the state in which they are employed.

As previously indicated, the trend in substantive due process or substantive rights has been toward an increased recognition of student constitutional rights. Corporal punishment has generally been upheld if not prohibited by statute. However, the punishment must be reasonable. In the event of a court case, each court in a sense defines and refines what is considered reasonable. In past court cases, courts have pointed out that consideration must be given to the age, sex, and size of the pupil; that the punishment must be in proportion to the offense; and that it must be administered without malice.

Lower court cases dealing with grooming have been decided, in some instances, in favor of the board of education—in support of their rules and regulations—and, in other instances, in favor of the student. A general principle seems to be that if the dress and grooming do not incite or cause disruptive behavior, the court ruling is likely to be sup-

4.   Lee O. Garber and Reynolds C. Seitz, *The Yearbook of School Law 1971* (Danville, Ill.: Interstate Printers and Publishers, 1971), p. 253.

portive of the student. Dress codes, once very much in vogue, are much less in evidence today. Although the United States Supreme Court has yet to address itself to a so-called long hair case, federal courts in every circuit have issued rulings in long hair cases, with half finding such regulations to be unconstitutional and with the other half upholding them. In the following states, federal courts have declared hair-length regulations unconstitutional:

Arkansas	Massachusetts	Pennsylvania
Connecticut	Minnesota	Rhode Island
Delaware	Missouri	South Carolina
Idaho	Nebraska	South Dakota
Illinois	New Hampshire	Vermont
Indiana	New Jersey	Virginia
Iowa	New York	West Virginia
Maine	North Dakota	Wisconsin

In the following states, federal courts have permitted—although certainly not required—school officials to regulate the length of students' hair:

Alabama	Kansas	Ohio
Alaska	Kentucky	Oklahoma
Arizona	Louisiana	Oregon
California	Michigan	Tennessee
Colorado	Mississippi	Texas
Florida	Montana	Utah
Georgia	Nevada	Washington
Hawaii	New Mexico	Wyoming

With regard to the student participation on athletic teams or in extra-curricular activities, the courts have generally refused to uphold dress and hair-length regulations, unless the school can prove that the hair or dress interfered with the student's ability to play the sport or perform the activity, as in *Long* v. *Zopp* (476 F. 2d 180, 4th Circuit 1973).

Sex Discrimination

Until recently, educational institutions could legally discriminate against females—whether students, staff, or faculty. In 1972, the Ninety-second Congress enacted Title IX of the Education Amendments Act to forbid sex discrimination against students and employees in federally assisted programs. The key provision in Title IX states: "No person in the United States shall, on the basis of sex, be excluded from participation in, be denied the benefits of, or be subjected to discrimination under any education program or activity receiving federal financial assistance." Title IX is enforced by the Office of Civil Rights of the Department of Health, Education, and Welfare (HEW). Individuals and organizations can challenge any discriminatory policy or practice by writing a letter of complaint to the secretary of HEW.

Schools at all levels are required to comply with Title IX. The statute does exempt military schools, some religious institutions, and admissions to private undergraduate schools. However, after admitting students of both sexes, a school cannot alter admissions policies in order to discriminate purposely on the basis of sex under the above cited exemption.

The Title IX regulation, which went into effect on July 21, 1975, details the impact of Title IX on students and employees: recruiting, admissions, financial aid, differential rules or regulations, housing rules and facilities, physical education and athletics, health care and insurance, student employment opportunities, extracurricular activities, counseling and testing, single-sex courses and programs, graduation requirements, vocational-education programs.

The employment section of the regulation covers all conditions of employment including part-time employment, maternity leave, and fringe benefits. In general, the employment provisions are similar to those of other nondiscrimination laws and regulations. Women's groups are highly critical of the regulation for being too weak. Some education administrators and some representatives of male athletic interests are highly critical of the regulations for being too strong. Others are simply confused.[5]

School Records   Prior to 19 November 1974, the effective date of the so-called Buckley Amendment, the law regarding the privacy of student records was extremely unclear. Many school administrators and a large majority of parents do not yet realize that the parents now have the right to view their children's educational records; students over the age of eighteen also have the right to see their school records for themselves. Many teachers are not yet aware that their written comments, which are submitted as part of the student's record, must be shown at a parent's request or at a student's request, if the student is eighteen.

The new law (Public Law 93–380 as amended by Public Law 93–568) requires that schools receiving federal funds must comply with the privacy requirements—or face loss of those funds. What must a school district do to be in compliance? Stated simply, the Buckley Amendment sets forth these main requirements; the school district must:

Allow all parents, even those not having custody of their children, access to each educational record that a school district keeps on their child;

Establish a district policy on how parents can go about seeing specific records;

Inform all parents what rights they have under the Amendment, how they can act on these rights according to school policy, and where they can see a copy of the policy;

Seek parental permission in writing before disclosing any personally identifiable record on a child to individuals other than professional per-

5. Lucy Knight, "Facts about Mr. Buckley's Amendment," *American Education* 13 (June 1977): 7.

sonnel employed in the district (and others who meet certain specific requirements).

These provisions were spelled out in a set of regulations published by HEW last June, a year and a half after the Buckley Amendment became law. . . . For a final word as to what is and what is not legal under the law or for further information on a particular point, the reader is referred to the regulations published in the June 17, 1976 *Federal Register*.[6]

Student Publications

A significant decision in the area of student newspapers was the case of *Scoville* v. *Board of Education* (1970) originating in Illinois. Students were expelled for distributing a newspaper named "Grass High" that criticized school officials and used vulgar language. The students were expelled under an Illinois statute that empowered boards of education "to expel pupils guilty of gross disobedience or misconduct." The board of education was supported by a federal court in Illinois; but, upon appeal, the Court of Appeals for the Seventh Circuit reversed the decision. The court concluded:

. . . absent an evidentiary showing, and an appropriate balancing of the evidence by the district court to determine whether the Board was justified in a "forecast" of the disruption and interference, as required under Tinker, plaintiffs are entitled to the declaratory judgment, injunctive and damage relief sought.

The *Scoville* decision undoubtedly has had an effect on institutional control over student publications.

Other recent cases concerning substantive rights have dealt with the legality of the practice of searching school lockers and the educational rights of married students. In general, the courts have ruled that lockers may be searched by school authorities. Courts have ruled quite consistently that marriage, in and of itself, is not a valid reason for expulsion. They have also said that, while school authorities may not bar married students from instructional classes, they may bar them from extracurricular activities. The opinions have been based on the doctrine that every child has a constitutional right to attend school. This right may be removed if a student's moral standards can legally be proved to be objectionable and deleterious to other students.

In summary, the doctrine of *in loco parentis* in public schools is being redefined: greater attention is being afforded to the constitutional rights of students. The *Tinker* case was the first decision in the history of the U.S. Supreme Court that involved pupil discipline but that was not related to a religious freedom.[7]

6.   Bernice Sandler, "Title IX: Anti-Sexism's Big Legal Stick," *American Education* 13 (May 1977): 6, 9.
7.   Lee O. Garber and E. Edmund Reutter, Jr., *The Yearbook of School Law 1970.* (Danville, Ill.: Interstate Printers and Publishers, 1970), p. 321.

**Teacher
Certification**

Teachers possess the same inalienable rights as other citizens. As public employees directly involved in the education of children, they are also in positions of great responsibility. This responsibility is legally recognized, in part, by requirements for state certification that are designed to assure qualified and competent teachers in the public schools.

All states have established qualification requirements necessary for teacher certification. The administration of certification is most often a function of a state certification board. It is its duty to make certain that the applicants meet the legal requirements and to issue the appropriate certificates. Certifying agencies may not arbitrarily refuse the issuance of a certificate to a qualified candidate. The courts have ruled that local boards of education may prescribe additional or higher qualifications beyond the state requirements, providing such requirements are not irrelevant, unreasonable, or arbitrary. A teaching certificate is a license or granted privilege to practice a profession—it is not a right. In addition to professional educational requirements, certification laws usually require evidence of citizenship, good moral character, and physical health. Frequently a minimum age requirement is stated.

Recently efforts have been made to establish performance-based teacher certification. In other words, teacher certification would be more closely related to demonstrated teaching competency rather than to the completion of specific courses, as has been the case historically. Perormance-based certification is likely to be related to performance-based teacher-education programs. The following excerpt from a pamphlet on performance-based teacher education explains the concept:

> In performance-based programs, performance goals are specified and agreed to in rigorous detail in advance of instruction. The student preparing to become a teacher must either be able to demonstrate his ability to promote desirable learning or exhibit behaviors known to promote it. He is held accountable, not for passing grades but for attaining a given level of competency in performing the essential tasks of teaching; the training institution is itself held accountable for producing able teachers. The emphasis is on demonstrated product or output. Acceptance of this basic principle has program implications that are truly revolutionary.[8]

Although much remains to be done to bring about performance-based teacher-education programs and, subsequently, performance-based teacher certification, the concepts have merit and will probably be implemented in some form in the next few years.

8. Stanley Elam, *A Résumé of Performance-Based Teacher Education, What Is the State of the Art?* (Washington, D.C.: American Association of Colleges for Teacher Education, 1972), p. 3.

Teacher Employment Contracts

The statutory authority to employ teachers is usually vested in boards of education. This authority includes the power to enter into a contract and to fix terms of employment and compensation. In some states, specific members of the school board are required to sign teacher contracts. When statutes confer the employing authority to boards of education, this authority cannot be delegated. It is usually the responsibility of the superintendent to screen and nominate candidates to the board. The board then takes official action as a group, meeting in official session, to enter into contractual agreement. Employment procedures vary from state to state, but the process is fundamentally prescribed by the legislature and must be strictly followed by local boards.

A contract usually contains certain basic essentials such as the following: the identification of the teacher and the board of education; a

Teacher power: teachers strike for common interests. (*Photograph by Eric A. Roth, The Picture Cube*)

statement of the legal capacity of each party to enter into contract; a definition of the assignment specified; a statement of the salary and the manner in which it is to be paid; and a provision for signature by the teacher and by the legally authorized agents of the board. In some states, contract forms are provided by state departments of education and the use of these forms is mandatory; in others, the use of the forms is permissive.

A teacher may not enter into legal contract unless he or she possesses a valid teaching certificate issued by the respective states. Funds may not be legally expended under a contract with a teacher not legally certified. The requirement of certification for the contract to be valid is intended to protect the public from incompetent teachers.

Frequently a new teacher will enter into a contract before receiving state certification, but he or she acquires certification before commencing teaching duties. A question may be raised as to whether such a contract is valid. The answer depends upon the specific wording and interpretation of the state statute. In some states, this practice is legally sanctioned. In general, "the weight of authority is that a certificate must be had at the time of making the contract unless the statutory language clearly indicates that it was the legislative intention that possession of a certificate at the time of beginning of teaching is sufficient."[9]

Teachers have the responsibility of making certain that they are legally qualified to enter into contractual agreements. Furthermore, they have the responsibility to carry out and to abide by terms of the contract. In turn, they have a legal right to expect proper treatment from their employer under the terms of the contract.

Teacher Tenure   Teacher tenure legislation exists in the majority of states. Most of the states plus the District of Columbia have tenure or fair dismissal laws that are mandatory and apply to all school districts without exception. Other states, including New York, California, and Texas, have more restricted tenure legislation that it is less than statewide. The New York law excludes rural districts, the California law is optional in districts with under 250 pupils, and the Texas law is permissive, giving all districts the option of coming under its provisions. Georgia, Kansas, Nebraska, Oregon, and Wisconsin have laws that apply to designated cities, counties, or school districts. Five states do not have any tenure laws: North Carolina, Mississippi, South Carolina, Utah, and Vermont. The various tenure laws differ not only in their extent of coverage but also in their provisions for coverage.

Tenure laws are intended to provide security for teachers in their positions and to prevent the removal of capable teachers by capricious action or political motives. Tenure statutes generally include detailed

9.   Robert R. Hamilton and Paul R. Mort, *The Law and Public Education* (Brooklyn: The Foundation Press, 1969), p. 359.

specifications necessary for the attainment of tenure and for the dismissal of teachers possessing tenure. These statutes have been upheld when attacked on constitutional grounds. The courts have reasoned that since state legislatures create school districts, they also have the right to limit their power.

Tenure is obtained by serving as a satisfactory teacher for a stated length of time. This period of time is referred to as the probationary period and varies in length from state to state. The actual process of acquiring tenure after serving the probationary period depends upon the applicable statute: in some states the process is automatic at the satisfactory completion of the probationary period; in other states official action of the school board is necessary to grant tenure.

The grounds and procedures for dismissal of teachers on permanent tenure are usually spelled out as part of the tenure statute. The grounds generally include incompetency, inefficiency, insubordination, immorality, and "other good and just" causes. Generalizations cannot be made on what constitutes these grounds; the decisions are made on the merits of each case. The procedures are designed to prevent arbitrary action by school boards, with provisions made for the filing of charges, for hearings, and for appeals. The specific rights that a teacher has under tenure do not generally preclude reassignment to another position for which he or she is qualified. However, demotions in rank and salary have been interpreted as removal and reemployment rather than reassignment.

Teacher tenure may be affected by teacher conduct outside as well as inside of school. This area, in a sense, deals with the personal freedom of teachers: their freedom to conduct themselves as other citizens in their personal behavior, their freedom to engage in political activities, and their academic freedom in the classroom. Teachers are more apt to be criticized than other citizens for their personal behavior and political activities. The present trend is toward a more liberal view in these areas.

Tenure laws come under frequent attack by those who claim they protect the incompetent teacher. There is undoubtedly some truth in this assertion; but it must be stated clearly and unequivocally that they also protect the competent and most able teachers. Teachers who accept the challenge of their profession and dare to use new methods, who inspire curiosity among their students, and who discuss controversial issues in their classrooms need protection from dismissal through political or capricious methods. The dismissal of incompetent teachers can be accomplished under the law by capable administrators. Tenure laws, though frequently attacked, are necessary in the current system of American education.

Although due process has been the rule for years in respect to tenured teachers, evidence is now starting to accumulate indicating that nontenured faculty also has, or should have, procedural due process rights. In some states, rather complete due process procedures for nontenured faculty are spelled out in the statutes; in most states, however, there are only perfunctory provisions providing calendar dates for nonrenewal of contracts. Landmark cases in Massachusetts (*Lucia* v. *Duggan,* 1969) and Wisconsin (*Gouge* v. *Joint School District No. 1,* 1970) both supported the necessity of following due process in the dismissal of nontenured teachers. In the *Lucia* case, the court said: "The particular circumstances of a dismissal of a public school teacher provide compelling reasons for application of a doctrine of procedural due process."[10] In the *Gouge* case, the court said:

> [A] teacher in a public elementary or secondary school is protected by the due process clause of the Fourteenth Amendment against a nonrenewal decision which is wholly without basis in fact and also against a decision which is wholly unreasoned, as well as a decision which is impermissibly based.

It has become increasingly apparent that the rights of procedural due process are applicable to nontenured as well as tenured faculty.

Academic Freedom   A most sensitive and vital concern to the educator is that of academic freedom—freedom to control what one shall teach and freedom to teach the truth as one discovers it, without fear of penalty. The United States Supreme Court dealt with an academic freedom issue in a case that arose in New Hampshire (*Sweezy* v. *State of New Hampshire,* 1957). A guest lecturer at the University of New Hampshire, upon being queried by the attorney general of the state of New Hampshire about the subject matter of his lectures, refused to answer the questions and was sentenced to jail for contempt. The Court reversed the contempt sentence, indicating an invasion of the lecturer's academic freedom. In *Pickering* v. *Board of Education* (1968), the United States Supreme Court dealt with academic freedom at the public school level. Pickering was a teacher in Illinois who, in a letter published by a local newspaper, was critical of the school board and the superintendent for the ways they had handled past proposals to raise and use new revenues for the schools. After a full hearing, the board of education terminated Pickering's employment, whereupon he brought suit under the First and Fourteenth Amendments. The Illinois courts rejected his claim. The United States Supreme Court, however, upheld Pickering's claim and in its opinion stated:

> To the extent that the Illinois Supreme Court's opinion may be read to suggest that teachers may constitutionally be compelled to relinquish the First Amendment rights they would otherwise enjoy as citizens to comment on matters of public interest in connection with the operation of the public schools in which they work, it proceeds on a premise that has been unequivocally rejected in numerous prior decisions of this Court.

10. Haskell C. Freedman, "The Legal Rights of Untenured Teachers," *Nolpe School Law Journal* 1 (fall 1970): 100.

The Court then addressed itself to the problem of dealing with cases involving academic freedom:

> The problem in any case is to arrive at a balance between the interests of the teacher, as a citizen, in commenting upon matters of public concern and the interests of the State, as an employer, in promoting the efficiency of the public services it performs through its employees.

It is difficult to define precisely the limits of academic freedom. In general, the courts strongly support the concept of academic freedom, yet they recognize the necessity of the practice of professional responsibility by teachers as they interact with youth. True academic freedom and professional responsibility are vital for the future of America and American education.

Right to Bargain Collectively

What are the rights of teachers to bargain collectively? This issue has received much attention in recent years. In the past it was common for teachers' groups to meet somewhat informally with boards of education to discuss salaries and other teacher-welfare provisions. The superintendent even frequently served as spokesperson for such teacher groups. In recent years, formal collective procedures have evolved. These procedures have been variously labeled collective bargaining, professional negotiation, cooperative determination, or collective negotiation. They represent the growing desire of teachers to participate officially and directly in policy making, particularly in matters relating to their welfare. Teachers are demanding a formalization of the procedures of employer-employee relationships in the form of officially adopted written procedural agreements.

Collective bargaining has been defined as

> a means for winning improved goals and not the goal itself. The existence of a contract means that decisions of salaries, working conditions, and other matters within the scope of the Collective Bargaining agreements can no longer be made unilaterally by the school administration. Instead, the contract outlines effective participation by the teachers' union and its members in the formulation of school policies and programs under which they work.[11]

The first teachers' group to enter into a collective bargaining agreement with its local board of education was the Maywood, Illinois, Proviso Council of West Suburban Teachers Union Local 571 in 1938. In 1957, a second local, the East St. Louis, Illinois, Federation of Teachers, was successful in negotiating a written contract. The major breakthrough, however, came in December, 1961, when the United Federation of Teachers, Local 2 of the American Federation of Teachers (AFT), won the right to bargain for New York City's teachers. Since that time, collective

11. Carl J. Megal, "Brief History of Collective Bargaining," *An AFT Guide for AFT Legislative Action and State Collective Bargaining Laws* (Washington, D.C.: American Federation of Teachers, 1970), p. 9.

bargaining agreements between boards of education and teachers' groups have grown phenomenally. Both the AFT and the NEA have been active in promoting collective bargaining. Today, approximately 75 percent of the nation's teachers are covered by collective bargaining agreements.

Both the NEA and the AFT have been very active in proposing bargaining legislation. Many states already have collective bargaining agreements; undoubtedly more statutes will be forthcoming. The details of the statutes and the proposed bills vary, but generally they include the right of public employees: to organize and to bargain collectively, to make provisions for the determination of the bargaining agent (in the case of teachers, usually either an AFT or an NEA affiliate, or a combination of both), to describe the scope of negotiations, and to provide an impasse procedure. In many negotiation statutes, strikes are prohibited. In some instances, where the statutes have called for exclusive representation of all employees by a single organization, election campaigns to select the bargaining organization have been bitterly waged. It can be expected that the courts and legislatures will be called upon frequently in the future to determine the rights of teachers and the rights of boards of education regarding collective bargaining.

When teachers obtain greater participation in educational policy making through unified action, they must assume commensurate responsibilities. The decision-making responsibilities are afforded to teachers by boards of education and administrators who recognize the democratic principle that those affected by policy should have a voice in determining policy. Such participation should involve a commitment on the part of teachers to abide by and adhere to cooperatively determined policies. Teachers, as professional educators and front-line workers in daily direct contact with pupils, possess knowledge that is valuable in educational policy making. Teachers, as specialists, have expertise that board members frequently do not have and are not expected to have. It is hoped that the thrust of these efforts will directly or indirectly provide educational benefits to school children.

Right to Strike   Courts have ruled on the legality of teacher strikes. The Supreme Court of Connecticut (*Norwalk Teachers' Association* v. *Board of Education,* 1951) and the Supreme Court of New Hampshire (*City of Manchester* v. *Manchester Teachers' Guild,* 1957) ruled that teachers may not strike. The court opinion in Connecticut stated that

> under our system, the government is established by and run for all of the people, not for the benefit of any person or group. The profit motive, inherent in the principle of free enterprise, is absent. It should be the aim of every employee of the government to do his or her part to make it function as efficiently and economically as possible. The drastic remedy or the organized strike to enforce the demands of unions of government employees is in direct contravention of this principle.

In general, the judicial view has been that public employees do not have the right to strike. An exception to this general view was expressed by a state district court in Minnesota, when it said that to hold the view that a public employee has no right to strike is

> to indulge in the expression of a personal belief and then ascribe to it a legality on some tenuous theory of sovereignty or supremacy of government. . . . The right to strike is rooted in the freedom of man, and he may not be denied the right except by clear, unequivocal language embodied in a constitution, statute, ordinance, rule, or contract.

The decision was upheld by the Supreme Court of Minnesota (*Board of Education of City of Minneapolis* v. *Public School Employees Union*, 1951). Shortly thereafter, the Minnesota legislature passed an antistrike law applicable to public employees. Two states, Hawaii and Pennsylvania, in their collective bargaining statutes, permit strikes. At least fifteen states have statutes that prohibit strikes. Whether or not there are specific statutes prohibiting strikes, boards of education threatened by strikes usually can obtain a court injunction forestalling them. Both the NEA and the AFT view the strike as a last-resort technique—but as a justifiable technique in some circumstances.

The 1960s revealed a phenomenal increase in the number of teacher strikes. There were 3 strikes in the 1960–61 school year; 181 strikes in the 1969–70 school year; and a total of 500 strikes during the decade. Over 500,000 teachers participated in strikes during the ten-year period, and more than five million teacher-days of instruction were involved. Thirty-three states and the District of Columbia experienced at least one strike during the decade. NEA affiliates called 331 strikes, and AFT affiliates called 135. A spectacular increase took place in the 1967–68 school year. In September, 1967, the schools of New York City, Detroit and many other Michigan cities, East St. Louis (Illinois), and Broward County (Florida) were not opened because of "extended vacations" as teacher groups negotiated with boards of education over salaries and working conditions. The New York City strike was the last to be settled, with schools closed from the time of their scheduled opening on September 11 until September 29. The strike violated the State of New York's recently enacted Taylor Law, which bars strikes by public employees. On 4 October 1967, the United Federation of Teachers was fined $150,000 and its president was sentenced to fifteen days in jail and fined $250 for criminal contempt of court. The Board of Education of the City of New York had obtained an injunction against the strike. The presiding judge termed the strike a "rebellion against government," rejecting the union's position that the work stoppage was a mass resignation rather than a strike. The Taylor Law in this case obviously did not prevent a strike, but it most certainly provided the means for punitive action against the union for violating the court injunction that had prohibited the strike.

Although schools continued to be plagued with work stoppages in the seventies, the total number of strikes during the 1976–77 school year was 152 (130 called by the NEA; 22 called by the AFT), a decline from the high of 194 strikes during 1975–76. The 1977–78 school year began with the fewest number of strikes for the previous four-year period (40 called by the NEA; 10 by the AFT). One could speculate that the early eighties may be the beginning of an era of school board militancy that may deter strikes. The reduced number of strikes may also indicate a trend to keep tempers cool in labor relations and in contract negotiations. In some schools, contracts are being negotiated that will continue in effect for more than one year, thus reducing the total number of possible work stoppages. The oversupply of certified teachers may be another influence that is curbing teacher militancy. Finally, recent court decisions upholding the authority of school boards to bring sanctions against striking teachers may be dampening the enthusiasm of teachers to use the strike as a viable tactic.

Lawyers are increasingly involved in working out legal aspects of teacher and student rights. (*Photography by Eric A. Roth, The Picture Cube*)

Recently the U.S. Supreme Court, by a six to three vote, ruled that boards of education can discharge teachers who are striking illegally. The ramifications of this decision, involving a Wisconsin public school, are potentially far-reaching: the Court viewed the issue of discharge as a policy question rather than as an adjudicative decision: "What choice among the alternative responses to the teachers' strike will best serve the interests of the school system, the interests of the parents and children who depend on the system, and the interests of the citizens whose taxes support it?" The Court said that the state law in question gave the board the power to employ and dismiss teachers "as a part of the balance it has struck in the area of municipal labor relations" (*Hortonville Joint School District No. 1* v. *Hortonville Education Association*, 96 S. Ct. 2308, 1976).

One can argue that strikes are illegal and unlawful when in violation of statute; that the courts, in their decisions, have questioned the right of public employees to strike; and that some teachers and teacher organizations consider strikes to be unprofessional. The question before teachers seems to be whether or not the strike is a justifiable and responsible means—after all other alternatives have been exhausted—to call attention to and attempt to remedy abominable educational and working conditions.

The strike undoubtedly should be a last-resort technique. Emphasis by teacher organizations would be better directed toward developing negotiation procedures on both local and state levels. Teacher organizations and school authorities should work together to obtain adequate sources of funds for public schools. The political arena, long avoided by teachers, must become a familiar habitat for them; through this kind of involvement, they can improve the quality of education and their own professional status.

Liability With nearly fifty million students enrolled in elementary and secondary schools, it is almost inevitable that some will be injured as they participate in educational activities. Each year some of these injuries will result in lawsuits in which plaintiffs seek damages. Frequently these suits are brought against both the school districts and their employees. These actions seeking monetary damages for injuries are referred to as *actions in tort*. Technically a tort is a legal wrong—an act or the omission of an act that violates the private rights of an individual. Torts generally result from and are based upon alleged negligence; the basis of tort liability or legal responsibility is negligence. An understanding of the concept of negligence is essential to an understanding of liability.

Legally, negligence results from a failure to exercise or practice due care. It includes a factor of foreseeability of harm. Court cases on record involving negligence are numerous and varied; the following two are illustrative. In California, in a high school chemistry class, pupils were injured while doing an experiment that involved the manufacture of gunpowder (*Mastrangelo* v. *West Side Union High School District*, 1935). The teacher was in the room and had supplemented the laboratory manual instructions with his own directions. Nevertheless, an explosion occurred, allegedly resulting from the failure of pupils to follow directions. A court held the teacher and the board of education liable. Negligence in this case consisted of the lack of strict supervision of laboratory work. In Oregon, a child was injured by a log while attending a school outing at a beach (*Morris* v. *Douglas County School District*, 1966). Children were playing on a large log in a relatively dry space on the beach. A large wave surged up on the beach dislodging the log, which began to roll. One of the children fell off the log on the seaward side; the receding wave pulled the log over the child, injuring him. In the subsequent court action, the teacher was declared negligent for not foreseeing the possibility of such an occurrence. The court said:

> The first proposition asks this court to hold, as a matter of fact, that unusual wave action on the shore of the Pacific Ocean is a hazard so unforeseeable that there is no duty to guard against it. On the contrary, we agree with the trial judge, who observed that it is common knowledge that accidents substantially like the one that occurred in this case have occurred at beaches along the Oregon coast. Foreseeability of such harm is not so remote as to be ruled out as a matter of law.

Although negligence is a rather vague concept involving due care and foreseeability, it is defined more specifically each time that a court makes a decision. In each instance, based somewhat on past decisions, courts decide what constitutes reasonable due care and adequate foreseeability.

In the absence of statutes imposing liability, school districts generally are not held liable for torts resulting from the negligence of their officers, agents, or employees while the school districts are acting in their governmental capacity. This concept is based on the doctrine that the state is sovereign and cannot be sued without consent; a school district, as an arm of state government, is therefore immune from tort liability. Employees of school districts frequently are not protected by the immunity enjoyed by school districts: every teacher is liable for his or her own action. Teachers must act as reasonable and prudent people, foreseeing dangerous situations. The degree of care that is required increases with the immaturity of the pupil. Lack of supervision and of foreseeability form the basis of negligence charges.

Some states have made provisions to protect teachers from financial loss arising out of claims or suits, by reason of alleged negligence, while carrying out their educational duties. Connecticut, Massachusetts, New Jersey, and New York have laws that protect teachers from suits brought by parents or students. These laws either authorize or require school districts, at their own expense, to defend teachers against suits that charge teachers with negligence. Further, under these laws, districts are also either authorized or required to pay any judgments rendered against the teacher. An Illinois law charges boards of education with the following duty:

> To indemnify and protect school districts, members of school boards, employees, and student teachers against death and bodily injury and property damage claims, and suits, including defense thereof, when damages are sought for negligent or wrongful acts alleged to have been committed in the scope of employment or under the direction of the board. No agent may be afforded indemnification or protection unless he is a member of a school board, an employee of a board or a student teacher.[12]

Further, Illinois school boards are empowered:

> To insure against any loss or liability of the school district, members of school boards, employees and student teachers by reason of death and bodily injury and property damage claims and suits, including defense thereof, when damages are sought for negligent or wrongful acts allegedly committed during the scope of employment or under the direction of the school board. . . .[13]

Many states have laws similar to the Illinois law authorizing school districts to carry liability insurance.

Although the doctrine of governmental immunity still prevails in most states, there is a definite trend toward making school districts liable for negligence. This trend, in opposition to historical precedent, assumes that school funds can be diverted from their imposed educational use and basically supports the idea that governmental immunity is an outmoded and illogical concept. It seems logical that the concept of negligent behavior should apply to both private and governmental activities.

Membership in the state affiliates of the NEA and membership in the AFT permit teachers to participate in liability insurance programs sponsored by these organizations. Teachers should carry liability insurance either on their own behalf or through their respective organizations.

Summary and Implications   As has been pointed out in this chapter, the frequency of court cases dealing with education has substantially increased in the last few years. The courts appear to be increasingly responsive to cases that deal with both students' and teachers' rights and responsibilities. Students and teachers should be aware that if they encounter what might be considered a specific abuse of their rights, legal assistance should be sought.

12. *The School Code of Illinois* (Springfield, Ill.: Office of the Superintendent of Public Instruction, 1969), Section 10–20.20, p. 102.
13. *The School Code of Illinois,* Section 10–22.3, p. 105.

Teachers often enlist the aid of their teacher organizations; in addition, a number of other agencies, such as the American Civil Liberties Union (ACLU), may be solicited by either teachers or students for legal assistance.

From the many court decisions related to education, a framework has evolved for acceptable conduct of teachers within the school setting: the contemporary teacher may no longer assume that his or her ignorance of such acceptable standards of conduct will be overlooked by the courts when adjudicating a suit brought against the teacher. Nor should the contemporary teacher be intimidated by the courts when reasonable rules of conduct are now being evolved for the practice of pedagogy. Courts do not start hearings on their own efforts: school boards, school employees, and teachers must be sued before a court case can develop. On the other hand, prospective teachers need to be deliberately sensitive to the parameters of the legal aspects of teaching. Although beginning teachers need not have the knowledge and expertise of a lawyer, considerable knowledge of the law as related to education might contribute in more than an incidental way to one's becoming a successful teacher.

Discussion Questions

1. Legally parents and students over 18 are now granted the right to check their personal school files to determine the accuracy of the information. How will this affect teacher behavior?
2. In what ways are the expanding legal decisions related to students' rights and responsibilities infringing upon teachers' rights and responsibilities?
3. What are the legal considerations that apply to corporal punishment of students by teachers?
4. How have the courts served as guardians of academic freedom in the classroom? Cite court decisions in your answer.
5. How would you justify the implementation of busing programs when such programs might cause disruption in the neighborhoods? What are the pros and cons of busing students to integrate the schools?

Supplemental Activities

1. Invite to your class individuals or groups who have filed legal suits against the schools. (Staff members of the American Civil Liberties Union may respond to such a request.) In addition, consider inviting a lawyer who is employed by a school district to class to explain his or her role in serving the school system.
2. Examine a copy of your local or state school code to study and evaluate certification standards, tenure legislation, and curricular requirements.
3. Form a discussion group to report to your class on the topic of "Student Rights and Responsibilities."
4. Accompany a truant officer to a court hearing of a school truancy case; report the specific findings of your trip to class. Discuss the relationship of the courts and the schools.
5. Invite members of nearby teacher organizations to class to discuss the ways in which teacher organizations advocate teachers' rights.

Bibliography

Carter, David G., et al. "Student and Parents Rights: What Are Their Constitutional Guaranties?" *NOLPE School Law Journal* (1976): 45–60.

Cary, Eve. *What Every Teacher Should Know about Student Rights*. Washington, D.C.: National Education Association, 1975.

Discipline Crisis in Schools. Washington, D.C.: National Education Association, 1975.

McCarthy, Martha M. "Is the Equal Protection Clause Still a Viable Tool for Effecting Educational Reform?" *Journal of Law and Education* (April 1977): 159–182.

McCune, Shirley, and Matthews, Martha. *Programs for Educational Equity: Schools and Affirmative Action*. Washington, D.C.: U.S. Department of Health, Education, and Welfare, 1975.

Papke, David Ray. "Is There a Lawyer in the House?" *Change* (April 1977): 14–16.

Pepe, Thomas J. *A Guide for Understanding School Law*. Danville, Ill.: Interstate Printers and Publishers, 1977.

Piele, Phillip K. *The Yearbook of School Law: 1976*. Topeka, Kan.: National Organization on Legal Problems of Education (NOLPE), 1976.

School Code of Illinois. Springfield, Ill.: Office of the Superintendent of Public Instruction, 1976.

Sherman, Robert R. *Tenure under Attack*. Washington, D.C.: American Federation of Teachers, AFL-CIO, n.d.

CHAPTER 5

Teacher Organizations

MOST TEACHERS IN THE UNITED STATES IDENTIFY JOHN DEWEY AS perhaps the most important educational philosopher of the twentieth century. It is also a matter of record, though most teachers may not be aware of it, that John Dewey was in favor of strong teacher organizations. Dewey, a staunch advocate of the schools as a social force, believed that teachers should ally themselves with organized labor for their own good and the good of education. Although there has been considerable disagreement among teacher organizations regarding the merits of alliance with organized labor, teacher organizations have grown as instruments of social force and are able to exert pressures on behalf of members.

Prior to the sixties, little attention was given to the activities of the various teacher organizations; teacher organizations had not yet emerged as the powerful groups they are today. This lack of power was not merely a matter of small membership: as a matter of fact, large numbers of teachers have always joined organizations. Mandatory membership in state education associations was a condition of the teaching contract in many, if not most, school districts. Teachers, like other professionals, have always desired to belong to groups organized to serve their common needs and to seek solutions to their problems. Teachers continue to be solicited for membership in numerous and varied types of organizations. Further, most teachers continue to join some kind of teacher organization.

Teacher Power For many years, the large membership in teachers' organizations remained as a latent force; this force emerged as "teacher power" during the sixties. As teacher power developed even greater strength during the seventies, teacher organizations became more and more militant in their approach to salary issues and various other teacher concerns. As teachers worked together to identify themselves more clearly as members of a homogeneous professional group, their most common conscious and desirable group goals were also identified. The concept of teacher power emerged as teacher groups worked to organize activities and to implement what were recognized as common goals.

The two major teacher organizations, which have been rivals for teacher membership throughout the United States, are the National Education Association (NEA) and the American Federation of Teachers (AFT). Prior to the period of teacher militancy during the sixties, the NEA espoused a stance of nonstriking professionalism and abhorred the unionistic stance of the AFT—an affiliate of the AFL-CIO. Over the years, the NEA has refused to join the AFL-CIO, which the AFT refuses to leave. At the same time, the AFT leaders remain opposed to a union that admits principals and other supervisors, as some NEA locals do. During this time, the AFT also stressed the need for collective bargaining contracts such as those gained in Maywood, Illinois (1948); Pawtucket, Rhode Island (1951); and Butte, Montana (1953). During the fifties, the rivalry between the NEA and the AFT increased in intensity. In some school systems, the NEA stance began to become more strongly associated with the union point of view. The first collective bargaining election between the NEA and the AFT, which took place in East St. Louis, Illinois, in 1957, was won by the AFT.

Most teachers are members of both a local and a national teachers' organization. (*Photograph by Owen Franken, Stock, Boston*)

In the fall of 1961, the teachers in New York City conducted an election to determine which organization was to serve as the sole bargaining agent in their behalf in discussions with the Board of Education. The United Federation of Teachers (UFT), affiliated with the AFL-CIO, won the election over the Teachers' Bargaining Organization (TBO), which was supported by the NEA. This election may be viewed, in retrospect, as the most significant contest of what has grown to be the emergence of organized power for teachers. Although such bargaining elections were rare in the early sixties, teacher organizations have since directed much of their resources to organizing and concentrating the combined influence of their members for desired goals.

By 1967, the NEA reported 389 agreements covering 208,000 teachers. By 1973, this total had swelled to roughly 4,200 agreements covering 1.4 million teachers.[1] Although every school district does not have a bargaining agreement, membership figures reported by the NEA and AFT in the late seventies indicate that most teachers do belong to one of the two unions.

Patterns of Organization

Teacher organizations in the United States developed first on a local and then on a statewide basis. In Philadelphia, on 26 August 1857, ten state teacher associations organized to form the National Teachers' Association in order to elevate "the character and advance the interests of the profession of teaching. . . ." The name of the association was changed in 1870 to the National Education Association (NEA). This association has become the largest teacher organization in the United States, with more than 1.5 million members.

The second largest teacher organization in the United States is the American Federation of Teachers (AFT), an affiliate of the AFL-CIO; the AFT has approximately 500,000 members. Of the remaining 1.5 million teachers who are neither NEA nor AFT members, many belong to various religious education associations, associations related to their teaching specialties, organizations of administrators, college organizations, or nonaffiliated local organizations. Some teachers, of course, do not belong to any kind of teacher organization.

National Education Association (NEA)

The NEA is a highly developed organization with many departments, divisions, and commissions. The basic purpose of the NEA, as stated in Section 2 of the charter, is "to elevate the character and advance the interests of the profession of teaching and to promote the cause of education in the United States." Figure 5–1 traces the organizational chronology of the NEA from its founding in 1857 as the National Teachers' Association. In 1870, the NTA united with the National Association of School Superintendents, organized in 1865, and the American Normal School Association, organized in 1858, to form the National Educational

1. Myron Lieberman, "Negotiations: Past, Present and Future," *School Management* 17 (1973): 14.

National Education Association
1857–1870

The National Teachers' Association
Organized August 26, 1857, in Philadelphia, Pennsylvania.
Purpose—*To elevate the character and advance the interests of the profession of teaching and to promote the cause of popular education in the United States.* [The word "popular" was dropped in the 1907 Act of Incorporation.] The name of the Association was changed at Cleveland, Ohio, on August 15, 1870, to the "National Educational Association."

1870–1907
National Educational Association
Incorporated under the laws of the District of Columbia, February 24, 1886, under the name "National Education Association," which was changed to "National Educational Association," by certificate filed November 6, 1886.

1907–
National Education Association of the United States
Incorporated under a special Act of Congress, approved June 30, 1906, to succeed the "National Educational Association." The Charter was accepted and Bylaws were adopted at the Fiftieth Anniversary Convention held July 10, 1907, at Los Angeles, California.

Figure 5–1.
Organizational
chronology of the
National Education
Association (NEA).

Source: NEA Handbook for Local, State, and National Associations, 1976–77 (Washington, D.C.: National Education Association, 1977), p. 147.

Association. The organization was incorporated in 1886 in the District of Columbia as the National Education Association and in 1906 was chartered by act of Congress. The charter was officially adopted at the Association's annual meeting of 1907, with the name of National Education Association of the United States. The original statement of purpose of the National Teachers' Association remains unchanged in the present NEA charter, as quoted above.

NEA Policy-making and Governing Bodies

Overall policies of the NEA are made by the officers and the governing bodies. A recent *NEA Handbook* describes the relationships between the Representative Assembly, the Executive Officers, the Board of Directors, and the Executive Committee:

The Representative Assembly is the primary legislative and policy-making body of the Association. It derives its powers from and is responsible to the membership. The Representative Assembly elects officers; adopts the program budget; votes on proposed amendments to the constitution, Bylaws, and Rules; receives committee reports; and approves resolutions and new business.

The Representative Assembly consists of some 9,000 delegates of state and local affiliates as well as representatives of retired teachers, Student NEA, and school nurses. In addition, all executive officers and members of the Board of Directors and Executive Committee are delegates to the Representative Assembly.

The Executive Officers of the Association are the president, vice-president, and secretary-treasurer. They are elected by the Representative Assembly and are subject to the policies established by the Representative Assembly, Board of Directors, and Executive Committee. They are on full-time leave from their educational positions and maintain offices in NEA Headquarters in Washington, D.C. . . .

The Board of Directors and Executive Committee are responsible for the general policies and interests of the Association. The Board and Executive Committee are subject to policies established by the Representative Assembly and derive their authority from the Constitution and Bylaws.

The Board consists of one director from each state affiliate, plus an additional director for each 20,000 active NEA members within that state affiliate. The executive officers and other members of the Executive Committee are ex-officio members of the Board.

The Executive Committee consists of nine members—the three executive officers and six members elected at large by the Representative Assembly.

The Board meets at least 4 times a year, including one meeting in conjunction with the Annual Meeting as specified in the Bylaws. The Executive Committee meets approximately 10 times a year. Usually meetings are held at NEA Headquarters. Meetings are open to all members, and provision is made for individual members to register as observers.[2]

NEA Organizational Structure The NEA organizational structure is composed of several types of units, including councils, committees, departments, associated organizations, and joint committees. Figure 5–2 is the organization chart of the NEA, which shows the various subdivisions. The councils conduct investigations, recommend standards, build support programs for better programs of education, and work for freedom of teaching and learning. Joint committees provide cooperation between the NEA and other organizations with mutual interests in specific problems.

Many of the special needs of teachers are met through the departments, national affiliates, and associated organizations. A number of these special interest groups were originally organized as national organizations separate from the NEA, and they continue to choose their own officers and plan their own programs. Departments serve general interests such as the Association of Classroom Teachers (ACT), national affiliates represent separate disciplines such as music educators, while associated organizations represent groups such as school administrators.

NEA Income and Expenses The national headquarters of the NEA, located at 1201 Sixteenth Street, N.W., Washington, D.C., is headed by the Executive Director. Several hundred persons are employed by the association and its affiliated departments. The sources of the association's income are: dues from

2. *NEA Handbook for Local, State, and National Associations*, 1976–77 (Washington, D.C.: National Education Association, 1977), pp. 11–12. Reprinted by permission.

Figure 5–2. Organization chart of the National Education Association for the United States.

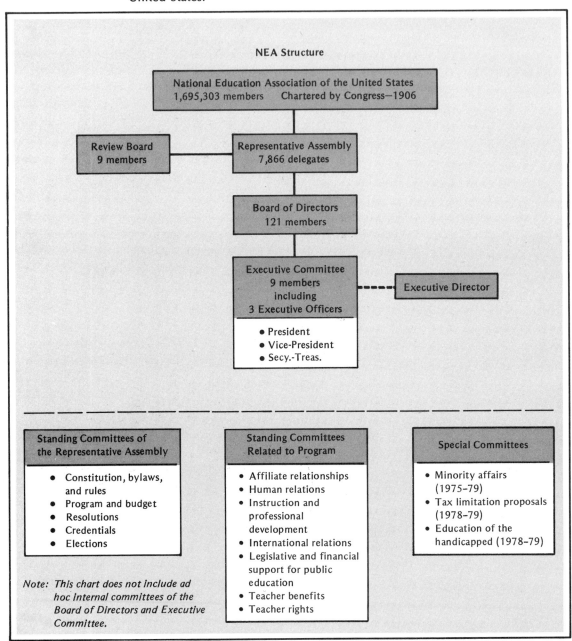

NEA Structure

National Education Association of the United States
1,695,303 members   Chartered by Congress—1906

Review Board
9 members

Representative Assembly
7,866 delegates

Board of Directors
121 members

Executive Committee
9 members
including
3 Executive Officers
- President
- Vice-President
- Secy.-Treas.

Executive Director

Standing Committees of
the Representative Assembly

- Constitution, bylaws, and rules
- Program and budget
- Resolutions
- Credentials
- Elections

Note: This chart does not include ad hoc internal committees of the Board of Directors and Executive Committee.

Standing Committees
Related to Program

- Affiliate relationships
- Human relations
- Instruction and professional development
- International relations
- Legislative and financial support for public education
- Teacher benefits
- Teacher rights

Special Committees

- Minority affairs (1975–79)
- Tax limitation proposals (1978–79)
- Education of the handicapped (1978–79)

Source: NEA Handbook, 1978–79 (Washington, D.C.: National Education Association).
Reprinted by permission.

members and affiliates, interest on bank deposits and on investments of general funds, fees, receipts from advertising and from sales of publications and services, and any other funds received by gift or bequest. Of these, membership dues provide most of the operating income. Recent dues increases, unifications, and membership growth have had the combined effect of increasing the profession's annual budget at the national level to $48.7 million for 1976–77.

American Federation of Teachers (AFT)

The AFT was organized on 15 April 1916 and became affiliated with the American Federation of Labor in May, 1916. John Dewey held the first membership card in the AFT. Teachers' unions had existed prior to 1916: for example, the Chicago Teachers' Federation was formed in 1897 and became affiliated with the American Federation of Labor in 1902. AFT membership grew steadily from 110,522 members in 1965 to 205,323 members in 1970—almost doubling. Membership exceeded 300,000 by 1972 and reached 470,491 in May, 1976 (Figure 5–3). The AFT has 931 local unions in the United States, Canal Zone, Guam, and the Armed Forces overseas schools for the dependents of military personnel. In addition to the national federations, state federations of teachers exist in a majority of the states. The national headquarters of the AFT is located at 1012 Fourteenth Street, N.W., Washington, D.C. 20005. The staff at national headquarters provides aid to local unions and members upon request.

AFT Policy-making and Governing Bodies

Local affiliated unions are the functioning units of the AFT. Their charters are issued by the national AFT Executive Council, and they form the basis for representation at the annual convention. The governing body of the AFT is the annual convention of delegates, who are elected by local union members. Each local is entitled to one delegate for twenty-five or fewer members. For each 100 members or major fraction thereof, one additional delegate may be elected. Additional delegates to the annual convention represent the area councils and state federations. Every two years the convention elects a president and thirty vice-presidents, who comprise the national Executive Council. In order to facilitate its business, the Executive Council elects five of its members in addition to the president to serve on the Executive Committee. The Executive Committee has no constitutional authority, but the Council refers financial matters, personnel matters, and the supervision and organizing of activities to it.

AFT Organizational Structure

Figure 5–3 shows the organizational structure of the AFT. The structure includes the president, thirty vice-presidents, the secretary-treasurer, an administrative staff, and ten departments, including organization, educational research, colleges and universities, collective bargaining services, legislation, international education, human rights and community

Figure 5–3. Table of organization for the American Federation of Teachers (AFT).

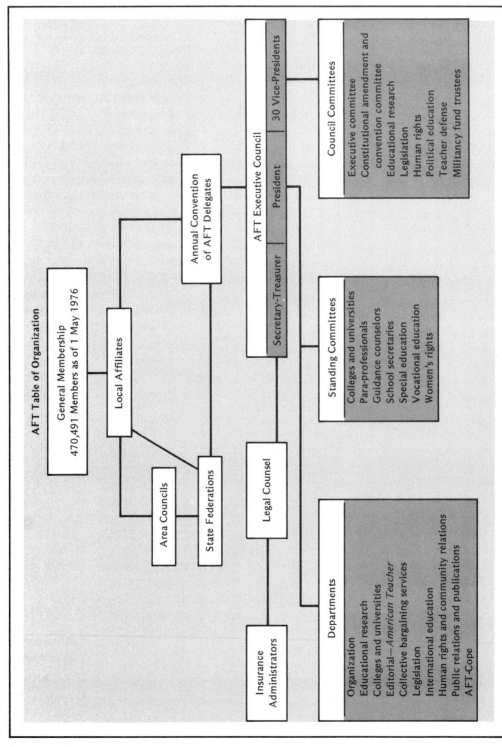

Source: *Constitution of the AFT, 1976.* Washington, D.C.: American Federation of Teachers, AFL-CIO.

relations, public relations and publications, and AFT-COPE. The Committee on Political Education (COPE) is becoming more active as the AFT moves toward greater participation in the political discussions related to educational decisions.

As previously mentioned, the AFT has always been affiliated with the AFL-CIO. The AFT boasts of this affiliation, since organized labor was a major force in establishing our system of free public schools and has actively supported school improvement programs at local, state, and national levels. Affiliation with organized labor gives the AFT the support of the more than 15,000,000 members of the AFL-CIO. The aid and support of local labor unions have often worked to the advantage of local AFT unions in gaining better salaries and improved fringe benefits from local boards of education.

AFT Income and Expenses The national AFT secretary-treasurer is required to make an annual financial report to the convention delegates. The report of the 1976–77 expenses is prefaced by a statement of budget problems:

> Our union has faced very severe financial problems during the year; although the expenditures were approximately what we had anticipated, our income was somewhat short primarily due to our problems involved with declining enrollment, school budget crises and the accompanying reduction-in-force of some of the larger cities. We did achieve significant collective bargaining victories and organized large numbers of new members. Without these victories the financial picture would have been worse.

While total income has increased from $8,917,508 in 1975 to $11,375,-348 in 1977, expenses have kept pace because of the costs of supporting strikes, the expanded needs of the organization, and the effects of inflation. The largest expense in the 1976–77 AFT budget was the allocation to "organization and servicing"; this expense, coupled with the allocation for "administrative and departmental" expenses, constituted 63 percent of the total 1976–77 AFT general fund expenditures.

Yearly Dues Classroom teachers who join teacher organizations pay yearly dues, which vary from $75 to $200 for national, state, and local membership. Both the NEA and AFT incorporate a unified dues plan whereby each member pays dues covering all three levels of membership. In Illinois, for example, the yearly dues are based upon the average yearly salary for teachers in the state. Membership dues in the local associations are determined by each local affiliate and therefore vary. A typical amount might be $10. Under the unified dues approach, each teacher is required to pay unified (national, state, and local) dues for the year; however, if a teacher belongs to other organizations affiliated with the NEA or AFT, dues for these memberships would be paid separately.

AFT and NEA Compared

During the sixties, the AFT was generally viewed as a collection of teacher unions that would willingly, though illegally in most states, close the schools by the strike method to gain their demands. Many educators, NEA members especially, looked upon the strike tactic as a labor union technique that should not be used by "professional" teachers. At that time the NEA used a procedure termed *sanction*. When sanctions were imposed against a school, the professional association advertised the school district as being an unacceptable place to work and discouraged association members from taking employment in the district. Teachers completed existing contractual agreements without closing the schools. Generally several months' notice was given before sanctions were invoked. Sanctions were applied by the NEA upon local districts and also upon entire states (Oklahoma and Utah). Technically, the NEA did not have a no-strike policy at that time, but it was strongly implied.

The strong competition between the AFT and the NEA for memberships and bargaining rights during the late sixties was vocally volatile and highly intense. Teacher militancy among members of both the NEA and AFT grew considerably. The strike tactic utilized by the AFT seemed to have greater immediate effect than the NEA sanctions. As a consequence, the NEA began to embrace the strike as a last resort rather than the sanction procedure. The NEA also came to embrace collective bargaining, which was first utilized by the AFT.

To serve its very large dues-paying membership, the NEA developed extensive field service and research services—available to all members and to all state and local affiliates. NEA members benefit from such field services as counseling, retirement planning, career development, strike strategy assistance, insurance programs, and so forth.

Thus the influences of the AFT and NEA on each other have resulted in a growing sameness of philosophy and purpose. Today most teachers, administrators, and board of education members consider both the AFT and NEA to be teacher unions employing those tactics proven to be most successful by the trade unions of organized labor.

Trends Toward Merger

In October, 1968, shortly after David Selden was elected president of the AFT on a "merger" platform, the AFT invited the NEA to enter into discussions of merger. A week later, the AFT invitation was declined by the NEA Executive Committee. Even though the first attempts at merger discussions failed to materialize at the national level, local actions along merger lines began to develop. In October, 1969, 1,800 NEA and AFT members joined together in Flint, Michigan. An important merger of major urban local affiliates of the NEA and the AFT occurred in February, 1970, in Los Angeles and was approved by an 8,999 to 5,042 vote by local teachers. After the Los Angeles merger, the New York Education Association (NEA) and the Empire State Federation of Teachers (AFT) merged in May, 1973, to form the New York State United Teachers Association with 200,000 members. In September, 1974, the Florida Education Association and the Florida AFT voted to merge. However, as a consequence, the NEA expelled the Dade County (Florida) Classroom Teachers' Association because the proposed merger included AFL-CIO affiliation, which violates NEA policy.

Following the annual convention of the AFT in Washington, D.C. (August, 1973), the general convention feeling was that the NEA-AFT merger was inevitable. At the same time, the then AFT President David Selden warned that several obstacles still remained in the way of merger. At about this time, the present AFT President, Albert Shanker of the New York City AFT, was emerging as a challenger to Selden's leadership. By March, 1974, the possibilities of merger were lessening. NEA President Helen Wise, following the break-off of merger talks, stated that "NEA wants teacher unity. AFT wants AFL-CIO membership."

The annual NEA convention in Chicago reported 1974 as a year of calm, with the possibility of merger with the AFT a faint and distant hope. NEA leaders openly expressed their hostility toward both the AFT and Albert Shanker, who was swept into the AFT presidency at the union's Toronto convention. After these two conventions, it was obvious that the NEA-AFT rivalry had resumed.

By the beginning of the 1977–78 school year, the NEA and AFT had once again drifted apart. The 1973 New York State merger has since split—with the NEA and AFT again competing for a position of dominance in numbers represented. With national memberships now declining as a consequence of declining enrollments, teacher layoffs, and school budget crises, the AFT has opened membership opportunities to

Many schools have strong local traditions that highlight the school year. (*Photograph by Talbot Lovering*)

interested noneducational workers, such as lawyers, who have expressed an interest in joining. The NEA views this development as unacceptable for its purposes. Seemingly the old issues of labor union affiliation and several new issues are surfacing—to delay, if not permanently set aside, the possibility of further NEA-AFT merger attempts.

Political Action   The most recent developments within teacher organizations are political action committees. The AFT has an active Committee on Political Education (COPE). A similar NEA committee is called the Political Action Committee for Education (NEAPAC) and is financed by NEA dues.

One reason for this recent thrust toward the political arena has been the success achieved by other unions and organizations through effective political action. In the past, many organizations used a kind of moral persuasion procedure, whereby delegates presented themselves to legislators or legislative committees to ask for legislation to meet organizational needs. The lessons of history demonstrate that this procedure does not work very well. Other organizations, including teacher organizations, have found a much more effective method is to assist in the election of political candidates who are sympathetic to their particular needs. Thus, for teacher organizations, the function of political action committees is to monitor the voting records of elected officials with regard to education bills and to analyze the various platforms of new candidates. Teacher organizations hope to support actively those candidates who will perform in accordance with the organizations' views. To analyze various candidates, the NEA appointed an ad hoc committee to outline the procedure for the endorsement of a 1976 presidential candidate. AFT-COPE was also active in outlining procedures for endorsing a 1976 presidential candidate. Both NEA and AFT endorsed the Carter-Mondale ticket.

The trend toward concentrated efforts for political action has caused some divisiveness within local teacher organizations and has further separated the two national organizations. Many individual teachers do not agree philosophically with the concept of collective political action. In addition, the AFT and the NEA take different positions on the formation of umbrella coalitions that include large organizations of other public employees. The NEA supports the movement to form the Coalition of American Public Employees (CAPE), which would include fire and police personnel, municipal and public employees, and other public workers. Ohio is an example of a state that has taken such a course. The AFT opposes such a coalition, feeling that such an umbrella organization of public workers would alienate the public. The AFT prefers to identify with the public employees of its parent AFL-CIO.

The various state and national political action committees sanctioned by both the NEA and AFT have as a common aim the promotion of education by encouraging teachers to participate in the political life of their local, state, and national communities. The Illinois Political Action Committee for Education (IPACE) indicates that the two most important jobs IPACE has are selecting and supporting candidates for public office who are committed to the goals established in the Illinois Education Association legislative platform. This committee and similar committees throughout the state are responsible for making recommendations on political endorsements to their respective boards of directors. Interestingly, the NEA and AFT political action committees were in almost identical agreement on which candidates to endorse during the 1976–77 national elections.

State and Local Teacher Organizations

Although the state and local units of both the NEA and AFT operate under the umbrella of the parent national offices, the bases of power reside with the state and local units. The local federation of teachers has the highest priority in the overall organizational scheme. However, the strength of any single local union resides in the solidarity in numbers, in resource personnel, and in services provided by the state organization.

For the most part, teachers participate directly in the affairs of local organizations. Solutions to the problems at hand are, therefore, primarily the concerns of local teacher groups. The influence of these groups obviously would be weakened without the support and resources of strong state and national parent organizations. However, there are widespread signs of unrest among local organizations by disgruntled members about their national affiliation. Several local chapters have taken steps to sever relations with their respective state and national affiliates. If it persists, continued local chapter withdrawal will serve to reduce membership—and thus reduce power—of the state and national organizations.

Religious Education Associations

The *Education Directory* lists forty-two religious education associations of various denominations. These national and regional religious education associations are listed under denominational or interdenominational control and do one or more of the following: operate sectarian schools attended by students who prefer them to public or private schools; supplement the public or private school program by offering educational activities for youth and adults; operate adult educational programs open to the public; and formally promote scholarships among their members in sciences and liberal arts. Each of the religious education associations, by itself, has a very small membership when compared with either the NEA or the AFT. However, when the memberships of all forty-two religious education associations are totaled, it is obvious that large numbers of teachers are members of these associations.

Summary and Implications   Prospective teachers will find concerted pressure placed on them to affiliate with the recognized teacher organizations. The advantages and disadvantages of such paid memberships must be decided upon by each teacher. In some districts, the climate of the working environment for teachers may be strongly likened to the unionistic climate of the trade unions. In other districts, the teachers attempt to maintain a more scholarly, professional climate analogous to that of the traditional professions—law, dentistry, medicine. Again, each teacher must determine the manner in which he or she will contribute to the organizational climate associated with a particular membership.

Discussion Questions

1. Do you feel that teachers have gone too far or not far enough in their attempts to gain power? Discuss the rationale for your answer.
2. In your opinion what would be the most significant advantages for the merger of the NEA and AFT? Disadvantages?
3. Teacher strikes are reported to have been at their lowest ebb in the past few years. What do you consider to be the reasons for the diminished number of teacher strikes?
4. In what ways do the politicians, at all levels, affect the nature of the teaching profession?
5. List and describe the pros and cons of membership in teacher unions. Discuss the rationale for the unified (national, state, local) dues structure as it is related to membership.

Supplemental Activities

1. Divide the class into interview teams for the purpose of interviewing local, state, and national politicians on the topic of the importance of maintaining our system of public education. Share the reports in follow-up class discussions.
2. Invite representatives of the NEA and AFT to class to discuss their organizations.
3. Invite a small group of local teachers to class to discuss the pros and cons of their teacher organizations.
4. Examine and discuss an agreement negotiated between a teacher organization and a school district.
5. Invite a group of trade union members to discuss the strike as a power strategy for employees.

Bibliography

American Federation of Teachers, AFL-CIO. *Constitution of the AFT,* 1976. Washington, D.C.: American Federation of Teachers, AFL-CIO, 1976.

Barbaro, Fred. "Mass Jailing of Teachers." *Clearinghouse* (September 1973): 11–18.

Browne, James. "Power Politics for Teachers, Modern Style." *Phi Delta Kappan* (October 1976): 158–164.

Collective Negotiation Agreements for Administrators. Arlington, Va.: Educational Research Service, 1978.

Geel, Tyll van. *Authority to Control the School Program*. Lexington, Mass.: Lexington Books, 1977.

Illinois Political Action Committee for Education. *Election and Surveying Handbook*. Springfield, Ill.: Illinois Education Association, 1976.

National Education Association. *NEA Handbook for Local, State, and National Associations, 1978–79*. Washington, D.C.: NEA, 1978–79.

Riccio, Alfred T. "Seven Questions (with Answers) That Boards Are Asking about Bargaining." *American School Board Journal* (November 1977): 36,54.

Shanker, Albert. "Where We Stand: High Court Limits Public Employee Rights." *New York Times*, 27 June 1976.

"Student Wrongs versus Student Rights." *Nation's Schools and Colleges* 2 (April 1975): 31–38.

"A Teachers' War That's Costing Millions," *U.S. News and World Report*, 5 April 1976, pp. 90–91.

PART II

School and Society

An examination of the history of the United States shows the school to be a significant institution within the culture of American society. The school has served as a common bond that has transmitted the commonality of American culture. All cultures are identified by commonly held customs, attitudes, and beliefs; compared with other more homogeneous nations of the world, the American culture remains unique in its diversity. Within the United States, the acceptance of individuality has helped to develop diversity of religious organizations, of political affiliations, and of social and economic institutions. The school has been given the special task of transmitting this cultural diversity.

We will now examine the role of the school within the culture of the United States and its relationship to other societal institutions. As an element of society, the school has its own culture, traditions, and customs. It deals with a constantly changing school population, rapidly changing technological demands, a continuing knowledge explosion, and diverse expectations from parents who entrust their children to the school.

In Part II, we will examine the multifaceted interactions between the school and the individual and the culture. In particular, we will study the school as a social institution and investigate how it copes with particular social problems endemic to the American culture. We will next discuss selected nationwide efforts in education mounted in an attempt to solve pressing social problems and will conclude with a treatment of international social impacts on education in American society.

CHAPTER 6

Culture, People, and the School

AS THE UNITED STATES OBSERVED ITS BICENTENNIAL IN 1976, IT could reflect upon a two-hundred-year history of societal support for, and recognition of the importance of, education in America. From a very meager beginning in the original thirteen colonies, the United States has built a fifty-state educational program that stands second to that of no other nation in the world. Fostering both a free and private system of education, the formal institution of school, in its many forms, has emerged as the primary agent for cultural preservation. This institution has gradually assumed many of the educational activities formerly provided by the home and the church. Although it has become a permanent social institution in its own right, it has been continually subjected to the conflicting pressures exerted by the larger society. It has not been privileged to enjoy the exclusive status of home or church.

Operating under the principle of separation of church and state, the church has not exerted any direct or significant influence upon public education in the United States. The earliest forms of education in this country, however, were affected by significant religious influences of the eighteenth and nineteenth centuries. The compulsory education laws of the twentieth century have brought about closer contacts between the school and home; these contacts have placed the school in a challenging position.

American schools tend to remain somewhat traditional. Although many elements of society tolerate and promote change, the majority of Americans still resists change from the norm or from the traditional. Although home living and general family behavior structure have changed rapidly since World War II, society has only permitted limited change in schooling. If the school attempts change and that change threatens the customs, traditions, and values of the home, the school will eventually revise its program. Thus the school is directed into a role of cultural transmission. Since a traditional role is the dominant feature of the school, an examination and discussion of culture in general and the culture of the school, in particular, are pertinent.

Culture and Anthropology   Much of the knowledge about culture regarding human development, relationships between races and subgroups of races, social customs, human ways of worshiping, their pursuits, constraints, and fears, comes from the scientific study of humankind called *anthropology*. Anthropologists study and examine the cultures of people, present and past. Four specialized branches of anthropology that have special significance to the school and society are physical anthropology, archaeology, cultural anthropology, and linguistics. Although specialization of study may require different methods of examination, the anthropological findings are shared so that a better understanding of mankind can develop. Charles Darwin's theory of evolution (1857) helped to motivate a flourishing study of anthropology. As research techniques have continued to advance and as increased numbers of anthropologists have been trained, a vast storehouse of findings has contributed to the current understanding of schooling as a social need.

Sociology   *Sociology* is the behavioral science that deals with the many facets of the individual's behavior while living as a member of a group. As a sociological concern, culture is defined as the sum total of the aspects of life of a group of people who have been or are living together. Specialized areas of study in sociology are: general sociology, social psychology, demography, the community, social organization, and social change. Of primary significance to educators is general sociology, which studies the ways people behave while members of all sorts of groups. The school is one such group. Sociology was named by a French philosopher, Auguste Comte (1798–1857). From his time on, interest in sociology spread rapidly and continues to thrive today. It provides teachers and related school personnel with knowledge related to the individual and personality, the home environment and its effect on students, and social class structure in the American culture. Further, it helps the teacher to understand the effect of class structure on the school's efforts and the effect that different value structures have on school programs.

Institutions and Arts   All cultures have several basic aspects in common. These commonalties may deal with the material needs of people such as food, shelter, and tools; or they may deal with nonmaterial activities such as manners, mores, and religion. Every culture depends upon common elements such as the use of tools to meet daily living needs, a system of communication (language), the systems or organized group activities called *institutions*, and a system of expressing the desire for beauty usually referred to as *the arts*. No culture has been discovered that did not utilize tools for such purposes as catching, growing, preparing, cooking, and eating food; and for constructing houses, making clothing, and altering the physical surroundings in many ways. Every culture maintains a system of language that provides communication within the culture. Languages grow and change as needs arise within the culture or as different cultures come in contact with each other. In every culture, there is a desire for beauty, expressed through a system of arts, including music, dancing, painting, sculpture, and rituals. In every culture, institutions have considerable stability since each centers around a cultural need. An institution unites a group of people who share a common need that is satisfied through that institution. The school is one of these cultural institutions.

Although cultures have many general characteristics in common, they also differ greatly. It is true that all cultures utilize tools; however, the nature of the tools and the way in which they are used varies considerably. Languages are obviously quite different from one another, as are institutions and art forms. A culture that does not come in contact with more advanced cultures may exist for hundreds of years with very little change. This has been seen in recent years with the study of southeast Asian, Australian, and African cultures. The study of Malayan tribes, isolated from much of the modern world, has revealed little change in their customs and practices for hundreds of years. One of the ways in which cultures grow and change is by borrowing from other cultures. Another way is by invention. While invention and borrowing induce cultural change, within every culture there is some inherent resistance to change. The fixed customs within a culture represent the desire to do things in the same manner and enforce conformity. In order for a culture to remain strong, there must be a balance of the forces of conformity and change. A reasonable amount of conformity is needed to keep groups of people working together, but growth and change are also needed in order to progress.

Acculturation   As a result of improved communication and rapid travel, the people of one culture can easily meet those of another. When cultures meet, there is a resultant exchange of ideas and materials. Frequently the people of a simple culture try to adopt a more complex culture, a process called *acculturation*. However, acculturation in its modern manifestation involves any adoption of change or adaptation to what the human encounters in the social process. Typically people tend to resist learning a new culture, causing the process of acculturation to be very slow. In the immediate past, and to some extent in the present, the influence of the Western world was felt through acculturation of many non-Western peoples who attempted to learn Western culture. There has emerged, however, a new sense of worldly consciousness in the Western world itself. This new consciousness is evidenced by Western world interests in and study of Eastern social, economic, political, and art forms. The concept of acculturation has been worldwide.

A new type of acculturation has emerged within the United States during the past decade. It might even be termed a new type of social consciousness affecting an expanding number of minority groups that are part of the American population. In a real sense, this social consciousness has fostered a different acculturation process, one that challenges the American "melting pot" notion. This new social consciousness within the United States society has become labeled *cultural pluralism*. The American culture is attempting to preserve the cultural differences of blacks, native Americans, Spanish-speaking Americans, and others who have contributed uniquely to the American civilization. This movement carries with it extensive societal implications for the schools.

Determinants of Class Structure

One feature of American society directly related to the school is the social class structure. Although American society is not a rigid caste system, in which no one can rise above the position into which he or she was born or placed by religious laws, America is a class society. Sociologists usually refer to six class divisions in the American social system: the upper-upper, the lower-upper, the upper-middle, the lower-middle, the upper-lower, and the lower-lower. The usual criteria used to determine social class in the United States are occupation, values, wealth, income, prestige, social contacts—and such intangibles as control over the actions of others. In American communities, extreme variances exist from community to community with respect to the proportion of people within the different classes. Examples of the different types of communities, which exhibit different proportions of social classes within them, are small communities that are not satellites of large cities, small rural communities, small cities of 5,000 to 15,000 people, large cities, and metropolitan areas. All will contain certain elements from the six class divisions but the distribution of the classes will be different.

The upper-upper and lower-upper classes consist of wealthy and socially prominent families. The distinguishing feature within the upper class is that the lower-upper class consists of the newest members of the class, whereas the upper-upper class is made up of established social register families of long standing. The upper-middle-class members are professional workers and businessmen who tend to associate with the upper classes but are not as wealthy or prominent. The lower-middle class consists of some professional workers, small businessmen, and white-collar workers. The upper-lower class is the largest group in the American class system and consists of skilled and unskilled workers. The lower-lower class is often looked down upon by the other classes and consists of manual laborers, migrant workers, and many unemployed.

Social Stratification   Various studies have been conducted in which the facets of social stratification were examined. In this context, social stratification is the general term that includes such characteristics as hierarchy and rank within the social class structure. Although social classes may be discussed as distinct groups, the various classes in American society are interrelated in a hierarchical structure. One may locate one's position in the structure by comparing one's own or one's group's characteristics to those ascribed by the community to the specific classes. In so doing, one recognizes one's rank as an individual or the rank of one's group in the community class structure, in terms of power and prestige, compared with other individuals or groups in the same community. In terms of the interrelatedness among social class groups, a particular individual or group will exchange communications with other individuals or groups having more or less influence within the same community. When studies of social stratification are undertaken, an attempt is made to measure specific aspects of the class structure such as prestige, occupation, wealth, social interaction, class consciousness, value orientations, and power.

Figure 6–1 illustrates the possibility of both upward and downward social mobility in the social structure typical of the American society. The dark heavier arrow within the Figure indicates that there is generally more upward than downward mobility in America. As suggested earlier, such mobility is not usually possible in a caste system. Although the several social classes are all a part of the large American culture, each class is a subculture with characteristics somewhat different from the other classes. As one moves from one class to another, either up or down, one must learn the characteristics of the somewhat different culture into which one is moving so that one may adjust to and function well within one's new environment. Teachers who understand the

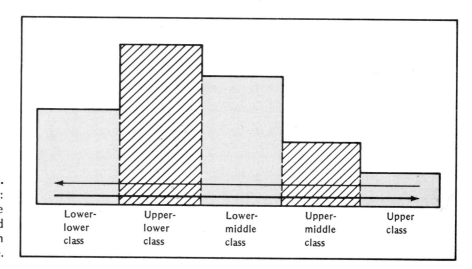

Figure 6–1. Social mobility: people may move freely, upward and downward, within the social structure.

Lower-lower class   Upper-lower class   Lower-middle class   Upper-middle class   Upper class

characteristics of the various social classes will be better able to work with students from each of these groups.

Mores and Folkways

Within each of the elements of social class structure, one can distinguish the mores and folkways of a class. *Mores* have generally been defined as rules that govern behavior. They are fixed customs of a particular group and tend to be classified as "good" or "bad." They are assumed to be laws of the culture, and to counter them or to violate their tenets is taboo. An example of middle-class taboos would be open, promiscuous social behavior.

Whereas mores tend to have good or bad associated with them, *folkways* tend to be couched around "corrects" or "incorrects" of conduct, etiquette, or dress. As such, it is not taboo to violate a folkway, but one may suffer some form of social censure when challenging the folkway of a particular class. An example of such a violation would be the personal dress of a teacher in a particular school district, which does not conform to the image that the teacher should maintain as a professional. As society and its various classes within the structure have continued to experience change, it has become exceedingly difficult to identify and to examine the mores and folkways. The exponential rate of change during the past two decades has created a cultural lag that has thoroughly shaken the confidence and comfort of the many societal reference groups.

Mobility

Mobility of the population (physical movement within the country) is related to factors of sex, destination, occupation, and education. In general, it can be said that younger people tend to move more. As the national and international economy stays healthy, professional, technical, and other white-collar workers tend to display the greatest mobility. In general, the moves of these occupational groups are associated with their levels of education: the greater the number of years of formal schooling, the more mobile the person. Table 6–1 shows the mobility status of Americans by geographic region within a five-year period.

School as an Institution

As a social institution, the school has a structure that helps it function properly. A graphic representation of the structure of the school as a social institution is shown in Figure 6–2. The dotted lines in the Figure outline the structure of the school and are used to suggest that the school is an open system accepting and exchanging information within its own environment. The structure has indentifiable components: role, purposes, areas of emphasis, operations, organization, human and material resources, and outcomes. In addition to a variety of external social forces that affect the school, societal conditions, curricular trends, and pupil attitudes have a significant impact on the school as an institution. Successful performance of the institution is wholly dependent upon the successful interaction of each of its structural com-

Table 6–1. Mobility status of the U.S. population: place of residence in 1975 compared to former residence in 1970.

	Number	Percent
Total Population: 5 Years Old and Over	193,512	100.00
Same house (nonmovers)	99,651	51.5
Different house in U.S. (movers)	79,838	41.3
Same county	46,835	24.2
Different county	33,003	17.1
Same state	16,349	8.4
Different state	16,354	8.6
Abroad or no report on mobility		7.2

Source: U.S. Bureau of the Census, *Current Population Reports*, series P–20, no. 285.

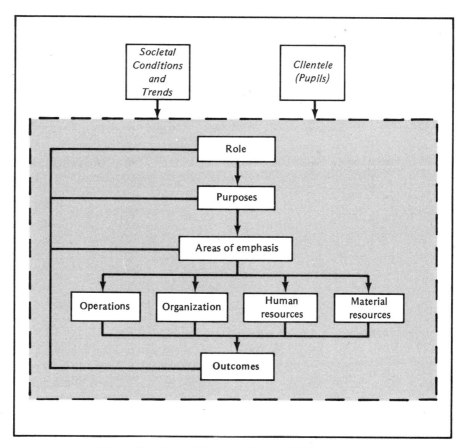

Figure 6–2. The school as an open institution.

Source: Adapted from *The Logical Structure Theory*, Norbert J. Nelson, Purdue University.

ponents. Each of these components will be discussed in the following sections.

Role of the School

The school attempts to emphasize one or a combination of three distinct roles. One of these is *reproduction,* in which the school serves as a preserver of traditions and heritage. Emphasis is oriented toward the past, and decisions on what to teach are based upon the customs and traditions of the past. A second role is *readjustment.* When the school assumes this role, it attempts to alter its program as is seen fit by society. Whereas change in the past was measured in periods, ages, or centuries, today—for educational purposes—it is measured in decades and years. This requires continuous change if the school is to keep itself alert to the present. A third role is *reconstruction,* in which the school is seen as an agent of change for society and assumes the responsibility for guiding the changes of the future. From this viewpoint, the moral and social ills of the past and present must be remedied; therefore, the school attempts to reconstruct society for the future.

As a present-day school attempts to seek its role in society, it should attend to three areas of special significance: universal education, equality of opportunity, and liberation within society. Compulsory attendance

This school is inscribed as an institution "dedicated to the preparation of youth for the responsibilities of life". (*Photograph by Eric A. Roth, The Picture Cube*)

laws, child labor laws, and other state and national social legislation have guided this nation in its attempts to bring about universal education. Despite the cry of certain contemporary critics who push for a return to basics, the school has in the past been able to provide the bulk of the population with the basic tools necessary for communicative and economic existence. If, however, the school is to keep pace with the present rate of technological change, universal education may have to include life-long learning programs for adults.

Schools should provide programs that assure quality and quantity to all who seek it. It is apparent that equality of opportunity has not always had the same meaning to all people. As will be discussed later, a turning point in education came with the *Brown* v. *Board of Education* decision (1954). Continued civil rights legislation and affirmative-action programs (equal rights for women and other minorities) have assisted the school in providing equality of opportunity in education. The recent Public Law 94–142 (1975), discussed in some detail in Chapter 8, continues a national trend toward equality of opportunity.

If an educational program is successful, it provides students with the tools needed to improve their status within society. Liberation permits social and economic mobility. In the United States, the liberation commitment has been partially met for ethnic groups, but it is still a long way from being achieved for racial groups. This is a problem that cannot be completely corrected by social legislation; the solution must partially evolve from an educated citizenry. These roles are discussed at greater length later in a presentation of aims and objectives of education.

Purposes of Schooling

Education seeks to satisfy *academic* and *psychological* needs of students. The basic academic needs are knowledge, understanding of alternatives, value judgments, and productive capability. The knowledge explosion has placed a greater emphasis on the tools of learning as they relate to the subject disciplines. The picture of the nuclear age, both exciting and foreboding, necessitates a keen sense of how to arrive properly at alternatives for shaping the future. As society changes, so do the mores and folkways that traditionally have aided us in making value judgments. As traditional mores and folkways change, the student has an even greater need to see them in the perspective of what they will lead to in the future. Every person has a need for economic productivity; it is one of the purposes of the school to provide the student with the proper tools.

The psychological needs that the school attempts to satisfy include the individual's need for status, security, affection, independence, and achievement. Students who do not have these needs satisfied become frustrated. Therefore, it becomes the special task of the teacher to help satisfy these psychological needs so the student can successfully pursue academic goals. It is realistic to assume that the psychological needs are seldom fully satisfied; however, if the level of frustration can be kept to a minimum, better learning is likely to occur.

Areas of
Emphasis

The broad areas of emphasis in education are *general* education, *exploratory* education, and *personal* education. General education is usually considered the tool or core area of formal learning. Although this type of education is present at all levels of learning, kindergarten through college, it is primarily associated with the elementary school. Exploratory education is usually a special function of the junior high school or middle school. At this level, the student is exposed, at his own rate of acceptance, to the many possible areas of specialization he may pursue in senior high school or post–high school education. Personal education is the primary function of the senior high school. It may come in the form of terminal work completed in the high school or of preparatory work for higher education usually associated with one of the professions. These areas, as functions of the educational institution, are explained in greater depth in Part VI, in the discussion of the function of the educational program.

Operations

Schools function within formalized patterns of organizational and legal behaviors. In addition to these behaviors, the area of operations includes the *methodology* of teachers and the *working relationships* of the four levels of rank within the institution. These four levels include the school board or public, the administration, the teachers, and the pupils. In terms of methodology, the operations area seeks answers to such questions as how can mathematics or English best be taught. Or in what kinds of organizational environment does maximal learning take place? These questions are not, by far, the only ones to be asked but are typical operational concerns. These operational questions pursue the monumental task of arriving at a comfortable yet productive theory of learning that meets the individual differences of all students as they strive for excellence.

Organization

Some basic concepts of the organization of school systems will be identified here briefly and developed more fully in Part III. These basic concepts are *horizontal and vertical span of control, school district organization, and boards of education.* Teachers need to acquaint themselves with the organizational structure of the system if they are to understand their role in it. The typical vertical structure of the educational system is *line and staff,* similar to a military structure. As teachers have become better educated and professionally competent, a definite trend has developed toward horizontal organization in which the staff has assumed wider responsibilities in program development. Much of the increased teacher participation in program development has come about as a result of stronger professional teacher organizations. It is important that the teacher understand organizational structure, in general, and how it may differ among the many local school systems.

Human and Material Resources

Education cannot function adequately without students, teachers, specialists, supervisors, administrators, and the school board. As society has become more specialized, a similar demand for specialization in education has been accommodated by its personnel policies. In that each member of the system increasingly has a more specialized function to perform, it becomes important that all members understand one another's function and assist in the cooperative effort of goal attainment.

Just as the school needs human resources to operate, it also needs material resources, including the physical plant, educational hardware (machines, projectors), and software (books, papers). It has become extremely important for school staffs to work cooperatively in planning and designing new facilities or in adapting and renovating old school buildings that will help to promote maximum learning. Within well-planned school buildings, teachers can create an atmosphere that capitalizes on the learning materials.

Pressures on Schools

The school as a social institution does not exist in a vacuum. Since education is still primarily a function of each state, there are fifty separate state school systems. Within each of these states, the schools are an integral part of the community and are subject to the likes and dislikes of the people who make up that community. Thus no two schools are completely alike. The beginning teacher must understand the various forces that come to bear on what is actually taught in the classroom. These forces may be classified as *legal forces* and *extralegal forces* at the local, state, regional, and national levels.

The legal forces are set in motion by state constitutions, statutes, legal opinions, court cases, and common law. The extralegal forces differ in that they have no legal origin. They are a mirror of the society in general and use societal pressure to exert their influence. Both the legal and extralegal forces have direct and indirect influence upon classroom instruction. At the local level, the direct legal force in public education is the school board. Indirectly, the people represent the legal forces in that they participate in the selection of the school board. Two extralegal forces operating directly at the local level are the PTA and the classroom teachers' association. As increasing numbers of states allow or mandate collective bargaining for teachers, the influence of teachers is moving from extralegal to legal pressure on the schools. Indirectly, groups such as the League of Women Voters, the local Chamber of Commerce, and the Rotary Club help to influence popular opinion and bring pressures to bear upon the school. Figure 6–3 shows the types of direct and indirect influences at the local, state, regional, and national levels.

This interplay of influence between the school system and the society establishes the educational policy affecting students and teachers. In

		Legal		Extralegal	
		Direct	Indirect	Direct	Indirect
Local		Local board of education	Superintendent of local school ——— People	PTA/PTO ——— Local teachers' association	Local Chamber of Commerce Churches DAR ACLU
State		Legislature ——— State school board	State courts ——— Attorney general	State PTA ——— State teachers' association	State Chamber of Commerce ——— American Legion
Regional		None	None	College and university accrediting agencies	
National		None	Departments: HEW Agriculture Treasury Defense	PTA NEA AFT	U.S. Chamber of Commerce and NAM

Figure 6–3.
Legal and extralegal
influences on the
school.

Source: Norbert J. Nelson, Purdue University.

addition to the legal and extralegal forces, other local social and economic factors tend to influence the action of all forces impinging upon
the school system. One such factor is the wealth of the community—and
the availability of this wealth for educational use. Wealth is related to
the industrial makeup of the community. Not only does wealth involve
financial ability but also, more importantly, financial effort, that is, the
effort made through local taxes to support the schools. In large cities, the
taxes on industries provide considerable revenue, but the cities are also
faced with providing increasing governmental services for their own
residents and for commuters who do not reside within the city. Such
service costs reduce the funds available for education. In the middle-
class suburban communities, with limited industry to support the tax
burden, homeowners have allowed themselves to be taxed heavily to
support the schools. However, homeowners are beginning to feel the
burden because of other increasing governmental costs caused by suburban growth.

Another factor affecting local influence is the social and ethnic
composition of the community. The upper-middle-class groups tend to
give more support to education and tend to play a more active role in the

development of educational policy. Lower socioeconomic groups typically do not take this same interest in education. Recently, however, there has been increased interest and participation of blacks and Spanish-speaking Americans in school concerns. A problem still remains: even though the lower socioeconomic group may be in the majority, the upper-middle class still may control the school program and the school board.

A third factor is the age structure of the community. If the community is dominated by young people with children, there is usually active and enthusiastic interest in the educational program, particularly in residential suburban communities. On the other hand, if the community has a majority of elderly people, the educational program may lack local support.

A fourth factor affecting local influence on the school system is the rate of population change within the community. This nation continues to be very mobile; when the majority of the community population is transient, the people tend to take less interest in the schools. The transient quality of a community also affects teacher attitudes; it frequently becomes difficult to hire and retain good teachers. With an expanding oversupply of teachers, however, problems caused by population mobility have been greatly reduced.

Regional beliefs and attitudes also exert influence on local school systems, as seen in the various ways integration problems have been handled regionally. Many areas of the South, for example, have experienced more integration than areas of the North. Likewise, conservative and traditional viewpoints have dominated education in the Midwest. Regional beliefs have also influenced what reading materials are to be used in the classroom: for example, in Kanaha County, West Virginia, fundamentalist religious groups challenged the use of contemporary reading materials.

The school as a social institution is subject to influences of all kinds. In order to maintain its equilibrium as an institution, it must learn to accommodate and purposefully direct these influences. In a 1976 national survey of public opinion, a Gallup poll identified the seven major problems facing public schools, as shown in Figure 6–4. As an open structure in society, the school cannot afford to resist or neglect public opinion that reflects prevailing attitudes toward the school. School and society are mutually dependent. Whereas the school finds itself wholly dependent upon society for its livelihood, society likewise is dependent upon the school to maintain and develop the culture it desires.

School as a Subculture   Most educators agree that the school has as one of its functions the transmission of the prevailing culture to the child. As a part of their description of the school as a social system, Havighurst and Neugarten have written directly on the topic of the culture of the school:

Figure 6–4. Public opinion on problems facing the public schools.

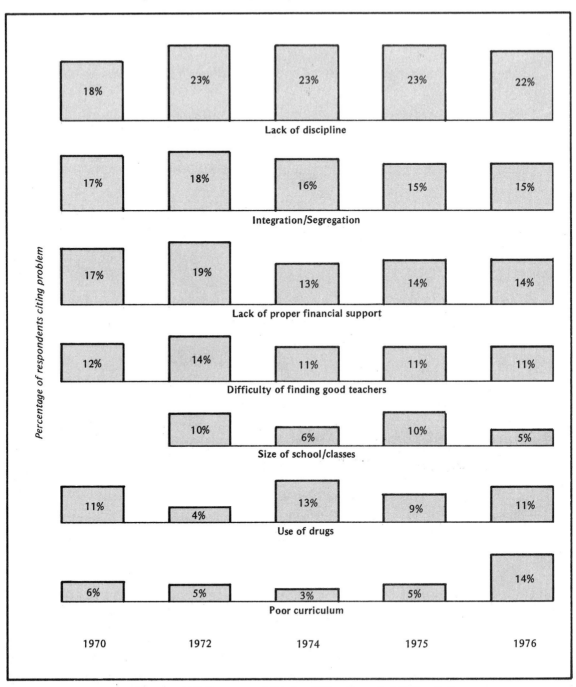

Source: U.S. Government Printing Office, Report of Gallup Poll.

The school has a subculture of its own—a complex set of beliefs, values and traditions, ways of thinking and behaving—that differentiate it from other social institutions. Education in the school, as compared with that in the family or in the peer group goes on in relatively formal ways; and even those activities that are least formal (as in children's play at recess) are evaluated in terms of their contribution to the learning situation. Groupings are formed, not on the basis of voluntary choice, but in terms of aptitudes for learning and teaching.

Differentiation develops gradually according to achievement. In the elementary school, achievement proceeds along two lines; the first is the "cognitive," or the learning of information and skills; the second is what Parsons calls "moral" or social—learning respect for the teacher, consideration of fellow-pupils, good work habits, initiative, and responsibility. In the secondary school, the emphasis is upon types, rather than levels, of achievement. With its variety of subject matter, personnel, and activities, the high school offers the student a wider range of choices along both the cognitive and the social axes of achievement.[1]

Subcultures   As Havighurst has suggested, the subculture of the school is composed of many elements. In most instances the mores and folkways of the school have withstood the test of time and have a direct effect on school plant, personnel, students, curriculum, laws, and values. Although increasing numbers of new physical plants for learning are suggestive of open-learning areas, the vast majority of school plants are still of the "egg crate" variety with single and double-loaded corridors of single classrooms. Teachers and other educational specialists must meet changing, but long-established, certification regulations that govern by credential examination who may or may not teach. Despite individual differences in ability, rate of learning, and personal interests, most students are subjected to the same type of information retrieval and processing, as determined by the many state curriculum regulations. The Carnegie Unit persists despite its very questionable validity. Special school laws regulate fiscal practice and structure, transportation, curriculum, and social and moral behavior. The school's own system of common law regulates classroom behavior, dress code, speech behavior, and other descriptive, local school-board policies. Common rituals for school practice are found in athletics, clubs, promotion exercises, and a whole host of special events, usually referred to as routine school activities. The signs and emblems of the school's own culture are displayed by school songs, colors, and cheers. The culture is basically middle class; and general values reflect that part of the larger society.

Formal Practices   Within the school operation itself, there are varied modes of formalized practices. Children are assigned to grade levels for learning on the basis of age rather than readiness, ability, or interests. In most instances

1.   Robert J. Havighurst and Bernice L. Neugarten. *Society and Education.* 4th ed. (Boston: Allyn and Bacon, 1975), p. 139.

all children start first grade at age six. This may vary by a year or less from state to state, but in general the practice is based on a traditional formality rather than on a rational or special set of collected data. Time modules of learning represent another school formality. Classes meet for certain periods of time each day of the week, and all learning occurs in these specified time blocks. Authority is adult-centered, with the learner having little or no direct input into his learning situation. Boys and girls are grouped together for learning despite a vast store of knowledge that has suggested very strongly that there are different maturation rates related to sexual differences. The whole reporting system of educational achievement represents yet another example of school formality. Traditional letter grades are awarded to students on the basis of some comparison with other learners who have received the same type of learning stimuli. This grading system is referred to as a *norm-referenced* reporting system. Only recently have significant attempts been made to reduce the formalism in education by creating open-space learning centers, nongraded learning programs, and individualized learning packages based upon readiness and interests. Newer grading systems attempt to judge learning perfomance on the basis of the individual's entry and exit learning behavior and are referred to as *criterion-referenced* reporting systems. These two reporting systems are discussed further in Chapter 23.

Cultural Variations To be sure, there are variations in the culture of the school. These variations may be associated with regional influences, school location (rural, urban, suburban), length of operation of the school, or social structure of the community. Regional influence may have a profound effect on certain athletic programs. For example, in some areas of the Midwest, basketball is generally thought to be the state sport. In one particular midwestern state, it even carries a "hysteria" label. In some areas of the East, this type of fierce athletic competition has a somewhat lower priority—with wrestling and gymnastics equally popular. The great high school marching bands of many southern schools take high priority in the local school curriculum. Rural schools may place great emphasis on Future Farmers of America clubs, agriculture programs, and 4-H Clubs, while urban schools seldom sponsor such activities. A type of regional isolationism often reflects itself within the school program.

Traditions Older schools have stronger traditions than newer schools, and thus variations are apparent even within large growing communities. These variations may be found in feelings of pupil pride or of resignation to mediocrity. In addition, these feelings are often carried over to the adult part of the community and may have both a positive or negative effect upon the school. Local traditions may be reflected in the emphasis given to sports or academic programs; they may cause significant problems of balance in the school program.

There is little doubt that the culture of the school must be taken into account if its contribution to the total culture of society is to be analyzed and studied. Values of students, teachers, and parents interact significantly upon the total operation of the school and its contribution to societal development.

Values   Since the dawn of civilization, scholars have studied the domain of values associated with humans as individuals and humans as members of a group. *Axiology* is a branch of philosophy that describes the nature of and kinds of values and describes the values worth holding. (Axiology as a branch of philosophy is discussed more fully in Chapter 15.) If one's personality is demonstrated by one's behavior, it may be said that one's behavior is to a considerable degree based upon the values one holds. Some personal frustration may arise from such a premise, since one's individual behavior is often influenced by the value structure of one's membership group as well as by one's personal value system. It is imperative for each of us to focus upon our personal value system for the purpose of gaining a conscious awareness of the priority of the values we possess if our behavior is to be consistent with these values.

To a considerable degree, as with personality, individual values are formed and affected by the social class position one occupies. Our American schools are, in turn, influenced by the values held by those who manage the schools and teach the pupils. Since most school board members are from the upper-middle and lower-upper classes, and since most American teachers are from middle-class backgrounds, it is natural that the public schools are predominantly influenced by middle-class value systems. This kind of influence presents no problem so long as the students are of middle-class origin. Perhaps the biggest problem facing city schools is the clash of value systems in institutions dominated by middle-class personnel and attended by minority pupils. To ensure success in the classroom, the beginning teacher must not only become familiar with the value standards of the several social, ethnic, and racial classes but also must be able to teach the individual pupil who holds a value system that differs from the teacher's. All too often in our schools, the only attention given to value systems is that of the discipline and management of pupils, and perhaps the management of their parents, while the school attempts to practice its major function of teaching skills and knowledge.

Community Schools   The community still serves as the dominant resource in the education of its children. Although both the state and federal government have regulatory influences on local schools, educators have given serious attention to the community school concept since the 1930s. Three types of community schools that remain readily identifiable are rural, sub-urban, and urban schools. The following sections examine the differences between the three major types of community schools and point to the unique qualities each possesses.

Rural Schools   Science and technology have helped to bring an end to the one-room schoolhouse of rural America. Although a few one-room schools still exist, developments in transportation and communication, for the most part, have helped to consolidate the small rural schools. Today many rural school systems compare favorably with their urban and suburban counterparts. One has only to drive through the rural areas of this nation to see some very modern and tastefully designed schools. However, the educational program of the rural schools is still the subject of much debate.

The rural sections of America have undergone considerable change in the past thirty years. The small farm has almost disappeared, and in its wake large-scale mechanized farming has emerged. Expensive machinery, new crop fertilizers, and irrigation have changed the nature of farm operations. Because of these developments, fewer farmers are needed; and the majority of rural youth must migrate to the cities for employment. The mass communication media of television, radio, magazines, and newspapers have helped to bring the rural areas into closer proximity with the city. All of this has helped speed the end of rural America as it was known prior to World War II. In order to be effective in meeting the needs of rural students, the rural school has had to adjust its educational program to prepare youth for pursuits other than farming. Many consolidated schools are proceeding in this direction, and rapid progress is being made.

Despite all of the change that has taken place, rural America still retains its distinctive patterns: the school is the center of rural life; values are more conservative; and the rural family tends to remain a cohesive unit. School children travel long distances each day to get to school, and social contacts at school become vital. Although families live considerable distances from one another, there is a close feeling of neighborliness. The social structure of the rural area is less stratified, and everyone tends to know everyone else.

During the decade of the 1970s, there has been a return to rural life. It has been estimated that the rural areas had an emigration rate of 12.3 percent during the 1960s but have experienced a net inflow of 2.9 percent during the 1970s. Many of those returning to the rural areas are young and well-educated people, fleeing from the complexities of metropolitan life to the simplicity and quiet of small rural farms and towns. This migration is a kind of renaissance for self-reliance, confidence, and cleaner environments. Since these people have come from urban and suburban areas, they bring different value structures and present new problems for the rural school.

Attempting to maintain its isolation from the big city, the rural school often takes a less sophisticated approach to education. The teachers are not expected to be highly intellectual; to be successful, they must adjust themselves to the rural or small-town pattern of life. Rural school boards remain dominated by farmers who still cling to the importance of agricultural education. Unless mandated by state law, these schools are lacking in specialized programs for the slow learner or the academically talented, and they frequently have inadequate vocational programs. The increase of new consolidated vocational-technical schools for county or intermediate school has helped to alleviate the lack of vocational training for rural youth. Academic programs have also been improved through the use of various funds provided by the U.S. Office of Education. Properly staffed guidance programs rarely exist, and the curricular offerings do not have the breadth of the urban and suburban schools. Because of the sparsity of population and cost involved, children in need of special attention frequently get little. The vast majority of teaching, although handled by teachers as well trained as their city counterparts, is still of the single textbook approach. Although the rural school has come a long way since 1900, it has much further to go. If its students are going to be increasingly compelled to compete with their city counterparts for college and vocational preparation, the rural school must offer programs that meet this challenge.

Suburban Schools

Suburban educational systems have spawned with the evolvement of modern American suburbia. In an attempt to escape the so-called evils of the big city, the large middle class of our nation continues to migrate to the fringe areas. Here they may enjoy the aesthetic pleasure of the unobstructed view of a blue sky and still be within the service area of the city. In effect, the city dweller has been transplanted to a semirural setting. The major growth in this area has come since World War II and has been concentrated around the nation's largest cities— New York, Boston, Chicago, Washington, and Los Angeles. This growth pattern has resulted in what demographers now call the *megalopolis*. A person traveling between Washington, D.C., and Boston observes very little countryside. The same may be said for the traveler from Michigan City, Indiana, to the Milwaukee, Wisconsin, complex.

The key to the social pattern in suburbia has been housing development. Where the city dweller has tended to be segregated by religion, nationality, or race, the suburban dweller is segregated by income. The row houses of the city exist in kind in suburbia—but with a larger lawn. What was once the rich man's retreat has now become a center of urban decentralization. Many of the city problems have also moved to suburbia. The suburban family has in many ways turned to matriarchal supervision because the father spends little time at home. The reduction of the number of work hours per week has been consumed by commuting time to and from the place of work in the city. When he is home, the suburban father has precious little time for family living. He seems driven to compete with his neighbors on such mundane pursuits as a beautiful lawn; he is involved in the process of continuous maintenance of his house in order to protect his investment. Civic activity, clubs, and recreation also compete for father's time. Psychologists suggest that many of the problems that children bring with them to school can be traced to this changing pattern of family life.

Since suburban youth are somewhat isolated from school and recreational facilities, they have become dependent upon the car and telephone. The suburban family now feels a need for two cars and either an extension phone or a private phone for the children. Teen-agers are on the move, and a car is considered a necessity.

As the suburbs have grown in number and size, so have the schools. Suburban school building has become a big business. These schools utilize the newest furniture, devices, and equipment. They also attempt to employ the best teachers available. The programs reflect what the middle-class family feels is necessary education for their children's success in life. Where guidance and special education are found lacking in rural America, such is most often not the case in suburbia. Suburban schools attempt to provide all services for all students. One has only to examine the activity program of the modern suburban high school to see that there are provisions designed to meet the needs of all students. The educational emphasis is structured toward preparation for college, and the parents have a keen interest in the operation of the school. Because of pressures for college entrance, the suburban school has been subjected to excessive parental influence. Parents often demand more homework and insist that their children be continuously challenged. The parental pressure for a return to the basics is greatest here.

With all this attention on education, suburban youth appear to develop in a passive and sheltered atmosphere. Everybody wants to be like everybody else. Preparation for a secure life is the by-product of the suburban school. One of the inherent weaknesses in this type of education is its hidden emphasis on conformity and social isolation. The problems of this nation are many, and suburbia cannot isolate itself from these problems. Social contact is needed between all strata of society if attempts at solving social problems are to be fruitful. With our mobile society, the interdependence of the immediate family (father, mother, and children) and other relatives (grandparents, aunts, uncles, cousins) has lessened. This forces the school to assume additional responsibilities for transmitting the culture of all societal levels to the vast middle class of suburbia.

Urban Schools   The migration to suburbia has hastened the decay of the inner city. City stores and recreational establishments are finding it profitable to locate elaborate branches in spacious and beautifully designed shopping centers adjacent to suburbia. It is much more convenient to shop near one's home than to trudge to the center of the city. Since wealth, or at least "credit wealth," is centered in the suburbs, business has to cater more to the needs of suburbia and less to the needs of the inner city.

With the egress of white city dwellers to suburbia, there has been an equal ingress of the black, brown, and yellow races to the inner city. These immigrants are primarily black, Puerto Rican, Mexican-American, and American Indian. More recently there have been increasing numbers of Korean and Vietnamese families coming into these areas. Where the inner city was once a temporary domicile for the white migrant, it has become a trap for its newer occupants. Restricted to certain areas of the city, these newer city migrants find it almost impossible to move elsewhere, even if they achieve a higher level of economic security. The typical urban child lives in a multifamily unit and is surrounded by thousands of people. The more deteriorated the slum is, the more inhabitants there are. The child who lives in the center of the slum is restricted by it and has few contacts outside his own block. Problems of the city are more acute toward the city center. Here there are too few and poorly kept parks, inadequate police protection, and old, poorly maintained schools.

The multiple social problems of the city have brought about increased problems for the urban school system. Although most middle-class people have gone to the suburbs to live, their value systems remain embedded in the city schools. Today many of the large-city schools resemble the suburban school; as a result, they fail to meet the needs of their different class of students. The curriculum is often geared to middle-class living, and the children are introduced to values and practices with which they seldom come in contact. In recent years, federal and state funds have provided inner-city learners with compensatory programs that are meaningful and enhancing to their way of life such as day-care operations, reading materials, and educational welfare programs for parents.

Because of the many social problems in the inner city, violence and disorder have increased in the schools. The arguments for the neighborhood-school concept have been severely attacked; in its place has come the demand for the busing of black students to all-white districts.

High-caliber teachers are difficult to hire and hold in city schools despite the high salaries that teacher organizations have secured for their members. Discipline problems, social class prejudice, low economic standards, increased use of drugs, and deplorable living conditions all contribute to what appear to be insurmountable problems of urban education. The financial plight of the large urban areas has caused many people to declare the cities potential disaster areas. School superintendents find their jobs next to impossible and have called upon the federal government to aid in a massive overhaul of urban education.

Since the sixties, the cities have attempted to modify the pervasive ills of the urban school systems. Some innovative changes have been the experiments of the store-front schools of New York and the Parkway Plaza Project in Philadelphia. Other alternative educational programs, funded privately or publicly, have begun—on a very small scale—to bring changes to urban education. In an attempt to make education relevant for urban students, these programs have deviated markedly from the traditional school curriculum found in typical city schools. As with other urban social and educational projects, the supporting funds for these programs have been seriously jeopardized by the general lack of economic stability of all American cities with large minority populations. These cities face even greater financial crises in the eighties. The financial plights of New York, Detroit, and Los Angeles were reported at the National Mayors' Conference in 1975. In 1975 and 1976, these and many other city schools faced early closings and late openings— until state legislatures came to the financial rescue.

School and the Individual

The culture of the school is believed to influence the personality development of students. Likewise, the sets of values held by students are influenced by the schools. Since we have a predominantly middle-class society, the schools are primarily oriented toward middle-class personality and value norms. The adult culture of schools is generally in agreement with the middle-class orientation toward personality development and values, since the adults associated with the schools are, for the most part, from middle-class environs. The peer culture of the schools is not generally in agreement with such a single-minded middle-class school orientation, however. Many contemporary students' concerns are more closely identified with individual development rather than with the middle-class social philosophy that emphasizes social relations.

Teachers are also influenced by the cultural aspects of schools and the society supporting the schools. As an individual within the society, the teacher assumes many roles. Most teachers have definite perceptions of what their roles should be in a given societal setting. Likewise, societal pressures suggest somewhat definite expectations of acceptable teacher behavior. In the simultaneous pursuit of both their personal and professional goals, teachers are influenced by their personal perceptions and societal expectations.

Personality Determinants

One's personality may be defined as the complex of characteristics that distinguishes an individual—or as the organization of the individual's distinguishing character traits. Scientists have noted that similarities of life experiences tend to produce similar personality characteristics in different people. On the other hand, individuals are unique: no two personalities are exactly alike. However, personality is not something that is fixed; rather, it continually grows and develops. Teachers have

Peer influence plays a strong role in the subculture of the school. (*Photograph by Talbot Lovering*)

considerable opportunity to guide and to strengthen the growth and development of their students' personalities.

Peer Influence   Though the peer group may reflect adult society, it also influences other members of its group and adults with regard to several personality factors. Personality determinants such as role, values, behavior, socialization concepts, status, and experiences of all kinds are learned by the child from the peer group. The school setting provides prolonged contact with the peer group away from the parents. When children make their first school contacts, they usually respond according to the patterns they have learned at home. While the early influences learned at home tend to be carried along with each child as the child develops, other influences from the peer group also affect personality development. For example, every individual has certain social needs that he or she strives to satisfy. Satisfaction of social needs strongly influences positive personality development. Strong peer group associations tend to satisfy strong social needs, such as approval from others, desire for success, and yielding to the feelings of others.

Teacher Role   Teachers assume many roles in the community: the teacher may be a spouse, parent, church member, club member, and participating citizen. Also teachers have many subroles they fulfill in their professional capacity that are related to their behavior in the community and with their students. If the beginning teacher wishes to be successful in a professional capacity, he or she must develop an understanding of role perception and role expectation. Specifically teachers should have predetermined perceptions of what their role in society should be. Likewise, society expects a certain role performance from the teacher. A potential danger for the beginning teacher is a conflict of role identity. When the role expectations of a community deviate from the role perceived by the teacher, the possibility for tension and conflict is self-evident. This possibility is further increased when teachers reside outside the community in which they are employed, as is often the case in both urban and suburban areas.

The teacher is a well-educated individual, possessing many skills that may be profitably utilized in the community. At one time, a primary community expectation for teachers was participation in Sunday-school activities, choir membership, or service organizations. At present, it is not uncommon to find teachers active in welfare or social organizations, local governmental duties, and occasionally active partisan politics: teachers serve on school boards, city councils, and state and national legislatures. There are some communities, however, that still attempt to restrict teachers from participating in community government. Generally, however, teacher participation in an ever-widening range of community activities has grown steadily in the recent past. One reason for this growth is the increasing number of people from all social levels entering the teaching profession.

One of the teacher's many subroles is that of protector of morality. The level of community feeling regarding this role is dependent upon the particular community. On the whole, however, parents expect teachers to provide a special kind of model behavior for their children. Although the parents' habits may be unethical, and at times illegal, they do not want the teacher to exhibit such behavior. Since teacher behavior is held up for public display, teachers must use absolute discretion in their personal life. Exemplary behavior is vital for the young teacher. Most students tend to hold their teachers in high esteem and to emulate their behavior as they do their parents'. Other subroles that the teacher may be expected to fulfill in the community are those of a cultured individual who is widely read and traveled, an explorer of knowledge who works for the continual improvement of society, a preserver of tradition and the status quo, and an expert in the methods of child growth and development. Needless to say, some of these roles conflict.

Conflict of Roles One of the role conflicts that a teacher faces relates to economics: the teacher is expected to be a model of dress and appearance, to live in a respectable house within the school community, and to participate financially in church, club, and welfare organizations. All too often teachers are expected to maintain a certain standard of living on salaries that are not commensurate with their needs. These community pressures have contributed to an increased rate of moonlighting among teachers, especially male teachers who are the sole source of income for their families.

In addition to being an employee of the school board, a subordinate of the principal, an advisee to superiors, and a colleague to fellow teachers, the teacher fulfills many specific roles in the classroom. Teachers serve as transmitters of knowledge and directors of learning. They enter the classroom to teach, and if there is any role they can perform best, it should be this one. They have acquired thorough understanding of their teaching area and have received special training through professional work in teaching methods, curriculum, philosophy, and psychology. The teacher has been specially trained to perform the teaching function to promote maximum learning. Our schools have traditionally divided subject matter into courses. Teacher success is usually examined in light of pupil success in the subject matter courses.

Teachers also serve as directors of discipline. They strive to guide children toward appropriate behavior. This guidance may be carried out in various ways. Some teachers become strict disciplinarians; some attempt to solicit the voluntary cooperation of students; still others give students a great deal of freedom to act as they wish. Many teachers never learn to control students successfully. Discipline problems plague many beginning teachers. It is difficult to learn the techniques of disciplining students since this is an area that does not lend itself to special training in teacher-preparation programs. As indicated earlier, the public views the lack of discipline to be the most urgent problem in the schools at the present time. Teachers who have a firm background in their teaching areas, in educational philosophy, and in psychology of learning must also develop their own techniques for handling classroom discipline.

The teacher is an evaluator. Like discipline, evaluation is another difficult task for the teacher. Children receive grades and are passed, or retained in a grade, based on the decision of the teacher. In addition, the teacher determines what is appropriate moral and ethical behavior for students. In many respects teachers are entrusted with the authority of judge and jury; they must call upon their total capabilities to evaluate each child fairly.

In many instances the teacher also performs as a substitute for the parent. In most states the teacher stands *in loco parentis* while the child is in school. Teachers are not only expected to discipline a child as the parent might and at the same time teach but also are expected to help the child manage his or her own personal problems. The teacher performs a multitude of varied duties—ranging from helping little children with their clothing to helping older students adjust to the excitement, problems, and anxieties of adolescence. Occasionally the teacher becomes the special confidant of students—when, for example, students have difficulty communicating with their parents about particular personal problems.

All the foregoing does not imply that the teacher must fill all roles equally well in order to be successful. Various situations will dictate specific emphases for appropriate teacher behavior. Teachers must determine their proper role as they perceive it, and they must understand the expectations and limitations that accompany that role.

Summary and Implications

Schools and society are dependent upon each other for survival. The diversity of our social classes, the types of schools society envisions, and the social setting of the schools add to the complexity of the school as a social institution. It is imperative that all prospective educators develop an understanding and appreciation of this diversity if they wish to function effectively in the milieu called school. The future of the school as an institution is wholly dependent upon how it responds to the demands of the society it serves. Although some may continue to urge less formal schooling or the deschooling of society, the fact remains that cultural transmission is best protected by the school. Since the church and the home have continued to abandon their formal educative roles, the school must meet the challenge of filling these voids. Teachers and administrators must continue to seek harmonious ways in which to educate the young people of society beyond simply providing students with factual or rote knowledge and must provide them with a humanistic outlook, if society is to survive in an acceptable direction. Unless educators remain knowledgeable about the sociological implications of schooling, the schools will not meet this challenge.

Discussion Questions

1. In what way can the school be used as an instrument of change in society?
2. How can the school provide equality of opportunity when each community school is directed to serving a particular student body?
3. Discuss the major areas of concern in the changing role of the teacher.
4. How can the schools counter the public image of ineffective discipline practices?
5. Discuss some potential cures for the problems of the inner-city school.

Supplemental Activities

1. Visit a local high school and interview a student about the subculture of the school.
2. Attend a PTA meeting and discuss your observations with your class.
3. Compare a community's expectations for an elementary teacher and for a secondary school teacher. Note any differences.
4. Interview a Chamber of Commerce member and detail his or her expectations for the community school.
5. Meet with a school administrator and find out how the administrator responds to community pressures. Discuss in class.

Bibliography

Cove, William M., and Chesler, Mark A. *Sociology of Education*. New York: Macmillan, 1974.

Cusick, Phillip A. *Inside High School*. New York: Holt, Rinehart and Winston, 1973.

Glatthorn, Allan A. *Alternatives in Education: Schools and Programs*. New York: Dodd, Mead, 1975.

Kozol, Jonathan. *Free Schools*. Boston: Houghton Mifflin, 1972.

Liska, John A. *Schooling and Education*. New York: D. Van Nostrand, 1976.

Schimmel, David, and Fischer, Louis. *The Civil Rights of Students*. New York: Harper & Row, 1975.

Schwartz, Audrey James. *The Schools and Socialization*. New York: Harper & Row, 1975.

CHAPTER 7

The School and Social Problems

THERE IS CONSIDERABLE DEBATE ABOUT THE EXTENT TO WHICH the schools can, or should, help solve our country's social problems. Some people feel that our schools should only be concerned with the academic development of students; others feel our schools are in a unique position to help solve many of our nation's pressing social problems—and should do so.

Although this debate remains unresolved, the fact that social problems affect our students and our schools seems indisputable. This chapter explores some of the social problems our country is currently facing and examines the effects these problems are having on our students and on our schools.

Poverty The poverty problem in the United States is extremely complex: it is very difficult, if not actually impossible, to sort out and to analyze the various factors that presently contribute to poverty. The following discussion is devoted to an examination of some of the more identifiable causes of poverty in the United States.

Poverty is not new. It has existed since the human race appeared on earth and probably will be around as long as humans are around; however, the nature of poverty is continually changing. Whereas poverty may at one time be defined in terms of physical hunger or even starvation, it may at another time be defined in terms of a lack of luxuries. In other words, poverty is a relative matter. It is not the mere fact that some people are literally starving to death in the United States that defines our poverty problem; rather, it is the stark contrast between those who have relatively little and those who have so much. The problem is that conditions of extreme poverty exist in the midst of abundance. Since poverty is a relative matter, it is interesting to specu-

Table 7-1. Money income—percent distribution of families and individuals by income level and race, in constant (1975) dollars, 1955–75.

Item and Income Level	White			Black and Other Races		
	1955	**1965**	**1975**	**1955**	**1965**	**1975**
Families						
Under $3,000	10.8	6.3	3.7	30.7	17.6	11.4
$3,000—$4,999	9.5	7.2	6.5	18.4	16.9	14.9
$5,000—$6,999	12.3	8.2	7.9	18.2	17.0	11.8
$7,000—$9,999	23.0	14.8	12.6	18.2	17.9	15.4
$10,000—$11,999	15.6	11.3	8.9	7.7	8.2	9.3
$12,000—$14,999	11.9	16.7	13.8	4.1	9.6	10.9
$15,000—$24,999	13.9	26.5	31.7	2.6	11.3	20.1
$25,000 and over	3.0	8.9	15.1	0.1	1.6	6.4
Unrelated Individuals						
Under $1,500	31.9	21.4	7.9	44.0	30.3	15.0
$1,500—$2,999	20.4	20.7	19.6	22.3	22.3	29.3
$3,000—$4,999	15.9	15.8	21.9	18.7	16.3	18.1
$5,000—$6,999	13.3	11.2	13.5	10.2	10.8	10.7
$7,000—$9,999	11.6	13.7	15.3	3.4	12.1	11.7
$10,000—$14,999	5.2	11.4	13.5	1.1	7.0	10.8
$15,000 and over	1.7	5.7	8.6	0.2	1.1	4.3

Source: U.S. Bureau of the Census, *Current Population Reports,* series P–60, no. 103.

late whether poverty—at some future time—will be defined in terms of having only one car, of living in a home with only three bedrooms, or of not having enough money to vacation in Europe.

There is less poverty today in the United States than in the past. The government's definition of poverty is based on changing economic conditions—further adjusted by such factors as family size, sex of family head, number of children, and farm or nonfarm residence.[1] Table 7–1 presents a national survey of the income level of families and unrelated individuals by percent distribution from 1955 to 1975. This table vividly illustrates the great difference in incomes in this country, the income trends over the past twenty years, and the differences between black and whites in the income picture.

Table 7–2 contains information on national poverty and indicates that, as of 1975, 25.9 million Americans (12.3 percent of the population, or

1. U.S. Bureau of the Census, *Statistical Abstracts of the United States: 1976,* 97th ed. (Washington, D.C.: Bureau of the Census, 1976), p. 392.

Table 7–2. Persons below poverty level, by race, 1965–75.

	Number below Poverty Level (millions)			Percent below Poverty Level		
	1965	**1970**	**1975**	**1965**	**1970**	**1975**
All persons	33.2	25.4	25.9	17.3	12.6	12.3
White	22.5	17.5	17.8	13.3	9.9	9.7
Black and other races	10.7	7.9	8.1	47.1	32.0	29.3
Black	not available	7.5	7.5	not available	33.5	31.3

Source: U.S. Bureau of the Census, *Current Population Reports,* series P–60, no. 106.

about one in eight) were below the poverty level. This table also shows that there is a far greater percentage of nonwhite than white people affected by poverty. Approximately 29.3 percent of the nonwhite and 9.7 percent of the white people in the United States now live in poverty. Although there is a higher percentage of nonwhite families living in poverty, numerically there are many more impoverished white families.

There are other segments of the population that suffer severely from poverty. For instance, according to a report by the President's Appalachian Regional Commission, one-third of the Appalachian white families earn less than $3,000 per year. The per capita income for this segment of the population is 35 percent less than for the rest of the country. More than one million Appalachian adults are unemployed, an understandable statistic when we realize that 10 percent of the Appalachian adults have less than five years of schooling. The Appalachian subculture has created a way of life that keeps these mountain people impoverished. Farming and mining have been their traditional sources of livelihood; however, the mountain farms are no longer productive enough to provide a good living, and automation has largely replaced men in the coal mines. Those who have migrated from the mountains to large cities have found that their education and skills do not qualify them for the available jobs.

In general, the amount of income that people earn is directly related to the amount of education they have received. The average lifetime earnings for American men with less than eight years of education are approximately $200,000. Men with a high school diploma have an expected earnings of $375,000; men who have four years of college education have an average life income of approximately $425,000.[2] It

2. *The Conditions of Education, 1977* (Washington, D.C.: National Center for Educational Statistics, 1977), p. 120.

is obvious that providing more education for the poverty-stricken will help to alleviate the poverty problem.

Many people feel that education alone cannot solve the poverty problem. A few researchers, such as Christopher Jencks, even suggest that education has little impact on a person's lifetime income. In any event, education alone cannot solve the complex problem. There are many other immediate needs such as employment, housing, medical care, and legal advice, which must be met through other means. Although this kind of immediate assistance is absolutely essential in the war on poverty, it will not solve the long-range problem. Only education can do that.

Fortunately, Americans have become concerned with the poverty problem that exists in the United States. It has been demonstrated that tax money spent to eradicate poverty is a profitable investment. It is cheaper to help people lift themselves out of poverty than it is to pay the consequences of allowing them to remain impoverished. One needs only to check the cost of social-welfare programs and crime fighting to be convinced of this finding.

It is equally fortunate that the nation's current war on poverty is being waged largely through education. One of the many federal educational programs currently directed toward solving the poverty problem is the Elementary and Secondary Education Act, passed in 1965. This act has provided several billion additional dollars per year for the American school system. The purpose of the act, known as Public Law 89–10, is "to strengthen and improve educational quality and educational opportunities in the nation's elementary and secondary schools." It provides for this under five Titles: Title I draws the most money and is intended to help educationally deprived children. This money is allocated to state departments of education, which, in turn, release it to local school districts requesting it to pay for specific projects developed by local authorities. There is no limit to the kinds of programs that can be financed under this Title—except that the money cannot be used to replace local school funds.

In conclusion, it is important to realize that if we are to eradicate poverty, we must treat the disease itself and not just the symptoms. In fact, we must attempt to prevent the disease from occurring in the first place. The most effective "vaccine" that we have at our disposal is education. It is an ironic contradiction that a nation that has amassed far greater material wealth than any other nation in history can still contain such severe pockets of poverty. Poverty prevents a person from being a productive citizen, from pursuing excellence, and from developing a sense of dignity. If we are committed to the importance of these three ideals, then we must continue to work toward the eradication of poverty in the United States.

The fact that our nation has recognized the poverty problem, that we have begun to realize the democratic, human, and economic necessity for solving the problem, and that we have initiated many immediate and long-range programs aimed at eradicating the problem—many of which involve education—makes us optimistic about the possibility of substantially reducing poverty.

Minority Groups   There are a number of so-called minority groups in American society today, including Afro-Americans, Spanish-speaking Americans, Indians or native Americans, and Asian-Americans. There are, in fact, within our society an infinite number of groups—economic, social, religious, political, agrarian, educational, and nationality groups.

Table 7–3, showing the United States population by race, indicates that, although whites constitute a sizable majority, significant numbers of other racial groups are present in our society.

Table 7–4 shows the languages spoken in households throughout the United States. The fact that over ten million school-age children (one out of eight) come from non-English-speaking homes presents an interesting challenge to the nation's schools—particularly indicating the need for bilingual education.

Blacks   Approximately 11 percent of all the people in the United States are blacks. Black Americans suffer considerably from many of the nation's social problems—racial discrimination, violence, school dropouts, drugs, alcohol, unemployment, housing, and unequal educational opportunities.

A 1954 Supreme Court decision (*Brown* v. *Board of Education of Topeka*) made it illegal for schools to practice *de jure* segregation—that which is "deliberate." However, nearly all school systems build neighborhood schools that serve only the children living in a particular

Table 7–3.   United States racial population, 1970.

Race	Number	Percent
White	177,749,000	87.4
Negro	22,580,000	11.1
Indian	793,000	.4
Japanese	591,000	.3
Chinese	435,000	.2
Filipino	343,000	.2
Other	721,000*	.4
TOTAL	203,212,000	100 percent

*Aleuts, Asian Indians, Eskimos, Hawaiians, Indonesians, Koreans, Polynesians, and other races not shown.
Source: U.S. Bureau of the Census, 1970, vol. I.

Table 7–4. Household languages of the population, July 1975.

Language Spoken in Households	Total Population, 4 Years Old and Over	School-age Population, 4 to 25 Years Old
Total	196,796,000	83,150,000
English only	167,665,000	71,404,000
Non-English as usual or other language	25,347,000	10,639,000
Spanish	9,904,000	5,162,000
French	2,259,000	967,000
German	2,269,000	794,000
Greek	488,000	189,000
Italian	2,836,000	952,000
Portuguese	349,000	117,000
Chinese	534,000	219,000
Filipino	377,000	174,000
Japanese	524,000	213,000
Korean	246,000	107,000
Other	5,559,000	1,741,000
Not reported	3,786,000	1,106,000

Source: National Center for Education Statistics, July 1975, Survey of Languages.

neighborhood. Since blacks tend to live together and only in certain neighborhoods, black children usually end up attending black schools. This type of segregation is called *de facto* segregation—that which is not necessarily "deliberate." It has not yet been determined whether the 1954 Court decision forbids de facto segregation. However, in 1961, a federal district court ruled that the attendance lines drawn by a school board are illegal if these lines promote de facto segregation (*Taylor* v. *Board of Education* in New Rochelle, New York). This decision has prompted integrationists to work toward the abolishment of de facto segregation, particularly in larger northern cities. Some school systems have transported children to other neighborhood schools in an attempt to minimize de facto segregation. In 1977, some larger city school districts, such as Louisville, Kentucky, reorganized with nearby suburban districts to facilitate racial integration in their schools. More detailed information on the legal aspects of racial desegregation of the schools is presented in Chapter 10 of this book.

The problem of racial integration is one that affects schools throughout the United States. Whereas blacks once tended to live in the South, Table 7–5 shows that they now live throughout the country and in many different locations. The social problems of black Americans are found throughout the entire United States and seriously affect the entire population.

Table 7–5. Black population, by region and residence, 1940–74.

Region	1940	1974	Residence	1974
Percent distribution	100	100	Population . . . millions	23.5
North	22	39	Metropolitan areas	17.8
Northeast	11	18	Central cities	13.7
North Central	11	20	Outside central cities	4.1
South	77	53	Nonmetropolitan areas	5.7
West	1	9		
Percent of all classes	10	11	Percent distribution	100
North	4	9	Metropolitan areas	76
Northeast	4	9	Central cities	58
North Central	4	8	Outside central cities	17
South	24	19	Nonmetropolitan areas	24
West	1	5		

Source: U.S. Bureau of the Census, *U.S. Census of Population: 1970*, vol. I, part B; and *Current Population Reports*, series P–23, no. 54.

Spanish-speaking Americans

The current status of the Spanish-speaking minorities in the United States is as follows:

- Spanish-speaking Americans comprise 6.9 percent of the United States population, or 14.4 million people (not including an estimated 5 million immigrants, migrants, and illegal aliens).
- Spanish-speaking Americans consist of 8.7 million Mexican-Americans, 4.8 million Puerto Ricans, 877,000 Cubans, and 123,000 other Latin Americans.
- 88 percent of Spanish-speaking Americans live in urban metropolitan areas.
- The average family is relatively large, consisting of six people.
- Family income is barely above poverty level—about $4,000 for an urban family of four.
- Because of, at least in part, cultural pride, large percentages of Spanish-Americans choose to speak Spanish at home (75 percent of the Puerto Ricans, 85 percent of the Cubans, and 48 percent of the Mexican-Americans).

Most of the Spanish-speaking minority groups are suffering from poverty, including the Puerto Ricans who have migrated to large cities in the United States. Approximately 15 percent of the population of New York City is made up of Puerto Ricans; a great number of Puerto Ricans also live in Chicago, many of whom are second-generation mainlanders.

Puerto Ricans generally pride themselves on being self-sufficient. Unfortunately handicaps such as language barriers, poor job skills, and lack of education keep most of these people in poverty. Children from these

Equal opportunities for native Americans and all minorities will continue to be a concern of educators. (*Photograph by Talbot Lovering*)

families frequently do poorly in school because of language difficulties, impoverished cultural backgrounds, and the fact that many are highly transient.

There are also a considerable number of Mexican-Americans who live in poverty. Many of these people have recently moved to the United States in hopes of finding a better life. Their cultural background makes it difficult for them to realize economic success in a highly technical society. These immigrants usually come from the poor sections of Mexico, and most have had little formal education or special job training. A great number of Mexican-Americans live in the southwestern part of the United States; many others travel throughout the country as seasonal workers.

Migrant workers—Mexican-American and others—pose a particularly difficult social problem. Approximately one million migrant workers and their families move frequently—following the growing season as it progresses northward each year. Historically the pay and the living conditions for these migrant workers have been poor. Because of constant moving, it has been difficult for the migrant worker's child to attend school or to receive an adequate education.

By 1978, some tangible improvements in the form of better pay and healthier living conditions had been made for migrant workers; however, most still face an uncertain future. The migrant child, moving from school to school as the parents follow their work, still has serious school problems. Bilingual education, discussed later, represents one promising effort to help solve some of the pressing social problems of the Spanish-speaking student.

Native Americans   Native Americans constitute yet another impoverished segment of the United States population. Since losing their lands to the white man, American Indians have suffered the additional loss of their native heritage and have lived largely on government subsidies. Although their cultural background is different from other minority groups, native Americans still suffer from the same basic problems—lack of education and of special skills that would permit them to realize economic success in a technological society.

Indian children have more than their share of educational problems. At present, the average educational level for all Indians is 8.4 years; the school dropout rate is over 40 percent; school achievement levels are low; and 25 percent of all Indian children start school unable to speak English.

The Indian Education Act of 1972 and its 1974 amendments are designed to help native Americans help themselves. Each year over a quarter of a million Indian schoolchildren in over a thousand school districts now receive some benefits from the Indian Education Act. These grants are aimed at providing bilingual and bicultural enrichment activities—such as cultural-awareness curricula—coupled with reading programs, guidance services, and transportation. Other grants attempt to involve Indian parents and Indian communities in educational activities; still other parts of the act are aimed at providing inservice training programs for teachers in Indian schools, financial aids for Indian college students, adult Indian education, and tribal improvement projects.

Although these recent steps are encouraging, a great deal remains to be done if the nation is to solve the immense social problems of its native American citizens.

American Women   In 1972, Title IX of the Education Amendments was enacted, stating: "No person in the United States shall, on the basis of sex, be excluded from participation in, be denied the benefits of, or be subjected to discrimination under any educational program receiving federal financial assistance." Although women clearly constitute the majority of the United States population, they still suffer from subtle and sometimes overt sex discrimination in education, job placement, individual rights, and general status within the social structure of the nation.

One of the major reasons that women work is economic. It is also true that some women with high levels of education and training work for reasons of self-fulfillment rather than for purely economic reasons. It is estimated that four out of every ten mothers are now part of the United States labor force—a 33 percent increase from the 1960 labor market report. Table 7–6 shows the sharp increase in the percentage of American women who have joined the labor force.

Table 7–6. Women in labor force by age groups.

Age Group	Percent	
	1947	1974
20 to 24 years	45	63
25 to 34 years	32	52
35 to 44 years	36	55
45 to 54 years	33	55
55 to 64 years	24	41

Source: *Manpower Report of the President,* April 1975; percents are of all women in the listed age groups.

There were over 37 million American women employed in 1978. In all probability, the one million annual divorces in the United States contribute to the large number of women in the labor force. Only 14 percent of all divorced women are awarded alimony, and child support payments are usually less than half of what it takes to support a child.

Additional information about the occupational status of American women is provided by Table 7–7. This table shows that the percentage of women employed is relatively high in clerical work and service work—and is relatively low in managerial, administrative, and blue-collar work.

Other statistics reveal the condition of women now working in America:

- 43 percent of all married women (husbands at home) are working.
- 46 percent of all women with children under 18 are working.
- 63 percent of all working mothers have children between 6 and 17 years.
- 19 percent of all working mothers have children under 3 years.
- 62 percent of mothers without husbands are working.
- 6.8 million families (12 percent of all families) are headed by women.
- 5.1 million women in the labor force have children under 6 years of age.
- 26.8 million children have working mothers.
- 4.6 million children have working mothers who are heads of households.

This information has particular significance for the schools as they attempt to provide for the needs of children.

Although they may be well educated and highly qualified, some women do not enjoy equal job competition with men. Except for the professional areas of teaching, nursing, library services, and social work, males dominate professional and technical fields; discrimination against women for white-collar and sales positions still persists. Women tend to be concentrated in the less skilled, less well-paying jobs of the labor

Table 7–7. Occupations of employed men and women by race.

	White		Minority	
	Men	**Women**	**Men**	**Women**
Total Employed (thousands)	47,340	29,280	5,179	4,136
Percent	100	100	100	100
Professional and technical	15	15	9	12
Managers and administrators	15	5	5	2
Sales workers	6	7	2	3
Clerical workers	6	36	7	25
Blue-collar workers	46	15	57	20
Service workers	7	19	15	37
Farm workers	5	2	4	1

Source: Justice for American Women, National Commission on the Observance of International Women's Year, 1976, p. 337.

market. When women do constitute any sizable number within a given profession, they suffer from inequality of pay when compared with men. Federally required *affirmative action* programs are the first government attempts to reduce discrimination in the hiring, paying, and promoting of women.

Since many women in the past had few options other than to marry and to raise children, women are often stereotyped as housekeepers and mothers. Although recent legislation has attempted to correct the myth of ability differences, the roles of wife and mother, still the societal expectation for women, will only gradually be restructured.

Among a growing number of groups, the National Organization for Women (NOW) and the Women's Equity Action League (WEAL) have pressed American society for an awakening to sex discrimination. This recent movement has had a marked effect on all aspects of American society. In addition, the feminist movement has gained national recognition with the support of a feminist press. The KNOW Press, Inc., ERIC Women Studies reports, and Betty Friedan's *The Feminine Mystique* have all questioned Whitney Darrow's children's tale:

> Boys have trucks. Girls have dolls.
> Boys are doctors. Girls are nurses.
> Boys are presidents. Girls are first ladies.
> Boys fix things. Girls need things fixed.
> Boys build houses. Girls keep houses.[3]

3. Whitney Darrow, *I'm Glad I'm a Boy. I'm Glad I'm a Girl* (New York: Simon and Schuster, 1970).

Although the Civil Rights Act of 1964, Title VII, prohibited discrimination, it was not until the 1970s that women began to receive equal treatment under the law. New federal guidelines from the Departments of Labor and Health, Education, and Welfare—and federal court cases—have helped women to combat sex discrimination within all levels of society. The nation's schools are beginning to focus some attention on nonsexist education. Although these steps are essential and encouraging, much yet remains to be done if women are to receive equal rights.

Racial Discrimination The 1954 United States Supreme Court decision that public schools could not practice racial segregation represented the first time that the *separate but equal* doctrine, established in the *Roberts* v. *Boston* case (1849) and solidified in the *Plessy* v. *Ferguson* case (1896), was held to be unconstitutional. The 1954 Supreme Court held that it was completely immaterial whether or not separate schools were equal in terms of buildings, equipment, and teachers. The significant issue was that education is "a principal instrument in awakening the child to cultural values, in preparing him for later professional training, and in helping him to adjust normally to his environment." The Court went on to say that when black children are forced to attend segregated schools—even though these schools may be equal—they may well develop "a feeling of inferiority as to their status in the community that may affect their hearts and minds in a way unlikely ever to be undone." The Court added that when a child does develop this sense of inferiority, he or she is apt to be less motivated to learn. The mere fact that a child is forced to attend a segregated school—even if that school provides an excellent education—is likely to cause the child to receive an inferior education. The Court summarized: "We conclude that in the field of public education the doctrine of separate but equal has no place."

Title VI of the 1964 Civil Rights Act states that racial discrimination must end in all programs receiving federal financial assistance in order that they may qualify for future federal aid. The U.S. Office of Education, responsible for administering much of this provision, requires that all school districts seeking federal aid must comply by any one of the following three means: (1) by filing an "Assurance of Compliance" form, declaring that no discrimination whatsoever is practiced within the school district; (2) by showing that there has been a final federal court order directing the complete racial integration of the school system by 1967; or (3) by submitting approved plans for the integration of the school system. The substantial federal aid provided under the Elementary and Secondary Education Act of 1965, along with the Civil Rights Act of 1964, stimulated the desegregation of American public schools. The legislative and judicial aspects of racial desegregation are discussed in greater detail in Part III of this book.

Most school districts have now taken steps to integrate their schools physically. Table 7–8 provides information on school desegregation col-

Table 7–8.   Districts that desegregated, by source of intervention and by year of greatest desegregation.

Time period	Courts No.	%	HEW No.	%	State/Local No.	%	Total No.	%
1901–53	0	0	0	0	7	3	7	1
1954–65	13	6	18	12	53	21	84	13
1966–67	8	4	19	12	46	18	73	12
1968–69	53	26	42	28	34	13	129	21
1970–71	107	51	61	40	46	18	214	35
1972–73	12	6	5	3	38	15	55	9
1974–75	15	7	7	5	31	12	53	9
TOTAL	208	100	152	100	255	100	615	100

Source: Desegregation of the Nation's Public Schools, report of the United States Commission on Civil Rights, 1976, p. 135.

lected in a 1976 national survey of a random sample of about 8 percent of the nation's school districts.

This table shows that serious school desegregation efforts did not start until the mid-1950s—in all likelihood a result of the 1954 U.S. Supreme Court decision. Table 7–8 also shows the three major sources of intervention that brought about desegregation in these school districts. These were, in order, state and local forces, court orders, and the U.S. Department of Health, Education, and Welfare (HEW). It is interesting to note that both the courts and HEW were actively promoting desegregation in 1970 and 1971.

Although relatively good progress has been made in physically integrating the various racial groups in the schools, educators are finding that this physical integration, in and of itself, does not automatically bring about effective integration. Unfortunately, in most racially mixed classrooms, black, white, and Spanish-speaking students are far from achieving the friendship and understanding that is the true goal of integration. In fact, more often than not, the bulk of students will form racial cliques within the school and, in many instances, have little more interaction with the other races than they had in segregated schools. Solving this problem represents the next great challenge for educators— in their struggle to achieve racial equality and racial understanding within the school systems.

School Dropouts   Though somewhat different in nature, the two major types of school dropouts—high school dropouts and college dropouts—both represent a substantial loss to our society.

In most states, students are required to attend school until the age of sixteen. This, of course, prevents them from dropping out of school during the early part of high school; however, once past the compulsory attendance age, a frightening percentage of students drop out of school. The rate of dropouts is disturbing for many reasons: there are no jobs for most of these students; a high proportion of them get into trouble with the law; many of them cannot qualify for military service. In general, most of them are not yet prepared to be productive citizens, and a large number of them are destined to become social liabilities.

Figure 7–1 shows the dropout picture in America in recent years: the dropout rate has remained relatively constant but is still considerably higher for black students than for white students.

A recent survey of Philadelphia High School dropouts reveals just how bleak the employment picture is for dropouts. Only about 20 percent of the black dropouts and 43 percent of the white dropouts were able to find employment. Three-fourths of these had full-time jobs with an average wage of $2.50 an hour. The female dropouts—many owing to pregnancy—fared even less well in the job market. This survey further found that 40 percent of these dropouts left school on their own—

Figure 7–1.   High school dropouts.

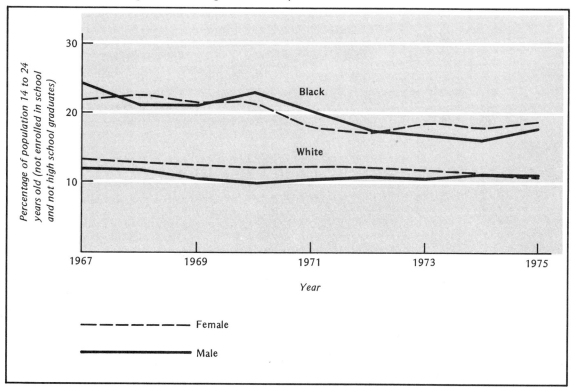

Source: Bureau of the Census, 1977.

without discussing this major decision with family, friends, or school personnel. The major reasons these students gave for quitting was that school "turned them off" and was a dead end that led nowhere.

It is estimated that 75 percent of all juvenile delinquents under seventeen years of age are school dropouts. A recent District of Columbia study revealed that 57 percent of that city's criminals had been high school dropouts.

All of these studies point to the desperate need for the schools and for society at large to find ways to keep children in school—not only for the good of the students themselves but also for the good of the entire society. The economic cost of ignoring this problem is sizable. A recent research study estimates that the failure to complete high school among American males (now ages 25 to 34) costs the nation $237 billion in income over the lifetime of these men and $71 billion in lost government revenues ($47 billion federal and $24 billion state and local).[4] This study, in contrast, determined that the estimated cost of a minimum high school education for these men would have been only $40 billion; thus the net loss in national income from the inadequate education of these males was about $200 billion greater than the initial investment required to prevent this condition.

These data clearly show that the money spent to keep our children in school and prevent dropouts is not, in fact, an expense but rather an excellent long-term investment that returns handsome dividends.

The gifted high school graduate who does not go on to college represents another type of school dropout. It is estimated that each year somewhere between 60,000 and 100,000 high school graduates who were in the upper third of their class fail to go to college. It is also estimated that about 60,000 students drop out of college each year. In fact, half of the students who enter college never graduate. Although many of these students leave college for academic reasons, a great number of them have exceptional academic ability. Approximately one-fifth of the high school dropouts have IQs of 120 or above; only about one-half of the college-age students in the upper 10 percent of the IQ range ever graduate from college. The underdeveloped talent of these gifted students represents a substantial loss to society. It is important to realize that this loss results only because these students fail to develop their fullest potential—not because they fail to enter a particular field of work. It is apparent that our society and our schools have a long way to go before resolving the dropout problem.

Violence   A *juvenile delinquent* is commonly defined as a youth between the ages of ten and eighteen who is brought into court and found guilty of breaking a law. It is estimated that well over two million American

4. *The Costs to the Nation of Inadequate Education,* a study conducted by Prof. Henry M. Levin for the Senate Select Committee on Equal Educational Opportunity.

youths between the ages of ten and eighteen are picked up by police each year. Two-thirds of these young people are let go with warnings and released to their parents. Of the approximately 700,000 juveniles brought to court each year, nearly half are traffic cases of various sorts. Approximately 20 percent of the youth who are arrested are charged with more serious offenses—11 percent are charged with burglary, 7 percent with auto theft, 1 percent with aggravated assault, and 1 percent with robbery. The incidence of juvenile delinquency among girls is less than one-tenth that of boys. The juvenile delinquency rate is nearly four times greater in cities than in rural areas.

It is difficult to pinpoint the precise causes of juvenile delinquency; however, a number of associated factors have been identified. For instance, a high proportion of delinquents come from the lower social classes. It is possible, however, that police are more lenient with young people from the middle and upper classes than with those from the

Dropouts face a bleak future in the job market. (*Photograph by Tania D'Avignon*)

lower classes. On the other hand, there is undoubtedly a great deal of delinquency by youth from the lower social classes that goes unde-tected.

Another factor associated with juvenile delinquency is how often it involves school dropouts. A study in New York City found that 95 per-cent of all the seventeen-year-old juvenile delinquents were school dropouts and that 85 percent of all the sixteen-year-old juvenile delin-quents were dropouts. Various studies of delinquency have also shown that a large proportion of delinquents did failing work while in school and that they were often of lower intelligence than nondelinquents. The interrelationship between lower social class, school dropout, school failure, and lower intelligence (as measured by existing tests) is so com-plex that it is difficult to assess the contribution of each factor toward juvenile delinquency.

Perhaps the most common characteristic shared by juvenile delin-quents is a poor family relationship. Sheldon and Glueck have found five different home characteristics that prove good predictors of juvenile delinquency: lack of affection of the father for the boy; lack of affec-tion of the mother for the boy; lack of supervision by the mother; over-strict, erratic, or lax discipline by the father; and a general lack of cohesiveness in the entire family.[5] The *Glueck Delinquency Prediction Scale,* which utilizes these five family characteristics to identify potential delinquents, has proved to be a good predictor. However, the inability to identify potential delinquents early enough to allow preventive ac-tion remains one of the main obstacles to solving the problem.

Crime   It is sad but true that many of today's juvenile delinquents will be to-morrow's criminals. Statistics on crime in the United States are stagger-ing: estimates of the cost of crime run as high as $30 billion per year. A breakdown of this figure indicates that crime costs each American family about $400 a year. A report from the President's Commission on Law Enforcement and Administration of Justice revealed that organized crime has grown in size and sophistication to where it now involves narcotics, prostitution, murder, gambling, protection rackets, real estate, confidence games, politics, stock market manipulations—nearly every facet of American life.

Serious crime has increased every year since 1947—with the excep-tion of 1972 when it decreased slightly. In recent years, serious crime has been increasing somewhere between 10 and 20 percent each year; crimes by women are also increasing dramatically. To make matters worse, fewer than one in four serious crimes lead to arrest; in other words, three-fourths of the people who commit crimes do not get arrested.

5.   Sheldon and Glueck, "Early Detection of Juvenile Delinquents," *Journal of Crim-inal Law, Criminology, and Policy Science* 47: 174–182, 353–364.

Violent Schools   Just as our society at large has become more violent, so have our schools. In fact, violence and vandalism have become major problems in many of our schools. Consider these statistics:

- The Chicago school district currently spends $10 million each year combating violence and vandalism.
- The Dade County schools in Florida, during a recent one-year period, experienced a sharp increase in school violence: assaults rose from 566 to 830; robberies jumped from 119 to 195; rapes increased from 6 to 22; and physical attacks on teachers rose to 225.
- The Detroit school district stations police officers in many schools and spends $230,000 a year on alarm systems alone.
- A recent U.S. Senate Committee on Delinquency reports that the nation loses $600 million to school vandalism each year.
- An estimated 70,000 serious physical assaults are made on teachers each year; several hundred thousand assaults are reported on students.

These statistics suggest the magnitude of the problem that the schools are facing of increased vandalism and violence. Unfortunately very few solutions to these problems have been found. Some schools have hired policemen, adopted strict rules, expelled troublesome students, and taken a determined stance. Other schools have solicited the help of students and parents, have attempted to change the curriculum to make it more interesting and relevant to students, have gone to great lengths to keep all students in school, and have generally adopted a democratic, humanistic, and sympathetic attitude. Frankly, few schools have been successful in solving the problem of violence—probably for two major reasons. First, few schools have the financial resources required to make a serious, concerted attack on the problem. Second, violence has become so prevalent in American society that some social scientists feel there is simply no way to keep it out of the schools. Violence, crime, and a general disregard and disrespect for the rights and welfare of others have become commonplace in America. The magnitude and diversity of this problem can only be understood by analyzing related problems such as child abuse and neglect, wife beating, juvenile delinquency, television and movie violence, illegitimate births, divorce rates, tax fraud, governmental corruption, welfare cheating, price fixing, stock manipulation, organized crime, business crime, and stealing by employees. Crime and violence have indeed become a part of almost every facet of American life. Until the basic values of society change, the schools will reflect these same basic problems—and be violent schools in a violent society.

Drugs   One of the most tragic social problems in America today is that centered around the misuse of drugs by young people. It has been said that drugs are now a $20-billion-a-year habit that the United States has not been able to throw off. The extent of our nation's drug problem is indicated by these statistics:

- Among the 18 million students in the nation's public secondary schools, somewhere between 20 and 35 percent of them—the estimate of most doctors, educators, and drug-abuse authorities—are experimenting with drugs.
- Up to 6 million high school students are taking drugs illegally.
- Some 12 to 15 percent (up to 2.7 million) high school students are taking marijuana and other so-called soft (generally nonaddictive) drugs on a regular basis.
- From 2 to 3 percent (or some 500,000 youngsters) are hopelessly addicted to hard drugs like heroin.
- In the Haight-Ashbury Clinic in San Francisco, more than 50,000 patients, whose average age was twenty, have been served in the past three years. Forty percent took drugs without even knowing what the drugs were.
- In Pennsylvania, a survey by the state health department showed that 11 percent of the state's high school population, or 123,000 students, are frequent users of illicit drugs.
- Of the more than 100,000 heroin addicts in New York City alone, approximately 25,000 of them attend the city's public schools.

Manufacturers in the United States turn out 1 million pounds of tranquilizers, 10 billion sedative dosages, 500 tons of barbiturates, 8 billion amphetamine tablets, and 34 million pounds of aspirin every year. Some 200 million prescriptions for sedatives, stimulants, and tranquilizers serve more than 30 million people each year, with Americans paying $250 million for tranquilizers alone.

In an attempt to solve their drug problems, many schools have embarked on various programs to help to provide their students with basic information about drugs so that they may understand the dangers of drug abuse and develop an informed, healthy attitude that will lead to a conscious decision not to use illicit drugs. Generally the drug-education programs that have been adequately funded, that involve parents and students, that are taught by well-trained teachers, and that avoid preaching and moralizing, have been the most successful.

Alcohol   During the 1960s, there was a decline in the use of alcohol by American teen-agers. Some authorities attributed this decline to the fact that many students were switching from alcohol to drugs during the period. Unfortunately, most studies indicate that in recent years there has been a sharp increase in student use of alcohol. For instance, a recent study in California's San Mateo County showed that 25 percent of the students in grades 9 through 12 drank at least 50 times per year, while 50 percent drank at least 10 times per year. A similar study of the New York City high schools found that young people are now drinking at an

Alcoholism is a hidden problem affecting many teen-agers. (*Photography by Franklin Wing, Stock, Boston*)

earlier age and that a frightening number of these early drinkers become teen-age alcoholics. Supporting this finding is the astonishing fact that twenty-five chapters of Los Angeles County Alcoholics Anonymous are now composed solely of teen-agers. An administrator of the Dubuque, Iowa, school system reports that it is now rather common to have to remove drunken students from school activities. Many schools now have numerous students consuming alcohol in school buildings during the school day. Medical authorities report a rapid rise in "polydrug" abuse—the use of combinations of drugs and alcohol—among students. For instance, alcohol and barbiturates, sedatives, or tranquilizers, when used together, can heighten each other's effects—and can cause death. Some authorities believe that alcohol has now become the foremost drug problem for young people in America.

Smoking Millions of American students regularly smoke cigarettes. If educators are concerned about the growing evidence of physical damage caused by smoking and if they are concerned about the health of young people, they will be forced to deal with this alarming problem. Figure 7–2 shows the estimated percentage of the nation's teen-agers who smoke regularly. This figure shows that roughly 10 percent of 12 to 14 year olds, 20 percent of 15 to 16 year olds, and 35 percent of 17 to 18 year olds smoke cigarettes regularly. It also reveals that the problem of smoking is not restricted to boys but affects very large numbers of girls as well. Translated into actual figures, Figure 7–2 means that each year about one million young people take up cigarette smoking and that over four million school-age youngsters smoke on a regular basis.

Many people feel that the school is the only agency that has a fighting chance to reduce teen-age smoking significantly. An increasing number of schools are accepting this challenge. Some schools are including a systematic study of the effects of smoking as part of their curriculum. The most promising approach to smoking education seems to be that in which the youngsters themselves run their own antismoking campaigns. Some schools have joined forces with parent groups, the American Cancer Society, the American Heart Association, and the National Tuberculosis and Respiratory Diseases Association to combat teen-age smoking. Unfortunately most schools have not yet made a serious effort to attack this social problem, which affects millions of young people.

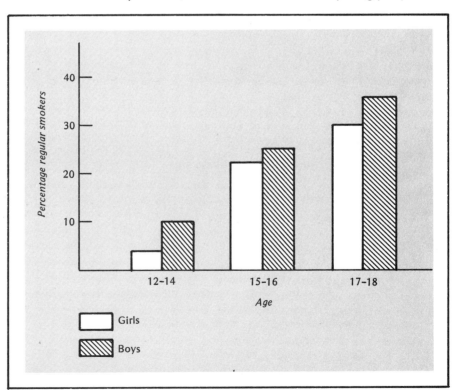

Figure 7–2.
Teen-age cigarette
smoking.

Source: National Clearinghouse for Smoking and Health, U.S. Department of Health, Education, and Welfare.

programs as the Manpower Retraining Program and through various other adult-education programs, society already has begun to assume some degree of this responsibility.

The second major theory regarding the long-range effects of automation is that a considerable percentage of the eliminated jobs are permanently lost to the labor market. If this latter theory is true, then the social problem becomes not only one of retraining workers but also of readjusting the labor market in such a way that society can accommodate itself to automation.

That this nation still receives a considerable number of immigrants each year adds yet another complicating factor to the automation-unemployment problem. Approximately 2,500,000 immigrants came to the United States between 1951 and 1960. Since most of these immigrants must join the unskilled and skilled labor force, they too must compete with automation for jobs.

American society has changed in many ways since 1900; similarly, the demand for various types of workers has changed considerably. Since 1970, there has been a 5.8 percent increase in white-collar workers—from 43.2 to 49 percent of the total labor force. The percentage of blue-collar workers has decreased from 50.4 percent in 1960 to 47.5 percent at the present time. Farm workers made up 6.5 percent of the labor force in 1960, whereas now less than 3.5 percent of the labor force is engaged in farming. Almost without exception, those occupations for which there is a decreasing demand are the occupations that require less formal education. In the future, there will be a need to retrain people—in some cases several times during their lives—for different occupations created by a rapidly changing society.

Table 7–9 shows the recent history of unemployment rates in the United States. The unemployment rate is, of course, influenced by many factors other than automation and immigration. For instance, the relatively high unemployment rate in 1975 was in large part brought about by an economic recession. In fact, the general economic condition of the country probably has more to do with unemployment than any other

Table 7–9.   Unemployment rates in the U.S.

Year	Percent
1950	5.3%
1955	4.4%
1960	5.5%
1965	4.5%
1970	4.9%
1975	8.5%

Source: U.S. Bureau of Labor Statistics.

single factor. However, other considerations also influence the employment picture. The fact that many additional women are entering the labor force (approximately 50 percent more women have entered the labor market since 1966), that fewer young people are now in military service, and that trends in college enrollments are changing all contribute to the country's unemployment rates.

Certain groups within our society are more affected by unemployment than others, as Figure 7–4 vividly points out. Although actual unemployment rates change from year to year, the relative unemployment picture for the groups represented in Figure 7–4 has remained about the same in recent history. Women, non-whites, and teen-agers generally experience higher unemployment rates.

Figure 7–5 reveals yet another dimension of the nation's unemployment problem—one that should be of particular interest to educators. The story told by this figure is a simple but extremely important one—that unemployment rates are significantly higher for people with less formal schooling.

Leisure   One outgrowth of advanced technology and of increased productivity has been a decrease in the length of the workweek. In 1850, the average workweek was sixty-six hours; today it is less than forty hours. Furthermore, the workweek will continue to decrease in the future.

Americans spend three times more money on leisure (approximately $160 billion) each year than they spend on education; this spending not only indicates the amount of leisure time that these citizens enjoy but also, parenthetically, substantiates the contention that they can afford as good an educational program as they wish to have. In 1900, approximately 25 percent of the nation's time was devoted to leisure. Today the average American spends about 35 percent of the time in leisure activities. Each year, approximately 314 million Americans attend sporting events, 78 million visit museums, 62 million attend at least one performance of live theater, 16 million collect stamps, 37 million families

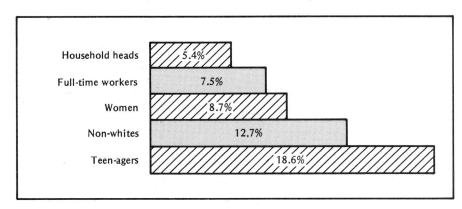

Figure 7–4.
Unemployment of
selected groups.

Source: U.S. Department of Labor Statistics, 1976.

Figure 7–5.   Unemployment rate, by education attainment and age.

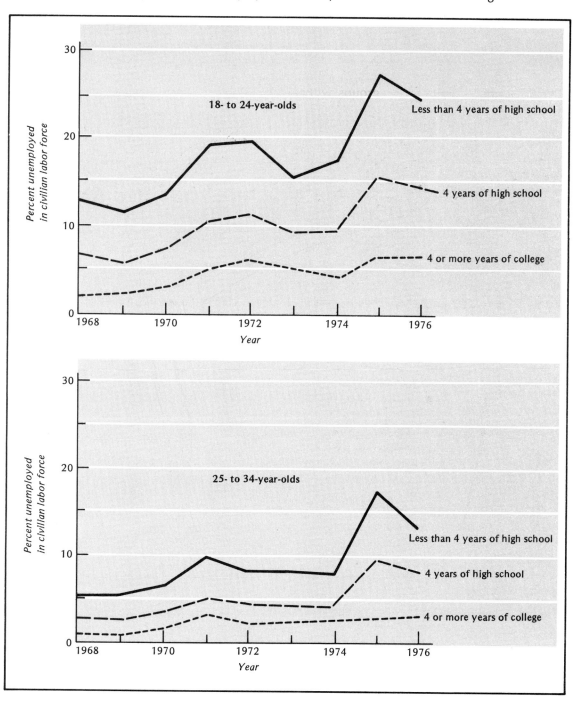

Source: Bureau of Labor Statistics

plant gardens, 10 million carry out genealogical research, 3 million are rather serious photographers, 58 million go camping, 30 million play tennis, 40 million do volunteer charitable work, and so forth.

Not only is the percentage of leisure time increasing for the average American, but so is life expectancy. Life expectancy has increased from forty-eight years in 1900 to approximately seventy-five years today. The combination of a shorter work week, a higher standard of living, a longer life expectancy, less child labor, and earlier retirement enables today's average American to spend more than one-third of his life at leisure.

This increased free time presents a challenging educational problem. In the first place, many Americans have not been "educated" to use free time purposefully. Leisure time can be a burden as well as a blessing if one has not developed any productive leisure-time interests. One out of ten Americans lives in such poverty that he or she cannot afford the minimum essentials—much less any leisure-time activities. And ironically, owing to unemployment, it is usually the poverty-stricken who have the most leisure time.

Educators have begun to respond to the challenge of providing experiences that will lead to the productive use of leisure time. Education for leisure has opened avenues for the student to develop an interest and a degree of proficiency in chosen forms of recreation; however, many interests cannot be pursued and refined in adult life, unless adequate provision is made for recreational areas. In a nation where population continues to increase and industry continues to expand, the urgent need for land conservation should be given a high priority. Recent attempts by local, state, and national agencies to reclaim previously exhausted land sites and to correct polluted air and water resources suggest the national concern to provide the much-needed recreational areas. Expanded efforts along these lines are necessary if the interest and the proficiency in recreational activities promoted by the schools are to bear fruit.

Additional attempts have been made by educators to provide for the future leisure of the population by stimulating interests in the fine arts—art, music, and literature. The attempts already made in this direction should not suggest, however, that the task has been accomplished. The challenge of today will be even greater tomorrow. Schools, as one social institution in society, must continue to search for imaginative ways to help prepare students for the productive use of leisure time. Adult-education classes are growing throughout the country by leaps and bounds. Whereas in 1970 approximately 13 million Americans attended school part-time, today over 20 million do so. There seems to be a genuine interest on the part of citizens to use part of their leisure time exploring new fields. Our educational system is in a unique position to help them do so.

Education should
provide skills for
leisure activities
in adult life.
*(Photograph by
George N. Peet,
The Picture Cube)*

Pollution   An increasingly serious problem in America is the widespread pollution
of the environment. Unfortunately, although this may well be one of
the most serious problems affecting society, the general public until
recently has not been sufficiently concerned about it to take steps toward a solution. Perhaps the most promising step taken toward allevi-
ating this problem was the nearly unanimous passage of the Environmental Education Act in 1970.

As it has done so often in the past, the government has looked to
the nation's schools to help solve a pressing social problem—this time
the problem of cleaning up our badly polluted environment. The passage of the Environmental Education Act is predicated on the belief that

pollution problems will only be solved when citizens are educated to the point at which they will develop new attitudes and new behaviors regarding the environment.

The following statistics underline the need for the nation to marshal its forces to attack pollution problems:

- About a billion pounds of chemicals are added to food items in America each year, amounting to five pounds per person.
- Over 12,000 chemical substances are now listed on the government's list of toxic substances; many of these chemicals are still commonly used throughout American industry.
- The World Health Organization estimates that between 70 and 90 percent of all human cancer might well be traceable to environmental pollution.
- Each day a billion pounds of chemicals (pesticides, herbicides, and fungicides) are released into the atmosphere. Parenthetically, without them, farm output would drop 25 percent and food prices would jump 50 percent.
- Over twenty of the nation's major rivers are now rated "unswimmable" by the Environmental Protection Agency owing to pollution problems.
- The Council on Environmental Quality estimates that it will cost over $270 billion during the next ten years to mount a serious national attack on pollution.

World Resources Much is written today about the energy shortage. As serious as this problem is, it is only part of the even larger problem of the rapid depletion of many of the essential resources of the world. Consider these few statements:

- The most optimistic predictions suggest that the world will, for all practical purposes, run out of crude oil before the year 2100. Conservative predictions, based on rapidly increasing consumption, suggest that known crude oil supplies will last only fifty years.
- Only seven nations in the entire world—with only 8 percent of the world's population—grow a surplus of food. In contrast, one-third of the world population lives in countries that not only cannot grow enough food but also cannot afford to import enough food to provide adequate diets for their citizens.
- Tonight the world will have 215,000 more mouths to feed than it had last night. Based on present growth rates, the world's population will double in the next forty years.
- A natural resource that is more essential and more precious to humans than oil—water—is in increasingly short supply in many parts of the world.

- The National Institute for Occupational Safety and Health (NIOSH) estimates that 100,000 deaths occur each year in the United States from on-the-job pollution.

This list, indicating the rapid depletion of natural resources, could continue at length. A more detailed listing of the absolutely shocking statistics would reveal the magnitude of this serious worldwide problem. Suffice it to say that people simply cannot continue to deplete and mismanage the natural resources of the world if they are concerned about the health and, in fact, the very existence of future generations.

This worldwide problem has a number of implications for American schools. For instance, the dramatic increase in the cost of energy is sapping school budgets, which are increasing at the rate of about 25 percent each year. This additional $250 million, if not spent on energy, would fund about 20,000 additional and badly needed teaching positions.

But perhaps the most far-reaching implication of the energy problem for schools is not as much financial as curricular. Today's students, who are tomorrow's adults, need to be thoroughly educated about world resources—supply, rate of consumption, finiteness, value, indispensability, potential substitutes, and so forth. Today's students also need to explore and to come to grips with many moral issues related to the conservation of world resources such as: the right of Americans to use proportionately more natural resources than other nations simply because they can afford them; or the right of future generations to have a fair share of natural resources preserved for their use. Unfortunately most school systems have not yet devised or instituted such programs.

Summary and Implications   There are many serious social problems in the United States that have a dramatic impact on our schools. Schools cannot adequately meet the educational needs of their students without taking into account the society from which the young people come. In fact, our schools and our society are so intimately related that any problem affecting one affects the other; therefore, the schools alone cannot solve many of the problems confronting young people. The implication here is clear: if we are serious about solving the problems facing young people, both our society at large and our schools must work together in a concerted, purposeful way—probably not yet envisioned by planners—to accomplish the task. This effort would require that much more money be spent on education than is now the case. It would require that parents work much harder and much more closely with educators than is now the case. It would require a much deeper and broader commitment to education on the part of American society than is now the case.

Discussion Questions

1. In your estimation, what steps remain to be taken to achieve the American ideal of equality of opportunity in our public schools?
2. What do you believe to be some practical solutions to our environmental pollution problem?
3. How serious do you believe alcohol and drug problems are among American youth?

How can the schools contribute to the solution of these problems?
4. What effects will the current population trends in the United States have on the public school system?
5. Given a free hand, how would you use the schools to help people better utilize their leisure time?

Supplemental Activities

1. Visit a local high school and record the socioeconomic status of the learners as you observe them. Check the accuracy of your observations with the teacher.
2. Visit a culturally deprived area, rural or urban, and identify special programs that the community provides to compensate its disadvantaged.
3. Visit the schools of a culturally deprived area to contrast their conditions and problems with those of an advantaged area.
4. Develop and carry out a class project de-

signed to survey the environmental pollution problems in your immediate geographical area. Decide how the results of your class project could be utilized by the local public school system in an "environmental education program."
5. Make arrangements for a former drug addict to visit your class. Discuss the topic "Youth, Drugs, and the Public Schools."
6. Spend a day with a local community social worker and record the cases that are investigated.

Bibliography

Havighurst, Robert J., and Neugarten, Bernice L. *Society and Education,* 4th ed. Boston: Allyn and Bacon, 1975.

Johnson, Kenneth R. *Teaching the Culturally Disadvantaged.* Palo Alto: Science Research Associates, 1970.

Luce, Clare Boothe. "The 21st-Century Woman —Free at Last?" *Saturday Review,* August 1974, pp. 58–62.

Marland, Sidney P., Jr. "Environmental Education Cannot Wait." *American Education* (May 1971).

Miller, Harry L. *Education for the Disadvantaged.* New York: The Free Press, 1967.

Ornstein, Allan. *An Introduction to the Foundations of Education.* Chicago: Rand McNally, 1977.

Roberts, Edwin A., Jr. "The Middle Class Does the Work, Pays the Bills, and Gets Blamed for Everything." *Today's Education* 59 (January 1970).

Sarason, Seymour B. *The Culture of the School and the Problem of Change.* Boston: Allyn and Bacon, 1971.

Seckinger, Donald S. *A Problems Approach to Foundations of Education.* New York: John Wiley, 1975.

Taylor, Charlotte P. *Transforming Schools, A Social Perspective.* New York: St. Martin's, 1976.

Wolk, Donald J. "Youth in Trouble: Drug Abuses." *Today's Education* 60 (November 1971).

CHAPTER 8

National Educational Priorities

DURING THE PAST TWO DECADES, THE FEDERAL GOVERNMENT HAS provided considerable financial assistance to the schools in an attempt to solve national educational problems. Most of these efforts have been compensatory in nature, but others have given direction to new national priorities in education. This chapter presents, in some detail, a few of the most recent attempts of the federal government to solve pressing social and educational problems. In addition, earlier federal projects are highlighted—to serve as examples of national funding efforts in education.

Public Law 94–142
In 1967, Congress created the Bureau of Education for the Handicapped (BEH) and began providing the states with funds to create, to improve, and to operate compensatory programs for the millions of handicapped children in the United States. For over a ten-year period (1967 to 1977), the federal government allocated over three hundred million dollars each year to train and retrain special education personnel and to establish research and development operations. All of this effort has been directed toward helping children handicapped by mental retardation, speech problems, emotional disorders, deafness, blindness, and other related health disabilities. There is little doubt that the BEH programs have had a significant effect on improving the conditions of the handicapped in the United States. Despite all of these efforts, however, great differences still exist between the various state programs because BEH-sponsored programs have remained voluntary rather than mandatory. The mainstreaming laws of many states during the late 1970s helped to equalize compensatory efforts within individual states, but the national differences remain acute. Handicapped children in some states are more fortunate than those in other states in receiving help. Public Law 94–142 was badly needed.

Perhaps the most significant single piece of legislation during the past decade has been the passage of Public Law 94–142, the Education for the Handicapped Act. Ascertaining that eight million handicapped children existed in the United States, Congress passed the Act in 1975 and scheduled mandatory partial implementation for 1978. Although the bill was conceived of and passed for the improvement of school programs for handicapped children, it has—because of its due process implications—paved the way for individualized programs for all learners encountered by the schools. It has been suggested that this bill has even helped to speed development of early childhood programs because it requires early identification of youngsters needing help. The major features of the Act are as follows:

- All handicapped learners between the ages of three and eighteen are to be provided with a free public education.
- Each handicapped child is to have an individualized program, developed jointly by a school official, a teacher, the parents or guardian, and if possible, the learner himself or herself.
- Handicapped children are not to be grouped separately—unless severely handicapped, in which case separate facilities and programs would be deemed more appropriate.
- Tests for identification and placement are to be free of racial and cultural discrimination biases.
- School districts are to maintain continuous efforts at identifying handicapped children.
- School districts are to establish priorities for providing educational programs.
- Placement of the handicapped requires parental approval.
- Private schools are also covered by the Act.
- Retraining and inservice training of all personnel are required.
- Special federal grants are available for school building modifications.
- State departments of education are to be designated the responsible state agency for all programs for handicapped.[1]

The due process concerns of this Act touch the very core of the process of education in the United States. Successful mass education in this country has significantly raised the mean level of achievement, literacy, and school-level completion for all U.S. citizens. At the same time, however, the school has had to resort to teaching and learning practices directed at group goals. Despite an awareness of the benefits of individualized programs for all children, the schools have been unable to develop such programs because of money constraints and of the sheer masses of school-age children. A due process question for educators naturally arises: if handicapped children are required to have

1. Leroy V. Goodman, "A Bill of Rights for the Handicapped," *American Education* 12 (July 1976): 7.

individually tailored programs to meet their needs and interests, why not provide such programs for all learners? No two children are alike and, therefore, each should have his or her own program. As the constitutionality of Public Law 94–142 is upheld and strengthened, the rights of all learners to have individual programs will have to be considered by the schools.

Career Education

Career education was given national support by former U.S. Commissioner of Education Sidney P. Marland, following his appointment in 1971. During the first five years of their existence, career-education programs, conceived of as a national educational effort, expanded and still effectively promulgate the concept of "education for work" as a basic goal of education. Kenneth Hoyt, director of the U.S. Office of Education's Office of Career Education, has provided outstanding leadership in spreading the concept of career education throughout the school systems of the United States. There were, for example, over four hundred career-education programs in operation in 1976.[2]

Career education is commonly defined as helping learners become familiar with the knowledge and the values of a work ethic society. It is hoped that as learners acquire this knowledge, they will make wiser choices of life occupations where job choice becomes related to social, leisure, and interpersonal roles. In the program of the National Institute of Education (NIE), career education is presented as having three major objectives:

1. To reduce unemployment
2. To reduce low-income employment
3. To reduce alienation in employment.[3]

This concept for career education is intended to begin in the early years of a learner's life and continue into the retirement period. Both the Office of Education and NIE support the philosophy of preoccupational, occupational, and postoccupational planning for career education.

Donald Super describes the stages of a career over the total life span.[4] He sees these as: the growth stage, the exploratory stage, the establishment stage, the maintenance stage, and the decline stage. The growth and exploratory stages are assigned as priorities for the elementary and secondary schools. In addition to the development of career awareness, the learner is encouraged and helped through these two stages to develop a fixed occupational preference, whether it be in paid or unpaid employment. The last three stages pertain to the work

2. Shirley B. Neill, "Clearing the Air in Career Education," *American Education* 13 (March 1977): 6.
3. Donald E. Super, *Career Education and the Meaning of Work* (Washington, D.C.: HEW, 1976), p. 17.
4. Ibid., pp. 22–24.

market, the maintenance of the career choice, and the graceful decline through the retirement years.

Arizona, Oregon, Minnesota, and California have developed a variety of career-education programs that range from state-mandated efforts to the efforts of local schools and businessmen. In addition to the use of specially developed curricula for learners, these programs provide for inservice training of teachers and for community participation in development and implementation of career-education goals. In 1976, Sidney Marland, who had become president of the College Entrance Examination Board, reported, "The impressive number of school districts implementing or interested in career education indicates there probably never in our educational history has been such enormous movement toward a central concept of reform over such a brief span of time." A national educational priority has been established.

Adult Performance Level (APL) Study

Despite prolonged efforts to bring about mass education in this country, it has been estimated that one in five adults lacks the skills and knowledge needed to function effectively in society. A literacy problem continues to exist. In an attempt to combat the literacy problem of adults in this country, a team of adult-education researchers, sponsored by the U.S. Office of Education, set out to identify the coping-skills competencies needed by adults. Conducted at the University of Texas, the study took four years to complete. The findings of this study indicate:

- One out of five adults (19.8 percent) lack basic coping skills.
- Thirty-three percent of all adults are marginally competent in coping with everyday problems.
- Less than half of all Americans are functioning with any degree of skill or knowledge competence.[5]

Adult competence has been classified into two broad areas for identification—*knowledge areas* and *general skills areas*. The knowledge areas are: occupational knowledge (career education), consumer economics, law and government, health, and knowledge of resources in the community. The general skills areas are: reading, writing, computing, speaking, listening, and problem solving. The APL study team established sixty-five generic competencies for the knowledge areas and general skills areas. These stated competencies have become the basis on which many statewide programs for adult education have been developed.

The major difference between APL-type programs and the usual General Equivalent Diploma (G.E.D.), or other night-school education programs, is the credit given to adults for what they already know and

5. Edith Roth, "APL: A Ferment in Education," *American Education* 12 (May 1976): 6.

can do. The typical adult-education program assesses its students on the Carnegie Unit-type system and then assigns a program of study (with courses and hours comparable to regular secondary school) for the adult to complete. There is no credit given for knowledge or skills gained through the so-called school of hard knocks. On the other hand, APL assesses an adult's basic competencies in the knowledge and skills areas and then provides programs to shore up or eliminate areas of weakness. Programs vary in length and may range from formal class settings to very informal means of gaining competency. The test is a demonstration of the desired competencies—however they may be gained.

APL programs have spread across the nation, with notable programs in New York, California, Alabama, Texas, Pennsylvania, and Mississippi. With programs supported by both federal and private grants, these states have developed what are called *external diploma* programs. These programs are offered through community colleges, vocational schools, and regular public school districts. Highly individualized, the programs allow the adult learners to move at their own pace. APL has opened many new doors for millions of adults and has helped to remove the social and economic stigmas attached to illiteracy.

Bilingual-Bicultural Education

The Bilingual Education Act, Title VII of the Elementary and Secondary Education Act, was enacted into law in 1968. At the present time, the federal government actively continues to support its commitment to bilingual-bicultural education. During the late 1970s, the federal government increased its financial support to the program and stepped up its efforts to enforce the *Lau* v. *Nichols* decision. This landmark Supreme Court case mandated that school districts provide all non-English-speaking students with special language instruction to equalize their educational opportunity.[6]

The Bilingual Education Act and its various amendments were enacted to help with the special needs of growing numbers of American children whose first language is not English. Originally the Act was intended to focus on low-income learners, early childhood education, adult education, dropouts, and vocational students. In addition, funds were provided for the preservice and inservice training of teachers for these programs. In 1974, the low-income requirement was dropped with the passage of the Equal Educational Opportunity Act.

Bilingual-bicultural education is formal instruction for learners using their native language for learning all subjects until second-language (English) skills have been developed. This approach increases the equal educational opportunity of minority children. Today approximately 25 percent of the United States population speaks a language other than

6. Richard V. Teachner, "Bilingualism and Bilingual-Bicultural Education," *Hispania* 60 (March 1977): 116.

Bilingual-bicultural education for adults is available in many communities. (*Photograph by Paul Conklin; courtesy of OEO*)

English as a native tongue. People of Spanish, German, and Italian descent make up the majority of this group—with the Spanish-speaking people who migrated from Latin America and Puerto Rico by far the largest group. The Asian population has increased because of repealed immigration legislation. Native American numbers have swelled as their total population has increased. Over 30 percent of American Indians speak a native language as their first language.

English monolingual schools have helped to deny to non-English speakers equal access to education and to job opportunities. Hindered by language barriers in schooling, these minority Americans have suffered from illiteracy problems. The much-publicized Coleman Report (1966) showed that non-English-speaking learners were desperately behind the national achievement norms in reading, mathematics, and verbal ability. Language difficulties were cited as the source of the problem and were used to support the need for bilingual-bicultural legislation.

English as a Second Language (ESL) programs have been used with minority groups to compensate for the lack of English skills. Learners in these programs receive all their instruction in English, but special attention is given to language development as subject areas are studied. In the elementary school, ESL has been used to replace art or music; at the secondary level, ESL has been substituted for English composition or literature. The major emphasis is on learning oral language skills—listening and speaking. One of the major goals is to help non-English speakers acquire skills that will help them communicate with their teachers.

Bilingual-bicultural education helps learners to strengthen their identity by including their historical, literary, and cultural traditions in the regular curriculum. Positive reinforcement of self-concept is emphasized: these include identity, success in learning, and reduction of cultural shock for the learner. Special preservice and inservice training of teachers stresses the need for positive teacher-student interaction in the learning process. Early studies in bilingual-bicultural programs reported that healthy self-concept and active student participation helped to increase the achievement of non-English learners significantly.

As bilingual-bicultural programs continue, there is little doubt that the language incompatibility between the school and the language-minority student will decrease. The school must continue, however, to provide a significant mainstream approach so as not to foster what could become ethnic separateness.

Reading One of the most ambitious attacks of the war on poverty has been associated with Title I of the Elementary and Secondary Education Act—the reading programs for poverty children. Nationally supported reading programs began during the 1960s and have continued through the 1970s; these federally supported programs have reached all parts of the nation.

Although Title I is a federal program and is maintained as a high priority in education, it is administered through the states. Each state is allocated a fixed sum of support, based upon poverty figures, and is charged with administering the distribution of funds and with evaluating the program on the basis of federal criteria.

Because of continued shifts in the economy over the past six or seven years and because of increased inflation, the poverty level has risen steadily. As a result, Title I reading programs have reached increasing numbers of children in the form of compensatory programs. These programs provide additional reading specialists, a variety of materials, and in many cases, increased use of teacher aides. It has not been uncommon for teacher-pupil ratios to be reduced to one teacher to five pupils in elementary schools and one to ten in secondary schools. Wherever possible, parents are involved in the program.

Title I programs direct their efforts toward "continuous progress learning," that is, toward diagnosing the child at a given performance level and then moving the child individually through the program. This may be accomplished through the regular program or in special facilities where the child leaves the classroom for a period of reading instruction. After a child begins to demonstrate reading performance at a given grade level, the child is then maintained in the regular reading program of the classroom. Reading programs are aimed at taking care of those with the greatest need first. A philosophy of early intervention has led to fewer dropouts, more positive school attitudes, and reading performances that allow the child to progress normally within the regular school environment.

Day Care   As more and more mothers continue to enter the labor market, the pressing need for child care mounts. Although the reasons for entering the labor market may be varied, the impact on child rearing is significant. The day-care center has grown in increasing numbers across the nation. Initiated with the early Head Start programs of the 1960s, federal day-care legislation has increased the compensatory programs now available throughout the country. As a Title IV program, day care has incorporated newer theories of learning for young children, ages one to five, in nursery settings. The need for such programs has been tied closely to the women's liberation movement. As continued new job opportunities for women have appeared, greater needs for child care have emerged, particularly among the middle class where the consciousness level has been raised to such a degree that some women wish to pursue careers before their children begin formal schooling.

Common arrangements for children under three years of age are often made with a day-care mother, who cares for the child in a private home. Supervised by a state department of welfare or other social agency, these day-care homes are licensed and inspected for health, safety, food, light, heat, equipment, fences, and the like. The day-care mother may or may not be licensed, depending upon the particular state. Perhaps the biggest weakness with this program is that federal criteria for day-care homes do not require some form of teacher licensing; yet there is much formal teaching taking place in the home.

Day-care centers are more formal in nature than private homes—and also tend to be more stable. Usually they are staffed by trained early-childhood specialists, operate with a professional director, and can be found in a variety of settings—including churches, store fronts, homes, and settlement houses. These centers, or early childhood schools, are inspected and licensed by welfare departments in many states; in some states, they also are licensed as private or public schools by state departments of education. These programs tend to be more formal than the day-care home and usually are designed to care for somewhat older but still prekindergarten children.

Debate over day care continues today. As federal welfare legislation, day-care programs vary financially with each presidential administration, subject to the dominant welfare philosophy of the moment. There is little doubt, however, that day care has become an essential element of welfare-reform plans of the federal and of many state governments.

Summary and Implications

Although this chapter illustrates only a few national priorities, the federal government's activities and influence can be readily seen in education. The government's participation in education has increased significantly during the past two decades. Many of the federal programs were begun during the 1960s; during the 1970s, these programs were expanded significantly and supported by increased amounts of funding. Spawned by the need for social and welfare changes, many of the federal programs in education have been of a compensatory nature. It appears that the federal government is able to respond more quickly to national needs in education than state and local school systems. It must be remembered, however, that federal funds allocated to the support of public education still account for a very small amount of the total dollars now spent on education. Whether the federal share of support will increase in the future remains difficult to assess. As "due process" and "equal opportunity" pressures continue to expand within the society, it seems apparent that federal interest in meeting these pressures will continue. As school enrollments continue to decline into the next decade, new priorities for federal participation will probably emerge.

Discussion Questions

1. Discuss some of the due process implications of Public Law 94–142.
2. Why is the concept of career education so important for the young learner?
3. In what way does APL have implications for the secondary school?

4. Why should the federal government participate in a public educational program that is the individual responsibility of the fifty states?
5. Discuss the assertion that "too strong an emphasis on bicultural education will produce separatism in the United States."

Supplemental Activities

1. Visit a day-care home and report on the activities.
2. Investigate with a high school guidance counselor career-education opportunities.
3. Prepare a list of priority areas in education where the federal government should become involved.

4. Visit a local school and discuss how a handicapped learner's individualized program is established.
5. Create a collage depicting the federal government's role in financially supporting education during the last two decades.

Bibliography

Blanco, George M. "Competencies Needed by Bilingual Education Teachers," *Educational Leadership* 35 (November 1977).

Cole, Robert W. and Dunn, Rita. "A New Lease on Life for Education of the Handicapped," *Phi Delta Kappan* 59 (September 1977).

Educational Testing Service. *Focus No. 3: Early Education*. Princeton: Educational Testing Service, 1977.

Graney, Marshall. "Role Models in Children's Readers." *School Review* 85 (February 1977).

Olson, Paul A., Freeman, Larry, and Bowman, James. *Education for 1984 and After*. Lincoln: Nebraska Curriculum Development Center, 1974.

U.S. Department of Health, Education, and Welfare. *Full Educational Opportunity Under the Law*. Washington, D.C.: U.S. Government Printing Office, 1975.

CHAPTER 9

Education in a World Setting

PEOPLE HAVE ALWAYS FACED THE PROBLEM OF LEARNING TO LIVE with their neighbors. In recent history, however, as transportation and communication have improved, world trade increased, and population mushroomed, it has become even more essential that people learn to live in peace. In fact, in view of the nuclear weapons that now exist, human survival on earth literally depends upon the ability of neighbors to get along. Many people believe that education in each nation throughout the world has an extremely significant role to play in world peace. This chapter will explore some of the dimensions of education in a world setting.

Ideological and Economic Conflict
Recent international relations have been characterized by two basic differences among nations—one ideological and the other economic. In the one case, world power has been divided into two major factions: those nations adhering to socialism or communism and their corresponding economic philosophies, and those nations adhering to democracy and its corresponding economic philosophy. The Soviet Union has exhibited strong influence as a proponent of communist doctrines, while the United States has advocated democracy. While there are many differences in the basic tenets of communism and democracy, the basic issue is *freedom*. As currently practiced, communism is government by a few—a form of dictatorship. Freedom embodies choice without coercion; it means, for example, that developing nations should be permitted to plan their own forms of government without threat. The foreign policy of the Soviet Union has not favored freedom of choice to developing nations; its philosophy has been the expansion of communism—a direct threat to freedom-loving people.

Ideology and Education

The relationships between ideology and education are strong and direct: educational systems are based upon and promote the ideologies of the nations in which they are located. As they develop, new nations may either follow existing ideological and educational patterns or develop new ones. One thing is certain, however: it is self-evident that education is significant in the development of all nations—even though the means and ends of education vary considerably from nation to nation. Education is an effective agent for transmitting ideologies and for encouraging nationalism.

Education and Peace

The United Nations represents a major effort toward international peace and understanding. Its charter reads, in part, that it exists:

1. To take effective collective measures for the prevention and the removal of threats to peace;
2. To develop friendly relations based on respect for the principle of equal rights and self-determination of peoples;
3. To cooperate in economic, social, cultural, and humanitarian matters and to promote respect for human rights and fundamental freedoms for all.

Numerous agencies are directly related to the United Nations and operate under its auspices to foster world understanding. Some of these agencies are: the World Health Organization (WHO), primarily inter-

UNESCO provided technical assistance to allow this school to be built in a previously malaria-ridden jungle in India. (*Photograph courtesy of UNATIONS*)

ested in promoting personal health, mental and physical, and in developing desirable conditions of public health and sanitation; Food and Agricultural Organization (FAO), concerned with the standard of living and with nutrition as influenced by the production of farms, forests, and fisheries; United Nations Children's Fund (UNICEF), actively engaged in child welfare; and the International Bank for Reconstruction and Development (IBRD), interested in international trade and foreign investments to facilitate development and reconstruction.

UNESCO   One agency directly related to education is the United Nations Educational, Scientific, and Cultural Organization (UNESCO). Its preamble reads, in part:

> The Government of the States Parties to the Constitution on Behalf of their Peoples Declare:
>
> > that since wars begin in the minds of men, it is in the minds of men that the defenses of peace must be constructed;
> >
> > that ignorance of each other's ways and lives has been a common cause, throughout the history of mankind, of that suspicion and mistrust between the peoples of the world through which their differences have all too often broke into war; . . .
> >
> > that the wide diffusion of culture, and the education of humanity for justice, liberty, and peace are indispensable to the dignity of man and constitute a sacred duty which all nations must fulfill in a spirt of mutual assistance and concern; . . .
>
> *For these reasons:* the States parties to this Constitution, believing in full and equal opportunities for education for all, in the unrestricted pursuit of objective truth, and in the free exchange of ideas and knowledge, are agreed and determined to develop and increase the means of communication between their peoples and to employ these means for the purpose of mutual understanding and a truer and more perfect knowledge of each other's lives . . .

Although UNESCO has been involved in many educational, scientific, and cultural projects, it has perhaps been most successful in helping to improve teacher-education programs in many countries. UNESCO represents a definite united effort by member nations to achieve peace and security in the world through education.

World Confederation of Organizations of the Teaching Profession   The aims of the World Confederation of Organizations of the Teaching Profession (WCOTP) are:

to foster a conception of education directed toward the promotion of international understanding and good will, with a view to safeguarding peace and freedom and respect for human dignity; to improve teaching methods, educational organizations, and the academic and professional training of teachers so as to equip them better to serve the interests of youth, to defend the rights and the materials and moral interests of the teaching profession, to promote closer relationships between teachers in the different countries.

Membership in the WCOTP is representative of over ninety-five nations. The American Federation of Teachers, the American Teachers' Associations, and the National Education Association of the United States are members. In a recent questionnaire-type study sponsored by the WCOTP, many educational problems common to all nations were identified, including the lack of funds, the shortage of excellent teachers, the need for school buildings, and the need for compulsory and free education. The WCOTP, facing these problems with determination, holds an Assembly of Delegates once each year. Resolutions of the delegate assembly have ranged widely "from intensive literary programs to free education at all levels, from increased availability and status of technical education to special and adequate provision for the educational and medical needs of the physically and mentally handicapped." WCOTP also sponsors regional conferences; in the past, these conferences have dealt with such topics as the status of the teaching profession in Niamey, Niger; the teaching of science in elementary schools in Asia; and the role of teachers in nation building. WCOTP's bulletin *Echo,* designed to promote international understanding, is published in thirteen languages. *Educational Panorama,* another WCOTP publication, is published in English, French, Spanish, Japanese, and Arabic.

Student Exchange

Student and teacher exchange programs represent another effort toward international understanding. It is hoped that these programs will foster better understanding of various cultures, increase tolerance, encourage cooperation, reduce human suffering, and reduce world tensions. It has been estimated that 20 percent of the universities and colleges in the United States operate such programs. The growth of such programs has been rapid; for example, in the 1957–58 school year, there were 157 programs; in 1970, there were over 600 programs—two-thirds of them carried on during the academic year. Although at a less dramatic rate, these programs have continued to increase right up to the present time.

Secondary school exchange programs are also increasing. It has been estimated that over 5,000 young students from foreign countries study in the United States each year and that over 20,000 high school students from the United States study abroad each year. Most of the American high school exchange students are in summer programs. The U.S. Department of Defense operates a school system for the children of American servicemen abroad. This school system, United States Dependents School, European Area (USDESEA) is the nation's nineteenth largest school system, with an enrollment of 116,000 students in 217 schools.

Teachers for the USDESEA come from every state in the Union. Although not officially organized as an international education program, USDESEA affords opportunities for the broadening of cultural experiences between citizens of the United States and those of other nations.

Opportunities for Americans to teach abroad are increasing. Teacher shortages in other nations, combined with a surplus of teachers in the United States, have increased opportunities for foreign employment. Recruiters from West Germany and Australia, for example, have visited many college and university campuses seeking teachers from the United States.

A concise summary of opportunities for studying or teaching abroad can be found in *Educational and Cultural Exchange Opportunities,* a booklet published by the U.S. Department of State, Bureau of Educational and Cultural Affairs, Washington, D.C. 20520.

Agency of International Development The government of the United States, apart from its United Nations affiliation and from various student exchange programs, has been engaged in specific international educational efforts. Two major governmental efforts aimed at assisting developing nations are currently being made through the Agency of International Development (AID) and the Peace Corps.

AID is the governmental agency responsible for the administration of foreign aid or assistance programs. It is housed within the Department of State and headed by an administrator who is responsible to the Secretary of State. The purpose of AID is to help developing and poor nations in their social and economic development through loans, grants, and technical assistance in many fields. AID, founded on the precepts of self-help and mutual assistance, is a cooperative endeavor in which our government helps others to help themselves. AID has faced difficult decisions as to what is the best way to help a developing nation socially and economically.

Typical programs that AID has been involved in are: building and staffing of modern teacher-training programs, renovating university academic programs, establishing new agricultural and engineering colleges, constructing new school buildings, and modernizing ministries of education. The programs administered by AID have received both criticism and praise. Some of the criticisms include: a lack of specific focus for human development, superficial programs that only scratch the surface of a problem and may actually accentuate it, weaknesses in the partnership of self-help arrangements, lack of long-term commitments necessary for success, failure to recognize the help that nations other than the United States can provide, and lack of success in mobilizing, utilizing, and maintaining native academic talent. On the other hand, AID has been credited with initiating new and promising programs, with creating an atmosphere of ferment inducive to change, and with tapping the university communities of the United States through contract devices. Programs of assistance such as those attempted by AID are difficult to assess because the results from such programs are usually neither immediate nor tangible.

AID and its predecessors have assisted schools now enrolling over 23 million students, trained more than 500,000 teachers in their own countries, brought more than 150,000 students and specialists to the United States, and helped to build hundreds of thousands of classrooms and to distribute millions of textbooks. Yet, much remains to be done. For example, two out of three adults in developing nations are unable to read and write. AID is exploring innovative methods for helping developing countries. Three new thrusts are envisioned: to explore the potential of educational technology for achieving major breakthroughs in the quantity, quality, and cost of education in the less developed countries; to evaluate nonformal educational programs; and to foster research in educational finance and in methods of increasing the accuracy and usefulness of economic measurement tools in educational planning, decision making, and management.

The Peace Corps   The Peace Corps, a part of ACTION, represents another important international educational endeavor. ACTION was created in 1971 by executive order of the president. The Peace Corps program is carried out by volunteers who are first given specialized training in the language and culture of a given country and are then sent to that country to work intimately with its people in enterprises such as farming, teaching, engineering, or health. The program emphasizes Americans actually "doing" and demonstrating, not merely advising—as a means of helping others help themselves. Peace Corps volunteers live under conditions similar to those with whom they work in order to understand the culture of the communities and the attitude of its citizens and to suggest the egalitarian image of democracy. Peace Corps volunteers are assigned to many nations, with particularly large numbers in Latin America, Africa, the Far East, the Near East, and South Asia.

As a result of experiences learned from the Peace Corps venture, the following thrusts are now being developed.

1. More volunteers are being assigned to the high-priority needs of developing nations, as identified by the developing nation.
2. Volunteers are being recruited with the skills necessary to meet the high-priority requests. Older volunteers and those with families are more likely to be recruited and accepted. It is interesting to note that President Carter's mother, Miss Lillian, served with the Peace Corps in India.
3. A greater effort is being made to create a genuine partnership with the host country. The Peace Corps must avoid engaging in a kind of volunteer colonialism. A new goal calls for 50 percent of the Peace Corps overseas staff positions to be filled with local citizens.

A Peace Corps worker involved in a construction project in Venezuela. (Photograph by Donald Patterson, Stock, Boston)

4. Volunteer service by international and multinational teams are being organized.
5. A stronger effort is being made to relate Peace Corps activities to similar problems in the United States.

Peace Corps workers are now serving in sixty countries; a total of 80,000 Americans have served in the Peace Corps since its inception in 1961.

The Peace Corps and AID have cooperated in developing school-to-school partnerships, especially in less technically developed nations. The program provides American school children, parents, and teachers with an opportunity to help foreign villages build schools of their own. The emphasis in this area is on fostering self-help. In addition to school construction, the program encourages exchanges of books, equipment, students, and teachers.

Summary and Implications Each year the world grows smaller and nations become more interdependent upon one another. The solution to many of our most serious worldwide problems, such as those of energy, pollution, and health—to name just a few—will be found only through better education for people throughout the world. And perhaps world peace will depend, ultimately, on the success of education on a worldwide scale. What are the implications for American citizens, teachers, and schools? For one thing, it would seem sensible for our government and citizens at large to assign a higher national priority to the promotion and development of international understanding and peace. Our teachers and schools must work harder to develop excellent programs that will help students learn more about other countries and develop desirable attitudes about international understanding and world peace. Such programs will take considerable effort and will be costly. The question is not whether we can afford to do so, but rather can we afford *not* to do so.

Discussion Questions

1. What are some of the things you feel could be done through the American school system to promote world peace?
2. Which countries have the best school systems in your estimation? What makes these systems the best?

3. What new efforts would you like to see our government make to insure world peace?
4. Discuss ways that education could be improved around the world.

Supplemental Activities

1. Interview several foreign students regarding the school systems in each of their countries. Contrast these foreign school systems with ours.
2. List what you believe to be the strengths and weaknesses of the Peace Corps.
3. Discuss with a number of people who have lived in foreign countries their views on human rights, on the importance of education, and on comparative governments.

4. Go to the library and locate some additional information on the educational activities of UNESCO. Read and evaluate this material.
5. Write a brief proposal for an instructional unit on "peace education" that could be taught at the high school level.

Bibliography

Belding, Robert E. "Career Education in Sweden." *American School Board Journal* (July 1975): 37–38.

DeVault, M. Vere, and Kato, Koji. "Gakushu-juku: Japan's Second System of Education." *Phi Delta Kappan* (June 1977): 735–737.

Fraser, Stewart E. "The Four R's of Vietnamese Education: Resolution, Ramification, Reconciliation, and Redevelopment." *Phi Delta Kappan* (June 1977): 730–735.

Henderson, George. *Education for Peace: Focus on Mankind.* Washington, D.C.: Association for Supervision and Curriculum Development, 1973.

Kazamias, Andreas M., and Masslalas, Byron G. *Tradition and Change in Education: A Comparative Study*. Englewood Cliffs, N.J.: Prentice-Hall, 1965.

Rose, Charles J. "The International Baccalaureate after Ten Years." *Phi Delta Kappan* (May 1977): 708.

Taylor, Harold. *The World and the American Teacher*. Washington, D.C.: American Association of Colleges for Teacher Education, 1968.

Weidner, Edward. "U.S. Institutional Programs in International Education." *Phi Delta Kappan* 51 (January 1970).

PART III

Control, Organization, and Support of American Education

The control of education in the United States involves three levels of government—federal, state and local. Federal control is authorized through the United States Constitution and specific federal laws related to education. Correspondingly, the control function in the various states emanates from their respective constitutions and state laws, while local boards of education, as agents of the state, function under delegated authority from the states—with some discretionary power.

Legally, under the Tenth Amendment of the United States Constitution, education is a function of the states, yet the actual operation of the schools is carried out by local government. The federal government has a strong interest in education, particularly as it relates to national security, national domestic problems, and the rights of citizen as guaranteed by the United States Constitution and federal laws.

The organization of education within the United States is characterized by decentralization. Local boards of education in each of approximately 16,000 local school districts in the United States have the responsibility, delegated to them by their respec-

tive states, of providing education for their citizens. These local boards must abide by the federal and state constitutions and laws; but they may with their discretionary power make policies and decisions that are appropriate and unique to their own districts. As the United States has matured as a nation from colonial days to the present, the relative degree of centralized control has increased. Increasingly, local boards of education are generally perceived as having less control over education. This decrease in local control has resulted in part from federal and state legislation, court decisions, the complexities of our society, and the quest for equality of opportunity in education.

The traditional roles of local, state, and federal government in education have changed over the years. It is quite likely that these roles will continue to change and that new patterns of governmental interrelationships, as they apply to education, will emerge from this tripartite control.

In Part III, the functions of each level of government will be considered as they apply to the legal, organizational, and financial aspects of American education. Decisions made at any of the three levels of government regarding either legal, administrative, or financial matters are likely to serve as a stimulus to further interactive decisions. The concomitant effects of these multilevel decisions must assure to all citizens their inalienable rights as Americans.

Specifically, these chapters consider the legal basis and the control of education in the United States; local, state, and federal roles are examined. Attention is directed toward the current interpretations of the United States Constitution as they apply to the issues of separation of church and state and of school desegregation.

The organizational pattern of education in the United States will be examined, with particular attention given to the newly developing roles of the federal, state, regional, and local governments in the educational enterprise. The changing pattern of the financing of public education will be scrutinized in the light of its vital relationship to equality of educational opportunity.

CHAPTER 10

The Law and American Education

THE EDUCATIONAL SYSTEMS OF THE UNITED STATES, BOTH PUBLIC and nonpublic, are governed by law. The United States Constitution provides the basic law of the nation, and state constitutions provide the basic law of the respective states. Since a constitution is created by the people, a state legislature has no right to change that constitution without the consent of the people. State legislatures make laws applicable to education; these laws must be in accordance with both the federal Constitution and the applicable state constitution. The enabling and legislative control agents of education are illustrated in the top portion of Figure 10–1. It is not unusual for conflicts to occur in this system of control. In such instances, state and federal court systems make legal interpretations that result in a body of case or common law. The lower portion of Figure 10–1 is illustrative of interpretive and administrative agents.

The initial part of the discussion of legal foundations in this chapter deals primarily with public schools and briefly considers the roles of the federal government, state legislatures, and boards of education in the legal control of education. The latter part considers some basic, persistent, and current legal issues as they relate to the administration of American education.

Constitutional Provisions for Education   In contrast to nonpublic schools, public schools are created by law, supported by general taxation, and controlled by elected officials. The United States Constitution makes no specific provision for public education; however, the Tenth Amendment has been interpreted as granting this power to the states. It specifies that "the powers not delegated to the United States by the Constitution, nor prohibited by it to the states, are reserved to the states respectively, or to the people." Education is considered legally a function of the respective states; however, education as a legal function of the states must be practiced in accordance with other provisions of the United States Constitution: the First and the Fourteenth Amendments have been applied to the operation of education in the various states. The Fourteenth Amendment provides for the protection of specified privileges of citizens. It reads, in part, "No state shall make or enforce any law which shall abrogate the privileges or immunities of citizens of the United States; nor shall any state deprive any person of life, liberty, or property without due process of law; nor deny to any person within its jurisdiction the equal protection of the laws." The First Amendment ensures freedom of speech, religion, the press, and the right to petition. It specifies that "Congress shall make no law respecting an establishment of religion or prohibiting the free exercise thereof; or abridge the freedom of speech or of the press; or the right of the people peaceably to assemble and to petition the government for redress of grievances." Specific instances of the application of these amendments to education will be considered later in Part III.

Each state has made provisions for education in either its constitution or its basic statutory law. Article X of the 1970 Constitution of the State of Illinois reads:

SECTION 1.   GOAL—FREE SCHOOLS

A fundamental goal of the People of the State is the educational development of all persons to the limits of their capacities.

The State shall provide for an efficient system of high quality public educational institutions and services. Education in public schools through the secondary level shall be free. There may be such other free education as the General Assembly provides by law.

The State has the primary responsibility for financing the system of public education.

The current Constitution of the State of Michigan in Section 2, Article VIII, states:

The Legislature shall maintain and support a system of free public elementary and secondary schools as defined by law. Each school district shall provide for the education of its pupils without discrimination as to religion, creed, race, color, or national origin.

The Constitution of the State of Utah in Section 1, Article X, reads:

The Legislature shall provide for the establishment and maintenance of a uniform system of public schools, which shall be open to all children of the State, and be free from sectarian control.

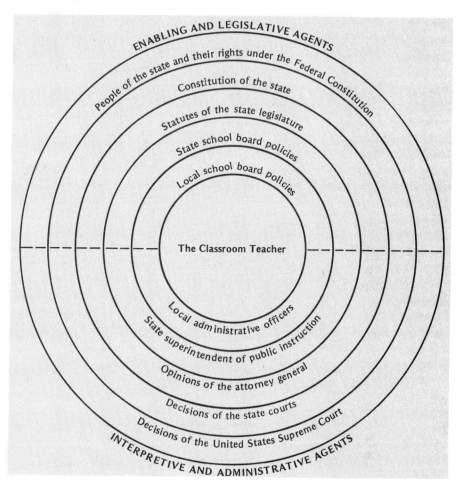

ENABLING AND LEGISLATIVE AGENTS

People of the state and their rights under the Federal Constitution

Constitution of the state

Statutes of the state legislature

State school board policies

Local school board policies

The Classroom Teacher

Local administrative officers

State superintendent of public instruction

Opinions of the attorney general

Decisions of the state courts

Decisions of the United States Supreme Court

INTERPRETIVE AND ADMINISTRATIVE AGENTS

Figure 10–1. Sources of legal control in American education as they affect the classroom teacher.

Source: Jefferson N. Eastmond, *The Teacher and School Administration* (Boston: Houghton Mifflin, 1959), p. 97.

Through such statements the people of the various states have committed themselves to the responsibility of education. The state legislatures have the obligation of fulfilling the educational commitment.

State Legislatures and Political Action

State legislatures are generally responsible for the creation, operation, management, and maintenance of the state school systems. The legislatures are the state policy makers for education. State departments of education are created by legislatures to serve as professional advisors and to execute state policy. State legislatures, though powerful agencies, also operate under controls: the governors of many states have veto power over school legislation as they do over other legislation; and the attorney general and the state judiciary system, when called upon, will rule on the constitutionality of educational legislation.

State legislatures make a variety of decisions. These decisions generally are concerned with the organizational pattern of education within the state; the certification standards and tenure rights of teachers; programs of studies; standards of building construction for health and safety; financing of schools, including tax structure and distribution; and pupil conduct and control, including compulsory attendance laws.

In their school legislative deliberations, state legislatures are continually influenced by special interest groups. These groups, realizing that the legislature is the focus of legal control of education, exert considerable influence on individual legislators. Some of the representative influential groups, as illustrated in Figure 10–2, include state teachers' associations; state associations of school administrators; state school board associations; various labor, business, professional, and agricultural organizations; patriotic groups; horticultural, temperance, and humane societies; taxpayers' federations; and religious groups.

It is not uncommon for over one thousand educational bills to be introduced each year in a state legislative session. Many of these bills had their origin in special interest groups. Throughout the nation in the past

Figure 10–2. Legislative decision making.

few years, state legislatures have dealt with educational proposals concerned with a wide range of topics such as accountability, state aid, textbooks, adult basic education, negotiations, strikes, consumer education, lotteries, education for the gifted, establishment of legal holidays, aid to parochial schools, performance certification of teachers, scholarships, sex education, fire drills, and civil and criminal liability. There is little doubt that many important decisions affecting education are hammered out in the political arenas of state legislatures.

Local Boards of Education

Local school boards are agents of the state, created by and responsible to the state for the operation of education within a specified local school district. They possess only those powers granted to them by statutes, or those implied by the statutes, which are necessary to enable them to carry out their responsibilities. Powers usually granted or implied to local school boards include the power to obtain revenue to maintain schools, to purchase sites and build buildings, to purchase materials and supplies, to organize and provide a program of studies, to employ necessary personnel and regulate their services, and to admit and assign pupils to schools, and to control their conduct.

The preceding statements, which briefly outline the legal structure under which American education functions, are basic to the understanding of federal-state-local interrelationships. The local operation of schools in terms of the law must abide by the constitutional and statutory provisions of the state and, at the same time, assure the rights of individuals as stated in the Constitution of the United States. Conflicts arise when state constitutional and statutory provisions for education are not in harmony with the United States Constitution or when individuals feel that their rights as United States citizens are being infringed upon or are not being fully granted. From these conflicts, court cases arise; the decisions from such cases result in a body of case law that further interprets constitutions and statutes. A number of these conflicts and resultant cases have centered around the issue of separation of church and state.

The First Amendment— Church and State

Historically, the United States has maintained a strong tradition of separation of church and state. This basic principle expressed in the First Amendment was designed by our forefathers to assure each citizen the freedom to choose and practice religion in his or her own manner. Education, a governmental function necessary for the survival of an effective democracy, must be carried on in such a manner in order to preserve this basic right of religious freedom.

Our nation also has a strong religious heritage. In colonial times, education was primarily a religious matter; furthermore, a good deal of colonial education was conducted in private schools. Many private schools today are still religious in nature, and many students receive their education in private schools. It has been estimated that approximately one-tenth of the total elementary school population is, and will continue to be, enrolled in nonpublic or private schools through 1984.[1]

Court cases concerned with the separation of church and state most frequently involve both the First and Fourteenth Amendments of the United States Constitution. The First Amendment is made applicable to the states by the Fourteenth Amendment. For example, a state law requiring the reading of a daily prayer in classrooms throughout the state could be interpreted as establishing a religion or, at least, "prohibiting the free exercise thereof," and would be in violation of the Fourteenth Amendment, since states are not permitted to make laws that abridge the privileges of citizens of the United States. The privilege of free practice of religion is assured by the First Amendment.

Court cases related to the separation of church and state can be classified into three categories: those dealing with the use of public funds to support nonpublic education; those dealing with the practice of sectarian religion in public schools; and those dealing with the rights of parents to provide private education for their children. In the late 1960s and 1970s, renewed attention was given to the use of public funds for parochial education.

Public Funds—Parochial Education

The question of the use of public funds to support private or sectarian schools has been raised on many occasions. Typically, state constitutions prohibit the use of public funds for sectarian institutions or schools. However, public funds have been used to provide transportation for students to church schools and to provide textbooks for students in private schools. The use of funds for these purposes has been challenged in many instances.

The landmark case in respect to the use of public funds to provide transportation for students to church schools was *Everson* v. *Board of Education,* ruled upon by the United States Supreme Court in 1947. The Court held that the use of tax-raised funds by a New Jersey school district to reimburse parents for bus fares expended to transport their children to church schools did not violate the establishment clause of the First Amendment. The majority of the Court viewed the New Jersey statute permitting free bus transportation to parochial school children as "public welfare legislation" to help get the children to and from school safely and expeditiously.

Since the *Everson* decision, the highest courts in a number of states, under provisions in their own constitutions, have struck down enactments authorizing free busing of children attending denominational schools. Other state supreme courts have upheld enactments providing

1.   Kenneth A. Simon and Martin M. Frankel, *Projections of Educational Statistics to 1984–85* (Washington, D.C.: U.S. Government Printing Office, 1976).

for the use of public funds for the transportation of students to denominational schools.

In 1975, the United States Supreme Court affirmed a federal district court decision in Missouri (*Luetkemeyer* v. *Kaufman*) that although a state may provide free transportation to parochial school students (*Everson* v. *Board of Education*), principles of equal protection do not require a state to do so merely because such services are provided to public school pupils.[2]

It is apparent from the court decisions and legislation in the various states that distinctly different opinions exist regarding the proper and valid use of public funds for private school transportation.

A similar situation exists regarding the use of public funds to provide textbooks for private schools. The landmark case relating to the use of public funds to provide textbooks for private schools originated in Louisiana. A Louisiana statute provided for textbooks to be supplied to nonpublic school children free of charge. The statute had been upheld by a state court on the theory that the children, and not the nonpublic schools, were the beneficiaries.

In *Cochran* v. *Louisiana State Board of Education* (1930), the United States Supreme Court held the Louisiana textbook statute valid under the Fourteenth Amendment. The Court discounted taxpayers' contentions that furnishing textbooks purchased with tax-raised funds to private school pupils was a tax for a private rather than a public purpose and constituted a deprivation of taxpayers' money without due process of law. This decision did not rest on the First Amendment, having been rendered before the Supreme Court ruled that the First Amendment is applicable to the states under the Fourteenth Amendment.

In a later case (*Board of Education of Central School District No. 1, Towns of Greenbush et al.* v. *Allen* (1966), the United States Supreme Court, upon appeal (1968), upheld the constitutionality of a New York textbook statute. The New York law required boards of education, upon individual request, to lend textbooks free to children in grades seven through twelve who were in private schools, if these schools are complying with state compulsory attendance law. The majority of the Court reasoned as follows:

> The express purpose of Sec. 701 was stated by the New York Legislature to be furtherance of the educational opportunities available to the young. Appellants have shown us nothing about the necessary effects of the statute that is contrary to its stated purpose. The law merely makes available to all children the benefits of a general program to lend school books free of charge. Books are furnished at the request of the pupil and ownership remains, at least technically, in the State. Thus no funds or books are furnished to parochial schools, and the financial benefit is to parents and

2. Thomas J. Flygare, "State Aid to Parochial Schools: Diminished Alternatives," *Phi Delta Kappan* 57 (November 1975): 204.

children, not to schools. Perhaps free books make it more likely that some children choose to attend a sectarian school, but that was true of the state-paid bus fares in *Everson* and does not alone demonstrate an unconstitutional degree of support for a religious institution.

In 1974, the Missouri Supreme Court held that it was a violation of the state constitution for the state to loan textbooks free of charge to parochial school students. The United States Supreme Court denied review of the case, thereby preserving the state court decision. "Thus, although a state *may* lend textbooks to parochial school students, the Court declined to *compel* a state to do so if it is supplying free books to public school pupils."[3]

The United States Supreme Court, in its decision in the *Everson* case and again in the *Allen* case, has made it quite clear that providing transportation or textbooks per se is not in violation of the First Amendment.

Recently over twenty states have considered legislation providing for a variety of forms of direct aid to nonpublic schools. In 1968, Pennsylvania enacted legislation to supply aid for the purchase of secular education services; these services were defined as consisting of courses in mathematics, modern foreign languages, physical science, and physical education. Aid was to be in the form of reimbursement for teachers' salaries, textbooks, and instructional materials. Provisions were made in the law for approval of textbooks and teachers by the superintendent of public instruction. Payments were to be made directly to the school, and school accounts were subject to audit.

In 1969, Rhode Island enacted legislation providing for salary supplements to eligible teachers in nonpublic schools. A teacher requesting supplementary salary had to satisfy certain eligibility requirements such as being certified, teaching only those subjects taught in public schools, and using only materials used in public schools.

Both the Pennsylvania and Rhode Island laws were challenged, and the cases were eventually heard by the United States Supreme Court. The Court ruled in both the Pennsylvania case (*Lemon* v. *Kurtzman*, 1971) and the Rhode Island case (*DiCenso* v. *Robinson*, 1971) that the respective laws were unconstitutional. Justice Burger, who wrote the majority opinion, stated: "We conclude that the cumulative impact of the entire relationships arising under the statutes in each State involves excessive entanglements between government and religion." Entanglements were anticipated in accomplishing the necessary state supervision to ensure that the state aid would support only secular education. The Court pointed out that a further defect of the Pennsylvania statute was that it provided for the aid to be given directly to the school. In the *Everson* and *Allen* cases, the aid was provided either to the student or to his parents—not to the church-related school.

After the Pennsylvania case (*Lemon* v. *Kurtzman*) and the Rhode

3. Ibid.

Island case (*DiCenso* v. *Robinson*), the United States Supreme Court in 1972 struck down an Ohio plan for direct tuition payments to parents of children in private schools. In 1973, the Court also ruled against a Pennsylvania tuition payment proposal, a New York tax credit plan, and a New York state financing plan for record keeping and testing in parochial schools.

In 1975, in *Meek* v. *Pittenger*, the United States Supreme Court again struck down an effort by Pennsylvania to aid its numerous parochial schools. Pennsylvania had proposed three separate aid programs: (1) the provision of auxiliary services—such as counseling, psychological services, speech and hearing therapy—by public school employees to nonpublic school pupils; (2) the direct loan of instructional materials and equipment to nonpublic schools; and (3) the loan of textbooks without charge to nonpublic school pupils. The law was drafted by the Pennsylvania legislature to avoid the pitfalls of *Lemon* v. *Kurtzman*. The Court upheld the textbook provision, basing its opinion on *Board of Education of Central School District No. 1, Towns of Greenbush et al.* v. *Allen*, but struck down the provision of auxiliary services on the basis of "excessive entanglement" and the provision of instructional materials inasmuch as the materials and equipment become subsumed in the "religious mission" of the schools.

Most recently, the United States Supreme Court in *Wolman* v. *Walter* (1977), a case originating in Ohio, affirmed that providing nonpublic school pupils with books, standardized testing and scoring, diagnostic services, and therapeutic and remedial services is constitutional. The proposals for instructional materials and field trip services were ruled unconstitutional.

The Court cited *Allen* and *Meek* in approving the textbook provision. Numerous cases were cited in respect to standardized testing and scoring, diagnostic services, and therapeutic and remedial services. The Ohio law proposed "to supply for use by pupils attending nonpublic schools within the district such standardized tests and scoring services as are in use in the public schools of the state." The Court noted that (1) the tests are used to measure the progress of students in secular subjects; (2) nonpublic school personnel are not involved in either the drafting or the scoring of the tests; and (3) the statute does not authorize any payment to nonpublic school personnel for costs of administering the tests. In respect to diagnostic services, the Court noted that (1) speech, hearing, and psychological services are to be provided within the nonpublic school; (2) personnel who perform the services (with the exception of physicians) are employees of the local school system; (3) physicians may be hired on a contract basis; (4) the purpose of the services is to determine the pupils' deficiency or need for assistance; and (5) treatment of any defect would take place off the nonpublic school premises. The Court concluded that "providing diagnostic services on nonpublic school premises will not create an im-

The Supreme Court ruled in many significant cases of desegregation. (*Photograph courtesy of Ackad Studio, Washington, D.C.*)

permissible risk of the fostering of ideological views. It follows that there is no need for excessive surveillance, and there will not be impermissible entanglement."

In considering the provision of therapeutic services and remedial reading, the Court noted that the Ohio proposal, in contrast to *Meek*, called for the services to be rendered in public schools, public centers, or in mobile units located off nonpublic school premises. It concluded: "It can hardly be said that the supervision of public employees performing public functions on public property creates an excessive entanglement between church and state."

The United States Supreme Court in reversing the Ohio district court in the provision of instructional materials referred to *Meek*. Although the Ohio proposal differed from *Meek* in that it purported to provide the materials to the pupils rather than the school, the Court reasoned: "In the view of the impossibility of separating the secular education function from the sectarian, the state aid inevitably flows, in part, in support of the religious role of the schools." Major points made by the Court in reversing the district court in the provision on field trips were (1) "Nonpublic schools control the timing of the trips, their frequency, and destination, therefore the schools rather than the children are the recipients of the service"; (2) "The field trips are an integral part of the educational experience, and where the teacher works within and for a sectarian institution, an unacceptable risk of fostering religion is an inevitable byproduct." In concluding, the Court said, "Moreover, the ·public school authorities will be unable adequately to insure secular use of the field trip funds without close supervision of the nonpublic teachers. This would create excessive entanglement."

The issue of public aid to private and church-related schools is still evolving. While it is clear that aid for certain secular services (such as transportation, textbooks, and under prescribed circumstances, testing, diagnostic, therapeutic, and remedial services) can be provided, it is not as yet absolutely clear what further aid will be approved. It is apparent that increasing numbers of state legislatures are attempting to find ways to provide aid to nonpublic schools without violating the First Amendment. It is quite probable that other laws will be developed based on findings from the *Lemon* v. *Kurtzman*, *DiCenso* v. *Robinson*, *Meek* v. *Pittenger*, and *Wolman* v. *Walter* cases. It is also quite probable that the laws developed will be challenged; and further rulings from the courts will be forthcoming.

Child Benefit Theory

In general, the decisions supporting the use of public funds to provide transportation and textbooks for students in private schools were based on *child benefit theory*, in which the Supreme Court reasoned that the transportation and books provide benefit to the children and not to the school or religion. Those opposed to child benefit theory argue that aid to children receiving sectarian education instruction is, in effect, aid to the institution providing instruction.

Child benefit theory, as supported by the United States Supreme Court, has penetrated federal legislation. The Elementary and Secondary Education Act of 1965 provides for assistance to both public and nonpublic school children. Title I, which deals with assistance for the education of children from low-income families, states that children from these families attending private schools must be provided services in proportion to their numbers. Title II, which deals with school library resources, textbooks, and other instructional materials, also states that nonpublic as well as public school pupils must receive benefits.

Religion in the Public Schools

Another issue related to the separation of church and state is centered around religious activities practiced in public schools. The providing of released time by public schools for religious instruction has been challenged and acted upon by the United States Supreme Court. In 1948, the Court held that the released-time program of the Champaign schools violated the principle of separation of church and state (*People of State of Illinois ex rel. McCollum* v. *Board of Education of School District No. 71, Champaign, Illinois*, 1948). The program in Champaign was a cooperative program between the schools and a voluntary association of members of Jewish, Roman Catholic, and Protestant faiths. Classes were held in the public school classrooms. Pupils were released from their regular classes to attend religious classes; those who did not elect to take religious instruction were not excused from regular class duties. In its decision, the Court pointed out that not only were tax-supported public school buildings being used for sectarian instruction but also the compulsory education law was facilitating religious instruction by providing pupils.

A released-time program in New York was challenged a few years after the *McCollum* case; in this case (*Zorach* v. *Clausen,* 1952), the United States Supreme Court upheld a New York statute that provided for released time. The major difference between the Champaign and the New York case was that in New York students were released from school to go to religious centers to receive religious instruction, whereas in Champaign the instruction was given in public school class-rooms. The Court indicated that the precise type of released-time program is significant: programs differ in the extent of school cooperation and in the degree of sectarianism. It can be concluded that the concept of released time in and of itself is not necessarily in violation of the First Amendment.

The courts have also rendered opinions on Bible and prayer reading in the public schools. In 1962, the United States Supreme Court (*Engle* v. *Vitale*) held that a prayer composed by the New York State Board of Regents and used as a part of the opening exercises of school was in violation of the United States Constitution. The prayer read as follows: "Almighty God, we acknowledge our dependence upon Thee, and we beg Thy blessings on us, our parents, our teachers, and our country." Pupils who objected to the reading of the prayer could be excused. The Court based its decision on the establishment clause of the First Amendment: "Congress shall make no law respecting an establishment of religion, or prohibiting the free exercise thereof." Justice Hugo Black, who wrote the decision, stated:

> The constitutional prohibition against laws respecting an establishment of religion must at least mean that . . . it is no part of the business of government to impose official prayers for any group of American people to recite as a part of a religious program carried on by the government.

In June 1963, the United States Supreme Court rendered a most significant decision in which it outlawed the reading of the Bible and the recitation of the Lord's Prayer in public schools. The Court indicated that these are religious ceremonies and, as such, are violations of the First and Fourteenth amendments of the Constitution. The opinion emphasized that government must remain neutral in matters of religion. The United States Supreme Court decision resulted from the appeals of two lower court decisions, one from Pennsylvania (*Schempp* v. *School District of Abington Township,* 1963) and the other from Maryland (*Murray* v. *Curlett,* 1963), which held that reading the Bible and saying the Lord's Prayer were not illegal.

The United States Supreme Court may eventually hear another case dealing with the practice of religion in public schools.[4] A Massachusetts law passed by the legislature in 1973 reads:

> At the commencement of the first class of each day in all grades in the public schools the teacher in charge of the room in which each such class is held shall announce that a period of silence not to exceed one minute in duration shall be observed for meditation or prayer, and during any such period silence shall be maintained and no activities shall be engaged in.

In January, 1976, the school committee of Framingham, Massachusetts, voted to comply with the law and adopted guidelines for use by classroom teachers in supervising the period of silence. Immediately a lawsuit was filed by the American Civil Liberties Union of Massachusetts on behalf of twelve Framingham school children and their parents. The plaintiffs charged that the law and the guidelines established a religious exercise in the public schools and are in violation of the establishment clause of the First Amendment.

The three federal judges who were impaneled to hear the case unanimously upheld the constitutionality of the law and the guidelines. The three-judge court found that the law and the guidelines did not have the primary effect or purpose of advancing religion. The phrase "meditation or prayer," the court noted, "indicates a legislative sensitivity to the First Amendment's mandate to take a neutral position that neither encourages nor discourages prayer." The judges concluded: "The fact that the Framingham program provides an opportunity for prayer for those students who desire to pray during the period of silence does not render the program unconstitutional." This case could very well signal the beginning of a new series of controversies on prayers in the courts.

The rulings of the United States Supreme Court that forbade obligatory prayer and Bible reading have prompted attempts to amend the Constitution to permit voluntary prayer. The late Senator Everett Dirksen (R., Ill.) tried unsuccessfully in 1966 and 1967 to secure congressional approval of a prayer amendment. In 1971, Representative Chalmers P. Wylie (R., Ohio) also introduced a prayer amendment that was subsequently defeated.

Private Education —an Alternative   The court cases having to do with the right of parents to provide private education for their children are closely related to those having to do with compulsory education. Compulsory education laws appear in the statute books of all states. They generally require parents or whoever has custody of a child, between specific chronological ages, to "cause said child to attend school." The constitutional objection raised re-

---

4.   Thomas J. Flygare, "Federal Court Upholds Minute of Silent Prayer or Meditation in Public Schools," *Phi Delta Kappan* 58 (December 1976): 354–355.

garding compulsory attendance laws is that they infringe upon the individual liberty guaranteed by the Fourteenth Amendment. The constitutionality of compulsory education laws has been attacked in numerous cases, but the principle has been uniformly upheld. In general, courts have reasoned that education is so necessary to the welfare of our nation that compulsory school attendance laws are valid and desirable. However, compulsory education does not mean compulsory public education.

The issue of whether a state could compel children to attend a public school was settled in a case in Oregon. In 1922, the legislature of Oregon passed a law requiring all children to attend public schools. The United States Supreme Court ruled that such a law was unconstitutional in that it infringed upon the rights of parents to control the education of their children (*Pierce* v. *Society of Sisters*, 1925). This ruling of the Court established a precedent permitting parents to have their children educated in private schools. In this same case, the Court also established beyond doubt that the state may reasonably regulate all schools, public and private, and require the teaching of certain subjects. It was established that private schools have a right to exist; that pupils may meet the compulsory attendance laws by attending private schools; and that private schools are subject to regulation by the state.

The courts have also ruled that education in a child's home can meet the requirement of compulsory education. In a case in Indiana (*State* v. *Peterman*, 1904), the Court specified that a school is a place where education is imparted to the young; therefore, a home can be a school if a qualified teacher is engaged in instruction as prescribed by the state. It should be noted that the state controls home instruction and that the instruction generally must be equivalent to that provided by a school. Home instruction must be carried out in good faith and not practiced as a subterfuge to avoid sending children to school. In a court case in New Jersey (*Stephens* v. *Bongart*, 1937) regarding equivalent home instruction, the opinion was rendered that the home instruction in this instance was not equivalent to that provided by a public school. Most compulsory education laws make provisions for children who are physically or mentally unable to attend school.

Although the courts have generally upheld compulsory education, a recent decision by the United States Supreme Court has altered the position slightly. In *Wisconsin* v. *Yoder*, the Court ruled that the Amish religious sect is exempt from state compulsory education laws that require children to attend school beyond the eighth grade. This 1972 decision of the Court was its first in holding a religious group immune from compulsory attendance requirements. The Court held that state laws requiring children to attend school until they are sixteen years of age violate the rights of the Amish to free exercise of religion. The Court stressed the 300-year resistance of the Amish to modern influences. Justice Burger wrote:

It cannot be overemphasized that we are not dealing with a way of life and a mode of education by a group claiming to have recently discovered some "progressive" or more enlightened process for rearing children for modern life.

The interpretation of compulsory education laws indicates the seeking of a reasonable balance between the rights of the individual and the rights of the state. Parents who desire a religious education for their children may meet the requirement of compulsory education by enrolling their children in private parochial schools. At the same time the state reserves the right to regulate private schools reasonably.

The Fourteenth Amendment— Desegregation
The Constitution guarantees certain specific rights to all citizens, and the various state constitutions make provisions for free educational opportunities. Under our form of government, ideally each citizen is afforded an equal opportunity to pursue education. This opportunity or right, however, is not and cannot be provided without commensurate citizen responsibility. The success of our decentralized educational system with its strong local emphasis depends heavily upon local support, participation, and cooperation; local citizens have the responsibility of assuring quality education in their areas. As citizens of their respective states and of the United States, they have the responsibility to provide equal opportunities for education to all children throughout the United States.

Local boards of education, under powers granted to them by the states, may assign students to a particular grade or classification and to a particular school or attendance center within the school district under their jurisdiction. Courts have held that boards of education acting in good faith must have the discretionary power to assign pupils in order to maintain the orderly administration of the school system. It should be noted that boards of education are expected to use this power by acting in good faith. They have the responsibility to assure, to the best of their ability, that each pupil in his or her assignment has an equal opportunity to pursue education. Both pupils and parents have this right.

Closely allied to the power of boards of education to assign pupils to schools is the issue of segregated schools. It should be recognized that segregation in its broadest meaning refers to different races and peoples of a variety of descents. In recent years, attention has been centered on the American black. In 1896 (*Plessy* v. *Ferguson*), the Supreme Court upheld a Louisiana law that required that railway companies provide separate but equal accommodations for the white and black races. The Court indicated in its opinion that the Fourteenth Amendment implied political, not social, equality. This separate but equal doctrine appeared to be the rule until 17 May 1954, when the Supreme Court repudiated the separate but equal doctrine (*Brown* v.

Board of Education of Topeka). The Court said that in education the separate but equal doctrine has no place and that separate facilities are inherently unequal. In 1955, the Court rendered the second *Brown* v. *Board of Education of Topeka* decision requiring implementation of the principles of the first decision.

De Jure   The *Brown* decision referred explicitly to *de jure* segregation, that is,
Segregation segregation by law or by official action. At the time of the *Brown* decision, many southern and border states required segregated schools by law. The existence of segregated schools has also resulted from neighborhood housing patterns. Many neighborhoods are made up predominantly of blacks and their neighborhood schools have predominantly black enrollments. This type of segregation is legally referred to as *de facto* segregation and is relatively common in most of the larger cities of the North. The United States Supreme Court has never ruled specifically on de facto segregation; it has only ruled on de jure segregation.

From the time of the *Brown* decision in 1954 until 1964, little progress was made in eliminating segregated schools. On 25 May 1964, the Supreme Court in reference to a situation in Prince Edward County, Virginia, said: "There has been entirely too much deliberation and not enough speed in enforcing the constitutional rights which we held in *Brown* v. *Board of Education.*" The Civil Rights Act of 1964 added legislative power to the 1954 judicial pronouncement. The Act not only authorized the federal government to initiate court suits against school districts that were laggard in accomplishing desegregation but also prohibited the use of federal funds for programs that discriminated as to race, color, or national origin.

Many segregated school systems have attempted to meet federal desegregation demands by adopting "freedom of choice" or "open enrollment" plans. Under these plans, pupils are permitted to choose the public schools they desire to attend. In 1968, the United States Supreme Court in *Green* v. *County School Board,* a case originating in Virginia, held that a "freedom of choice" plan was not unconstitutional in and of itself, but that, in this case, freedom of choice was not bringing about effective desegregation. Under the freedom-of-choice plan— after three years of operation—no white child had chosen to attend the black school, and 85 percent of the black children still attended the black school. Specifically, the Court said:

> In other words, the school system remains a dual system. Rather than further dismantling of the dual system, the plan has operated simply to burden children and their parents with a responsibility which *Brown II* placed squarely on the School Board. The Board must be required to formulate a new plan, and in light of other courses which appear open to the Board, such as zoning, fashion steps which promise realistically to convert promptly

to a system without a "white" school and a "Negro" school, but just schools.

A further ruling of the United States Supreme Court on de jure segregation resulted from a case arising in Charlotte-Mecklenburg County, North Carolina, in April 1971. A United States district judge had ordered extensive busing of pupils to achieve integration. The goal, as expressed by the judge, was to achieve a ratio of seventy-one whites to twenty-nine blacks in each school in an effort to approximate the racial ratio in the entire district. In its deliberations, the Court cited four main legal questions:

1. To what extent racial balance or racial quotas may be used as an implement in a remedial order to correct a previously segregated system;
2. Whether every all-black and all-white school must be eliminated as an indispensable part of a remedial process of desegregation;
3. What are the limits, if any, on the rearrangement of school districts and attendance zones, as a remedial measure;
4. What are the limits, if any, on the use of transportation facilities to correct state-enforced racial school segregation.

In its rulings the Court said: "The Constitutional command to desegregate schools does not mean that every school in every community must always reflect the racial composition of the school system as a whole." However, the Court continued: "The use made of mathematical ratios was no more than a starting point in the process of shaping a remedy, rather than an inflexible requirement." The Court upheld "the very limited use made of mathematical ratios" as being within the equitable remedial discretion of the district court.

In respect to one-race schools, the Court said: "In some circumstances certain schools may remain all or largely of one race until new schools can be provided or neighborhood patterns change." Further, "the existence of some small number of one-race or virtually one-race schools within a district is not in and of itself the mark of a system which still practices segregation by law." However, the Court cautioned that "the District judge or school authorities should make every effort to achieve the greatest possible degree of actual desegregation and will thus necessarily be concerned with the elimination of one-race schools."

In terms of limits on the rearrangement of school districts and attendance zones, the Court emphasized that "no per se rule can adequately embrace all the difficulties of reconciling the competing interests involved, but in a system with a history of segregation the need for remedial criteria of sufficient specificity to assure a school authority's compliance with its constitutional duty warrants a presumption against schools that are disproportionate in their racial composition." The Court recognized majority-to-minority optional transfers with the provision

Busing has been used widely as a means of integrating the public schools. (*Photograph by Wide World Photos*)

of free student transportation, remedial altering of attendance zones, and "clustering" as legitimate means of desegregating schools. The Court stated: "The remedy for such segregation may be administratively awkward, inconvenient, and even bizarre in some situations and may impose burdens on some; but all awkwardness and inconvenience cannot be avoided in the interim period when remedial adjustments are being made to eliminate the dual school systems."

The *Charlotte* case dealt with desegregation within a single school district. In January, 1972, U.S. District Court Judge Robert R. Merhige, Jr., ordered the consolidation of the Richmond, Virginia, schools with the suburban Henrico and Chesterfield County school systems. Richmond schools were approximately 70 percent black; the school systems of Henrico and Chesterfield Counties were about 90 percent white. In his opinion, Judge Merhige concluded that the constitutional rights of equality override the rights of cities and counties to establish educational boundaries. Judge Merhige reasoned that consolidation was the most promising remedy to bring about effective integration. In June 1972, the Fourth U.S. Circuit Court of Appeals reversed the order of Judge Merhige, stating that he had exceeded his authority in ordering a merger of city and county school systems to improve racial balance.

In 1973, the Richmond metropolitan desegregation case was heard by the United States Supreme Court. By a 4–4 tie vote, with Justice

Powell disqualifying himself, the Court upheld the Fourth U.S. Circuit Court of Appeals reversal of the metropolitan plan.

In a similar fashion, U.S. District Judge Stephen J. Roth ordered the desegregation of schools in Detroit and its surrounding suburbs. This case (*Milliken* v. *Bradley*) eventually reached the United States Supreme Court. In July, 1974, the Court in a 5–4 vote overturned lower court orders requiring the cross-busing of children between the Detroit city school system and fifty-three suburban school districts. Chief Justice Warren Burger, in delivering the opinion of the Court, said:

> Before the boundaries of separate and autonomous school districts may be set aside . . . it must first be shown that there has been a constitutional violation within one district that produces a significant segregative effect in another district. Specifically, it must be shown that racially discriminatory acts of the state or local school districts or of a single school district have been a substantial cause of interdistrict segregation. . . . Without an inner-district violation and inter-district effect, there is no consitutional wrong calling for an inter-district remedy.

The dissenting justices (Douglas, White, Brennan, and Marshall) saw the decision as a "giant step backward." Justice Douglas wrote: "When we rule against the metropolitan area remedy, we take a step that will likely put the problems of the blacks and our society back to the period that antedated the 'separate but equal' regime of *Plessy* v. *Ferguson*." Justice Marshall noted: "The rights at issue in this case are too fundamental to be abridged on grounds as superficial as those relied on by the majority today . . . unless our children begin to learn together, there is little hope that our people will ever learn to live together."

Since the Detroit decision, a number of cases involving metropolitan desegregation have been heard in various courts; the most significant of these originated in Wilmington, Delaware, and Louisville, Kentucky. In the fall of 1975, the U.S. Supreme Court upheld an earlier federal court order calling for the urban-suburban desegregation of the Wilmington, Delaware, area schools. The major factor in this case, which resulted in a ruling that differed from the Detroit case, was that state school reorganization involved school districts other than the Wilmington city district in actions that resulted in the segregation of blacks in Wilmington itself. Therefore, the Court reasoned that other districts should be involved in the solution.

In the Louisville case, the U.S. Sixth Circuit Court of Appeals, in effect, required the Louisville city school system and the Jefferson County school districts to eliminate "all vestiges of state-enforced discrimination" through the use of metropolitan integration. The appeals court determined that in the Louisville area a pattern of interdistrict actions had the effect of maintaining segregated schools. In the spring of 1975, the U.S. Supreme Court decided not to review the Louisville case. In July, 1975, a federal district court ordered implementation of a metropolitan plan—ordering the Louisville city and county school systems to desegregate their schools jointly by transporting students across the lines dividing the respective districts. Approximately one-sixth of the two district's 121,000 students needed to be bused to achieve a black enrollment of 12 to 40 percent in every school. Although Louisville suffered considerable turmoil in implementing metropolitan desegregation, the task was accomplished.[5] The segregation in both Wilmington and Louisville was viewed by the courts as *resulting from governmental actions* either by the state or by multiple school districts.

In June, 1977, the U.S. Supreme Court, in a segregation case related to the Dayton, Ohio, public schools, ruled that the evidence presented by the district court did not justify a systemwide remedy. A plan developed by a district court and approved by the United States Court of Appeals for the Sixth District as a systemwide remedy required

> beginning with the 1976–77 school year, that the racial composition of each school in the district be brought within 15 percent of Dayton's 48 percent–52 percent black-white population ratio, to be accomplished by a variety of desegregation techniques, including the "pairing" of schools, the redefinition of attendance zones, and a variety of centralized special programs and "magnet schools."

The United States Supreme Court, in remanding the case back to the district court, pointed out that

> the finding that the pupil population in the various Dayton schools is not homogeneous, standing by itself, is not a violation of the Fourteenth Amendment absent a showing that this condition resulted from intentionally segregative actions on the part of the Board. . . . It was thus not demonstrated that the systemwide remedy, in effect imposed by the Court of Appeals, was necessary to "eliminate all vestiges of the state-imposed school segregation."

In a second significant decision, also made in June, 1977 (*Milliken* v. *Bradley* II), the United States Supreme Court held:

> As part of a desegregation decree, a district court can, if the record warrants, order compensatory or remedial educational programs for school children who have been subjected to past acts of *de jure* segregation. Here the District Court, acting on substantial evidence in the record, did not abuse its discretion in approving a remedial plan going beyond pupil assignments and adopting specific programs that had been proposed by local school authorities.

The remedial programs included remedial reading, an inservice program for teachers and administrators, the development of an unbiased

5. For further elaboration of this case, the reader is referred to Roger M. Williams, "What Louisville Has Taught Us About Busing," *Saturday Review*, 30 April 1977, p. 6.

testing program, and the provision of counseling and career guidance programs for students. The costs of these programs were to be borne by the Detroit School Board and the state. *Milliken* v. *Bradley II* (1977) was the first time the U.S. Supreme Court had addressed directly the question of whether federal courts can order remedial education programs as a part of a school desegregation decree.

Private Academies

It has been estimated that "there may be as many as 4,000 of the basically segregationist academies in the Deep South, enrolling about 750,000 students.[6] Many of these academies were established as a means to escape from desegregation; however, they now appear to be an attempt to recreate the schools the parents knew as students. A suit is currently before the Internal Revenue Service urging revocation of the tax exempt status of organizations that support schools with discriminatory policies.[7]

A 1976 ruling of the United States Supreme Court (*Runyon* v. *McCrary*) held that exclusion of students from private schools on the grounds of race was a statutory violation. A statute passed shortly after the Civil War was determined applicable to the case. The impact of the decision may be minimal since the great majority of private schools have no policy of racial exclusion.

Busing

Busing is an extremely controversial issue. A number of school districts have been ordered to bus school children to end segregation, including San Francisco, Los Angeles, Pontiac, Kalamazoo, Indianapolis, Seattle, Tulsa, Oklahoma City, Louisville, Austin, Dayton, and Boston. Proponents view busing as a necessary and as oftentimes the only way to achieve equality of opportunity in education for children of all races. They further argue that an integrated society is essential and that, if people are going to live in an integrated society, a part of their preparation must take place in public school systems. Opponents of busing claim that it does not, in fact, improve the quality of education, and that busing requires large expenditures of monies that might be better used in compensatory education claims. As indicated in the previous discussion of *Milliken II* (1977), the U.S. Supreme Court has recognized both compensatory education and pupil assignment (which may involve busing) as legitimate remedies for past acts of de jure segregation.

In summary, the *Charlotte-Mecklenburg* (1971) case, which approved busing as a desegregation remedy, has been the basis for subsequent busing decisions. The Louisville busing order involved metropolitan desegregation and was based on the determination that a pattern of

---

6. "Private Academies: A Thorn for Public Education," *Education USA* 19 (February 1977): 177. Reported from *The Schools That Fear Built*. (Washington, D.C.: Acropolis, 1976).

7. Ibid., p. 184.

interdistrict action had had the effect of maintaining segregated schools. In the Dayton case, the U.S. Supreme Court pointed out that the existence of segregation in the Dayton school district in and of itself was not sufficient evidence for a total systemwide remedy. Sufficient evidence had not been shown to prove that the segregated schools resulted from intentional actions by the school board. Future decisions will, without doubt, define and refine the circumstances necessary for the courts to require busing as a remedy to segregation.

While the various courts and federal agencies have made rulings in respect to busing, the executive and legislative branches have also entered the debate. Former Presidents Nixon and Ford both have spoken publicly against busing as a means of achieving racial balance. Two laws have recently been enacted to limit busing: one law states that federal agencies must try all alternative methods of desegregation before resorting to busing; the other prevents the Department of Health, Education, and Welfare from ordering a plan that requires the assignment of children to schools other than those nearest their homes. Antibusing amendments to the Constitution have been proposed by Congress.

White Flight   In 1975, James Coleman, professor of sociology at the University of Chicago and author of the well-known U.S. Office of Education study *Equal Educational Opportunity*, completed another study, *Trends in School Segregation, 1968–73*.[8] In this latter study, Coleman concluded that (1) within-system segregation decreased in the South and Southeast, with the major reduction occurring in small districts; in effect, the remaining segregation had a profile similar to the North, that is, high segregation in large cities, little in smaller school districts; and (2) between-district segregation increased, particularly in metropolitan areas, as whites moved to districts with fewer blacks.[9]

In considering the policy implications of his research, Coleman pointed out that metropolitan desegregation was a possible solution; however, this approach assumes emerging residential segregation as a given fact. As an alternative approach—and one that eliminates mandated busing—he suggested that each child have the right to attend any school in a metropolitan area, so long as the school chosen had no higher proportion of his or her race than the neighborhood school.

Coleman's research and recommendations have been criticized; Green and Pettigrew reviewed the work of Coleman and other researchers, and offered the following six results of their analysis:[10]

8.   James S. Coleman, Sara D. Kelly, and John Moore, *Trends in School Segregation, 1968–73*. (Washington, D.C.: Urban Institute, 1975).

9.   James S. Coleman, "Racial Segregation in the Schools: New Research with New Policy Implications," *Phi Delta Kappan* 57 (October 1975): 76–77.

10.   Robert L. Green and Thomas F. Pettigrew, "Urban Desegregation and White Flight: A Response to Coleman," *Phi Delta Kappan* 57 (February 1976): 401–402.

1. There has been a long-term trend of whites leaving the central cities and of blacks migrating into these areas.
2. All the studies agree that desegregation and white flight are not related in the smaller cities.
3. In the metropolitan school districts, desegregation has little or no effect on white flight.
4. Court-ordered desegregation has not had effects on white flight different from desegregation resulting from other factors, such as residential or neighborhood transition.
5. The loss of white *and black* students from large central-city districts is related to the proportion of black students attending those districts. In part, the "proportion black" variable is a surrogate for a range of other variables, from eroding tax bases to old housing stocks.
6. While extensive school desegregation may hasten the white flight phenomenon, particularly in the largest nonmetropolitan districts in the South, the effect, if it obtains at all, may only be observed temporarily during the first year of desegregation, and then only for those families which have already made plans to move.

Wegmann, after a review of research, also offered some tentative conclusions on the topics of white withdrawal and *resegregation*.[11] Resegregation most commonly refers to a situation wherein an integrated school population becomes an almost totally black school population. Sometimes resegregation occurs within a school when the neighborhood from which the school's population is drawn changes from an integrated to a predominantly black neighborhood. If the population of a city becomes predominantly black, the schools in the city will also become predominantly black. In many instances the growth of the black population proceeds from the inner city toward the outer fringe areas of the city. Resegregation can also occur after a governmental desegregation order. In such instances white students may withdraw or simply not reenter when the next term begins. Further, white families may also move to another area not affected by the desegregation order. Wegmann concluded:

1. Whites do not necessarily withdraw from desegregated schools. Some schools maintain a high level of integration for years, some change slowly, and some resegregate very rapidly. Others may experience some white withdrawal followed by stability or even by white reentrance.
2. Racially mixed schools located in areas bordering the inner city present some markedly different patterns of resegregation from school districts which have experienced districtwide desegregation. It is important not to extrapolate from the one situation to the other.
3. In situations where there has been no governmental action to bring about desegregation, white withdrawal seems to be linked more than anything else to the underlying demographic consequences of increased

11. Robert G. Wegmann, "White Flight and School Resegregation: Some Hypotheses," *Phi Delta Kappan* 58 (January 1977): 393. Used with permission.

minority population growth. This growth takes place primarily in the neighborhoods located on the edge of the inner city, as area after area "turns" from white to black. The schools "turn" more quickly than the area generally, and play a significant role in making this process relatively rapid and apparently irreversible. Stable school integration seems to be a necessary, if not sufficient, precondition for stable neighborhood integration.

4. Decisions on where to purchase a home or where to send one's children to school are made not only on the basis of the present situation, but on estimates of what is likely to happen in the future. The belief that presently integrated schools and neighborhoods will shortly resegregate is a major barrier to attracting whites to integrated settings.

5. Little formal research has been done on the motivations behind white withdrawal from desegregated schooling. Worries about the quality of education, student safety, and social-status differences may be among the chief causes. To the extent that this is true, it could be expected that—other things being equal—school integration would more likely be stable and successful when combined with programs of educational improvement, in settings where concerns about safety are adequately met, and when programs of which parents can be proud are featured.

6. School desegregation ordinarily creates situations which have the potential for both racial and class conflict. The degree of white withdrawal to be expected when there is governmental intervention to desegregate schools may vary, depending on the proportion of minority students who are being assigned to a given school and on the social-class gap between the minority and white students.

7. White withdrawal from desegregated schooling has widely varying costs in different settings. Moving to a nearby segregated suburb, moving outside a county school district, attending a parochial school, attending a private school, transferring to a segregated public school within the same system, or leaving the state are examples of options which may or may not be present in a given situation. Each of these options, if available, will have different costs for different families, just as families will have varying abilities to meet these costs. So long as school desegregation is feared (or experienced) as painful, threatening, or undesirable, it can be expected that the number of families fleeing the desegregated school will be proportionate to these costs and their ability to pay these costs.

8. Although there is a certain degree of racial mixing in many public schools, there may also be a notable lack of cross-racial friendship, understanding, and acceptance. Superintendents in desegregated districts tend to describe racial relationships as "calm" or characterized by few "incidents." Few claim that they have attained anything like genuine community, nor is there much indication that extensive efforts are being made toward this end.

The issue of busing is far from being resolved. It is hoped that further research and experience will contribute answers to this facet of integration.

De Facto Segregation

Although the Supreme Court in the *Charlotte* case again dealt only with de jure segregation, it did, however, allude to de facto segregation. The Court said:

> We do not reach in this case the question whether a showing that school segregation is a consequence of other types of state action, without any discriminatory action by the school authorities, is a constitutional violation requiring remedial action by a school-desegregation decree. This case does not present that question and we therefore do not decide it.
>
> Our objective in dealing with the issues presented by these cases is to see that school authorities exclude no pupil of a racial minority from any school, directly or indirectly, on account of race; it does not and cannot embrace all the problems of racial prejudice, even when those problems contribute to disproportionate racial concentrations in some schools.

Lower courts have dealt with and ruled upon what has appeared to be de facto segregation. It is difficult in practice to differentiate clearly between de jure and de facto segregation. In all probability, in the instance of segregated schools, both types of segregation are present in varying degrees. In June, 1967, a major ruling was made in which a lower court addressed itself to the subject of de facto segregation. Judge J. Skelly Wright of the U.S. Court of Appeals for the District of Columbia, sitting as a district judge, ruled in *Hobson* v. *Hansen* that the segregation of black pupils in the District of Columbia schools that results from population patterns is unconstitutional. The judge pointed out in his ruling that Washington was formerly a de jure segregated school district. In a 4–3 decision, a court of appeals upheld many of Judge Wright's orders. The case was complicated by the time of the appeal: the method of selection of school board members for the District of Columbia had changed from appointment to election. The appeals court made it clear that it did not wish to bind the new board to former plans; rather, it preferred to maintain the opportunity for the board to evolve new programs.

A more recent case heard by the United States Supreme Court that approached the issue of de facto segregation was *Keys* v. *School District No. 1, Denver, Colorado*. Announcing its decision in June, 1973, the Supreme Court sent the suit back to a district court, which was to decide if school authorities had intentionally segregated a substantial portion of the school system. If proof affirmed that the school district was operating a duel system (segregated), even though there had never been any de jure or legal provisions for school segregation, then the entire system would be required to desegregate. In the spring of 1974, Judge William E. Doyle of the Tenth U.S. Circuit Court of Appeals ordered integration of the city's 70,000 children. The Supreme Court, however, had not resolved the de jure/de facto segregation dichotomy. Justice Powell, in a separate opinion, stated: "We should abandon a distinction which long since has outlived its time, and formulate constitutional principles of national rather than merely regional applications." The Supreme Court did, however, change the nature of the concept of de facto segregation by turning over to federal and state trial courts the discretion to determine, as an issue of fact and not as a question of law, whether or not a local school board presides over a de facto or de jure segregated school district. In a sense, the Supreme Court broadened the concept of de jure segregation.

While questions might be raised as to whether segregated schools were created by law, or were being perpetuated by state or school board actions (de jure), or whether they were the result of residential population patterns (de facto), or what the role of the judiciary might be in ordering the end of de facto segregation, it is clear that equality of educational opportunity is a basic right in the United States and must be attained. This right permits maximum intellectual growth and social mobility. All citizens of our democracy must have the opportunity to achieve their utmost potential, and education provides this opportunity. The Supreme Court has said basically that equality of educational opportunity cannot be provided in segregated facilities, even though the facilities appear to be equal in such tangible assets as buildings, curricula, and staffs. Boards of education must proceed with deliberation and determination to desegregate schools—a most difficult task because in many instances residential neighborhoods are segregated. New patterns of school attendance centers must be evolved. The efforts by local boards of education to assure the constitutional right of equality of opportunity to all citizens of all races will need the strong support of local citizens to accomplish the goal. The goal will not be easily or quickly realized.

Reverse Discrimination

Discrimination can be defined as a determination that an individual or a group of individuals, for example, blacks, women, or handicapped persons, has been denied their constitutional rights. In common usage, it generally refers to various minorities or individual members of a minority group who have suffered a lack of rights typically accorded to the members of a majority group. The term *reverse discrimination* implies that a majority group or an individual of the majority group has not been accorded certain rights because of different or preferential treatment provided to a minority group or an individual of a minority group.

Most recently the term *reverse discrimination* has been used in respect to admissions to law and medical schools. It has also been used in connection with affirmative action, that is, positive efforts undertaken by society to integrate the races and to provide equal opportunities. The most recent case to come to the attention of the courts is that of Allan Bakke, a white male, who claimed that he was discriminated against when he was denied admission to the University of California Medical School at Davis. In the medical school's class of one hundred, sixteen spaces were set aside for minority applicants. The supreme court of California upheld Bakke's claim and ordered him admitted. Regents of the university appealed to the United States Supreme Court to overturn the state ruling.

In general, the arguments supporting the denial of Bakke's admission point out that (1) special admissions programs based on race are not quotas but goals; (2) color-sensitive admissions policies are necessary to bring minorities fully into the mainstream of American society; (3) benefits accrue to society at large from special admissions; (4) merit alone, determined by academic grades and test scores, has not been the single criterion of selection for schools; and (5) the denial did not violate the equal protection clause of the United States Constitution. The arguments supporting Bakke's admission emphasize that (1) the special admissions program was a racial quota; and (2) quotas are harmful to society and are unconstitutional.

In June, 1978, the United States Supreme Court made its ruling in the Bakke case. In effect, the Court ruled, 5–4, that the University of California at Davis admissions program, which reserved sixteen places in each class for minorities, was illegal. At the same time, the Court accepted the use of minority status as a factor in admissions along with grades, test scores, and personal skills. The decision has been referred to by many legal authorities as a landmark decision that will be used as a precedent for interpreting the role of affirmative action in the future.

Summary and Implications

This chapter dealt with the law and its relationship to American education: the legal responsibilities of each level of government were discussed. Particular emphasis was placed on interpretations of the Constitution by the United States Supreme Court as the justices had made their rulings in cases related to education. Cases presented in this chapter dealt primarily with the First and the Fourteenth Amendments. The First Amendment ensures freedom of speech, religion, the press, and the right to petition. The use of public monies to support nonpublic education and the practice of sectarian religion in public schools have been persistent issues in American education.

The Fourteenth Amendment provides for the protection of specified privileges of citizens. Segregated schools functioned in the United States for many years. The era of desegregation began in 1954 with the U.S. Supreme Court ruling on *Brown* v. *Board of Education of Topeka*. These societal issues have decided impacts on the operation of schools.

Local boards of education must develop and adopt policies in harmony with federal and state legislation and court decisions. These board policies provide direction to administrators and teachers as they carry out their responsibilities. Policy making on sensitive issues such as religion and desegregation is often not easy. Yet it must be done, and policies so adopted must be implemented.

The rights of students as citizens must be protected; teachers should be knowledgeable of these rights and protective of them. Teachers, influential as they are in shaping the attitudes of students, play a vital role in the development of American society.

Discussion Questions

1. Why has the federal government played an increasingly strong role in education in recent years?
2. What should be the role of the private school in America?
3. What has been the supporting rationale for using public monies to supply transportation and textbooks to students attending private schools?

4. How has the United States Supreme Court influenced the operation of public education?
5. How do the court decisions and the federal legislation discussed in this chapter affect the responsibilities and behavior of classroom teachers?

Supplemental Activities

1. Interview officials from private schools in your area to discuss the role of private education in America.
2. Visit a racially integrated school and record your observations.
3. Procure and study the policy statements of a local school district; look specifically for federal or state influence.

4. Interview a public school superintendent and inquire about the effects of federal legislation and court decisions on the operations of a local school district.
5. Interview the individual at your college or university who has the responsibility for implementing affirmative-action policy.

Bibliography

Arons, Stephen. "The Separation of Church and State: *Pierce* Reconsidered." *Harvard Educational Review* 46 (February 1976).

Berke, Joel S., et al. *New Era of State Education Politics.* Philadelphia: Ballinger, 1977.

Bolmeier, Edward C. *Landmark Supreme Court Decisions on Public School Issues.* Charlottesville, Va.: Mickie, 1973.

Campbell, Roald F., Bridges, Edwin M., Nystrand, Raphael O. *Introduction to Educational Administration.* Boston: Allyn and Bacon, 1977.

Coleman, James S., Kelley, Sara D., and Moore, John. *Trends in School Segregation, 1968–73.* Washington, D.C.: Urban Institute, 1975.

Erickson, Donald A. *Educational Organization and Administration.* Berkeley, Calif.: McCutchan, 1977.

Flygare, Thomas J. "Austin and Indianapolis: A New Approach to Desegregation?" *Phi Delta Kappan* 58 (May 1977).

McDonald, Laughlin. "Has the Supreme Court Abandoned the Constitution?" *Saturday Review,* 28 May 1977.

Persell, Caroline H. *Education and Inequality.* Riverside, N.J.: The Free Press, 1977.

Williams, Roger M. "What Louisville Has Taught Us About Busing," *Saturday Review,* 30 April 1977.

CHAPTER 11

Organization and Administration of Public Education

IN THE DISCUSSION OF THE LEGAL FOUNDATIONS OF EDUCATION, the educational system was examined primarily from a judicial and legislative viewpoint. In this chapter, it is considered from an organizational and administrative viewpoint. Education in the United States is an immense enterprise. Currently, approximately 50 million students are enrolled in public and private elementary and secondary schools, 2.5 million teachers are employed to provide instruction for these students, and close to $75 billion are spent to conduct the enterprise. Nearly three out of every ten persons in the nation are direct participants in the educational process either as students, teachers, or supervisors.[1] Projections of similar data for 1985 indicate approximately 46 million students, 2.4 million teachers, and $100 billion total expenditures (in terms of 1975–76 dollars).[2] The enterprise is carried out in approximately 16,000 local school districts as a function of fifty state governments. This chapter considers the separate and interrelated funtions of all levels of government in the operation of education nationwide.

Local School Districts

A school district is a governmental unit empowered by state law to administer the school system of a local community. It is controlled by a governing board composed of citizens residing in the geographical area that makes up the district.

School districts are similar in purpose but differ widely in their characteristics. Some districts provide only elementary education; others,

1. W. Vance Grant and C. George Lind, *Digest of Educational Statistics, 1976* (Washington, D.C.: U.S. Government Printing Office, 1977), pp. 1–2.
2. National Center for Education Statistics, "Statistics of Trends in Education" (Washington, D.C.: U.S. Government Printing Office, January 1977).

only high school education; still others provide both elementary and secondary education. Approximately 27 percent of the districts have less than 300 pupils, and their total enrollment makes up less than 2 percent of the total national enrollment. Only 1 percent of the districts have enrollments in excess of 25,000 students, yet these enroll about 28 percent of the total. Thousands of school districts have only one attendance center, while a few urban districts may have as many as five hundred.

Local districts provide one of the few opportunities for citizens to participate directly in public decision making. Board members are local people, frequently citizens having day-to-day contact and known to one another on a "first-name" basis. The administration of the schools concerns people deeply and deals directly with their most cherished possession, their children; it also deals directly with their money in the form of taxation. In many cases the local district provides the most intimate relationship a citizen has with a governmental agency. Americans for the most part value this relationship. Some look upon the local district and its schools as the opportunity to determine their own destiny; others see the local district and local control as one of the few remaining opportunities to control public expenditures. The local district does have advantages: it permits citizens to have schools better than the prescribed state minimums, and it provides the opportunity for citizens to develop a program responsive to local needs.

Local control is stressed as an important and unique feature of American education; however, the value of local control of education has been challenged recently. It has been argued that the mobility of our population and the interdependence of our society have undermined the traditional concept that local people should have a strong role in determining education. It has also been argued that our national survival requires policies and programs that are determined by centralized authority.

It should be pointed out that local control, in a sense, is challenged each time that a decision by a local board or by a local school district is taken to the courts. As indicated in the previous chapter, many of the court decisions that dealt with the relationships of religion to the public schools or with desegregation were, in effect, a response to local control. Local control, combined with the traditional system of financing education, has resulted in inequality of educational opportunity—rather than equality. The alternative to local control is centralization. Ironically, education in large cities and urban areas is already centralized, and many of these areas are attempting to solve some of their problems by decentralization. Frequently centralization of government results in reduced responsiveness to citizen needs and demands. Ex-officio boards and councils for local community or neighborhood schools, which serve in an advisory capacity to official large city or county boards, represent efforts to maintain a form of local control within large centralized systems.

The control of education today is still predominantly local, carried out under the powers delegated by the states. Direct federal involvement (through court decisions) and indirect federal involvement (through federal aid) have been increasing. The problem of local-state-federal relationships in the control of education is a complicated one that must be faced and somehow resolved. New and intricate relationships are emerging.

Efforts have been made in the past to reorganize school districts to obtain both more effective and more efficient school districts. The major emphasis has been to reduce, through consolidation, the number of small rural districts. The number of school districts in the United States has decreased from approximately 100,000 in 1945 to approximately 16,000 today. California, Illinois, Nebraska, and Texas have in excess of 1,000 districts. Progress has been made in district consolidation and undoubtedly will continue to be made. It is a slow but inevitable process.

State legislatures have the power to effect school district reorganization, but they have been reluctant to do so. Frequently, school district reorganization legislation is permissive. Districts may consolidate with the blessing of the legislature, but with very little inducement to do so. Financial incentives have been incorporated into some reorganization legislation, but still reorganization proceeds slowly. In a few instances, mandatory school district reorganization laws have been passed. These laws usually set time limits for reorganization, provide for local community committees to study and present proposals for state review, and offer financial incentives for reorganizations. Some laws have stated that, in the event of a public impasse or the presentation of weak proposals, the state has the power to intercede and to effect reorganization.

It is apparent that local citizens tend to resist school district reorganization. Reasons for their resistance include sentimental feelings about their school, a desire to maintain local control, failure to realize the inferiority of their schools, the importance of the school as a significant social and recreational facility in the area, and fear of potential tax increases. As has been pointed out, progress has been made, but greater progress in school district reorganization is needed to meet current educational needs.

A recent study performed under a contract from the National Institute of Education raises questions about the value of consolidation of small rural schools.[3] Basically, the researchers assert, after reviewing the literature dealing with rural consolidation, that:

3. Jonathan P. Sher and Rachel B. Tompkins, *Economy, Efficiency and Equality: The Myths of Rural School and District Consolidation* (Washington, D.C.: National Institute of Education, U.S. Department of Health, Education, and Welfare, 1976).

1. The purported economies to be gained are frequently offset by "diseconomies," such as increased transportation costs and the cost of administering and distributing products procured through bulk purchasing;
2. Equalization of taxable wealth among districts has not occurred despite massive reorganization over four decades;
3. Quality of education has not improved. (The researchers base this assertion primarily on the relationships of school size to pupil achievement.)

They make three recommendations:

1. Small schools deserve more research;
2. Alternatives to consolidation and reorganization, such as regionalization, should be seriously considered;
3. Research done to demonstrate the value of proposed reforms should be scrutinized carefully.

More research does need to be done to verify the proclaimed benefits of consolidation and reorganization. The number and kinds of variables necessary to be controlled—particularly if pupil achievement is to be the measure of effectiveness of school reorganization—make it extremely difficult to conduct such research. Further, school reorganization, in and of itself, is probably one of the least powerful variables affecting pupil achievement—falling far behind such variables as native intellect, home environment, socioeconomic status, and motivation. It is interesting to note that even after massive reorganization, 27 percent of the school districts in the United States today still have less than three hundred pupils.

Urban districts also present reorganization problems. Rapid growth in urban areas, combined with unplanned and indiscriminate land use, has created immense problems. Wealthy districts, with few pupils are contiguous to poor districts with many pupils. The desires and expectations of the residents for their schools vary tremendously from district to district. Communication between the citizens and school authorities can become distant and distorted.

Efforts have been made recently to decentralize urban school systems to enable them to become more responsive to the desires of the residents. The teachers' strike in New York City in the fall of 1968 focused upon this issue and illustrated the complexities that may result from urban decentralization. There is no doubt that improvement can be made, but it presents an overwhelming and complicated task.

The legal authority to operate local school systems is given to local boards of education through state statutes. The statutes prescribe quite specifically the method for selection of school board members and the duties and responsibilities of the members after they are in office. The statutes also provide for such matters as the length of terms of board members, procedures to be used to select the officers of the board, duties of the officers of the board, and procedures for filling vacancies should they occur. It should be pointed out that school board members, while local citizens, are also agents of the state.

Ninety-five percent of the school boards in the United States are elected by popular vote, with the majority of these elected in special elections on a nonpartisan basis. Approximately 5 percent are appointed. The percentage of appointed school boards is higher in school districts enrolling over 25,000 pupils; yet even in these large districts, approximately three-fourths of the board members are elected. New York City and Chicago both have appointed school boards.

Elected board members generally must petition for a place on the ballot. If a candidate meets the legal requirements to serve as a school board member and follows proper petitioning procedures, he cannot be denied a place on the ballot. In some areas an extralegal caucus committee approves a slate of candidates. This committee is usually made up of representatives of community organizations. Members approved by a caucus committee must follow the same procedure as any other candidate in order to be placed on the ballot. The caucus process represents an attempt to nominate well-qualified candidates for board membership, but the caucus process recently has been charged with recommending persons for board membership who will perpetuate the inequities of the past. Frequently minority groups are not represented on the caucus committees. It should be noted that the caucus procedure is an extralegal procedure. A candidate on a partisan ticket is selected by the local party committee. School board members are most commonly elected from the district at large rather than from wards or precincts.

Appointments to boards of education are made by city councils, mayors, state legislatures, county boards, and other agencies. The most common procedure is appointment by a city council or mayor. It is not unusual for an appointing official to utilize an extralegal committee of citizens, who submit a list of names of individuals to be considered for the vacancies. This procedure is an attempt to separate partisan politics and education and, at the same time, to obtain highly qualified persons as board members.

Candidates for boards of education, elective or appointive, are frequently recruited from citizens who have expressed an interest in the schools by serving on citizen advisory committees to boards of education. Local PTAs also serve as a source of potential candidates.

The members of boards of education generally come from the proprietary and professional occupations. The number of farmers serving is steadily decreasing. Board members tend to have at least a high school education; many have college educations. The income level of board members is higher than the average, and generally they are representative of middle-class society.

A recent study conducted by the National School Board Association investigating board membership in the nation's fifty-one largest school districts revealed:

1. Compared to ten years ago, five times as many professional educators serve on school boards—but only half as many attorneys.
2. Minority representation has increased 3 percent in the past three years.
3. Sixty-nine percent of the board members are male, with an average age of forty-nine.

(These trends may or may not prevail in smaller school districts.)

It should be pointed out that teachers cannot be board members in the district in which they are employed; however, they can be board members in districts where they reside while teaching in a different district. The trend toward increased board membership by teachers is most likely a result of the proactive stance of professional associations to secure seats on school boards.

The powers and duties of school boards vary from state to state, but the school codes of the respective states spell them out in detail. The general powers and duties of local boards were discussed in Chapter 10. It should be pointed out that some of the duties are mandatory; others are discretionary. Some duties cannot be delegated; for example, if boards are given the power to employ teachers, they must do this; the power cannot be delegated even to a school superintendent. However, boards can delegate much of the hiring process to administrators and then act officially upon administrative recommendations for employment of personnel. An illustration of a discretionary power left to

Local control by local school boards has had a long historical tradition in America. (*Photograph by Talbot Lovering.*)

the local board would be the decision of whether or not to participate in a nonrequired school program—for example, a program of competitive athletics. Another illustration of discretionary power would be the decision to employ only teachers who exceed minimum state certification standards.

Powers and duties granted to boards of education are granted to the boards as a whole, not to individual members. An individual member of a board has no more authority in school matters than any other citizen of the community, except in instances where the school board may legally delegate a task, through official action of the board, to a specific member. A school board, as a corporate body, can act officially only in legally held and duly authorized board meetings, and these meetings usually must be open to the public. Executive or private sessions may be held, but ordinarily only for specified purposes such as the evaluation of staff members or the selection of a school site. It is usually required that any official action on matters discussed in private session must be taken in an open meeting.

One of the primary duties of the local board is to select its executive officer, the local superintendent of schools. In Illinois, the school code is specific in granting this power and in delineating the superintendent's duties and the working relationship between the board and the superintendent. The Illinois law reads that a superintendent is to be employed

> . . . who shall have charge of the administration of the schools under the direction of the board of education. In addition to the administrative duties, the superintendent shall make recommendations to the board concerning the budget, building plans, and locations of sites, the selection of teachers and other employees, the selection of textbooks, instructional material, and courses of study. The superintendent shall keep or cause to be kept the records and accounts as directed and required by the board, aid in making reports required of the board, and perform such other duties as the board may delegate to him.

Many states are not as specific as Illinois. While the Illinois statute is quite specific for a statute, basically it provides only guidelines for the development of local policies necessary to establish further board-superintendent working relationships. The cooperative development of specific policies helps in establishing the roles of both the board of education and the superintendent and, therefore, avoids conflict in this crucial relationship. Generally, boards are policy-making groups, and superintendents are executive officers. In many instances the distinction is very difficult to make.

The quality of the educational program of a school district is influenced quite strongly by the leadership that is provided by a board of education and its superintendent. Curriculum programs over and above state required minimums are discretionary. Local authorities, board members, and their superintendent frequently must convince communities of the need for specified school programs.

The superintendent of schools works with his staff to carry on the program of education. The size of the staff, of course, varies with the size of the school district. Some form of organization is necessary, and many school systems use a basic line-and-staff organization. Figure 11–1 illustrates a typical line-and-staff school organizational pattern. In this pattern, line officers are those who hold administrative power as it flows from the local board of education down to pupils. Superintendents, assistant superintendents, and principals are line officers vested with authority over those shown below them on the chart. Each individual is directly responsible to the official above him and must work

Figure 11–1.   Typical line-and-staff organization.

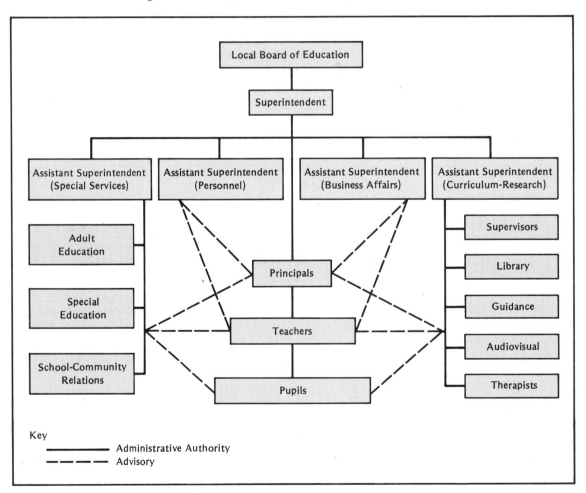

through him when dealing with a higher official. This arrangement is frequently referred to as the *chain of command.*

Administrative staff personnel are shown in Figure 11–1 as branching out from the direct flow of authority. Staff personnel include librarians, instructional supervisors, guidance officers, transportation officers, and many others, depending upon the size of the school district. They are responsible to their respective superior but generally serve in an advisory capacity. Staff personnel generally have no authority and issue no orders. They assist and advise others with their special competencies. Teachers are generally referred to as staff persons even though they are in the direct flow of authority. Their authority in this arrangement prevails only over pupils.

This strict type of organizational structure has received some criticism in recent years. Critics have said that it tends to stifle the contribution the teachers can make and that it is antagonistic to the concept of professional equality. Psychologists and authorities in "group dynamics" have indicated that a more flexible organization can be more effective in accomplishing desired goals. They suggest that effectiveness is related to the personal satisfactions gained in employment. Teacher groups, through "teacher power" utilized at the bargaining table, are asking for and in many instances are granted greater say in the policies and operating procedures of school systems. More recent organizational structures provide for wider participation of teachers and staff in administrative decision making. Figure 11–2 provides an illustration of a school organizational structure permitting wider participation in decision making.

In this structure, an administrative council exists that includes not only the various assistant superintendents but also a local educational policies commission. This commission may include members from the local teachers' group, members from the nonteaching staff, pupils, and, in some instances, members from the principals' group. The commission permits direct advisory input from staff at all levels. The "line" relationships are similar to those in Figure 11–1. For simplicity in the model, lower echelon central administrative personnel in Figure 11–2 have been referred to as administrative staff; it should be noted, however, that their relationship to principals is an advisory one. Advocates of this structure cite the following advantages: wider participation results in more ideas; pooled thinking is likely to produce higher quality decisions; all possible leadership potential is tapped; policies evolved are more likely to be implemented because of commitment; participants gain an understanding of the complete operation; and human relationships are likely to be improved. Some school systems have adopted a structure similar to Figure 11–2 to provide for this wider participation.

Any organizational structure must operate within the law. A structure that permits wide participation in the decision-making process must necessarily recognize that certain decisions are by law the responsibility

Figure 11–2.   Modified line-and-staff chart showing administrative council.

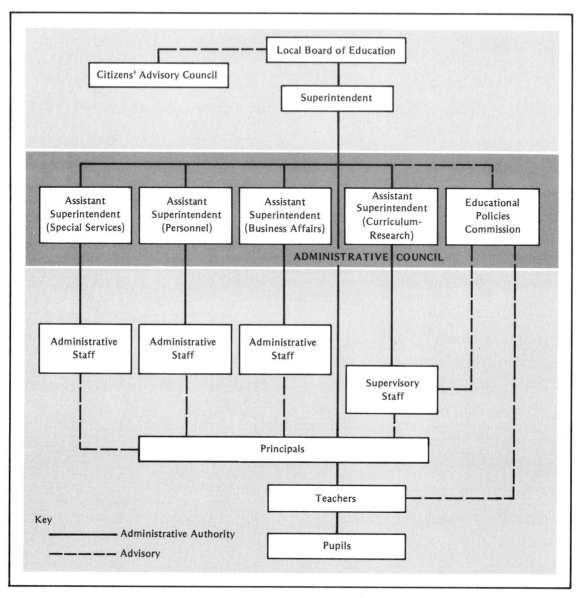

of the board of education and in some cases that of the superintendent. A board or a superintendent cannot shift legal authority or responsibility to another group. They can, however, solicit advisement in these areas; wide participation provides for this advisement.

The success of a wide-participation organizational structure depends to a large extent on the commitment of the school board and super- intendent to this plan of action. They must create opportunities for participation and be willing to accept the results, if at all possible under the law. Teachers must be willing to participate. Some teachers feel that their duties should be classroom responsibilities only and that administrative matters should be resolved by administrators. Other teachers feel quite strongly that their input should be formally negotiated and made official: they seek a participatory role that is stronger than advisory. The wide-participation plan requires committed participants.

Up to this point, this chapter has concentrated on the formal organization and structure of local school districts. There are many forces, both legal and political, that impact on local schools. It seems appropriate to digress to consider how viable local control really is. The next few pages provide a brief historical review of local control and a brief look at contemporary political forces, such as teacher power, emergent parent power, and the educational lobbies. The discussion of local schools concludes with a description of attendance centers.

Local Control: A Myth?

For many years local control was perceived as the bulwark and the unique feature of the successful American education enterprise. To what extent does local control really exist? In the last decade, it has been said that local control is a myth. Those said to be in actual control include professional administrators, teachers' organizations, and the federal courts.

A recent report notes four phases of control in the history of American education:[4]

Phase 1: Lay Control (1835–c.1900)
Phase 2: Control by Local Professionals (1900–c.1968)
Phase 3: The Nationalization of Education (1954–1975)
Phase 4: Education and the Social Goal (1975–present)

Phase 1 functioned with a mandate to educators to pursue limited educational goals that would enable individuals to function in their own small communities. Lay boards of education representative of the community in effect administered the schools. During this phase, the nation had over 100,000 school districts; school board members represented relatively homogeneous and unambiguous constituencies. There was ample opportunity for the citizens to interact with their board members and to hold the board accountable for its actions.

Phase 2 was ushered in during a rapid growth in school population, particularly in urban areas. Board members found they could no longer devote sufficient time to administrative tasks; consequently, the position of superintendent of schools emerged. During this period, the responsibilities for education were shifted from lay control to local pro-

4. L. Harmon Zeigler, Harvey J. Tucker, and L. A. Wilson, "How School Control Was Wrested from the People," *Phi Delta Kappan* 58 (March 1977): 534–539.

fessionals, mainly administrators. This change was partially inspired by the scientific management movement then taking place and by the desire of local citizens, including board members, to reduce the amount of political influence on education. Major structural modifications included: consolidation of school districts, centralization of school administration, election of fewer board members at large (rather than on a ward basis), election of board members by nonpartisan ballots, and the separation of board elections from other municipal and state elections. The mandate in Phase 2 was expanded over Phase 1 to include the development of skills and values necessary to construct a larger homogeneous society. Phase 2 was characterized as a period of stability, during which schools were perceived as agents of the transmission of knowledge, culture, and social norms.

Near the end of Phase 2, the seeds for Phase 3 were planted. The decision in *Brown* v. *Board of Education* (1954) was an initial step toward the school becoming viewed as an agent of social and economic change —the mandate of Phase 3. Subsequent court decisions, federal and state legislation, and infusions of federal and state aid (with accompanying control for the use of such funds) have all contributed to greater control by the federal government and other nonlocal units of government. The local administrative control of Phase 2 was gradually eroded; also contributing to the erosion was the influence gained by teacher unions through collective bargaining.

The Ziegler study concludes that Phase 3 governance cannot achieve the Phase 3 mandate.[5] He bases this conclusion partially on the research of James S. Coleman, which indicated that school quality and individual achievement are essentially unrelated; the research of Christopher Jencks who stated that school reform "cannot bring about significant social changes outside the schools"; and that of Raymond Bouden who concluded that "educational growth as such has the effect of increasing rather than decreasing social and economic inequality, even in the case of an educational system that becomes more equalitarian."[6] In effect, the goals of Phase 3 will not be attained in Phase 4.

It is clear that local school boards do not have the power they once had. Recent attempts to gain local control over education include those of teachers, parents, and consolidated professional organizations.

Teacher Power   Teachers have power—power to influence the direction of American education. Collective bargaining agreements of local teacher associations—NEA or AFT affiliates—are being expanded to include not only salaries but also course content, curriculum change procedures, teacher evaluation, and teaching procedures. Teacher organizations have backed many successful candidates for political offices and have recently en-

5.   Ibid., p. 539.
6.   Ibid.

dorsed presidential candidates. The membership of teachers on boards of education has increased fivefold in the last decade. Teachers serve on certification boards in many states and on evaluation teams for the accreditation of teacher-education programs in colleges and universities. They were influential in framing and passing federal legislation for teacher centers, which will provide inservice education for teachers and will be controlled by a board made up of a majority of teachers. A federal collective bargaining bill has been proposed for the past few years by the NEA.

Teachers have learned to make their collective influence felt through political action. The NEA and the AFT are now powerful political organizations: in the past few years they have gained increasing control of education at the local, state, and federal levels.

Parent Power   Over the last decade, parents have indicated their desire to have a much stronger voice in education for a number of reasons, including pronounced dissatisfaction with school programs and with high taxes. The immediate target is the local district board of education. Parents exert their power locally through organized campaigns to oust board members they are displeased with and by supporting other candidates they feel will foster their viewpoints.

A recent parents' concern is the collective bargaining movement, which is perceived by parents as reaching beyond collective bargaining and working conditions. A study conducted by the Institute for Responsive Education at Boston University recommended five alternatives to the closed system of collective bargaining:[7]

> A responsive board which holds open hearings before and during the negotiation process; multilevel bargaining, where the central board and teachers negotiate a master contract and district boards negotiate on more specific issues; 'individual third force' in which representatives of the public actually participate in negotiations; an ombudsman, who would represent the public in all aspects of policymaking, including negotiations; and limited scope bargaining, which would confine negotiations to economic questions.

At a recent conference of parents and citizens, concern was expressed that "parents and citizens are being locked out of collective bargaining sessions which are determining a widening range of education policies."[8] The conferees felt that parents should have a say in student discipline, curriculum, and general education policy. A report distributed at the conference by the Institute for Responsive Education (IRE) stated that "the introduction of a third force—parents/citizens—in education

---

7.   *Education USA* 17 (November 1974).
8.   *Education USA* 19 (December 1976), p. 108. A report on the first National Conference on Parent Involvement.

decision making can improve the shape, character and quality of public schooling."[9]

In the past, it was not unusual for parents to be concerned about education, particularly at the local level, and to exert pressure through political activity at the local level. Their current activities indicate that parents may begin to exert greater political pressure at the state and national levels.

Educational Organization Lobbies

It is clear that much lobbying takes place to affect the policies of education at both the state and federal levels. The lobbying power of the various national educational organizations varies considerably. Among the national educational lobbying groups are:

- National Education Association (NEA)
- American Federation of Teachers (AFT)
- American Association of School Administrators (AASA)
- Council of Chief State School Officers (CCSSO)
- National Congress of Parents and Teachers (NCPTA)
- National School Boards Association (NSBA)
- National Association of State Boards of Education (NASBE)
- American Association of Colleges of Teacher Education (AACTE)

All of these organizations, with the exception of CCSSO, have state affiliates and most of them have local affiliates, which also engage in lobbying efforts at the state and local levels.

Many times these organizations have opposing viewpoints. For example, the teacher organizations (NEA, AFT) have both supported federal bargaining legislation, whereas the AASA and the NASBE have both opposed such legislation. Nevertheless, many times they do in fact have some common interests, such as adequate financial support for education. The "big six" (AASA, NEA, CCSSO, NCPTA, NSBA, NASBE), an alliance of organizations that have been communicating informally since 1957, has turned away from trying to agree on specific legislative goals and now concentrates, instead, on reaching a common understanding of major issues. The "big eight," a forum of educational leaders sponsored by the United States Office of Education (USOE) and made up of the big six plus the AFT and AACTE, has announced a policy statement on the role of public schools in early childhood development. The forum is made up of the presidents and past presidents of each organization. There is little doubt that these organizations with their active affiliates, along with the CCSSO organization, are powerful in state and federal legislatures, and, along with the courts, have eroded local control. Their legislative impact, for example, is felt in local school attendance centers. Politics is an inseparable part of education.

9. Ibid.

Attendance Centers— Neighborhood Schools

The school organization for pupils may be considered in two interrelated ways: *grade-level grouping* and *attendance-center grouping*. Common grade-level groupings include K8–4, K6–3–3, and K6–6. A more recent type of grade grouping is K4–4–4. The rationale for grade-level grouping is presumably based primarily on child growth and on developmental and curricular considerations; this rationale is explained further in Part VI. Attendance-center grouping frequently is identical to grade-level grouping—although it need not be.

An attendance center is a school, within a district, to which pupils from a designated geographical area are assigned. Figure 11–3 illustrates

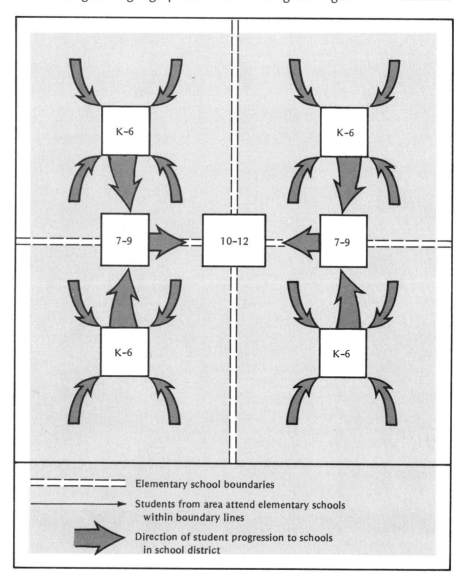

Figure 11–3. School attendance centers within a school district.

the attendance-center concept. In this illustration there are seven attendance centers: four K–6 centers, two 7–9 centers, and one 10–12 center. The attendance area for each of the K–6 centers is approximately one-fourth of the area of the school district. Their boundaries are represented by the respective exterior boundaries of the school district and the double dashed lines within the school district. Each 7–9 attendance center includes the area encompassed by two K–6 centers. The boundaries of the 10–12 center are coterminous with the district boundaries. It should be pointed out that, in reality, school districts and attendance centers are not nearly so geometrically perfect. Most often their boundaries are irregular and jagged. Occasionally they even have long peninsulalike projections extending deeply into other districts. The number of attendance centers in a district may vary from one in a rural area to more than five hundred in a heavily populated area.

School boards have the right to prescribe the boundaries for an at-

The principal is an integral part of both the traditional and the modified line-and-staff organization. (*Photograph by Cary Wolinsky, Stock, Boston*)

tendance center. Establishing these boundaries is a difficult task. Boards must be cautious in the exercise of this right, making certain that attendance areas are not determined on the basis of race, that the distances traveled by students either walking or being transported are not unreasonable, and that the safety of youngsters is not jeopardized.

The segregation issue has further complicated attendance-area decision making. Segregation exists by race, creed, economic status, nationality, and by many other characteristics. Neighborhood schools, frequently the most logical as attendance centers, are under attack as perpetuating de facto segregation. There is no doubt that in many instances, especially in urban areas, the neighborhood school is a segregated school. Attempts have been made to bus students from one neighborhood to another to accomplish balanced racial integration. In other instances voluntary transfer plans have been tried whereby students may elect to attend schools of their choice. Neither plan has met with a great measure of success. Recent proposals include the concept of educational parks built in carefully selected locations that would foster racial integration and that would permit enrollment to be drawn both from the city and its suburbs. The middle school, frequently composed of grades five through eight, while conceived of basically on a curricular rationale, also can serve in some instances as a means to accomplish racial balance by bringing together in an integrated setting children who were in segregated neighborhood elementary schools. These many attempts, however, seem to be chiefly stopgap and short-term solutions.

Intermediate Units

The *intermediate unit* of school organization is a unit functioning between the state department of education and the local school districts. Historically the intermediate unit served a liaison function between the state department of education and the local school districts. In rural areas, with a preponderance of small schools, it also served a direct educational function, such as providing guidance or special education services.

The basic purpose of the intermediate unit today is to provide two or more local districts with educational services that they cannot efficiently or economically provide individually; recently great strides have been made particularly in regard to cooperative provisions for special education and vocational-technical education. Area vocational-technical schools have been aided by relatively high infusions of federal monies. Other services that intermediate units can provide include audiovisual libraries, centralized purchasing, inservice training for teachers and other personnel, health services, instructional materials, laboratories, legal services, and special consultant services.

According to a recent Educational Research Services study, there has been a trend toward legislature-mandated regional centers in the last few years.[10] Eight states now require regional services, and four others have permissive legislation. Many earlier intermediate units, with the exception of county units, were voluntary consortiums. In Iowa, the fifteen area-education agencies have the same boundaries as community college and vocational districts. The Pennsylvania legislature recently dissolved county units, which served as intermediate units, and created twenty-nine intermediate units. Study is under way in Illinois to consider the feasibility of an intermediate-unit structure that can be more effective than the county units. Intermediate units or regional centers are developing closer ties with higher education institutions and with other regional government subdivisions and social agencies, such as mental health agencies. The Educational Research Services study also raises some interesting questions about regional centers. Do they tend to bolster school districts that should be reorganized? How should they be financed? What types of governing boards should they have? Should they have the power to levy local taxes?

State Functions   The state is the governmental unit in the United States charged with the responsibility for education. State legislatures, within the limits expressed by the federal Constitution and by respective state constitutions, are the major policy makers for education. State legislatures grant powers to state boards of education, state departments of education, chief state school officers, and local boards of education. These groups have only the powers granted to them by the legislature, implied powers from the specific grant of power, and the necessary powers to carry out the statutory purposes. A typical state organization for education is presented in Figure 11–4.

State Boards of Education   State boards of education have both regulatory and advisory functions. Authorities generally agree that the regulatory function of state school boards is of primary importance for consistent operation of local schools. Some of the regulatory functions include: establishing standards for issuance and revocation of teaching certificates, establishing standards for approving and accrediting schools, and developing and enforcing a uniform system for gathering and reporting educational data. Basically the advisory function includes considering the educational needs of the state, both long- and short-range, and making recommendations to the governor and the legislature on ways and means of meeting the needs. The advisory function that state school boards serve in studying school problems and in suggesting and analyzing proposals can be invaluable to the legislature, especially in light of the pressures applied to the legislative decision-making process. A state board

10. Robert Stephens, *Regional Educational Service Agencies* (Arlington, Va.: Educational Research Services, 1975).

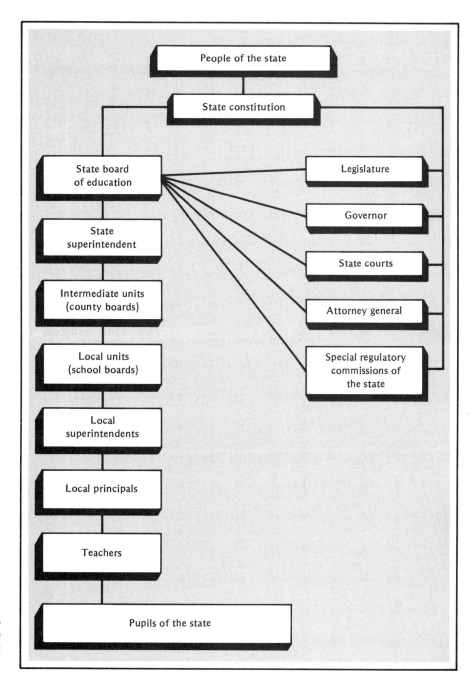

Figure 11–4.
Typical structure of a state school system.

People of the state

State constitution

State board of education

Legislature

Governor

State courts

Attorney general

Special regulatory commissions of the state

State superintendent

Intermediate units (county boards)

Local units (school boards)

Local superintendents

Local principals

Teachers

Pupils of the state

can provide a continuity of development for a program of education that is difficult to attain through the ordinary legislative procedures. A state board also can coordinate, supplement, and, in many cases, replace the various study commissions appointed by a legislature for educational advisement. These commissions frequently include groups studying textbooks, finance, certification, school district reorganization, school building standards, and teacher education.

Members of state boards of education attain their positions in a variety of ways, most commonly by appointment by the governor; other methods include election by the people, by the legislature, or by local school board members in regional convention. Table 11–1 illustrates the meth-

Table 11–1.   Methods of selection of state board members.

State	1947			1977		
	Elected by People or Representatives of People	Appointed by Governor	Other	Elected by People or Representatives of People	Appointed by Governor	Other
Alabama		X			X	
Alaska		X			X	
Arizona			X		X	
Arkansas		X			X	
California		X			X	
Colorado			X	X		
Connecticut		X			X	
Delaware		X			X	
Florida			X			X
Georgia		X			X	
Hawaii		X		X		
Idaho		X			X	
Illinois	(No State Board)				X	
Indiana		X			X	
Iowa	(No State Board)			X		
Kansas		X		X		
Kentucky		X			X	
Louisiana	X			X		
Maine	(No State Board)				X	
Maryland		X			X	
Massachusetts		X			X	
Michigan	X			X		
Minnesota		X			X	
Mississippi			X			X
Missouri		X			X	
Montana		X			X	
Nebraska	(No State Board)			X		

Table 11–1.   *(continued)*

State	1947			1977		
	Elected by People or Representatives of People	Appointed by Governor	Other	Elected by People or Representatives of People	Appointed by Governor	Other
Nevada	X			X		
New Hampshire		X			X	
New Jersey		X			X	
New Mexico		X		X		
New York			X	X		
North Carolina		X			X	
North Dakota	(No State Board)				X	
Ohio	(No State Board)			X		
Oklahoma		X			X	
Oregon		X			X	
Pennsylvania		X			X	
Rhode Island	(No State Board)				X	
South Carolina		X		X		
South Dakota	(No State Board)				X	
Tennessee		X			X	
Texas		X		X		
Utah			X	X		
Vermont		X			X	
Virginia		X			X	
Washington			X	X		
West Virginia		X			X	
Wisconsin	(No State Board)			(No State Board)		
Wyoming			X		X	
TOTALS	3	30	8	15	32	2

Adapted from David E. Elder and Milburn P. Akers, "A State Board of Education," *Illinois Education* 27 (January 1965): 214; R. F. Will, *State Education Structure and Organizations,* U.S. Office of Education, OE–23038, Misc., No. 46 (Washington, D.C.: U.S. Government Printing Office, 1964); and data made available by the Council of Chief State School Officers.

ods of selecting state school board members in each state.

In 1947, there were nine states without state boards of education; by 1977, there was only one. The 1970 Constitution of the State of Illinois created a state board of education; the method of selection of members is appointment by the governor. Iowa, New York, and Washington are unique in their elective procedures. In Iowa, conventions of delegates from areas within the state send nominations to the governor for his appointment; in New York, the Board of Regents is elected by the legislature; and in Washington, the state board is elected by members of boards of directors of local school districts. The terms of members are usually staggered to avoid a complete change in membership at any one time. Members usually serve without pay, but are reimbursed for their expenses. The policy of nonpayment, along with that of staggered terms, is considered a safeguard against political patronage.

Chief State   Every state has a chief state school officer. Currently twenty of these
School Officers   officers are elected by the people, twenty-six are appointed by state boards of education, and four are appointed by the governor. Table 11–2

Table 11–2.   Methods of selection of chief state school officers.

	1947			1977		
State	**Appt. by State Board**	**Appt. by Governor**	**Elected by People**	**Appt. by State Board**	**Appt. by Governor**	**Elected by People**
Alabama			X			X
Alaska	X			X		
Arizona			X			X
Arkansas	X			X		
California			X			X
Colorado			X	X		
Connecticut	X			X		
Delaware	X			X		
Florida			X			X
Georgia			X			X
Hawaii		X		X		
Idaho			X			X
Illinois			X	X		
Indiana			X			X
Iowa			X	X		
Kansas			X	X		
Kentucky			X			X
Louisiana			X			X
Maine		X		X		
Maryland	X			X		
Massachusetts	X			X		

Table 11–2.   (*continued*)

State	1947			1977		
	Appt. by State Board	Appt. by Governor	Elected by People	Appt. by State Board	Appt. by Governor	Elected by People
Michigan			X	X		
Minnesota	X			X		
Mississippi			X			X
Missouri	X			X		
Montana			X			X
Nebraska			X	X		
Nevada			X	X		
New Hampshire	X			X		
New Jersey		X			X	
New Mexico			X	X		
New York	X			X		
North Carolina			X			X
North Dakota			X			X
Ohio		X		X		
Oklahoma			X			X
Oregon			X			X
Pennsylvania		X			X	
Rhode Island		X		X		
South Carolina			X			X
South Dakota			X			X
Tennessee		X			X	
Texas			X	X		
Utah			X	X		
Vermont	X			X		
Virginia		X			X	
Washington			X			X
West Virginia			X	X		
Wisconsin			X			X
Wyoming			X			X
TOTALS	11	8	31	26	4	20

Adapted from David E. Elder and Milburn P. Akers, "A State Board of Education," *Illinois Education* 27 (January 1965): 216; R. F. Will, *State Education Structure and Organization*, U.S. Office of Education, OE–23038, Misc. No. 46 (Washington, D.C.: U.S. Government Printing Office, 1964); and data made available by the Council of Chief State School Officers.

illustrates the trend in the method of selecting chief state school officers. Arguments advanced in favor of electing the chief state school officer are based primarily on the concepts that, as an elected official, the individual will be close to the people, responsible to them, and free from obligations to other state officials. As an elected person, he or she would also be independent of the state board of education. Opponents to the election method argue primarily that this method keeps the department of education in the realm of partisan politics, that an elected official is obligated to other members of the same political party, and that many excellent candidates prefer not to engage in political contests. Furthermore, they feel that the chief state school officer, for efficient operation, should not be chosen independently of the state board of education.

Those who advocate that the chief state school officer should be appointed by a state board of education claim that policy making should be separated from policy execution, that educational leadership should not rest upon the competence of one elected official, and that the recruitment and retention of qualified career personnel would be enhanced.

Opponents of appointment by a state board of education claim mainly that the chief school officer selected under these circumstances is not responsible to the people. The major objection of gubernatorial appointment is the inherent danger of involvement in partisan politics. It should be noted that an elected state school officer is legally an "official" of the state, while an officer appointed by a state board of education is generally an "employee" and not a legal official. In instances where the chief school officer is elected, and hence is a legal official and theoretically responsible to the people of the state, the working relationship of this official with the state board is not as likely to be as clearly defined as it is in instances where the chief school officer is appointed by the state board of education, and hence is an employee of the board.

The chief state school officer can be a very influential person in education. This individual expresses his ideas of educational needs to the legislature, the governor, and the state board of education. He or she frequently reports to and suggests legislation to the legislature. Most often the chief state school officer is the executive head of the state department of education and, as such, through a staff, supervises and regulates the schools of the state. Specific duties of the office may include the following:[11]

- To serve as secretary and executive officer of the state board of education;

11. Edgar L. Morphet, Roe L. Johns, and Theodore L. Reller, *Educational Organization and Administration: Concepts, Practices, and Issues*, 3rd ed. (Englewood Cliffs, N.J.: Prentice-Hall, 1974), p. 264. By permission of Prentice-Hall, Inc., Englewood Cliffs, N.J.

- To serve as executive officer of any board or council that may be established to facilitate coordination of all aspects of the educational program;
- To select competent personnel for and serve as the administrative head and professional leader of the state department of education to the end that it will contribute maximally to the improvement of education;
- To arrange for studies and organize committees and task forces as deemed necessary to identify problems and to recommend plans and provisions for effecting improvements in education;
- To recommend to the state board of education needed policies, standards, and regulations relating to public education in the state;
- To recommend improvements in educational legislation and in provisions for financing the educational program;
- To explain and interpret the school laws of the state and the regulations of the state board of education;
- To decide impartially controversies and disputes involving the administration of the public school system; and
- To submit frequent reports to the public and periodic reports to the state board, to the governor, and to the legislature giving information about the accomplishments, conditions, and needs of the schools.

State Departments of Education

The activities of state government in education are carried on by state departments of education under the direction of the chief state school officer. These activities have been classified into five categories: operational, regulatory, service, developmental, and public support and cooperation activities.[12] Operational activities are those in which the state department directly administers schools and services, such as schools for the blind. Regulatory activities include the state department's overseeing that teacher certification standards are met, that school buses are safe, and that curricular requirements are being fulfilled. Service activities include advising and consulting, disseminating research, and preparing materials (on state aid, for example). Developmental activities are directed toward the improvement of the department itself and include planning, staffing, and researching in order to perform more adequately its operational, regulatory, and service functions. Public support and cooperation activities are those concerned with public relations, political activities with the legislature and governor, and relations with various other governmental and nongovernmental agencies.

Historically and traditionally, state departments have not exhibited strong leadership. Their activities have been concentrated mainly in the operational and regulatory categories. The Elementary and Secondary Act of 1965, under Title V, provides for monies to strengthen state departments of education. There is no question that departments have been strengthened, but the majority have not yet changed their traditional operational and regulatory roles. Specific suggestions have been

12. Roald F. Campbell, Gerald E. Sroufe, and Donald H. Layton, *Strengthening State Departments of Education* (Chicago: University of Chicago Press, 1967), p. 10.

made to state departments to change their roles, mainly from regulation to leadership, and to provide leadership in service, developmental, and cooperative activities. They must, for example, evolve a more creative relationship with their federal partner. As the problems of society change and as education is looked to for solutions, the roles of the partners in education—federal, state, and local—must change to meet these complex needs.

Federal Involvement

The role of the federal government in education can be considered in four parts: the United States Office of Education; programs operated directly by federal agencies; decisions of federal courts; and federal aid in various forms. Court decisions were considered in the previous chapter, and federal aid will be discussed under finance.

United States Office of Education

The United States Office of Education was established in 1867, largely through the diligent efforts of Henry Barnard, and was first known as the Department of Education. It has had a variety of names since then, including Office of Education (1869), Bureau of Education (1870), and Office of Education (1929). In 1870, the "Bureau of Education" was made a part of the Department of the Interior; in 1939, the "Office of Education" was made a part of the Federal Security Agency. In 1953, the Department of Health, Education, and Welfare replaced the Federal Security Agency, and its secretary was granted cabinet status. The Office of Education is now a unit of this department. The head of the Office of Education, called the commissioner of education, is appointed by the president. The purpose of the Department of Education, as stated in 1867, was:

> to collect such statistics and facts as shall show the condition and progress of education in the several States and Territories, and to diffuse such information respecting the organization and management of schools and school systems, and methods of teaching, as shall aid the People of the United States in the establishment and maintenance of efficient school systems, and otherwise promote the cause of education throughout the country.

Since its inception, the purposes and functions of the Office of Education have expanded. In addition to conducting research and providing services consistent with its original purpose, it now has a relatively strong role in administering federal grants to local school districts. This function, according to some authorities, allows the Office of Education to exercise a strong indirect control over education. There is no question that the administration of federal grants allows the Office of Education to be influential in implementing national goals for education. While some authorities feel that the current role of the Office of Education is too strong, others question whether it is strong enough. Perhaps the Office of Education should have a direct influence in school operations: it must be recognized that the socioeconomic forces in our society are not contained within local school districts or state boundaries. It has been suggested that a secretary of education in the president's cabinet is now needed. The current role of the Office of Education can best be described as emerging. The topic of federal grants will be discussed in greater detail in Chapter 12.

Educational Programs Operated by the Federal Government

The federal government directly operates some school programs. The public school system of the District of Columbia is dependent upon Congress for funds and for many years was under the control of a board of education appointed by the justices of the U.S. District Court for Washington, D.C. Currently, school board members are chosen by popular election.

The Department of the Interior has the educational responsibilities for children of national park employees, for Samoa (classified as an outlying possession), and for the trust territories of the Pacific, such as the Caroline and Marshall Islands. The schools on Indian reservations are financed and managed through the Bureau of Indian Affairs of the Department of the Interior.

The Department of Defense is responsible for the military academy at West Point, the naval academy at Annapolis, and the Coast Guard and Air Force academies. In addition, the Department of Defense operates a school system for the children of military personnel in areas where military personnel are stationed. The education supplied in the training programs, vocational and technical, of the military services has made no small contribution to the education of our nation. Many men transfer the technical and vocational skills acquired in the military to civilian occupations.

Interrelationships

Federal, state, and local governments all have a part in education. The federal government has an "interest" in education, which is a state "function" and a local "operation." Each level of government has a purpose to be accomplished through education. The emphasis at each level has been dependent upon the perspective at that level. Local school districts have been concerned with meeting immediate local educational needs; states have been concerned with promoting the welfare of the state and making certain that children have equal educational opportunity within the state; the federal government has been concerned with our national security, equality of educational opportunity, and the solution to national domestic problems. If local districts could and would completely meet all the needs of education—as perceived by the states and the federal government—then state and federal involvement in education would not be necessary. Federal and state involvement does seem necessary, however, to ensure that each individual will obtain his or her right to an equal opportunity to pursue excellence in education and to achieve personal dignity. It seems likely that American education will continue to be a local, state, and federal concern.

Summary and Implications

Chapter 11 has described the basic organization and structure of American education at the local, state, and federal levels. This chapter has also alluded briefly to the political nature of education and to the roles of parent organizations and professional organizations in shaping educational policies and legislation.

A knowledge of the formal organization of schools and of the political arena in which they operate is important to those who work in the schools. From initial certification, through their daily and yearly work, and finally during retirement, teachers are impacted by state regulations. Teacher organizations (NEA, AFT) are very active politically; as members of these organizations, teachers are expected to participate.

Teachers have made and will continue to make an impact on American education at local, state, and national levels. This impact is made at the local level through teaching in classrooms and through interaction with the community and with boards of education. The state and national teachers' organizations gain their basic strength at the local grass roots level. A knowledge of the organization and structure of education at the local level can be invaluable to teachers in their efforts to shape and to achieve the goals of American education—as well as to advance the goals of the teaching profession and its membership.

A knowledge of the state and national organization and structure of education is also essential. It is through political action at these higher levels that legislation affecting education and the teaching profession at all levels—local, state, and national—is developed. Teachers' organizations have been and will continue to be active at the state and national levels. Members of teacher organizations who are knowledgeable about the governance of education can be more effective participants in determining the future of American education and the teaching profession.

Discussion Questions

1. What improvements could be made in the governance of education at the local level?
2. How can teachers have an impact on the operation of local school districts?
3. What are the advantages and disadvantages of the selection of chief state school officers by election? What are the advantages of appointment by a state board of education?
4. How and why has local control of education been eroded?
5. How have teacher associations increased their power base in American education?

Supplemental Activities

1. Visit a meeting of a local board of education and write a critique of the meeting.

2. Examine and discuss educational bills considered by a recent session of a state legislature.

3.   Obtain and study a copy of the school code for your state.

4.   Examine policy manuals from local school districts in your area, looking particularly for policies that affect your behavior as a classroom teacher and those that deal specifically with student rights.

5.   Interview officers of local teachers' associations and inquire about their opinions on their role in local educational policy making.

Bibliography

Berke, Joel S., et al. *New Era of State Education Politics*. Philadelphia: Ballinger, 1977.

Broudy, Harry S. "The Demand for Accountability—Can Society Exercise Control over Education?" *Education and Urban Society* 9 (February 1977): 235–250.

Campbell, Roald F.; Bridges, Edwin M.; Nystrand, Raphael O. *Introduction to Educational Administration*. Boston: Allyn and Bacon, 1977.

Davies, Lee K. "The School Board's Struggle to Survive." *Educational Leadership* 34 (November 1976): 95–99.

Erickson, Donald A. *Educational Organization and Administration*. Berkeley, Calif.: McCutchan, 1977.

James, Tom. "Teachers, State Politics, and the Making of Educational Policy." *Phi Delta Kappan* 58 (October 1976): 165–168.

Knezevich, Stephen. *Administration of Public Education*. 3rd ed. New York: Harper & Row, 1975.

Morphet, Edgar L., et al. *Educational Organization and Administration*. 3rd ed. Englewood Cliffs, N.J.: Prentice-Hall, 1974.

Ryor, John. "The Case for a Federal Department of Education." *Phi Delta Kappan* 58 (April 1977): 594–596.

Stephens, Robert. *Regional Educational Service Agencies*. Arlington, Va.: Educational Research Services, 1975.

CHAPTER 12

Financing Public Education

MONEY TO SUPPORT EDUCATION COMES FROM A VARIETY OF taxes paid to local, state, and federal governments. These governments in turn distribute tax money to local school districts to operate their schools. The three major kinds of taxes used to provide revenue for schools are property taxes, sales or use taxes, and income taxes. In general, the property tax is a local tax, the sales tax is a state tax, and the income tax may be both a state and a federal tax.

The percentage of total school revenues provided from federal sources steadily increased from a low of .3 percent in 1919 to a high of 8.9 percent in 1971.[1] It is currently about 8 percent and is not expected to increase dramatically in the next few years. The major increase occurred in 1965 when the percentage increased from 4.4 to 7.9 percent. This increase was primarily a result of the passage and implementation of the Elementary and Secondary Education Act of 1965 (ESEA).

Across the nation, state sources have steadily increased from a low of 16.5 percent in 1919 to a current high of 43.7 percent. It is anticipated that, as more states implement legislative educational financial reform, the nationwide average of state aid will increase. Local sources have steadily decreased from a high of 83.2 percent in 1919 to the current low of 48.4 percent. The overall trend points toward a stabilization of federal support at a level of approximately 8 percent, accompanied by steadily increasing state support and steadily decreasing local support. This trend is in harmony with the recommendations of many recent studies and court rulings in the area of school finance, which in essence

1. W. Vance Grant and C. George Lind, *Digest of Educational Statistics, 1976* (Washington, D.C.: U.S. Government Printing Office, 1977), p. 71.

are directed toward achieving equal opportunity. A more complete discussion of this trend, and the reasons for it, will be provided later in this chapter.

The percentages of federal, state, and local revenues vary dramatically among states. Federal sources vary from a high of 21.2 percent in Mississippi to a low of 4.1 percent in Connecticut, Massachusetts, and New Jersey. State sources vary from a high of 92.7 percent in Hawaii; to a relatively high 65 percent in Alabama, Alaska, New Mexico, and North Carolina; to lows of 9.4 percent in New Hampshire, 14.2 percent in South Dakota, and 17.6 percent in Nebraska. New Hampshire, Nebraska, and South Dakota have the highest percentages of local revenues; correspondingly, Hawaii, Alabama, Alaska, New Mexico, and North Carolina have the lowest percentages of local revenues.[2]

Property Taxes— Local Revenue

The property tax is the basic source of local revenue for schools. It is based on the value of property, both real estate and personal property. Real estate includes land holdings and buildings such as homes, commercial buildings, and factories. Personal property consists of such things as automobiles, machinery, livestock, and intangible property such as stocks and bonds. The property tax is an old tax, based on an agrarian economy, when the measure of one's property was a measure of one's wealth.

The major advantage of the property tax is its stability. Although lagging behind other changes in market values, it provides a steady, regular income. Also property is fixed, that is, it is not easily moved to escape taxation such as income might be.

The property tax has a number of limitations. It bears heavily on housing; it tends to discourage rehabilitation and upkeep, since both of these would tend to raise the value of the property and therefore its taxes; it is often a deciding factor in the decision of where to locate business or industry; and it is not likely to be applied equally on all properties.

A major difficulty with the property tax is the determination of the value of property. In some areas, assessors are local people, frequently elected, with no special training in evaluating property. Their duty involves inspecting their neighbors' properties and placing a value upon them. In other areas, more sophisticated techniques involving expertly trained personnel are used for property appraisal. In any event, assessors are likely to be subject to political and informal pressures to keep values low. Appraisals generally take into account the location, area, and use of the property. Homes are judged by the number of rooms, facilities, type of foundation, building materials, and landscaping. In some areas,

2. Ibid., p. 69.

photographs of real estate are used for comparative purposes. Similar comparative scales are used to evaluate industrial and farm property. The value of real property is reviewed at regular intervals, frequently every four years, in an attempt to establish its current market value.

The assessed value of property is usually only a percentage of its market value. This percentage varies from county to county and from state to state. Attempts are made within states to equalize assessments or to make certain that the same percentage of full cash value is used in assessing property throughout the state. In recent years, attempts have been made to institute the use of full cash value for the assessed value. For the property tax to be a fair tax, equalized assessment is a necessity.

The property tax is most generally thought of as a proportionate tax, that is, one that taxes according to ability to pay. However, inequality of assessments and the fact that frequently the greatest wealth is no longer related to real estate property have in some instances made the property tax regressive. Regressive taxes, such as sales and use taxes, are those that have a relatively greater impact on lower income groups. There is some evidence to support the suspicion that persons in the lowest income groups pay a much higher proportion of their income in property taxes than persons in the highest income groups.

Inequities of the Property Tax

The major support for schools across the nation is provided by the property tax, which means basically that the total value of property within a school district when related to its number of pupils provides a basic index of the wealth of a school district. For example, a school district having an assessed valuation of $30 million and responsibility for the education of 1,000 pupils would have $30,000 of assessed valuation per pupil. Usually the number of pupils in average daily attendance is used as a divisor to determine assessed valuation per pupil. Since property tax rates are applied to assessed valuations, a district that has a high assessed valuation per pupil as compared to one that has a low assessed valuation per pupil is in a better position to provide quality education. For example, if school district A has an assessed valuation of $90 million and 1,000 pupils and school district B has an assessed valuation of $30 million and 1,000 pupils, a tax rate of $2 per $100 of assessed valuation would produce $1.8 million for education in district A and only $600,000 in district B. School district A could spend $1,800 per pupil, as compared to $600 per pupil in school district B with the same local tax effort.

Great differences exist in wealth per pupil from school district to school district. Concentrations of industrial developments increase valuations in one district, while a neighboring district may be almost completely residential with little valuation and a large number of pupils.

Differences in wealth and the concomitant differences in tax rates and per pupil expenditures were most dramatically pointed out in the *Serrano* v. *Priest* (1971) decision of the Supreme Court of California.

In *Serrano* v. *Priest,* the California Supreme Court was called upon to determine if the California public school financing system, with its substantial dependence on local property taxes, violated the Fourteenth Amendment. In a 6–1 decision in August, 1971, the court held that heavy reliance on unequal local property taxes "makes the quality of a child's education a function of the wealth of his parents and neighbors." Further, the court declared: "Districts with small tax bases simply cannot levy taxes at a rate sufficient to produce the revenue that more affluent districts produce with a minimum effort."

At the time of the *Serrano* v. *Priest* decision, for example, the Baldwin Park school district spent $577 per pupil, whereas the Beverly Hills school district spent $1,232. Yet the tax rate in Baldwin Park of $5.48 was more than double the rate of $2.38 in Beverly Hills. The discrepancies were a result of the difference in wealth between the two districts: Beverly Hills had $50,885 of assessed valuation per child; Baldwin Park had only $3,706 valuation per child—a ratio of thirteen to one. The inequities resulting from the property tax are at least twofold: the tax is oftentimes inequitably applied to the taxpayer, and in less affluent districts the tax frequently results in unequal opportunities for education —where education is a function of wealth.

Officially the California court ruled that the present system of school

The quality of education should not depend on the affluence of local taxpayers or school districts. (*Photograph by Eric Roth, The Picture Cube*)

financing in California was unconstitutional. Within a year of *Serrano* v. *Priest* (1971), five other courts—in Minnesota, Texas, New Jersey, Wyoming, and Arizona—made similar rulings.

In 1973, the United States Supreme Court consented to hear an appeal of the *San Antonio Independent School District* v. *Rodriguez* case, which originated in Texas. The elements of the *San Antonio Independent School District* v. *Rodriguez* case were similar to those of the *Serrano* v. *Priest* case. The Supreme Court, in a 5–4 decision, reversed the lower court in *San Antonio Independent School District* v. *Rodriguez* and thus reaffirmed the local property tax as a basis for school financing. Justice Potter Stewart, voting with the majority, admitted that "the method of financing public schools . . . can be fairly described as chaotic and unjust." He did not, though, find it unconstitutional. The majority opinion, written by Justice Lewis F. Powell stated: "We cannot say that such disparities are the product of a system that is so irrational as to be invidiously discriminatory." The opinion also noted: that the poor are not necessarily concentrated in the poorest districts, that states must initiate fundamental reform in taxation and education, and that the extent to which quality of education varies with expenditures is inconclusive. Justice Thurgood Marshall, in the dissenting opinion, charged that the ruling "is a retreat from our historic commitment to equality of educational opportunity."

Prior to the *San Antonio Independent School District* v. *Rodriguez* (1973) decision, but after *Serrano* v. *Priest* (1971), the National Legislative Conference Special Commission on School Finance recommended that "states could (should) assume responsibility for seeing that elementary and secondary schools are funded properly, and that 'equal opportunity' responsibility enunciated in *Serrano* v. *Priest* (1971) be accepted, regardless of the courts, because the Serrano principle is right."[3] By 1973, twelve states had made legislative financial enactments based in part on the principles identified in *Serrano* v. *Priest*. The twelve states were California, Colorado, Florida, Illinois, Kansas, Maine, Michigan, Minnesota, Montana, North Dakota, Utah, and Wisconsin.[4] It is interesting to note that, within nine months of *Serrano* v. *Priest*, ninety-nine commissions or committees were organized to study the school finance systems of the fifty states.[5] Undoubtedly changes are occurring in the state provisions for financial support for education. Since the flurry of legislation, however, the economic crunch has adversely affected the financial capability of states, and some states have not been able to live up to their commitments.

The property tax is only one part of an overall tax system. After a brief

3. Robert J. Wynkoop, "Trends in School Finance Reform," *Phi Delta Kappan* 56 (April 1975): 542.
4. Ibid., p. 544.
5. Ibid., p. 543.

look at local financial procedures, state and federal efforts in school finance will be discussed. Finally, a proposal for adequate and more equitable school financing in the future will be presented.

Local Planning and Budgeting

The property tax rate of a school district is determined essentially by the monetary needs of the district expressed in its budget. A budget is the financial plan of the school district. In a sense it can be conceived of as the educational program of the school district expressed in dollars and cents. Usually budgets are prepared on an annual basis, and they project the income and educational costs for a year. States generally prescribe specified forms and procedures to be used in preparing, administering, and adopting the school budget.

The superintendent of schools, assisted by a staff, usually prepares the budget. In many districts the process starts with teachers submitting budgetary requests. The approval of the budget and its final adoption usually require official action of the school board. In some states school budgets must be approved by the state. In many states a public hearing is required prior to adoption of the school budget.

The classification of budgetary expenditures has been standardized largely through the efforts of the U.S. Office of Education. Educational expenditures are classified in three headings: capital outlay, debt service, and current expenses. *Capital outlay* includes expenditures for land, buildings, and equipment; *debt service* includes the repayment of borrowed money and the interest on the debt; and *current expense* includes the expenditures necessary for daily operation and maintenance. The largest category of current educational expense is that of instructional expenses, which include teachers' salaries. This amount frequently exceeds 70 to 85 percent of the total budget. In its final form the budget expresses the amount of money that is necessary to operate the school system and, hence, determines the tax rate.

Planned-program budgeting, a new trend in budgeting, seeks to classify expenditures by school program rather than in the traditional categories of salaries, instructional materials, and administration. A program budget, for example, would project expenditures for categories such as the elementary school reading program, the high school mathematics program, or the vocational educational program. School districts under program budgeting need to identify their programs and keep their records accordingly. A major advantage of program budgeting is that of accountability—the relationships between educational costs and educational accomplishments become clarified. In an accountability approach, educational records of program accomplishment can be compared with the costs of the program. The accountability concept will be further discussed later in this chapter.

Provisions are usually made by the states to grant by law a basic minimum property tax rate for current expenditures for local school districts. Increases in tax rate limits frequently require voter approval.

In some states there is no state limit on the school tax rate. With local approval the rate can be raised as high as desired. In other states, the state establishes a maximum limit by law that cannot be exceeded, even with local approval. Frequently this maximum limit must in actuality be reached step by step with voter approval.

Limitations are usually set by states on the amount of capital outlay indebtedness that a school district may incur. These limits are established in various ways: in some states the limit is an established percentage of assessed valuation, 5 to 10 percent being common. In other states no limits are set, but the indebtedness must be approved by the legislature or by the state office of public instruction.

Limited tax rates for current expenses and limitations on indebtedness point out further the significance of assessed valuation as a factor in determining the quality of an educational program. A local school district can be making the maximum effort, taxing to the limit, and still not be able to offer a program comparable to that of a wealthier neighboring district exerting a medium effort. The effort made by a local school district is indicative of the value that its citizenry places on education; yet it is obvious that equal effort will not produce equal revenue or equal opportunity.

Expenditures per pupil vary widely, partly because of the differences in wealth between districts. States also differ in wealth and correspondingly in expenditures per pupil. Currently, the average annual expenditure per pupil in the United States is $1580. Alaska, New Jersey, and New York spend in excess of $2000 per pupil; Alabama, Arkansas, Kentucky, Mississippi, South Carolina, and Tennessee all spend less than $1200 per pupil.[6] It is anticipated that these expenditures will continue to rise. In dollars adjusted to 1975–76 purchasing power, expenditures per pupil have steadily risen from $350 per pupil in 1929 to $1580 in 1975–76.[7] If it is assumed that the conditions that prevailed in the last ten years will continue to prevail—including declining enrollments—it is likely that by 1981 the average per pupil expenditure (in 1975–76 dollars) in the United States will exceed $2000.

Assessment practices differ from state to state; hence it is·difficult to use assessed valuation per pupil as a measure to compare the wealth of states. A more accurate index is personal income per capita. States with per capita personal income greater than $6700 include Alaska, Connecticut, Illinois, and New Jersey; whereas Alabama, Arkansas, Mississippi, and South Carolina all have per capita personal incomes lower than $4700.[8] In general, higher per capita personal income results in higher expenditures per pupil.

6.   Grant and Lind, p. 78.
7.   Ibid.
8.   Ibid.

State Sources of Revenue

The major sources of tax revenue for states have been classified by the Department of Commerce into four groups: sales and gross receipts, income taxes, licenses, and other miscellaneous taxes. Sales and gross receipt taxes include those on general sales, motor fuels, alcohol, insurance, and amusements; income taxes include both individual and corporate; licenses include those on motor vehicles, corporations, occupations, vehicle operators, hunting, and fishing. The major miscellaneous classification includes property taxes, severance or extraction of minerals taxes, and death and gift taxes.

The average state receives 55.5 percent of its tax revenue from the sales and gross receipts category, 29.1 percent from income taxes, 9.0 percent from licenses, and 6.5 percent from other miscellaneous categories. Every state utilizes some form of sales tax, and a great many utilize individual and corporate income taxes.

Sales and Income Taxes

Sales and income taxes provide lucrative sources of state revenue and both are relatively easy to administer. The sales tax is collected bit by bit, in a relatively painless way, by the vendor who is responsible for record keeping. The state income tax can be withheld from wages, hence collection problems are eased. Some argue that this latter tax meets the criterion of a "good" tax because it is closely related to the ability to pay. Income taxes are referred to as progressive taxes because they frequently are scaled to the ability of the taxpayer to pay. Sales taxes are regressive taxes, since they have a greater impact on lower income groups. All persons pay the sales tax at the same rate, with the result that persons in lower income groups pay nearly as much tax as persons in high income groups. Part of the regressivity of the sales tax can be overcome by the exemption of food from taxation. Both sales and income taxes are direct and certain; they fluctuate with the economy; and they can be regulated by the legislature responsible for raising the money.

State Aid

State aid to local school districts is paid out of tax revenue raised by the state. The distribution of state aid is a complicated matter and varies considerably among states. State aid for education has resulted largely from three factors: the state has the primary responsibility for the education of its citizens; there is wide variation in the financial ability of local school districts to support education; and personal wealth is now less related to the ownership of real property than it once was. The first two factors have already been discussed in this section. The third factor relates to property tax—the major source of local income for school districts. Since a great deal of the individual wealth of the people is not in the form of real property and since it seems reasonable that taxation should be based on ability to pay, then it is apparent that the local property tax has serious limitations as a source of school funds. The progressive income tax appears to be more equitable. Monies so collected could be proportionately redistributed or shared by local school districts and also used to provide financial equalization for educational purposes.

State aid, in terms of its use, may be classified as general or categorical: *general aid* may be used by the recipient school district as it desires; *categorical aid* is earmarked for specific purposes. Examples of categorical aid include monies for transportation, vocational education, driver education, and handicapped children. Frequently categorical aid is given to encourage the development of specified educational programs, and in some states these aid programs are referred to as *incentive programs*. Categorical aid funds may be granted on a matching basis, wherein for each dollar of local effort the state contributes a specified amount. Categorical aid monies have undoubtedly encouraged the development of needed educational programs.

Historically general state aid was based on the concept that each child, regardless of his or her place of residence or the wealth of the district in which the child lives, should be entitled to receive essential, basic educational opportunities. General state aid was established on the principle of equality of opportunity and is usually administered through some type of *foundation program*. The administration of a foundation program involves determining the dollar value of the desired foundation education in a state, determining a minimum standard of local effort, and determining an equitable means for distributing the money to school districts in relationship to their local wealth. The foundation concept implies equity for taxpayers as well as equality of opportunity for students.

Figure 12–1 is a graphic representation of the operation of a foundation program. The total length of each bar represents the per pupil foundation level of education expressed in dollars. Each school district

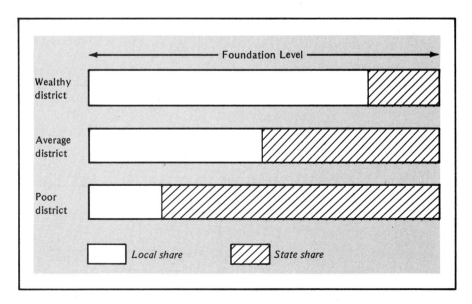

Figure 12–1.
Equalization and the foundation principle.

is required to put forth the same minimum local effort to finance its schools; this could be in the form of a qualifying tax rate that produces the local share of the foundation level. This tax rate will produce more revenue in a wealthy district than it will in a poor district; therefore poor districts will receive more state aid than wealthy districts. Local school districts do not receive general state aid beyond that amount established as the foundation level but are permitted to exceed foundation levels at their own expense.

The effectiveness of various state foundation programs in their attempts to achieve equalization has been limited. A major limitation is that the foundation level frequently is far below the actual expenditure level or far below the level needed to provide an adequate educational opportunity. For example, if a state established a per pupil foundation level of $600 and the average per pupil expenditures were $1000, it is apparent that equalization would not have occurred.

A second limitation is that most general state aid programs do not provide for the different expenditure levels for different pupil needs. For example, special education and vocational education both require more monies to operate than the usual per pupil expenditures for the typical elementary or secondary school pupil. These weaknesses and others—including the taxing inequities—have resulted in strong and determined research efforts to find a more satisfactory and acceptable system to finance American education. The findings and recommendations from these efforts will be discussed later in this chapter.

The method of distributing state aid differs from state to state. The percentage of current expenditures paid by state aid also differs from state to state, as does the ability of states to support schools.

In summary, the property tax is the largest local revenue producer, while sales and income taxes are the largest state revenue producers. State taxes may be used to equalize opportunity resulting from unequal local tax bases. The use of local, state, and federal funds to support education, by a variety of types of taxation, results in a tax system. It is important to look at each type of tax as a part of a system. As previously discussed, each individual kind of tax has its advantages and disadvantages, yet it is unlikely that any one of these taxes utilized by itself would be a panacea. In evaluating a system of taxes, one should consider the varying ability of citizens to pay, economic effects of the taxes on the taxpayer, benefits that various taxpayers receive, overall yield of the tax, economy of collection, degree of acceptance, convenience of paying, problems of tax evasion, stability of the tax, and the overall adaptability of the system. It is soon apparent that systems of taxation are complicated—an intricately interwoven, interdependent network.

The system of taxation exists to produce revenue for distribution. The distribution systems are equally complex; however, the educational theme applied to distribution is equality of educational opportunity. State equalization programs were designed to accomplish this objective;

although they have had some successes, it must be concluded that these successes have been limited.

Federal Aid   Many people have suggested that the logical solution to the inequities that exist in the ability of states to support education is federal aid. The United States has a long history of federal aid to education; however, it has been categorical and not general aid. It has been related to the needs of the nation at the time. Federal aid actually started prior to the adoption of the United States Constitution with the Ordinance of 1785, which provided land for public schools in "western territories," and has continued in a rather steady progression to the present time. It has been estimated that almost 200 federal aid-to-education laws have been passed since the Northwest Ordinance of 1785.[9] A discussion of federal aid prior to the enactment of the National Defense Education Act of 1958 is treated in Part IV.

Federal activity and funding have gained great momentum in the past few years. The Elementary and Secondary Education Act of 1965 (ESEA) approved and funded by the Eighty-ninth Congress was truly a landmark act among the federal acts designed to aid education. ESEA was categorical in nature yet came as close to general aid to education as any federal legislation has ever been. It was broad in its scope, and most school districts could qualify for funds. The basic purpose of the Act was to equalize educational opportunities. ESEA did not operate like typical state foundation programs; it had five titles, each designed for a specific purpose. Local agencies desiring to participate were required to plan and present proposals for action within the guidelines of the various titles. ESEA was amended in 1966, 1967, 1970—and each year from 1974 to 1978. ESEA represented an extensive federal effort to improve education throughout the United States. It recognized the importance of education in a democratic form of government, and in so doing, it sought to provide opportunities for every child to pursue educational excellence. It recognized the need for cooperative planning for education at the federal, state, and local levels.

New federal funding thrusts in recent years have included monies for adult, vocational, career, and bilingual education. The most recent major thrust is Public Law 94–142, known as the Education for All Handicapped Children Act, discussed in Part II.

In summary, the United States has a historical tradition of federal aid to education. It has been categorical, it has been related to the needs of the nation, and it has increased markedly in the past few years. Federal aid has been administered through various agencies; of late, the U.S. Office of Education has come into prominence in this respect.

9. Committee on Finance, *Financial Status of the Public Schools, 1971* (Washington, D.C.: National Education Association, 1971), p. 21.

Federal aid, while seemingly historically established, is still somewhat controversial. Advocates of federal aid point out that it is the logical answer to providing equality of educational opportunity for all children regardless of their place of dwelling. They point out that it is necessary for national defense and general welfare because these problems—in a modern nation with high mobility of population—cannot be resolved locally. They note it can be administered without federal control, as proved in the land-grant acts and the National Defense Education Act of 1958; and it provides the most equitable means—the income tax— of paying for public education. Opponents of federal aid point out that education is a state and local function. They argue that variations in fiscal ability to pay will always exist and that the distribution of federal funds will not guarantee that whatever differences now exist will be reduced appreciably. They point out that the nation is weakened by dependence on the federal government for funds, that categorical aid in and of itself is federal control, and that states can use the income tax as effectively as the federal government.

It seems logical that the federal government will continue its role in financing American education. Interrelated domestic, social, and economic problems of national magnitude must be resolved: these problems, for financial and a variety of other reasons, have not and probably will not be solved at local or state levels. The federal government has access to funds through the use of the most equitable tax—the progressive income tax, both personal and corporate. Personal and corporate income now account for the great majority of our national income; yet public schools in the main still are supported predominantly by the property tax, which is becoming increasingly less related to the taxpaying ability of the people. The inequality of the tax base of states can be equalized only through federal aid, and certainly the equality of educational opportunity is related to the ability of states to support education. The principle of local support for education served well for many years; and then, because of unequal tax bases, local support needed the help of state support. Federal support is now needed to bolster equality among the states. This support can be given with minor—if any—federal encroachment upon local school control; furthermore, it is proper that categorical funds—to effect their purposes—be controlled by the federal government.

Proposed Solutions to the School Finance Dilemma

It is clear that the current system of school finance—with its heavy reliance upon local support gained from the local property tax—cannot bring about a realization of equality of education opportunity. Further, the property tax itself in today's economy tends to be a regressive and an unfair tax. State equalization programs have not been successful in securing equality of opportunity. The federal effort, while stronger now than it has ever been before, is feeble in terms of the overall educational expenditure, contributing only about 9 percent at its peak in 1971–72. Recent thinking on new means of funding education follows in the next three sections.

Conducted and completed immediately prior to *Serrano* v. *Priest* (1971), the National Education Finance Project was based on assumptions that the researchers felt most Americans could agree upon as being appropriate and desirable:

1.   . . . that the opportunity to receive a good education should be equally available to everyone—that the level and character of a youngster's education should not depend on the district in which he happens to live, or the state, or on the wealth of his parents, or for that matter on the ignorance of his parents.
2.   . . . that education should be seen as helping to break down the barriers of caste and class, providing a path to success for everyone, no matter how humble his birth or circumstance, and excluding no one from the American dream.
3.   . . . that a government of the people, by the people, and for the people cannot succeed with an illiterate, ignorant citizenry.
4.   . . . that systems of taxation should be equitable—that people ought to be called upon to support education in proportion to their ability to pay.
5.   . . . that education is regarded not just as an expenditure—like buying a ticket to a movie—but as an investment . . . an investment in human capital, yielding substantial returns to the individual and to society as a whole.[10]

In essence, the project sought to provide methods of determining which school financing systems were consistent with the principles and premises that most Americans consider basic. The study examined state systems of finance from two perspectives: (1) how successful were the systems in equalizing the fiscal resources of many local school districts, irrespective of how wealthy or poor individual school districts might be; and (2) what attention was being given to cost differentials involved in educating special groups of children (for example, handicapped children) or in providing special kinds of educational programs (for example, vocational education). Among the conclusions were: (1) a weighted approach to allocating school funds (which allows for cost differential involved in educating special groups of children) is clearly more efficient and equitable than a system that relies almost entirely on average daily attendance figures; (2) the common practice by states of distributing funds to local school districts by flat grants keyed to average daily attendance—without regard to the differences in the resources of varying

10.   Roe L. Johns, "Toward Equity in School Finance," *American Education* 7 (November 1971): 3–6.

school districts or the varying needs of special kinds of children—is a major source of inequity in school financing; and (3) the end result of the heavy reliance on the property tax is that the quality of a child's education is largely determined by whether he or she had the good sense to be born of wealthy parents in a wealthy school district or whether he or she made the mistake of being born to poor parents in a poor district.[11] The authors conclude that the optimum model of school financing would be one involving some degree of local financing for the purpose of stimulating innovation and experimentation—but with primary funding from state and federal governments. To achieve what the general public desires, they estimated that the federal government should provide about 30 percent of school revenues, local school districts about 10 to 15 percent, the remainder to be provided by the state.

Post-*Serrano* Recommendations
As was indicated earlier, the *Serrano* decision was followed by many other court decisions dealing with school finance. Also the many commissions, created after the *Serrano* decision, filed their recommendations for the financing of schools. Table 12–1 presents guidelines that were extracted from the court decisions and commission reports—along with a clarification of each guideline and the origin of its support. In general, the guidelines are consistent with and supportive of the recommendations of the National Education Finance Project.

Another analysis by Joel Berke confirmed some of the findings of the National Education Finance Project and the post-*Serrano* guidelines listed in Table 12–1.[12] This study included the topic of federal aid as a source of reform and recommended: (1) the funding of Title I of the Elementary and Secondary Education Act should be increased; (2) in addition to the continuation of categorical aid programs aimed at specific national purposes, new federal aid programs should be designed to serve as levers to change the course of state policy; and (3) federal aid should help states to eliminate the disparities caused by wealth and need that characterize state patterns of raising and distributing revenues for education.[13]

In respect to Title I, Berke indicated that, while the educational benefits of Title I are mixed, "as a fiscal device it is clearly the best program in American educational finance."[14] Title I funds are concentrated on overburdened central cities and impoverished rural areas where needs are greatest. In respect to additional categorical aid, the study recom-

11. Ibid.
12. Joel S. Berke, *Answers to Inequity: An Analysis of the New School Finance.* (Berkeley, Calif.: McCutchan, 1974).
13. Ibid., pp. 169–176.
14. Ibid., pp. 169–176.

Table 12–1.   A model through which to view school finance reforms.

Guideline	Clarification of Guideline	Origin of Support
New school finance law should be fiscally neutral.	There should be an equal availability of taxable resources per pupil.	This guideline received the unanimous endorsement of the commission reports and the courts.
New school finance law should provide for variations to exist in the expenditure per pupil.	The state in its subventions and the local district in its expenditures should provide different resources to meet different needs of children.	This guideline received unanimous support from the commission reports and a heavy emphasis from the courts.
New school finance law should eliminate or greatly reduce local initiative required or permitted.	The amount of revenue raised by the local referendum to enable the school district to increase its expenditure should be curtailed or eliminated.	The guideline received heavy emphasis from the commission reports, but is loosely related to guidelines four and five, which both received heavy emphasis from the courts.
New school finance law should provide for the equalization of local revenue.	Equal tax efforts among districts should permit equal expenditures per pupil.	This guideline received heavy emphasis from both the commission reports and the courts.
New school finance law should fully fund the school finance model enacted by the state.	All revenue for the support of the schools should be raised by the legislature and not by the local school district.	This guideline received heavy emphasis from the commission reports and moderate support from the courts.

Source: Robert J. Wynkoop, "Trends in School Finance Reform," *Phi Delta Kappan* 56 (April 1975): 543. Reprinted by permission.

mended that the federal government require comprehensive educational priorities and also require that states systematically assess the outputs of their educational programs. In respect to federal aid eliminating disparities among states, the study suggested that "greater equality of educational opportunity will be greatly speeded up by requirements attached to a new program of federal funds: requirements to insure that state finance systems do not continue in the patterns of the past; with incentive funds to help pay for the initial costs of leveling up."[15]

15.   Ibid., p. 174.

Equity Actions
of States

The meeting of new equity standards in public school finance requires major revisions of state and local tax and spending policies. Some states are making strides in this regard; however, the 1974 and 1975 recession slowed the movement toward more equitable systems of public school finance. Nevertheless, elements of progress have been made in twenty-two states by means of new laws. In general, the new laws have demonstrated the following characteristics: substantial increases in funding for public schools have been obtained either by tapping budget surpluses or by raising the rates of existing state taxes; local school tax rates have been cut; distribution of aid has increasingly taken into account the presence of unusual educational needs or costs; limits have been set on local tax rates—or ceilings have been established on local school district expenditures; and pupil-weighting systems have provided more funding for educating children who are handicapped, who require bilingual education, or who are educationally disadvantaged.[16]

Establishing equitable financial regulations and providing equality of educational opportunity for all is a tremendous challenge for public education in the United States. Only with strong beliefs in public education—and in equality of opportunity—will the citizens of the nation be able to meet the challenge.

Accountability

Schools today are being called upon to be accountable. Although there are many definitions of the term *accountability*, it basically means that schools must devise a means that relates the vast expenditures of monies made available for education and their educational results. For many years in the past, the quality of education was measured by the numbers of dollars spent or the processes of education that were being used. In other words, a school system that had a relatively high cost per pupil, or used educational techniques that were judged to be effective, was considered to be an excellent school system. Seldom was the effectiveness of school systems judged by their output or by the educational accomplishments of their students. Accountability calls for schools to be judged by their output or by the educational attainments of their students. It further calls for a clear and definitive record of what those attainments cost.

Accountability has its roots in two very fundamental contemporary problems. One has been the continuous escalation of educational costs. Closely related to this has been the increasing loss of faith in educational results: in a sense, citizens have lost some of their blind faith in education. The failure of the American educational system, particularly in the inner cities, has been accurately documented. The expectations of citizens for their children have not been met. Although the American public schools have done the best job of educating the masses of any nation

---

16. Mary A. Golladay, *The Condition of Education* (Washington, D.C.: U.S. Government Printing Office, 1977), p. 138.

Accountability: educators must find reliable ways of measuring student progress. *(Photograph by Talbot Lovering)*

in the world, they still have failed for some of their constituents. Our goals have been high, which means that the educational expectations of our citizens have also been high. In the eyes of many of our citizens, we have not met their expectations, and we have been consuming more and more dollars. The percentage of educational expenses of our gross national product has been steadily increasing.

With the passage and implementation of the Elementary and Secondary Act of 1965, the federal government called for accountability: it asked to receive documented results of educational attainment. This thrust further fueled the call for accountability.

How can school systems become accountable? First, they must specify what their goals are and then translate these goals into specific instructional performance objectives for students. In other words, if one goal of an elementary school is "to have pupils learn to read," then this goal must be spelled out specifically for each grade level or child, whichever is most applicable, and a measure of success applied and reported. Only in this way can results or output be made meaningful to the public. The fact that many goals of education are subjective and not easily measured should not prevent educators from measuring and dealing precisely with those goals that do lend themselves to objectivity. When school systems can adequately report their results in "hard" data, the most difficult dimension of accountability will have been attained.

The second aspect, that of accounting for monies as they relate to educational results, is an easier task. Financial accounting systems designed to record expenditures by educational programs, as do planning, programming, and budgeting systems, can effectively reveal the costs of various educational programs. It is then a simple matter to report the cost of programs in terms of the accomplishments of the performance objectives of the program. Advanced computer technology has done much to assist in the task. The increased sophistication of an accountability reporting system has great possibilities for educational decision making and for regaining the public's confidence in the educational establishment. It may further help in determining those responsibilities that are clearly those of the schools and those that other agencies should accept.

A danger that lurks in the implementation of an accountability system is that goals that do not lend themselves to objective measurement will be dropped. Caution must be taken to avoid this. At the same time, great effort should be exerted to measure all goals as carefully as they can be measured.

Accountability is partially based on the premise that every child can be successful: the child can learn and his or her accomplishments can be reported. While educators can utilize computer technology and management systems that many believe are dehumanizing, they can also take advantage of accountability in an extremely humane way: each child will be expected to learn beginning at his or her threshold of achievement—rather than be marked for failure, as the child is in many schools today, because he or she is below the average upon entering school.

Performance Contracting

Performance contracting was a by-product of accountability. Industrial corporations indicated that they had the capability of assuring pupil attainment. For a specified sum of money, they would guarantee to a school system that they could accomplish stated instructional performance objectives. Their fees would be based on and scaled to pupil accomplishments. In other words, if the company succeeded in having the pupils achieve the agreed upon contractual objectives, the company would then receive the specified sum of money. If the contractor fell short of his goals, a lesser amount of money was paid. In some contracts, bonuses were paid if achievement was greater than that specified. It was usually specified that the educational achievement attained would be certified by an independent educational auditor for the benefit of both the contractor and the school system.

Educational Vouchers

Educational vouchers, like performance contracting, represented attempts to introduce educational reform. Under the voucher system, the parents of all school-age children in a community would be given a voucher roughly representing their child's share of the educational budget. The child could then use this voucher to attend any school he chose: public, private, or parochial. It would permit alternatives to the customary locked-in step system of neighborhood education wherein a child proceeds, usually without choice, from his neighborhood elementary school to junior and senior high schools, which still serve the same neighborhood. The rationale of the voucher system is that it would cause schools to be more responsive to their constituencies by introducing competition. In a sense, public schools are monopolies: students have no choice as to which school they may attend.

Public schools do not function in a social milieu that inspires innovation and responsiveness. They must, with very rare exceptions, accept students assigned to them; and the students, in turn, must attend these particular schools. In contrast, private schools may select their students; and students, if they can afford and desire private education, may select their school. The voucher plan sought to introduce the element of competition into public education: students would choose the best school in the area, and the weaker schools, in theory, would be forced to improve.

The use of federally funded voucher plans over the years has declined dramatically. However, the concept is still alive in the form of alternative schools and magnet schools within single school districts. It can be said definitely that performance contracting and educational vouchers did have positive residual effects on public school education.

Summary and Implications

This chapter presented the fundamentals of school finance. An emphasis was placed on the relationship of the overall system of finance, dependent on local, state, and federal sources, as that system relates to equality of educational opportunity.

The current trend in the United States is toward increased state financial support for education and toward decreased local financial support —along with a rather stable element of federal support. In many states, public education consumes more of the state budget than any other service, and additional funding for education is most likely to come from state than from other sources. When education issues are being debated by a state legislature, such issues frequently become money issues first and foremost. Other state services—such as welfare and highway construction—also need money and compete for the same usually limited funds. Further, legislators and governors are concerned with maintaining a fiscal balance necessary to keep a state solvent. Within this milieu, those participants with financial and political knowledge—and with clout and power—are likely to be the most successful.

Teachers are becoming an important influence in shaping legislation throughout the country. Their organizations are known and respected for the size of their constituency, their economic resources, their political activity, their research staffs, their legislative programs, and their lobbying efforts. Members of the profession should be knowledgeable about fundamentals of school finance in order to be both effective and responsible in the political arena.

Discussion Questions

1. What are the major advantages and disadvantages of the property tax?

2. What have been some of the noticeable effects of categorical aid—both state and federal—on the curricula of the local school districts in your area?

3. What changes are likely to occur in federal aid in the next decade?

4. What are the advantages and disadvantages of the increasing level of state support for education?

5. What factors other than equalized expenditures affect equality of opportunity?

Supplemental Activities

1. Study and evaluate the plan of state support for education in your state.

2. Interview members of local boards of education to determine their opinions on how schools should be financed.

3. Invite a tax assessor or supervisor of assessments to class to discuss the assessing process in your area.

4. Attend a budget hearing for a local school district.

5. Obtain and study a copy of a local school district budget. Prepare a list of questions about the budget and invite a local school official to class to answer your questions and to explain the budgeting process.

Bibliography

Benson, Charles. *Education Finance in the Coming Decade.* Bloomington, Ind.: Phi Delta Kappa, 1975.

Benson, Charles. *Equity in School Financing: Full State Funding.* Bloomington, Ind.: Phi Delta Kappa, 1975.

Berke, Joel S. *Answers to Inequity: An Analysis of the New School Finance.* Berkeley, Calif.: McCutchan, 1974.

Berke, Joel S. "Two Roads to School Finance Reform." *Society* 13 (January 1976): 67–72.

Campbell, Roald F., Bridges, Edwin M., and Nystrand, Raphael O. *Introduction to Educational Administration.* Boston: Allyn and Bacon, 1977.

Golladay, Mary A. "Financing of Public Elementary and Secondary Schools" in *The Condition of Education.* Washington, D.C.: U.S. Government Printing Office, 1977, pp. 124–138.

Harrison, Russel S. *Equality in Public School Finance.* Lexington, Mass.: D.C. Heath, 1976.

Legget, Stanton. "The Coming Battles over School Finance Reform." *Reader's Digest,* February 1977, pp. 21–27.

Pincus, John. "The *Serrano* Case: Policy for Education or for Public Finance?" *Phi Delta Kappan* 59 (November 1977): 173–179.

Wynkoop, Robert J. "Trends in School Finance Reform." *Phi Delta Kappan* 56 (April 1975): 542–545.

PART IV

Historical Foundations of Education

People have attempted to educate their offspring in one way or another since they have been on earth. Contemporary educators can learn much from these past educational efforts. It is through a careful study of the history of education that educators can avoid repeating past mistakes and can capitalize on past successes.

In Part IV, we will first explore some of the important antecedents to American education: many early educational practices in the American colonies were simply transplanted from Europe. Even today, many facets of our educational programs had their roots in other countries. We will then examine the highlights of educational development in the United States—from colonial times up to the recent past.

CHAPTER 13

Antecedents to American Education

Ancient World (up to A.D. 476) IT IS GENERALLY BELIEVED THAT HUMAN BEINGS HAVE BEEN ON earth for several million years. During 99 percent of this time, humans made very little progress toward civilization. It was not until about 10,000 years ago that they started to raise food, domesticate animals, build canoes, and live together in some semblance of community life. It was not until approximately 6,000 years ago that a written language was developed.

With the advent of a written language, humans developed a need for formal education. As their society became more complex and as their body of knowledge increased, people recognized a need for schools. Their increasing body of knowledge comprised the subject matter; the written language made it possible to record this knowledge and pass it on from generation to generation.

It is impossible to determine the exact date that schools first came into existence; however, the discovery of cuneiform mathematics textbooks that have been dated to 2000 B.C. suggests that some form of schools probably existed in Sumeria at that early date. There is also evidence to suggest that formal schools existed in China during the Hsia and Shang dynasties, perhaps as early as 2200 B.C. It was not until approximately 500 B.C., however, that society was sufficiently advanced to spawn an organized concern for education. This happened in Greece during what has been labeled the *Age of Pericles*.

Greece consisted of a number of city-states, one of which was Sparta. Sparta was a militaristic state, and her educational system was geared to support her military ambitions. Infants were exposed to the elements for a period of time, and if they survived the ordeal, they were judged to be sufficiently strong to make good soldiers or, in the case of females, to bear healthy children. From the ages of eight to eighteen, children became wards of the state. During this time they lived in barracks and received physical and moral training. Between the ages of eighteen and twenty, boys underwent rigorous war training, after which they served in the army. All men were required to marry at the age of thirty so that they might raise healthier children to serve the state. The aims of Spartan education centered around such ideals as the development of courage, patriotism, obedience, cunning, and physical strength. A later writer, Plutarch (A.D. 46–120), said that Spartan education "was calculated to make them subject to command, to endure labor, to fight, and to conquer." There was very little intellectual content in Spartan education.

In sharp contrast to the Spartan educational system was that of Athens, another Greek city-state, which developed an educational program that placed great stress on intellectual and aesthetic objectives. Between the ages of eight and sixteen, most Athenian boys attended a number of public schools. These schools included a grammatist school that taught reading, writing, and counting; a gymnastics school that taught sports and games; and a music school that taught history, drama, poetry, speaking, and science as well as music. Because of the need for all city-states to defend themselves against aggressors, Athenian boys received citizenship and military training between the ages of sixteen and twenty. Athenian girls were educated in the home. The aims of Athenian education placed stress upon the development of the individual, aesthetics, and culture.

It is interesting to note that the Western world's first great philosophers came from Athens. Of the many philosophers that Greece produced, three stand out above the rest—Socrates (470–399 B.C.), Plato (427–347 B.C.), and Aristotle (384–322 B.C.).

Socrates left no writings, but we know a good deal about him from the writings of Xenophon and Plato. Socrates developed a method of teaching that came to be known as the *Socratic method,* in which the teacher would ask a series of questions that led the student to a certain conclusion. The Socratic method is illustrated in the following account of a conversation between Socrates and city officials:

> The thirty tyrants had put many of the most distinguished citizens to death, and had encouraged others to acts of injustice. "It would surprise me," said Socrates one day, "if the keeper of a flock, who had killed one part of it and had made the other part poor, would not confess that he was a bad herdsman; but it would surprise me still more if a man standing at the head of his fellow-citizens should destroy a part of them and corrupt the rest, and were not to blush at his conduct and confess himself a bad magistrate." This remark having come to the ears of the Thirty, Critias and Charicles sent for Socrates, showed him the law, and forbade him to hold conversation with the young.
>
> Socrates inquired of them if he might be permitted to ask questions touching what might seem obscure to him in his prohibition. Upon their granting this permission: "I am prepared," he said, "to obey the laws, but

that I may not violate them through ignorance, I would have you clearly inform me whether you interdict the art of speaking because it belongs to the number of things which are good, or because it belongs to the number of things which are bad. In the first case, one ought henceforth to abstain from speaking what is good; in the second, it is clear that the effort should be to speak what is right."

Thereupon Charicles became angry, and said: "Since you do not understand us, we will give you something easier to comprehend: we forbid you absolutely to hold conversation with the young." "In order that it may be clearly seen," said Socrates, "whether I depart from what is enjoined, tell me at what age a youth becomes a man?" "At the time when he is eligible to the senate, for he has not acquired prudence till then; so do not speak to young men who are below the age of thirty."

"But if I wish to buy something of a merchant who is below the age of thirty, may I ask him at what price he sells it?"

"Certainly you may ask such a question; but you are accustomed to raise inquiries about multitudes of things which are perfectly well known to you; it is this which is forbidden."

"So I must not reply to a young man who asks me where Charicles lives, or where Critias is." "You may reply to such questions," said Charicles. "But recollect, Socrates," added Critias, "you must let alone the shoemakers, and the smiths, and other artisans, for I think they must already be very much worn out by being so often in your mouth."

"I must, therefore," said Socrates, "forego the illustrations I draw from these occupations relative to justice, piety, and all the virtues."[1]

Socrates traveled about Athens teaching the students who gathered about him. He was dedicated to the search for truth and at times was very critical of the existing government. Socrates was brought to trial for inciting the people against the government by his ceaseless questioning. He was found guilty and given a choice between ending his teaching or being put to death. Socrates chose the latter and thereby became a martyr for the cause of education. Socrates' fundamental principle, "Knowledge is virtue," has been adopted by countless educators and philosophers since his death.

Plato was a student and disciple of Socrates. In his *Republic,* Plato set forth his recommendations for the ideal society. He suggested that society should contain three classes of people: artisans to do the manual work, soldiers to defend the society, and philosophers to advance knowledge and to rule the society. Plato's educational aim was to discover and develop each individual's abilities. He believed that each man's abilities should be used to serve society. Plato wrote: "I call education the virtue which is shown by children when the feelings of joy or of sorrow, of love or of hate, which arise in their souls, are made conformable to order." Concerning the goals of education, Plato wrote: "A good educa-

1. Gabriel Compayre, *History of Pedagogy,* trans. W. H. Payne (Boston: D. C. Heath, 1888), pp. 24–26.

The Parthenon—the ancient world produced a flowering of philosophic inquiry. (*Photograph by George N. Peet, The Picture Cube*)

tion is that which gives to the body and to the soul all the beauty and all the perfection of which they are capable.''

Like Plato, Aristotle also believed that man's most important purpose was to serve and improve mankind. However, Aristotle's educational method was scientific, practical, and objective, in contrast to the philosophical methods of Socrates and Plato. Aristotle believed that the quality of a society was determined by the quality of education found in that society. His writings, which include *Lyceum, Organon, Politics, Ethics,* and *Metaphysics,* were destined to exert greater influence upon humankind up through the Middle Ages than the writings of any other man.

Insight into some of Aristotle's views concerning education can be obtained from the following passage taken from *Politics:*

That education should be regulated by law and should be an affair of state is not to be denied, but what should be the character of this public education, and how young persons should be educated, are questions which remain to be considered. For mankind are by no means agreed about the things to be taught, whether we look to virtue or the best life.

Neither is it clear whether education is more concerned with intellectual or with moral virtue. The existing practice is perplexing; no one knows on what principle we should proceed—should the useful in life, or should virtue, or should the higher knowledge be the aim of our training; all three opinions have been entertained. Again, about the means there is no agreement; for different persons, starting with different ideas about the nature of virtue, naturally disagree about the practice of it.

There can be no doubt that children should be taught those useful things which are really necessary, but not all things; for occupations are divided into liberal and illiberal; and to young children should be imparted only such kinds of knowledge as will be useful to them without vulgarizing them. And any occupation, art, or science, which makes the body or soul or mind of the freeman less fit for the practice or exercise of virtue, is vulgar; wherefore we call those arts vulgar which tend to deform the body, and likewise all paid employments, for they absorb and degrade the mind.[2]

The contributions that Greece made toward civilization and to education were truly outstanding.

In 146 B.C., the Romans conquered Greece, and Greek teachers and their educational system were quickly absorbed into the Roman Empire. In fact, many of the educational and philosophical advances made by the Roman Empire after that time were actually made by enslaved Greeks.

Prior to 146 B.C. Roman children had been educated primarily in the home, with some children attending the *ludi* school where the rudiments of reading and writing were taught. The Greek influence upon Roman education became pronounced between 50 B.C. and A.D. 200. During this time an entire system of schools developed in Rome. After learning to read and write in a ludi school, some children attended a grammaticus school to study Latin, literature, history, mathematics, music, and dialectics. These Latin grammar schools fulfilled a role somewhat similar to that filled by twentieth-century secondary schools. Students who were preparing for a career of political service received their training in a school of rhetoric. These rhetorical schools offered courses in grammar, rhetoric, dialectics, music, arithmetic, geometry, and astronomy.

The Roman Empire contained a number of institutions of higher learning that were continuations of former Greek institutions. For instance, a higher institution grew out of a library founded by Vespasian about A.D. 70. This institution later came to be known as the Athenaeum and

2. Paul Monroe, *Source Book of the History of Education* (New York: Macmillan, 1901), p. 282.

eventually offered studies in law, medicine, architecture, mathematics, and mechanics.

Quintilian (A.D. 35–95) was the most influential of all Roman educators. In a set of twelve books, *The Institutes of Oratory*, he described current educational practices, recommended the type of educational system needed in Rome, and listed the great books in existence at that time.

Quintilian had considerable insight into educational psychology; concerning the punishment of students, he wrote:

> I am by no means in favor of whipping boys, though I know it to be a general practice. In the first place, whipping is unseemly, and if you suppose the boys to be somewhat grown up, it is an affront in the highest degree. In the next place, if a boy's ability is so poor as to be proof against reproach he will, like a worthless slave, become insensible to blows. Lastly, if a teacher is assiduous and careful, there is no need to use force. I shall observe further that while a boy is under the rod he experiences pain and fear. The shame of this experience dejects and discourages many pupils, makes them shun being seen, and may even weary them of their lives.[3]

Regarding the motivation of students, Quintilian stated:

> Let study be made a child's diversion; let him be soothed and caressed into it; and let him sometimes test himself upon his proficiency. Sometimes enter a contest of wits with him, and let him imagine that he comes off the conqueror. Let him even be encouraged by giving him such rewards that are most appropriate to his age.[4]

These comments are as applicable today as they were when Quintilian wrote them nearly 2,000 years ago. Quintilian's writings were rediscovered in the 1400s and became influential in the humanistic movement in education.

The Romans possessed a genius for organization and for getting a job done. They made lasting contributions in the field of architecture: many of their roads, aqueducts, and buildings remain today. This genius for organization enabled Rome to unite nearly the entire ancient world with a common language, religion, and political bond—a condition that facilitated the spread of education and knowledge throughout the ancient world.

Middle Ages (476–1300) By A.D. 476 (the fall of the Roman Empire) the Roman Catholic church was well on the way to becoming the major power in government and education. In fact, the ascension of the church to a position of great power is often cited as a major cause of the Western world's plunge into

---

3. Quintilian, *The Institutes of Oratory*, trans. W. Guthrie (London: Dewick and Clark, 1905), p. 27.
4. Ibid., p. 13.

the *Dark Ages*. As the church stressed the importance of gaining entrance to heaven, life on earth, in a sense, became relatively unimportant. Many people viewed earthly life as nothing more than a means to a life hereafter. It is easy to see that a society in which this attitude prevailed would be unlikely to make intellectual advances, except perhaps in areas tangential to religion.

One can obtain insight into the loss of knowledge that took place during the Dark Ages by comparing writings from that period with earlier writings. During the seventh century, a Spanish bishop, Isidore of Seville, wrote an encyclopedia that supposedly contained all the knowledge in the world at that time. A map of the world, as it was then known, was included in this encyclopedia. Comparing Isidore's extremely crude map with a surprisingly accurate one drawn in the second century by Ptolemy vividly illustrates the loss of knowledge that had taken place over this 500-year period.

During the Dark Ages, one of the very few bright periods for education was the reign of Charlemagne (742–814). Charlemagne realized the value of education and, as ruler of a large part of Europe, was in a position to establish schools and encourage scholarly activity. In 800, when Charlemagne came into power, educational activity was at an extremely low ebb. The little educating that was carried on was conducted by the church mainly to induct people into the faith and to train religious leaders. The schools in which this religious teaching took place included *catechumenal* schools that taught church doctrine to new converts; *catechetical* schools that at first taught the catechism but that later became schools for training church leaders; and *cathedral* or monastic schools that trained clergy.

Charlemagne conducted an extensive search for a talented educator who would be capable of improving education in the kingdom. The man that Charlemagne finally selected for the job was Alcuin (735–804), who had been a teacher in England. While serving as Charlemagne's chief educational adviser, Alcuin became the most famous educator of his day. His main educational writings include *On Grammar*, *On Orthography*, *On Rhetoric*, and *On Dialectics*. In addition to working toward the general improvement of education in the kingdom, Alcuin headed Charlemagne's Palace School in Frankland. It is said that Charlemagne himself often would sit in the Palace School with the children, attempting to further his own meager education.

At one time Charlemagne and Alcuin issued a proclamation throughout the empire in an effort to encourage educational activity. Because this statement was one of the most important educational statements of that period and because it sheds a good deal of light on life at that time, it is reproduced here.

> Be it known to your Devotion, pleasing to God, that we and our faithful have judged it well that, in the bishoprics and monasteries committed by

Christ's favour to our charge, besides the due observance of a regular and holy life, care shall be had for the study of letters that those to whom God has given the ability to learn may receive instruction, each according to his several capacity. And this, that, just as obedience to the rule gives order and beauty to your acts, so zeal in teaching and learning may impart the like graces to your words, and thus those who seek to please God by living aright may not fail to please Him also by right speaking. For it is written "by thy words shalt thou be justified or condemned"; and though it is indeed better to do the right than to know it, yet it is needful also to know the right before we can do it. Every one, therefore, must learn what it is that he would fain accomplish, and his mind will the more fully grasp the duty which lies before him if his tongue errs not in the service of Almighty God. And, if false speaking should thus be shunned by all men, how much more must those exert themselves to shun it who have been chosen for this very purpose, to be the servants of the truth!

But in many letters received by us in recent years from divers monasteries, informing us of the prayers offered upon our behalf at their sacred services by the brethren there dwelling, we have observed that though the sentiments were good the language was uncouth, the unlettered tongue failing through ignorance to interpret aright the pious devotion of the heart.

And hence we have begun to fear that, if their skill in writing is so small, so also their power of rightly comprehending the Holy Scriptures may be far less than is befitting; and it is known to all that, if verbal errors are dangerous, errors of interpretation are still more so. We exhort you therefore, not only not to neglect the study of letters but to apply yourselves thereto with that humble perseverance which is well-pleasing to God, that so you may be able with the greater ease and accuracy to search into the mysteries of the Holy Scriptures. For, as in the sacred pages there are images and tropes and other similar figures, no one can doubt that the quickness with which the reader apprehends the spiritual sense will be proportionate to the extent of his previous instruction in letters. But let the men chosen for this task be such as are both themselves able and willing to learn and eager withal to impart their learning to others. And let the zeal with which the work is done equal the earnestness with which we now ordain it. For we desire that you may be marked, as behooves the soldiers of the Church, within by devotion, and without by wisdom—chaste in your life, learned in your speech—so that if any come to you to call upon the Divine Master, or to behold the excellence of the religious life, they may be not only edified by your aspect when they regard you, but instructed by your wisdom when they hear you read or chant, and may return home rejoicing and giving thanks to God Most High.[5]

It was roughly during Alcuin's time that the phrase *seven liberal arts* came into common usage to describe the curriculum that was taught in many schools at that time. The seven liberal arts consisted of the Trivium (grammar, rhetoric, logic) and the Quadrivium (arithmetic, geometry,

---

5. C. J. B. Gaskoin, *Alcuin, His Life and Work* (London: Cambridge University Press, 1904), pp. 182–184.

music, astronomy). Each of these seven subjects was defined rather broadly so that collectively they constituted a more comprehensive study than today's usage of the term suggests. The phrase *liberal arts* has survived the passage of time and is commonly used in the twentieth century.

In spite of the efforts of a few men such as Charlemagne and Alcuin, very little educational progress was made during the Dark Ages. However, between 1000 and 1300—a period that is frequently referred to as the *Age of the Revival of Learning*—humankind slowly regained a thirst for education. This revival of interest in learning was facilitated by two events: first, the rediscovery of and renewed interest in the writings of some of the ancient philosophers—mainly those of Aristotle; and second, the reconciliation of religion and philosophy. Prior to this time, the church had denounced the study of philosophy as contradictory to the teachings of the church.

The task of harmonizing the doctrines of the church with those of philosophy and education was largely accomplished by Thomas Aquinas (1225–1274), himself a theologian. Aquinas formalized *Scholasticism* (the logical and philosophical study of the beliefs of the church). His most important writing was *Summa Theologica,* which became the doctrinal authority of the Roman Catholic church. The educational and philosophical views of Thomas Aquinas were formalized into the philosophy *Thomism*—a philosophy that has remained important in Roman Catholic parochial education.

The revival of learning resulted in a general increase of educational activity and a growth of educational institutions—including the establishment of medieval universities. These medieval universities, the true forerunners of our modern universities, include: the University of Bologna (1158), which specialized in law; the University of Paris (1180), which specialized in theology; Oxford University (1214), and the University of Salerno (1224). By 1500, approximately eighty universities had been established in Europe.

Although it is generally true that the Middle Ages produced few educational advances in the Western world, we must remember that much of the Eastern world did not go through a "Dark Ages." Mohammed (569–632) led a group of Arabs through northern Africa and into southern Spain. The Eastern learning that the Arabs brought to Spain slowly spread throughout Europe through the writings of such scholars as Avicenna (980–1037) and Averroës (1126–1198). These Eastern contributions to Western knowledge included significant advances in science and mathematics—particularly the Arabic number system.

**Transition Period
(1300–1700)**

Two very important movements took place during the Transition Period —the *Renaissance* and the *Reformation.* The Renaissance represented the protest of individuals against the dogmatic authority exerted by the church over their social and intellectual life. The Renaissance started in

Erasmus possessed a good deal of educational discernment. (*Painting by Hans Holbein; The Bettman Archive*)

Italy (around 1130), when humans reacquired the spirit of free inquiry that had prevailed in ancient Greece. The Renaissance slowly spread throughout Europe, resulting in a general revival of classical learning, called *humanism*. Erasmus (1466–1536) was one of the most famous humanist educators; two of his books, *The Right Method of Instruction* and *The Liberal Education of Boys*, formed a humanistic theory of education.

Erasmus exhibited a good deal of educational insight; concerning the aims of education, he wrote:

The duty of instructing the young includes several elements, the first and also the chief of which is that the tender mind of the child should be instructed in piety; the second, that he love and learn the liberal arts; the third, that he be taught tact in the conduct of social life; and the fourth, that from his earliest age he accustom himself to good behavior, based on moral principles.[6]

His educational maxims indicated that Erasmus possessed a good deal of educational common sense:

> We learn with great willingness from those whom we love; Parents themselves cannot properly bring up their children if they make themselves only to be feared; There are children who would be killed sooner than made better by blows: by mildness and kind admonitions, one may make of them whatever he will; Children will learn to speak their native tongue without any weariness, by usage and practice; Drill in reading and writing is a little bit tiresome, and the teacher will ingeniously palliate the tedium by the artifice of an attractive method; The ancients moulded toothsome dainties into the forms of the letters, and thus, as it were, made children swallow the alphabet; In the matter of grammatical rules, instruction should at the first be limited to the most simple; As the body in infant years is nourished by little portions distributed at intervals, so should the mind of the child be nurtured by items of knowledge adapted to its weakness, and distributed little by little.[7]

The Protestant Reformation had its formal beginning in 1517, when Martin Luther (1483–1546) published his ninety-five theses that stated his disagreement with the Roman Catholic church. One of the disagreements that Luther had with the church held great implications for the importance of formal education: the church had come to feel that it was not necessary for each person to read and interpret the Bible for himself; rather, the church would pass on its interpretation to the laity. Luther not only felt that the church had itself misinterpreted the Bible but also that it was intended that people read and interpret the Bible for themselves. If one accepted the church's position on this matter, formal education remained rather unimportant. However, if one accepted Luther's position, education became necessary for all people so that they might read and interpret the Bible for themselves. In a sense, education became important as a means of obtaining salvation.

It is understandable that Luther and his educational coworker, Melanchthon (1497–1560), soon came to place great stress upon universal elementary education. Melanchthon's most important educational writing was *Visitation Articles* (1528), in which he set forth his recommendations for schools. Luther and Melanchthon felt that education should be provided for all, regardless of class; compulsory for both sexes; state-controlled and state-supported; and centered around classical languages, grammar, mathematics, science, history, music, and physical education.

6. Compayre, *History of Pedagogy,* pp. 88–89.
7. Ibid., p. 89.

Luther's following argument for increased governmental support for education has a familiar twentieth-century ring:

> Each city is subjected to great expense every year for the construction of roads, for fortifying its ramparts, and for buying arms and equipping soldiers. Why should it not spend an equal sum for the support of one or two school-masters? The prosperity of a city does not depend solely on its natural riches, on the solidity of its walls, on the elegance of its mansions, and on the abundance of arms in its arsenals; but the safety and strength of a city reside above all in a good education, which furnishes it with instructed, reasonable, honorable, and well-trained citizens.[8]

In an effort to combat the Reformation movement, Ignatius of Loyola (1491–1556) organized the Society of Jesus (Jesuits) in 1540. The Jesuits worked to establish schools in which to further the cause of the Roman Catholic church and to stem the flow of converts to the Reformation cause. Although the Jesuits' main interest was religious in nature, they soon grew into a great teaching order and were very successful in training their own teachers. The rules by which the Jesuits conducted their schools were stated in the *Ratio Studiorum*. A revised edition of the *Ratio Studiorum* still guides the operation of the Jesuit schools existing today. The improvement of teacher training was the Jesuits' main contribution to education.

Another Catholic teaching order, the Brothers of the Christian Schools, was organized in 1684 by Jean Baptiste de la Salle (1651–1719). Unlike the Jesuits, who were primarily interested in secondary education, de la Salle and his order were interested in elementary schools and in the preparation of elementary school teachers. De la Salle was probably the first educator to make use of student teaching in the preparation of teachers.

There were many other outstanding educators during the Transition Period, including Johann Amos Comenius (1592–1670). Comenius is perhaps best remembered for his many textbooks that were among the first to contain illustrations. Concerning a school that he operated, Comenius wrote: "We pursue a general education, the teaching to all men of all the subjects of human concern."[9] Comenius advocated that an entire system of schools should be created to serve the youth. In this regard, he wrote: "There should be a maternal school in each family; an elementary school in each district; a gymnasium in each city; an academy in each kingdom, or even in each considerable province."[10]

The invention and improvement of printing during the 1400s made it possible to produce books, such as those of Comenius, more rapidly and economically—a development that was essential to the growth of edu-

8. Ibid., p. 115.
9. Ibid., p. 128.
10. Ibid.

cation. Much of the writing of Comenius reflected the increasing interest in science that was taking place at that time.

Modern Period (1700–present) Two movements took place during the early Modern Period that greatly influenced the development of education. The first of these movements was a revolt of the intellectuals against the superstition and ignorance that dominated people's lives at that time. This movement has been called the *Age of Reason*. François Marie Arouet, who wrote under the name of Voltaire, was one of the leaders of this revolt. Those who joined in this movement became known as *rationalists* because of the faith they placed in human rational power. The implication for education in the rationalist's movements is obvious: if one places greater emphasis upon human ability to reason, then education takes on new importance as the means by which humans develop this power.

The second movement of the early Modern Period that affected education was the *emergence of common man*. Whereas the Age of Reason was a revolt of the learned for intellectual freedom, the "emergence of common man" was a revolt of common people for a better life—politically, economically, socially, and educationally. One of the leaders in this movement was Jean Jacques Rousseau (1712–1778), whose *Social Contract* (1762) became an influential book in the French Revolution. It has been suggested that the *Social Contract* was also the basal doctrine of the American Declaration of Independence.[11] Rousseau was a philosopher, not an educator, but he wrote a good deal on the subject of education. His most important educational work was *Émile* (1762), in which he states his views concerning the ideal education for youth. Rousseau felt that the aim of education should be to return man to his "natural state." His view on the subject is well summed up by the opening sentence of *Émile:* "Everything is good as it comes from the hand of the author of nature; but everything degenerates in the hands of man." Rousseau's educational views came to be known as *naturalism*. Concerning the best method of teaching, Rousseau wrote:

> Do not treat the child to discourses which he cannot understand. No descriptions, no eloquence, no figures of speech. Be content to present to him appropriate objects. Let us transform our sensations into ideas. But let us not jump at once from sensible objects to intellectual objects. Let us always proceed slowly from one sensible notion to another. In general, let us never substitute the sign for the thing, except when it is impossible for us to show the thing . . . I have no love whatever for explanations and talk. Things! Things! I shall never tire of saying that we ascribe too much importance to words. With our babbling education we make only babblers.[12]

Rousseau's most important contributions to education were his belief that education must be a natural, not an artificial, process and his com-

11. Paul Monroe, *History of Education* (New York: Macmillan, 1905), p. 283.
12. Compayre, *History of Pedagogy*, p. 299.

passionate, positive view of the child. Rousseau believed that children were inherently good—a belief that was in opposition to the prevailing religiously inspired belief that children were born full of sin. The contrasting implications for teaching methods suggested by these two views of children are self-evident, as is the educational desirability of Rousseau's view over that which prevailed at the time. Although Rousseau never taught a day of school in his life, he did more to improve education through his writing than anyone else of his time.

Johann Heinrich Pestalozzi (1746–1827) was a Swiss educator who put Rousseau's theory into practice. Pestalozzi established two schools for boys, one at Burgdorf (1800–1804) and the other at Yverdun (1805–1825). Educators came from all over the world to view Pestalozzi's schools and to study his teaching methods. Pestalozzi enumerated his educational views in a book entitled *Leonard and Gertrude* (1781–1785). Unlike most educators of his time, Pestalozzi believed that a teacher should treat students with love and kindness:

> I was convinced that my heart would change the condition of my children just as promptly as the sun of spring would reanimate the earth benumbed by the winter. . . . It was necessary that my children should observe, from dawn to evening, at every moment of the day, upon my brow and on my lips, that my affections were fixed on them, that their happiness was my happiness, and that their pleasures were my pleasures. . . .
>
> I was everything to my children. I was alone with them from morning till night. . . . Their hands were in my hands. Their eyes were fixed on my eyes.[13]

Key concepts in the Pestalozzian method included an expression of love, understanding, and patience for children; a compassion for the poor; and the use of objects and sense perception as the basis for acquiring knowledge.

One of the educators who studied under and was influenced by Pestalozzi was Johann Friedrich Herbart (1776–1841). While Pestalozzi had successfully put into practice and further developed Rousseau's educational ideas, it remained for Herbart to organize these educational views into a formalized psychology of education. Herbart's educational psychology stressed *apperception* (learning by association). The Herbartian teaching method developed into five formal steps: (1) preparation—preparing the student to receive a new idea, (2) presentation—presenting the student with the new idea, (3) association—assimilating the new idea with old ideas, (4) generalization—the general idea emerging out of the combination of the old and new ideas, and (5) application—applying the new knowledge. Herbart's educational ideas are contained in his *Science of Education* (1806) and *Outlines of Educational Doctrine* (1835).

Friedrich Froebel (1782–1852) was another European educator who

13. Ibid., p. 425.

TEACHER	Materials adapted for children	Attention to individual differences	Discipline based on love and interest	Personal bond with pupil	Analysis of abilities	Classification of pupils	Education to be fun	Development of both mind and body	Education as guidance of native abilities	Education as a science	Emphasis upon moral growth
Socrates				✓				✓			✓
Quintilian		✓	✓	✓	✓	✓		✓	✓		✓
Origen		✓	✓	✓	✓	✓					✓
Ausonius				✓				✓			
Jerome	✓			✓					✓		✓
Alcuin	✓	✓	✓	✓	✓				✓		
Abélard				✓			✓				
Vittorino	✓	✓	✓	✓	✓	✓		✓	✓		✓
Melanchthon		✓	✓	✓							✓
Ascham		✓	✓	✓	✓	✓		✓	✓		
Mulcaster		✓			✓	✓		✓	✓	✓	
Loyola		✓	✓		✓	✓		✓	✓	✓	✓
Comenius	✓	✓	✓		✓	✓		✓	✓	✓	✓
De la Salle		✓	✓	✓					✓		✓
Francke		✓	✓	✓				✓	✓		✓
Basedow	✓	✓		✓			✓	✓	✓	✓	✓
Pestalozzi	✓	✓	✓	✓	✓	✓	✓	✓	✓	✓	✓
Herbart				✓	✓	✓				✓	✓
Froebel	✓	✓	✓	✓			✓	✓	✓		✓
Seguin	✓	✓		✓	✓	✓		✓		✓	
Binet	✓	✓			✓	✓				✓	
Montessori	✓	✓	✓	✓	✓	✓	✓	✓	✓	✓	✓

Figure 13–1. Fundamental ideas about education.

Source: From *A History of Education: Socrates to Montessori* by Luella Cole, Ph.D., p. 637. Copyright © 1950 by Holt, Rinehart and Winston, Inc. Reprinted by permission of Holt, Rinehart and Winston.

was influenced by Rousseau and Pestalozzi and who made a sizable contribution to education. Froebel's contributions to education included: the establishment of the first kindergarten (or *Kleinkinder-beschäftigungsanstalt,* as he first called it in 1837), an emphasis upon social development, a concern for the cultivation of creativity, and the concept of learning by doing. He originated the idea that women are best suited to teach younger children. Froebel wrote his main educational book, *Education of Man,* in 1826.

Two developments in the last half of the nineteenth century were the last major European antecedents of American education. These were the maturing of the scientific movement, hastened by the publication of Charles Darwin's *Origin of Species* (1859), and the formalizing of educational psychology near the end of the century.

It is important for the student of educational history to realize that even though considerable educational advances had been made by 1900, the average European received a pathetically small amount of formal education—even at that late date. Historically education had been available only for the few who were fortunate enough to be born into the leisure class. Historically the masses of people in the working class had received little or no education up until that time. What little formal education the working person might have received was usually provided by the church for religious purposes.

Figure 13–1 lists some of the great European educators and indicates their views on a number of fundamental ideas concerning education.

Summary and Implications

The historical roots of our educational traditions can be traced to Europe. This chapter has attempted to present a brief overview of these antecedents to American education. Individuals mentioned in this survey who have helped to mold Western education include Socrates, Plato, Aristotle, Quintilian, Alcuin, Aquinas, Erasmus, Melanchton, Rousseau, Herbart, and Pestalozzi. These and other educational pioneers labored against overwhelming odds to advance the cause of education. Many of the educational concepts and practices developed by these early educators are still in use today; however, perhaps their greatest contribution was in helping humankind discover and appreciate the potential value of education.

In the next chapter, we will see how the ideas of these early educators were transported and adapted to America.

Discussion Questions

1. What do you believe were the major reasons humans developed the first schools?

2. What were the major differences between the Spartan and the Athenian school systems? Why did these differences exist?

3. What factors contributed to the decline of education between 500 and 1000?

4. What were the strengths and weaknesses of Jean Jacques Rousseau's ideas about children and education?

5. Which early European educators do you believe ultimately had the most influence on American education? Why?

Supplemental Activities

1. Read and discuss Quintilian's *Institutes of Oratory*.
2. Read and discuss Rousseau's *Émile*.
3. Read and discuss Pestalozzi's *How Gertrude Teaches Her Children*.

4. Read and discuss Froebel's *Education of Man*.
5. Read and discuss Herbart's *Science of Education*.

Bibliography

Armytage, W. H. G. "William Byngham: A Medieval Protagonist of the Training of Teachers." *History of Education Journal* 2 (1951): 107–110.

Butts, R. Freeman. *A Cultural History of Western Education*. New York: McGraw-Hill, 1955.

Chambliss, J. J., ed. *Nobility, Tragedy and Naturalism: Education in Ancient Greece*. Minneapolis: Burgess, 1971.

Cole, Luella. *A History of Education—Socrates to Montessori*. New York: Holt, Rinehart and Winston, 1950.

Compayre, Gabriel. *History of Pedagogy*. Translated by W. H. Payne. Boston: D.C. Heath, 1888.

Hillesheim, James W., and Merrill, George D., eds. *Theory and Practice in the History of American Education: A Book of Readings*. Pacific Palisades, Calif.: Goodyear, 1971.

Lucas, Christopher J. *Our Western Educational Heritage*. New York: Macmillan, 1972.

Meyer, Adolphe. *Grandmasters of Educational Thought*. New York: McGraw-Hill, 1975.

CHAPTER 14

History of American Education

Early Colonial Education

THE FIRST PERMANENT EUROPEAN SETTLEMENTS IN NORTH AMERica included Jamestown (1607), Plymouth (1620), Massachusetts Bay (1630), Maryland (1632), Connecticut (1635), and Providence Plantations (1636). The motives that prompted most of these settlers to move to America were religious, economical, and political in nature. Generally these people were not dissatisfied with education in their homelands. It is understandable, then, that nearly all educational practices and educational materials in early colonial America were simply transplanted from the old world.

The religious motive was very strong in colonial America, and it permeated colonial education. It was generally felt that a child should learn to read so that he or she could read the Bible and thus gain salvation. Beyond this, there was no demand for mass education. Since the clergy possessed the ability to read and write and since the ultimate utility of education was to read the Bible, it was logical for the clergy to do much of the teaching.

The early settlement of the East Coast fell into three general colonies: the Southern Colonies, centered in Virginia; the Middle Colonies, centered in New York; and the Northern Colonies, centered in New England.

The Southern Colonies soon came to be made up of large tobacco plantations. Owing to the size of the plantations, people lived far apart; few towns were established until later in the colonial period. There was an immediate need for cheap labor to work on the plantations and, in 1619, only twelve years after Jamestown was settled, the first boatload of slaves was imported from Africa. Other sources of cheap labor for the Southern Colonies included white Europeans from a variety of backgrounds, who purchased passage to the New World by agreeing to serve a lengthy period of indentured servitude upon arrival in the colonies. There soon came to be two very distinct classes of people in the South—a few wealthy landowners and a large mass of laborers, most of whom were slaves. The educational provisions that evolved out of this set of conditions were precisely what one would expect. No one was interested in providing education for the slaves, with the exception of a few missionary groups such as the English Society for the Propagation of the Gospel in Foreign Parts. Such missionary groups attempted to provide some education for slaves as a means to salvation. The wealthy landowners usually hired tutors to teach their children at home. Distances between homes and slow transportation precluded the establishment of centralized schools. When the upper-class children grew old enough to attend college, they were usually sent to well-established schools in Europe.

The people who settled the Middle Colonies came from a variety of national (Dutch, Swedes) and religious (Puritans, Mennonites, Catholics) backgrounds. This situation explains why the Middle Colonies have often been called the "melting pot" of the nation. This diversity of backgrounds made it impossible for those in the Middle Colonies to agree upon a common public school system. Consequently the respective groups established their own parochial schools. A number of children received their education through an apprenticeship while learning a trade from a "master" already in that line of work. Some people even learned the art of schoolteaching through an apprenticeship.

The Northern Colonies were settled mainly by the Puritans. In 1630, approximately one thousand Puritans settled near Boston. Unlike the Southern Colonies, people lived in close proximity to one another in New England. Towns sprang up and soon became the center of political and social life. Shipping ports were established, and an industrial economy developed that demanded a great number of skilled and semiskilled workers—a condition that created a large middle class.

These conditions of common religious views, town life, and a large middle class made it possible for the people to agree upon common public schools. This agreement led to very early educational activity in the Northern Colonies. In fact, in 1642, the General Court of Massachusetts enacted a law that stated:

> This Cot, [Court] taking into consideration the great neglect of many parents & masters in training up their children in learning . . . do hereupon order and decree, that in euery towne y chosen men . . . take account from time to time of all parents and masters, and of their children, concerning their . . . ability to read & understand the principles of religion & the capitall lawes of this country . . .

This law did nothing more than encourage citizens to look after the education of children. However, five years later (1647) another law was enacted in Massachusetts that required towns to provide education for the youth. This law stated:

> It being one chiefe proiect of y ould deluder, Satan, to keepe men from the knowledge of y Scriptures . . . It is therefore orded [ordered], ye evy [every] towneship in this iurisdiction, aft y Lord hath increased y number to 50 houshold, shall then forthw appoint one w [with] in their towne to teach all such children as shall resort to him to write & reade . . . & it is furth ordered y where any towne shall increase to y numb [number] of 100 families or househould, they shall set up a grammar schoole, y m [am] thereof being able to instruct youth so farr as they shall be fited for y university [Harvard] . . .

These Massachusetts school laws of 1642 and 1647 served as models for similar laws soon created in other colonies.

A number of different kinds of elementary schools soon sprang up in the colonies. These included the dame school, which was conducted by a housewife in her home; the writing school, which basically taught the child to write; a variety of parochial schools; and charity or pauper schools taught by missionary groups.

In 1635, a Latin Grammar School was established in Boston—the first permanent school of this type in what is now the United States. This school was established when the people of Boston, which had been settled only five years before, voted "that our brother Philemon Pormont, shal be intreated to become scholemaster, for the teaching and nourtering of children with us." The grammar school was a secondary school, and its function was college preparatory in nature. The grammar school idea spread quickly to other towns. Charlestown opened its first grammar school one year later, in 1636, by contracting William Witherell "to keep a school for a twelve month." Within sixteen years after the Massachusetts Bay Colony was founded, seven or eight towns had Latin grammar schools in operation. These schools, which were transplanted from Europe where similar schools had existed for a long time, were traditional in nature and designed to prepare youngsters for college and "for the service of God, in church and commonwealth."

Harvard was the first colonial college. It was established in 1636 for the purpose of preparing ministers. It may be of interest to note that by 1636 approximately fifty colleges and universities already existed in Central and South America. Other early American colleges included William and Mary (1693), Yale (1701), Princeton (1746), King's College (1754), College of Philadelphia (1755), Brown (1764), Dartmouth (1769), and Queen's College (1770). The curriculum in these early colleges was traditional in nature, with heavy emphasis on theology and the classics. An example of the extent to which the religious motive dominated the colonial colleges may be found in one of the 1642 rules governing Harvard College, which stated: "Let every Student be plainly instructed,

John Harvard bequeathed his library to the college named in his honor. (*Photograph by Daniel S. Brody, Stock, Boston*)

and earnestly pressed to consider well, the maine end of his life and studies is, to know God and Jesus Christ . . .''

The Struggle for Universal Elementary Education

By and large, colonial elementary schools were adaptations of schools that had existed in Europe for many years. When the colonists arrived in this country, they simply established schools similar to those with which they had been familiar in Europe. The objectives of colonial elementary schools were purely religious in nature. It was commonly felt that everyone needed to be able to read the Bible in order to receive salvation, and therefore parents were eager to have their children receive some type of reading instruction.

A good deal of insight into the nature of a colonial elementary school can be gleaned from the following account of a school that was conducted in 1750 by Christopher Dock, a Mennonite school teacher in Pennsylvania:

The children arrive as they do because some have a great distance to school, others a short distance, so that the children cannot assemble as punctually as they can in a city. Therefore, when a few children are present, those who can read their Testament sit together on one bench; but the boys and girls occupy separate benches. They are given a chapter which they read at sight consecutively. Meanwhile I write copies for them. Those who have read their passage of Scripture without error take their places at the table and write. Those who fail have to sit at the end of the bench, and each new arrival the same; as each one is thus released in order he takes up his slate. This process continues until they have all assembled. The last one left on the bench is a "lazy pupil."

When all are together, and examined, whether they are washed and combed, they sing a psalm or a morning hymn, and I sing and pray with them. As much as they can understand of the Lord's Prayer and the Ten Commandments (according to the gift God has given them), I exhort and admonish them accordingly. This much concerning the assembling of pupils. But regarding prayer I will add this additional explanation. Children say the prayers taught them at home half articulately, and too fast, especially the "Our Father" which the Lord Himself taught His disciples and which contains all that we need. I therefore make a practice of saying it for them kneeling, and they kneeling repeat it after me. After these devotional exercises those who can write resume their work. Those who cannot read the Testament have had time during the assemblage to study their lesson. These are heard recite immediately after prayer. Those who know their lesson receive an O on the hand, traced with crayon. This is a mark of excellence. Those who fail more than three times are sent back to study their lesson again. When all the little ones have recited, these are asked again, and any one having failed in more than three trials a second time, is called "Lazy" by the entire class and his name is written down. Whether such a child fears the rod or not, I know from experience that this denunciation of the children hurts more than if I were constantly to wield and flourish the rod. If then such a child has friends in school who are able to instruct him and desire to do so, he will visit more frequently than before. For this reason: if the pupil's name has not been erased before dismissal the pupils are at liberty to write down the names of those who have been lazy, and take them along home. But if the child learns his lesson well in the future, his name is again presented to the other pupils, and they are told that he knew his lesson well and failed in no respect. Then all the pupils call "Diligent" to him. When this has taken place his name is erased from the slate of lazy pupils, and the former transgression is forgiven.

The children who are in the spelling class are daily examined in pronunciation. In spelling, when a word has more than one syllable, they must repeat the whole word, but some, while they can say the letters, cannot pronounce the word, and so cannot be put to reading. For improvement a child must repeat the lesson, and in this way: The child gives me the book, I spell the word and he pronounces it. If he is slow, another pupil pronounces it for him, and in this way he hears how it should be done, and knows that he must follow the letters and not his own fancy.

Concerning A B C pupils, it would be best, having but one child, to let it learn one row of letters at a time, to say forward and backward. But with many, I let them learn the alphabet first, and then ask a child to point out a letter that I name. If a child is backward or ignorant, I ask another, or the whole class, and the first one that points to the right letter, I grasp his finger and hold it until I have put a mark opposite his name. I then ask for another letter, &c. Whichever child has during the day received the greatest number of marks, has pointed out the greatest number of letters. To him I owe something—a flower drawn on paper or a bird. But if several have the same number, we draw lots; this causes less annoyance. In this way not only are the very timid cured of their shyness (which is a great hindrance in learning), but a fondness for school is increased. Thus much in answer to his question, how I take the children into school, how school proceeds before and after prayers, and how the inattentive and careless are made attentive and careful, and how the timid are assisted.[1]

Christopher Dock's comments show the extent to which religion dominated the curriculum of colonial elementary schools. This account also points out that the curriculum of these schools was limited to the basic rudiments and that instructional materials were simple and meager.

In 1805, New York City established the first *monitorial* school in the United States. The monitorial school concept, which originated in England, represented an attempt to provide mass elementary education for large numbers of children. By 1840, nearly all these schools had been closed; the children had not learned enough to justify their existence.

A considerable amount of educational activity took place in the United States between 1820 and 1860: it was an "educational awakening" that was strongly influenced by Horace Mann. As secretary of the state board of education in Massachusetts, Mann helped to establish elementary schools (or common schools as they were then called) in that state. His educational accomplishments were great indeed; among other things, he published one of the very early professional journals in this country—*The Common School Journal*. Through this journal, Mann was able to keep the issue of elementary education before the public.

In 1852, Massachusetts passed a compulsory elementary school attendance law, the first of its kind in the country. Eventually other states passed similar compulsory attendance laws; by 1900, thirty-two states had passed such laws.

Pestalozzianism and Herbartianism made a considerable impact on elementary education when they were introduced into the United States in the latter part of the nineteenth century. Pestalozzianism emphasized that children should be taught with love, patience, and understanding. Furthermore, children should learn from objects and firsthand experiences—not from abstractions and words. Pestalozzian concepts soon spread throughout the country.

Herbartianism was imported into the United States at the Blooming-

1. Paul Monroe, *Source Book of the History of Education* (New York: Macmillan, 1901).

ton Normal School in Illinois by three students who had learned about the ideas of Herbart while studying in Germany. Herbartianism represented an attempt to make a science out of teaching. The system that Herbartianism lent to the poorly trained elementary teacher in the United States was badly needed. Unfortunately Herbartianism eventually contributed to a period of extreme formalism and rigidity that characterized American elementary schools in the early 1900s. This formalization was exemplified by the school administrator who would brag that at a given moment in the school day he or she knew exactly what was going on in all the classrooms. One can infer from this boast that teachers had a very strict and rigid schedule and curriculum imposed upon them. Since then, elementary education in the United States has been characterized by a tremendous growth in enrollment and by a refinement in program.

If we look back at the historical development of American elementary education, it is possible to make the following generalizations.

1.   Until the latter half of the nineteenth century, the motive, curriculum, and administration of elementary education were primarily religious in nature. The point at which elementary education became more secular than religious was the point at which states began to pass compulsory school attendance laws.
2.   Discipline has traditionally been harsh and severe in elementary schools. The classical picture of a colonial schoolmaster equipped with a stern look, dunce cap, stick, whip, and a variety of abusive phrases is a more accurate picture of colonial teachers than one might expect. It is no wonder that children have historically viewed school as an unpleasant place. Pestalozzi had much to do with bringing about a gradual change in discipline when he advocated that love, not harsh punishment, should be used to motivate students.
3.   Elementary education has traditionally been formal and impersonal. The ideas of Rousseau, Pestalozzi, Herbart, and Froebel helped to bring about a gradual change in this condition and make elementary education more "student-centered" about 1900.
4.   Elementary schools have traditionally been taught by poorly prepared teachers. This aspect of the history of education is discussed more fully later in this chapter under "The Preparation of Teachers."
5.   Though the aims and methodology have varied considerably from time to time, the basic content of elementary education has historically been reading, writing, and arithmetic.

The Need for Secondary Schools

The first form of secondary school in the colonies was the *Latin grammar school*, first established in Boston in 1635, only five years after colonists settled in that area. The Latin grammar school was largely concerned with the teaching of Latin and other classical subjects; this type of school was strictly college preparatory in nature, as illustrated by the wording of the "deluder Satan" law enacted in Massachusetts in 1647, previously quoted.

Harvard was the only university in existence in the colonies at that time. The entrance requirements to Harvard stated:

> When any Scholar is able to understand Tully, or such like classicall Latine Author extempore, and make and speake true Latine in Verse and Prose, suo ut aiunt marte; and decline perfectly the Paradigms of Nounes and Verbes in the Greek tongue: let him then, and not before, be capable of admission into the college.

European colleges and later colonial colleges also demanded that students know Latin and Greek before they could be admitted. For instance, in the mid-eighteenth century, the requirements for admission to Yale stated:

> None may expect to be admitted into this College unless upon Examination of the President and Tutors, they shall be found able Extempore to Read, Construe, and Parce Tully, Vergil and the Greek Testament; and to write true Latin in Prose and to understand the Rules of Prosodia, and Common Arithmetic, and Shal bring Sufficient Testimony of his Blameless and inoffensive Life.

With college entrance requirements such as these, and since Latin grammar schools were designed to prepare students for college, it is little wonder that the curriculum in these schools was so classical and traditional. Needless to say, a very small percentage of children attended the Latin grammar school because very few were interested in attending college. As late as 1785, there were only two Latin grammar schools existing in Boston, and the combined enrollment in these two schools was only sixty-four boys. Girls did not attend Latin grammar schools simply because colleges at that time did not admit girls; inasmuch as colleges existed largely to prepare ministers, it is understandable that they did not admit girls.

By the middle of the eighteenth century, there was a considerable need for more and better-trained skilled workers. Recognizing this need, Benjamin Franklin proposed a new kind of secondary school in Pennsylvania. This proposal resulted in the establishment of the first truly American educational institution—the American Academy. Benjamin Franklin established this school in Philadelphia in 1751 because he thought that the existing Latin grammar schools were not providing the practical secondary education needed by youth at that time. The philosophy, curriculum, and methodology of Franklin's academy were well explained in his proposal. Similar academies were established throughout America, and these institutions eventually replaced the Latin grammar school as the predominant secondary education institution in this country. These were usually private schools, and many of them admitted girls as well as boys. Later on, some academies even made an attempt to train elementary school teachers.

In 1821, a school that three years later changed its name to English High School was opened in Boston, and another distinctively American educational institution was launched. This first high school, under the direction of George B. Emerson, consisted of a three-year course in English, mathematics, science, and history. The school later added to its curriculum philosophy of history, chemistry, intellectual philosophy, linear drawing, logic, trigonometry, French, and United States Constitution. The school enrolled about one hundred boys during its first year.

The high school was established because of a feeling that the existing grammar schools were inadequate for the day and because most people could not afford to send their children to the private academies. The American high school soon replaced both the Latin grammar school and the private academy and has been with us ever since. Today there are approximately 31,000 high schools in the United States.

In about 1910, the first junior high schools were established in the United States. In 1916, a survey showed that there were fifty-four junior high schools existing in thirty-six states. One year later a survey indicated that the number had increased to about 270. Today junior high schools are a common part of the American school system. Recently some school systems have abandoned the junior high school in favor of what is being called *middle school,* which usually consists of grades six, seven, and eight. The evolution of the American secondary school is presented schematically in Figure 14–1.

The Aims of American Public Education

The aims and objectives of American public education have gradually changed over the years. During colonial times, the overriding aim of education at all levels was to enable students to read and understand the Bible, to gain salvation, and to spread the gospel. Almost all historical documents that have been preserved since colonial days reveal the dominance of the religious motive in education at that time.

After independence was won from England, the main goal of American education became that of unifying into a nation the multitude of immigrants who had so many different cultural backgrounds. This is not to say that the religious motive in American schools did not remain strong. Educational objectives such as providing Americans with a common language, attempting to instill a sense of patriotism, developing a national feeling of unity and common purpose, and providing the technical and agricultural training that our developing nation needed became important tasks for the schools.

In 1892, a committee was established by the National Education Association to study the function of the American high school. This committee, known as the *Committee of Ten,* made an effort to set down the aims and purposes of the high school at that time. This committee made

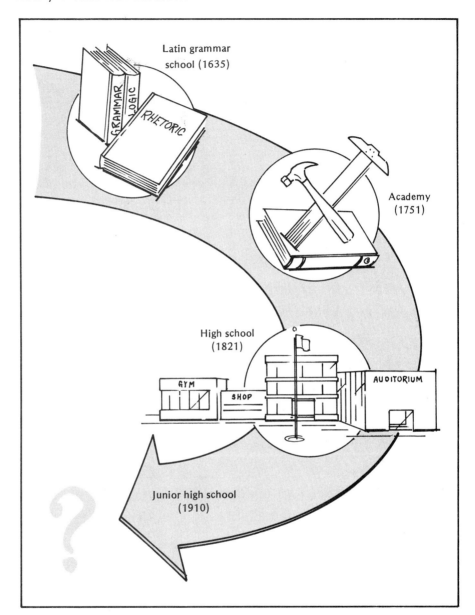

Figure 14–1.
Evolution of the
American second-
ary school.

the following recommendations for high schools at the turn of the century.

- High school should consist of grades seven through twelve.
- Courses should be arranged in sequential order.
- Students should be given very few electives in high school.
- One unit, called a Carnegie Unit, should be awarded for each separate course that a student takes each year, providing that course meets four or five times each week all year long.

The Committee of Ten also recommended that an effort be made to graduate high school students earlier to permit them to attend college sooner. At that time the inference from this recommendation was that high schools have a college preparatory function.

Before the turn of the century, teachers had relatively little direction in their work because most educational aims and goals were not stated in precise terms. This problem was partly overcome in 1918, when the Commission on Reorganization of Secondary Education published a report under the title "Cardinal Principles of Secondary Education"; these are usually referred to as the *Seven Cardinal Principles*. In reality, the latter constitute only one section of the basic principles discussed in the original text, but it is the part that has become most famous. These principles stated that the student should receive an education in the following areas:

1. Health
2. Command of Fundamental Processes
3. Worthy Home Membership
4. Vocation
5. Civic Education
6. Worthy Use of Leisure
7. Ethical Character

In 1920, the Committee on Standards for Use in the Reorganization of Secondary School Curricula stated that the ultimate objectives of American secondary education were as follows:

1. To maintain health and physical fitness
2. To use leisure in right ways
3. To sustain successfully certain definite social relationships, civic, domestic, and community
4. To engage in vocational and exploratory vocational activities

The American Youth Commission, in 1937, stated that the objectives of secondary education in modern America were to promote adequacy in the following six areas:

1. Citizenship
2. Home membership
3. Leisure life
4. Physical and mental health
5. Vocational efficiency
6. Preparation for continued learning

The following goals of education were listed by the Progressive Education Association in 1938; these "needs of youth" grew out of the Eight Year Study:

1. Physical and mental health
2. Self-assurance

3. Assurance of growth toward adult status
4. Philosophy of life
5. Wide range of personal interests
6. Esthetic appreciations
7. Intelligent self-direction
8. Progress toward maturity in social relations with age mates and adults
9. Wise use of goods and services
10. Vocational orientation
11. Vocational competence

Also in 1938, another attempt was made to set down the goals of American education when the Educational Policies Commission of the National Education Association (NEA) set forth the "Purposes of Education in American Democracy." These objectives stated that students should receive an education in the following areas:

THE OBJECTIVES OF SELF-REALIZATION

The Inquiring Mind.   The educated person has an appetite for learning.
Speech.   The educated person can speak the mother tongue clearly.
Reading.   The educated person reads the mother tongue efficiently.
Writing.   The educated person writes the mother tongue effectively.
Number.   The educated person solves problems of counting and calculating.
Sight and Hearing.   The educated person is skilled in listening and observing.
Health and Knowledge.   The educated person understands the basic facts concerning health and disease.
Health Habits.   The educated person protects his own health and that of his dependents.
Public Health.   The educated person works to improve the health of the community.
Recreation.   The educated person is participant and spectator in many sports and other pastimes.
Intellectual Interests.   The educated person has mental resources for the use of leisure.
Esthetic Interests.   The educated person appreciates beauty.
Character.   The educated person gives responsible direction to his own life.

THE OBJECTIVES OF HUMAN RELATIONSHIPS

Respect for Humanity.   The educated person puts human relationships first.
Friendships.   The educated person enjoys the rich, sincere, and varied social life.
Cooperation.   The educated person can work and play with others.
Courtesy.   The educated person observes the amenities of social behavior.

Appreciation of the Home.   The educated person appreciates the family as a social institution.

Conservation of the Home.   The educated person conserves family ideals.

Homemaking.   The educated person is skilled in homemaking.

Democracy in the Home. The educated person maintains democratic family relations.

THE OBJECTIVES OF ECONOMIC EFFICIENCY

Work.   The educated producer knows the satisfaction of good workmanship.

Occupational Information.   The educated producer understands the requirements and opportunities for various jobs.

Occupational Choice.   The educated person has selected his occupation.

Occupational Efficiency.   The educated producer succeeds in his chosen vocation.

Occupational Adjustment.   The educated producer maintains and improves his own efficiency.

Occupational Appreciation.   The educated producer appreciates the social value of his work.

Personal Economics.   The educated consumer plans the economics of his own life.

Consumer Judgment.   The educated consumer develops standards for guiding his expenditures.

Efficiency in Buying. The educated consumer is an informed and skillful buyer.

Consumer Protection.   The educated consumer takes appropriate measures to safeguard his interests.

THE OBJECTIVES OF CIVIC RESPONSIBILITY

Social Justice.   The educated citizen is sensitive to the disparities of human circumstance.

Social Activity.   The educated citizen acts to correct unsatisfactory conditions.

Social Understanding.   The educated citizen seeks to understand social structure and social processes.

Critical Judgment.   The educated citizen has defenses against propaganda.

Tolerance.   The educated citizen respects honest differences of opinion.

Conservation.   The educated citizen has a regard for the nation's resources.

Social Application of Science.   The educated citizen measures scientific advance by its contribution to the general welfare.

World Citizenship.   The educated citizen is a cooperating member of the world community.

Law Observance.   The educated citizen respects the law.

Economic Literacy.   The educated citizen is economically literate.

Political Citizenship.   The educated citizen acts upon an unswerving loyalty to democratic ideals.

In 1944, this same commission of the NEA published another statement of educational objectives, entitled "Education for All American Youth":

Schools should be dedicated to the proposition that every youth in these United States—regardless of sex, economic status, geographic location, or race—should experience a broad and balanced education which will:

1. equip him to enter an occupation suited to his abilities and offering reasonable opportunity for personal growth and social usefulness;
2. prepare him to assume full responsibilities of American citizenship;
3. give him a fair chance to exercise his right to the pursuit of happiness through the attainment and preservation of mental and physical health;
4. stimulate intellectual curiosity, engender satisfaction in intellectual achievement, and cultivate the ability to think rationally; and
5. help to develop an appreciation of the ethical values which should undergird all life in a democratic society.

In 1952, the Educational Policies Commission made yet another statement of educational objectives entitled the "Imperative Needs of Youth":

1. All youth need to develop salable skills and those understandings and attitudes that make the worker an intelligent productive participant in economic life. To this end most youth need supervised work experience as well as education in the skills and knowledge of their occupations.
2. All youth need to develop and maintain good health and physical fitness.
3. All youth need to understand the rights and duties of the citizen of a democratic society, and to be diligent and competent in the performance of their obligations as members of the community and citizens of the state and nation.
4. All youth need to understand the significance of the family for the individual and society and the conditions conducive to successful family life.
5. All youth need to know how to purchase and use goods and services intelligently, understanding both the values received by the consumer and the economic consequences of their acts.
6. All youth need to understand the methods of science, the influence of science on human life, and the main scientific facts concerning the nature of the world and of man.
7. All youth need opportunities to develop their capacities to appreciate beauty in literature, art, music, and nature.
8. All youth need to be able to use their leisure time well and budget it wisely, balancing activities that yield satisfactions to the individual with those that are socially useful.
9. All youth need to develop respect for other persons, to grow in their insight into ethical values and principles, and to be able to live and work cooperatively with others.

10. All youth need to grow in their ability to think rationally, to express their thoughts clearly, and to read and listen with understanding.

A recent White House Conference on Education concluded that American youth need an education that will develop the following traits:

1. Fundamental skills of communication, arithmetic, and mathematics
2. Appreciation for our democratic heritage
3. Civic rights and responsibilities
4. Respect and appreciation for human values
5. Ability to think and evaluate constructively
6. Effective work habits and self-discipline
7. Social competency
8. Ethical behavior
9. Intellectual curiosity
10. Esthetic appreciation
11. Physical and mental health
12. Wise use of time
13. Understanding of the physical world
14. Awareness of our relationship with the world community

These various statements concerning education objectives, made over the last century, sum up fairly well the history of the aims of American public education.

The Preparation of Teachers

One of the very first forms of teacher training grew out of the medieval guild system in which a young man who wished to enter a certain field of work would serve a lengthy period of apprenticeship with a master already in that line of work. Some young men became teachers by serving as an apprentice, sometimes for as long as seven years, to a master teacher.

The first teacher-training school of which there is any record was that mentioned in the following request to the king of England written by William Byngham in 1438:

Beseecheth ful mekely your poure preest and continuell bedeman William Byngham person of seint John zacharie of london, unto your souerain grace to be remembred how that he hath diuerse tymes sued unti your highnesse showyng and declaryng by bille how gretely the clergie of this youre Reaume, by the which all wysdom konnyng and gouernaunce standeth in, is like to be empeired and febled by the defaute and lak of Scholemaistres of Gramar, In so moche that as your seid poure besecher hath founde of late ouer the Est partie of the way ledyng from hampton to couentre and so fourth no ferther North ahan Rypon. ixx scoles voide or mo that weren occupied all at ones within .1. yeres passed bicause that there is so great scarstee of maistres of Gramar where of as now ben almost none nor none mower be hade in your Universitees ouer those that nedes most ben occupied still there: Wherfore please it unto your most souerain highnesse **and** plenteuous grace to considre how that for all liberall sciences used in you said Universitees certain lyflode is ordeyned and endued savying onely for gramar the which is rote and grounde of all the seid other sciences: And there upon graciously to graunte license to your forsaid besecher that he may yeve withouten fyn or fee (the) mansion ycalled Goddeshous the which he hath made and edified in your towne of Cambridge for the free herbigage of poure scolers of Gramer. . . .[2]

Byngham received this permission and established Godshouse College on 13 June 1439. Students at this college were required to give demonstration lectures to their fellow students as a rough form of practice teaching. Classes were even conducted during vacations so that country schoolmasters could attend. Byngham's college still exists today as Christ's College. It is interesting to find that, at the early date of 1439, Byngham made provision for two features still considered very important in teacher education today—namely, the scheduling of classes so that teachers in service may attend and the provision of some type of student teaching experience. Many contemporary educators would be surprised to find that these concepts have such a long history.

Teachers in colonial America were very poorly prepared to be educators. More often than not they had received no special training at all. The single qualification of most colonial school teachers was that they themselves had been students. Most colonial college teachers, private tutors, Latin grammar school teachers, and academy teachers had received some type of college education, usually obtained at one of the well-established colleges or universities in Europe. However, some of the teachers received their education at a colonial American college. Teachers in the various types of colonial elementary schools typically had only an elementary education, but a small minority had attended a Latin grammar school or private academy. It was commonly felt that to be a teacher required only that the instructor know something about the subject matter to be taught; consequently no teacher, regardless of the level taught, received training in the methodology of teaching.

Teaching was not looked upon as a very prestigious occupation. The pay was poor, and consequently many school teachers viewed their job as temporary employment until something better came along. For young ladies who taught elementary school, the "something better" was usually marriage. Men frequently left teaching for careers in the ministry or business. It was not uncommon to find career teachers in the colonies who were really quite undesirable people. Records show that many teachers lost their jobs because they paid "more attention to the tavern than to the school," or for stealing or swearing or for other conduct unbecoming a person in such a position.

---

2. W. H. G. Armytage, "William Byngham: A Medieval Protagonist of the Training of Teachers," *History of Education Journal* II (summer 1951): 108.

In its more rural past, the American elementary school was often run by one teacher who taught every age level. (*Photograph courtesy of the Library of Congress*)

Since many colonial schools were conducted in connection with a church, the teacher was often viewed as an assistant to the minister. In addition to teaching school, duties of some early New England teachers included, "to act as court messenger, to serve summonses, to conduct certain ceremonial services of the church, to lead the Sunday choir, to ring the bell for public worship, to dig the graves, to perform other occasional duties."

It was not uncommon in the colonies to use white indentured servants as teachers: many of the people who came to America purchased their passage by agreeing to work for a number of years as an indentured servant. The ship's captain would then sell the indentured servant's services, more often than not, by placing an ad in a newspaper. Such an ad appeared in a May 1786 edition of the *Maryland Gazette:*

Men and Women Servants
JUST ARRIVED

In the Ship *Paca*, Robert Caulfield, Master, in five Weeks from Belfast and Cork, a number of healthy Men and Women SERVANTS.

Among them are several valuable tradesmen, *viz.*

Carpenters, Shoemakers, Coopers, Blacksmiths, Staymakers, Bookbinders, Clothiers, Diers, Butchers, Schoolmasters, Millrights, and Labourers.

Their indentures are to be disposed of by the Subscribers,

Brown, and Maris,
William Wilson

Some colonial teachers learned the art of schoolkeeping by serving as an apprentice to a schoolmaster. Court records reveal a number of such indentures of apprenticeship as does the following, recorded in New York City in 1772:

This Indenture witnesseth that John Campbel Son of Robert Campbel of the City of New York with the Consent of his father and mother hath put himself and by these presents doth Voluntarily put and bind himself Apprentice to George Brownell of the Same City Schoolmaster to learn the Art Trade or Mastery—for and during the term of ten years . . . And the said George Brownell Doth hereby Covenent and Promise to teach and Instruct or Cause the said Apprentice to be taught and Instructed in the Art Trade or Calling of a Schoolmaster by the best way or means he or his wife may or can.

Benjamin Franklin, as noted earlier, proposed that an academy be established in Philadelphia. One of the justifications that Franklin had for such a school was that some of the graduates would make good teachers. Speculating on the need for graduates of such a school, Franklin wrote:

a number of the poorer sort [of academy graduates] will be hereby qualified to act as Schoolmasters in the Country, to teach children Reading, Writing, Arithmetic, and the Grammar of their Mother Tongue, and being of good morals and known character, may be recommended from the Academy to Country Schools for that purpose; the Country suffering at present very much for want of good Schoolmasters, and obliged frequently to employ in their Schools, vicious imported Servants, or concealed Papists, who by their bad Examples and Instructions often deprave the Morals and corrupt the Principles of the children under their Care.

That Franklin recommended that some of the "poorer" graduates would make suitable teachers reflects the low regard for teaching typical of the time. The academy that Franklin proposed was established in 1751 in Philadelphia, and many graduates of academies after that time did become teachers.

A number of educators had recognized this country's need for better-qualified teachers prior to the nineteenth century; it was not until 1823, however, that the first teacher-training institution was established in the United States. This private school, called a *normal school* after its counterpart in Europe, which had existed since the late seventeenth century, was established by the Rev. Mr. Samuel Hall in Concord, Vermont. Hall's school did not produce many teachers, but it did signal the beginning of formal teacher training in the United States.

The early normal school program usually consisted of a two-year course. Students would typically enter the normal school right after finishing elementary school. Most normal schools did not require high school graduation for entrance until about 1900. The curriculum was rather similar to the curriculum of the high schools existing at that time. Students would review the subjects they had studied in elementary school, study high school subjects, have a course in teaching or *pedagogy* as it was then called, and do some student teaching in a model school that was usually operated in conjunction with the normal school. The subjects offered by a normal school located in Albany, New York, in 1845, included English grammar, English composition, history, geography, reading, writing, orthography, arithmetic, algebra, geometry, trigonometry, human physiology, surveying, natural philosophy, chemistry, intellectual philosophy, moral philosophy, government, rhetoric, theory and practice of teaching, drawing, music, astronomy, and practice teaching.

Some states did not establish state-supported normal schools until the early 1900s. The dates when the various states accomplished this task are presented in Table 14–1. To a degree, this table also indicates the order in which each state decided that education was important—important enough to spend tax money to train better teachers.

During the early part of this century, a number of factors served to bring about a significant change in normal schools. For one thing, as the population of the United States increased, so did the enrollment in elementary schools; an ever-increasing demand for elementary teachers was thereby created. As more and more people attended high school, a demand was created for a greater number of high school teachers. To meet this demand, normal schools eventually expanded their curricula to include secondary teacher education. The establishment of high schools also created a need for teachers who were highly specialized in particular academic areas. To prepare such secondary teachers, normal schools established subject matter departments and developed more diversified programs with many courses in various academic areas. Then, too, the length of the teacher-education program expanded to two, three, and finally four years; this expansion helped to expand and diversify the normal school curriculum. The demand for teachers increased from about 20,000 in 1900 to more than 200,000 in 1930. Another factor that contributed to the growth of the

Table 14–1. Date of the establishment of the first state normal school in each state.

Massachusetts	1839	Texas	1879
New York	1844	North Dakota	1881
Connecticut	1849	South Dakota	1881
Michigan	1849	Oregon	1883
Rhode Island	1852	Virginia	1884
Iowa	1855	Louisiana	1884
New Jersey	1855	Arizona	1885
Illinois	1857	Wyoming	1886
Minnesota	1858	Florida	1887
Pennsylvania	1859	Nevada	1887
California	1862	Colorado	1889
Kansas	1863	Georgia	1889
Maine	1863	Washington	1890
Indiana	1865	Oklahoma	1891
Wisconsin	1865	Idaho	1893
Vermont	1866	Montana	1893
Delaware	1866	New Mexico	1893
Nebraska	1867	South Carolina	1895
West Virginia	1867	Maryland	1896
Utah	1869	Ohio	1900
Missouri	1870	Kentucky	1906
New Hampshire	1870	Alabama	1907
Arkansas	1872	Tennessee	1909
North Carolina	1876	Mississippi	1910

normal schools was that the United States had advanced technologically to the point at which there was a need for more and more college-educated citizens. The normal schools assumed the responsibility for helping to meet this need by establishing a number of academic programs in addition to teacher training. As normal schools increased their programs to four years and began granting baccalaureate degrees, they also changed their names to *state teachers' colleges*. For most institutions, the change in name took place during the 1930s.

Universities entered the teacher-preparing business on a large scale about 1900. Prior to that time, some of the graduates of universities had become high school teachers or college teachers; however, it was not until the turn of this century that universities established departments of education and added teacher education to their curricula.

Just as the normal schools expanded in size, scope, and function (during the 1920s) to the point at which they became state teachers' colleges, so did the state teachers' colleges expand in size, scope, and function to the point at which they became state colleges. This change in name and scope took place for most such institutions about 1950. The elimination of the word "teacher" from the name of these institutions really explains the story behind this transition. It was not that the new state college was no longer interested in the preparation of teachers; rather, this new institution was not interested *only* in teacher education. The state college became a new, multipurpose institution that combined teacher education, liberal arts, and graduate programs. One of the major reasons that this transition took place was that more and more students were coming to the colleges demanding a more varied education. The state teachers' colleges developed a more diversified program in an attempt to meet these demands. Many of these same state colleges have already evolved into state universities, some of which offer doctoral degrees in a wide variety of areas.

Figure 14–2 provides a reflective view of the evolution of American teacher-preparation institutions. If we look back on the history of teacher education, it becomes obvious that the establishment of the teaching profession has been a long and difficult task. A great many improvements have been made in the preparation of teachers from colonial times—when anyone could be a teacher—up to the present

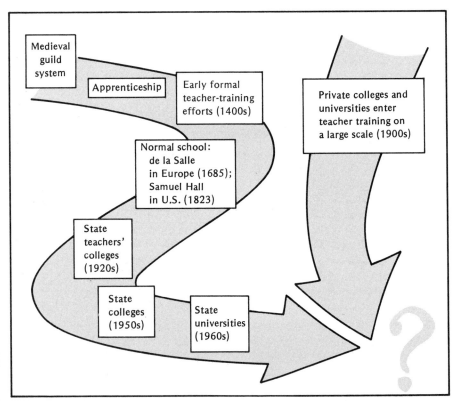

Figure 14–2.
Evolution of
teacher-preparation
institutions.

time when a number of states require five years of college training for permanent certification. Today approximately one-third of the high school teachers in the United States possess masters' degrees.

The Evolution of Teaching Materials

The first schools in colonial America were very poorly equipped. In fact, the first elementary schools were usually conducted by a housewife right in her home. The only teaching materials likely to be found in these early schools were a Bible or perhaps one or two other religious books, a small amount of scarce paper, a few quill pens, and *hornbooks*. The hornbook was the most commonly used teaching device in early colonial schools (Figure 14–3). While hornbooks differed widely from one another, many of them had a small hole in the handle of the paddle through which a leather cord was looped so that a student could hang the hornbook around his neck. Hornbooks provided the student with his first reading instruction. Records indicate that hornbooks were used in the Middle Ages in Europe and were commonly used until about 1760.

The first real textbook to be used in colonial elementary schools was the *New England Primer*. Records show that the first copies of this book

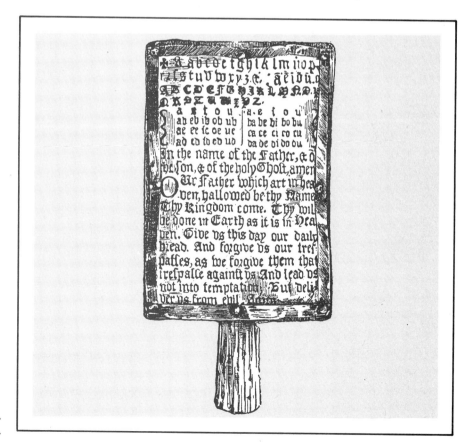

Figure 14–3.
A hornbook.

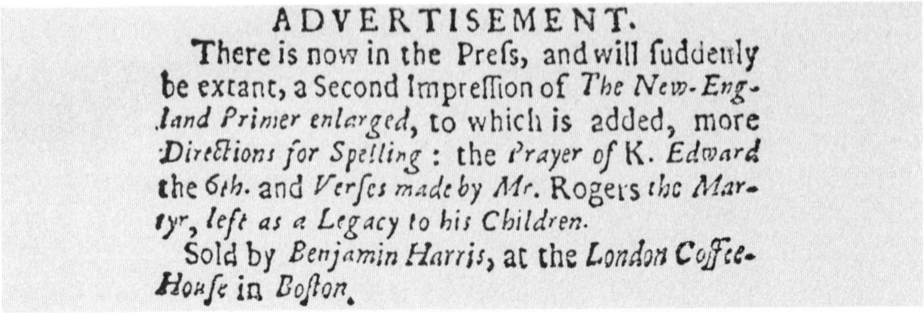

Figure 14–4.
Advertisement
from 1690
publication.

ADVERTISEMENT.
There is now in the Prefs, and will fuddenly
be extant, a Second Impreffion of *The New-Eng-
land Primer enlarged*, to which is added, more
Directions for Spelling : the *Prayer* of K. *Edward*
the *6th*. and *Verfes made* by *Mr.* Rogers *the Martyr*, *left as a Legacy to his Children*.
Sold by *Benjamin Harris*, at the *London Coffee-
Houfe in Bofton*.

were printed in England in the late 1600s. Copies of the *New England Primer* were also printed as early as 1690 in the American colonies. The book was advertised in the *News from the Stars Almanac*, published in 1690 in Boston (see Figure 14–4). The oldest extant copy of a *New England Primer* is a 1727 edition that is now in the Lenox Collection of the New York Public Library.

The *New England Primer* was a small book, usually about 2½ by 4½ inches, with thin wooden covers covered by paper or leather. It was from fifty to one hundred pages in length, depending upon how many extra sections were added to each edition. The first pages contained the alphabet, vowels, and capital letters. Next came lists of words arranged from two to six syllables, followed by verses and tiny woodcut pictures for each letter in the alphabet. A reproduction of such verses and pictures is presented in Figure 14–5. The contents of the *New England Primer* reflected the heavy religious motive in colonial education.

The primer was virtually the only reading book used in colonial schools until about 1800, when Noah Webster published *The American Spelling Book*, which eventually replaced the *New England Primer* as the most commonly used elementary textbook. This speller reportedly sold over 24,000,000 copies, and its royalties supported Noah Webster and his family while he prepared his dictionary. The book was approximately 4 by 6½ inches in size; its cover was made of thin sheets of wood covered with light blue paper. The first part of the book contained rules and instructions for the use of the book; next came the alphabet, syllables, and consonants. The bulk of the book was taken up with lists of words arranged according to syllables and sounds. The book also contained rules for reading and speaking, moral advice, and stories of various sorts. The book was about 160 pages long; Figure 14–6 shows a page from a *Blue-Backed Speller* printed about 1800.

There were a very limited number of textbooks available for use in colonial Latin grammar schools, academies, and colleges. Various religious books including the Bible were commonly used in these schools. A small number of books dealing with history, geography, arithmetic,

In Adam's Fall
We finned all.

Thy Life to mend,
This Book attend.

The Cat doth play,
And after flay.

A Dog will bite
A Thief at Night.

An Eagle' flight
Is out of fight.

The idle Fool
Is whipt at SchooL

Figure 14–5.
New England Primer.

Latin, Greek, and certain of the classics were available for use in colonial secondary schools and colleges during the eighteenth century. Harvard College had a rather large library for its day because John Harvard, its benefactor, bequeathed his entire library of 400 volumes to the school.

By 1800, nearly 200 years after the establishment of the colonies, school buildings and teaching materials were still very crude and meager. Some understanding of the physical features and equipment of an 1810 New England school can be obtained from the following description by a teacher of that school:

(A) The School Building: The school house stood near the center of the district, at the junction of four roads, so near the usual track of carriages that a large stone was set up at the end of the building to defend it from injury. Except in the dry season the ground was wet, and the soil by no means firm. The spot was particularly exposed to the bleak winds of winter; nor were there any shade trees to shelter the children from the scorching rays of the summer's sun, as they were cut down many years ago. Neither was there any such thing as an outhouse of any kind, not even a wood shed.

The size of the building was 22 × 20 feet. From the floor to the ceiling it was 7 feet. The chimney and entry took up about four feet at one end, leaving the schoolroom itself 18 × 20 feet. Around these sides of the room were connected desks, arranged so that when the pupils were sitting at them their faces were towards the instructor and their backs toward the wall.

or PRONUNCIATION. 85

FABLE I. *Of the Boy that stole Apples.*

AN old Man found a rude Boy upon one of his trees stealing Apples, and desired him to come down; but the young Sauce-box told him plainly he wou'd not. Won't you? said the old Man, then I will fetch you down; so he pulled up some tufts of Grass, and threw at him; but this only made the Youngster laugh, to think the old Man should pretend to beat him out of the tree with grass only.

Well, well, said the old Man, if neither words nor grass, will do, I must try what virtue there is in Stones; so the old Man pelted him heartily with stones; which soon made the young Chap, halten down from the tree and beg the old Man's pardon.

MORAL.

If good words and gentle means will not reclaim the wicked, they must be dealt with in a more severe manner.

Figure 14–6.
Blue-Backed Speller.

Attached to the sides of the desks nearest to the instructor were benches for small pupils. The instructor's desk and chair occupied the center. On this desk were stationed a rod, or ferule; sometimes both. These, with books, writings, inkstands, rules, and plummets, with a fire shovel, and a pair of tongs (often broken), were the principal furniture.

The windows were five in number, of twelve panes each. They were situated so low in the walls as to give full opportunity to the pupils to see every traveller as he passed, and to be easily seen. The places of the broken panes were usually supplied with hats, during school hours. A depression in the chimney, on one side of the entry, furnished a place of deposit for about half of the hats, and the spare clothes of the boys; the rest were left on the floor, often to be trampled upon. The girls generally carried their bonnets, etc., into the schoolroom. The floor and ceiling were level, and the walls were plastered.

The room was warmed by a large and deep fireplace. So large was it, and so efficacious in warming the room otherwise, that I have seen about one-eighth of a cord of good wood burning in it at a time. In severe weather it was estimated that the amount usually consumed was not far from a cord a week. . . .

The school was not infrequently broken up for a day or two for want of wood. The instructor or pupils were sometimes, however, compelled to cut or saw it to prevent the closing of the school. The wood was left in the road near the house, so that it often was buried in the snow, or wet with rain. At the best, it was usually burnt green. The fires were to be kindled about half an hour before the time of beginning the school. Often, the scholar, whose lot it was, neglected to build it. In consequence of this, the house was frequently cold and uncomfortable about half of the forenoon, when, the fire being very large, the excess of heat became equally distressing. Frequently, too, we were annoyed by smoke. The greatest amount of suffering, however, arose from excessive heat, particularly at the close of the day. The pupils being in a free perspiration when they left were very liable to take cold.

The ventilation of the schoolroom was as much neglected as its temperature; and its cleanliness, more perhaps than either. There were no arrangements for cleaning feet at the door, or for washing floors, windows, etc. In the summer the floor was washed, perhaps once in two or three weeks.

(B) The Instructors: The winter school usually opened about the first week of December, and continued twelve to sixteen weeks. The summer term commenced about the first of May. Formerly this was also continued about three or four months, but within ten years the term has been lengthened usually to twenty weeks. Males have been uniformly employed in winter, and females in summer.

The instructors have usually been changed every season, but sometimes they have been continued two successive summers or winters. A strong prejudice has always existed against employing the same instructor more than once or twice in the same district. This prejudice has yielded in one instance, so far that an instructor who had taught two successive winters, twenty-five years before, was employed another season. I have not been able to ascertain the number of instructors who have been engaged in the school during the last thirty years, but I can distinctly recollect thirty-seven. Many of them, both males and females, were from sixteen to eighteen years of age, and a few, over twenty-one.

Good moral character, and a thorough knowledge of the common branches, formerly were considered as indispensable qualifications in an instructor. The instructors were chiefly selected from the most respectable families in town. But for fifteen or twenty years, these things have not been so much regarded. They have indeed been deemed desirable; but the most common method now seems to be to ascertain, as near as possible, the dividend for that season from the public treasury, and then fix upon a teacher who will take charge of the school, three or four months, for this money. He must indeed be able to obtain a license from the Board of Visitors; but this has become nearly a matter of course, provided he can spell, read, and write. In general, the candidate is some favorite or relative of the District Committee. It gives me great pleasure, however, to say that the moral character of almost every instructor, so far as I know, has been unexceptional.

Instructors have usually boarded in the families of the pupils. Their compensation has varied from seven to eleven dollars a month for males; and from sixty-two and a half cents to one dollar a week for females. Within the past ten years, however, the price of instruction has rarely been less than nine dollars in the former case, and seventy-five cents in the latter. In the few instances in which instructors have furnished their own board the compensation has been about the same, it being assumed that they could work at some employment of their own enough to pay their board, especially the females.

(C) The Instruction: Two of the Board of Visitors usually visit the winter schools twice during the term. In the summer, their visits are often omitted. These visits usually occupy from one hour to an hour and a half. They are spent merely in hearing a few hurried lessons, and in making some remarks, general in their character. Formerly, it was customary to examine the pupils in some approved Catechism, but this practice has been omitted for twenty years.

The parents seldom visit the school, except by special invitation. The greater number pay very little attention to it at all. There are, however, a few who are gradually awakening to the importance of good instruction; but there are also a few who oppose everything which is suggested as, at the least, useless; and are scarcely willing their children should be governed in the school.

The school books have been about the same for thirty years. Webster's Spelling Book, the American Preceptor, and the New Testament, have been the principal books used. Before the appearance of the American Preceptor, Dwight's Geography was used as a reading book. A few of the Introduction to the American Orator were introduced about twelve years since, and, more recently, Jack Halyard.

Until within a few years, no studies have been permitted in the day school but spelling, reading, and writing. Arithmetic was taught by a few instructors, one or two evenings in a week, but, in spite of the most determined opposition, arithmetic is now permitted in the day school, and a few pupils study geography.[3]

About 1820, a new instructional device was introduced into American schools—the slate. These school slates were thin flat pieces of slate stone framed with wood. The pencil used to write on the slate was also made of slate and produced a light but legible line. The wooden frames of some of the slates were covered with cloth so that less noise

3. Paul Monroe, *Source Book of the History of Education* (New York: Macmillan, 1901), p. 282.

would be made as students placed the slates on the desks. There were even double slates made by hinging two single slates together with cord or leather. Students wrote their assignments on the slates, just as contemporary students write on tablet paper. Later on, large pieces of slate made up the blackboards that were added to classrooms.

In the same way that Noah Webster's *Blue-Backed Speller* had replaced *The New England Primer*, so did the McGuffey *Reader* eventually replace the *Blue-Backed Speller*. These readers were carefully geared to each grade level and attempted to instill in children a respect for hard work, thrift, self-help, and honesty. McGuffey's *Reader* dominated the elementary school book market until approximately 1900, when they were gradually replaced by a variety of newer and improved readers written by David Tower, James Fassett, William Elson, and others.

During the twentieth century, teachers have gradually adapted a wider and wider variety of tools to assist them in the job of educating American youth. This has come about partly through the influence of Pestalozzi, John Dewey, and others who demonstrated that children learn best by firsthand experiences. School buildings have become larger, more elaborate, and better designed to facilitate learning.

Today, many schools are equipped with an impressive array of books, laboratory equipment, movie projectors, filmstrip projectors, tape recorders, television devices, single concept films, teaching machines, programmed materials, and learning devices of all kinds. Some of the modern school buildings are not only excellent from an educational viewpoint but are also magnificent examples of architecture. One cannot help but be awed by the contrast between American education as it exists today and as it was at its humble and crude beginning 360 years ago. Figure 14–7 presents a diagrammatic summary of the evolution of the textbook.

The Education of American Blacks

In 1619, only a dozen years after the establishment of Jamestown, the first boatload of slaves arrived in the colonies. This event was recorded for history when, in that year, John Rolfe wrote in his *Journal* that the captain of a Dutch ship "sold us twenty Negroes." These slaves were imported as a source of cheap labor for the new colonies.

The number of slaves who were imported steadily increased to the point at which, between 1700 and 1750, thousands of blacks were brought to the American colonies each year. By the time of the Revolutionary War, there were approximately 700,000 blacks in the colonies; by 1860, there were 4,441,830 blacks.

Probably the first organized attempt to educate the blacks in colonial America was that of French and Spanish missionaries.[4] These early mis-

4. Much of the material dealing with the history of American blacks up until the signing of the Emancipation Proclamation (1863) was taken from the doctoral dissertation of Samuel Davis, "Education, Law, and the Negro" (University of Illinois, 1970).

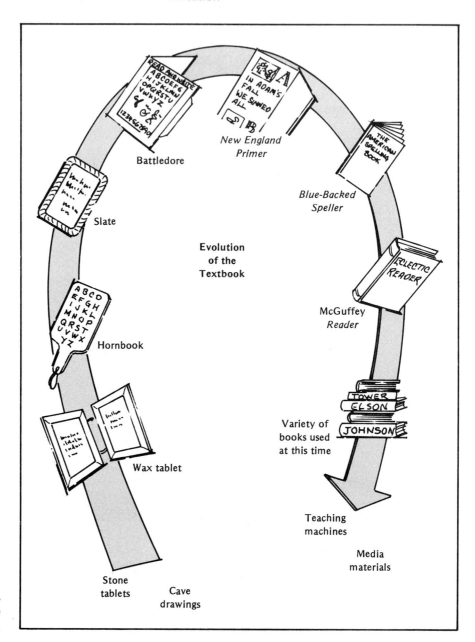

Figure 14–7. Evolution of the textbook.

sionary efforts set an example that influenced the education of black people throughout the colonies. In their endeavors to swell the ranks of the church, they provided instruction for blacks as well as the numerous offspring who were the result of mixed breeding. The education of slaves posed an interesting moral problem for the church. The English colonists had to find a way to overcome the notion that conversion of a slave to Christianity might logically lead to the freeing of a slave. The dilemma they faced was how to eliminate an unwritten law that a Christian should not be a slave. The issue was resolved by legislation on the part of the church's governing bodies and by formal declarations by the Bishop of London that conversion did not lead to manumission.

However, the organized church provided the setting in which black people were allowed to develop skills at reading, leadership, and education of their brethren. In many instances, blacks and whites attended church together. Eventually, some preachers were former slaves who had demonstrated exceptional skill in "spreading the gospel." The Baptists, in particular, allowed blacks to assume a rather active role in the church by encouraging a form of self-government that favored the growth of black congregations. Because of these features of Baptist church policy, the enslaved, as well as the free, black was given an opportunity for education and development not provided by many other denominations.

The efforts of the English to educate black slaves were largely carried out by the Society for the Propagation of the Gospel in Foreign Parts—a missionary organization. The Society was created by the Established Church of London in 1701. In 1705, the Reverend Samuel Thomas, of Goose Creek Parish in South Carolina, established a school

Tuskegee Institute was one of the few early black colleges in America. (*Photograph courtesy of the Library of Congress*)

fostered by the Society and enrolled sixty black students. Nine years later, the Society opened a school in New York City where 200 black pupils were enrolled. Despite stringent opposition from many whites who felt that educating slaves was a "dangerous business," the Society went on to establish other schools for black people. The degree of success of early efforts to educate blacks varied greatly. Initially, society was not violently opposed to the educating of blacks. Education, however, seemed to make the slaves aware of their plight. In the South, much of the unrest concerning slavery was attributed to the education of slaves. Insurrections, uprisings, and threats to overseers, masters, and their families produced fear among the whites. Some states even passed legislation that eliminated any and all forms of education for the slaves.

The Industrial Revolution in England, the invention of the cotton gin, the aftermath of the American Revolution, black insurrections, the extension of slavery into new territories, and the migration of black people to the North had dramatic effects on the education of blacks at the turn of the nineteenth century.

Prior to the invention of the cotton gin, the Southern states took a strong stand against the abolition of slavery. The nation's leaders who met in Philadelphia in 1775 at the first Continental Congress brazenly talked of the abolition of slavery in the colonies. In the final analysis, however, Southern leadership opposed these views, and the Congress compromised by not mentioning the issue of slavery in the Constitution. The Compromise of 1850, after much turmoil and debate by Clay, Calhoun, Douglas, Seward, and Chase, consisted of the following agreement:

- California should enter the Union as a free state;
- The other territories would be organized without mention of slavery;
- Texas should cede certain lands to New Mexico and be compensated;
- Slaveholders would be better protected by a stringent fugitive slave law; and
- There should be no slave trade in the District of Columbia.

The eventual migration of large numbers of blacks from the South to the North and West held vast implications for black education. In moving North and West, blacks were seeking economic independence. The small number of blacks who had previously populated the North and West did not constitute a great threat to the white worker. But large numbers of migrant blacks, a substantial portion of whom were unskilled, threatened to replace some white workers. Retaliation took the form of rioting, and unions organized to oppose the black worker. Some of this union opposition to the black man on the labor front has existed to the present time. This labor opposition represented yet another reason why many whites were generally reluctant to provide equal educational opportunities for blacks.

The black man's individual success in acquiring an education, as well as his group efforts to establish schools, was greatly enhanced by sympathetic and humanitarian white friends. John Chavis, a free black, born in 1763 in Oxford, North Carolina, was an example of a black helped by whites. Chavis became a successful teacher of aristocratic whites. His white neighbors sent him to Princeton "to see if a Negro would take a college education." His rapid advancement under Dr. Witherspoon soon indicated that the adventure was a success. He returned to Virginia and later went to North Carolina, where he preached among his own people. The success of John Chavis, even under experimental conditions, represented a small step forward in the education of American blacks.

Phyllis Wheatley was a slave girl brought from Africa in 1761. She was placed in the service of the household of John Wheatley of Boston and, without any formal training, learned to read and speak English fluently. She eventually became well known for her poetry, which was published and read widely.

Benjamin Banneker, a distinguished black man, was born in Baltimore County, Maryland, in 1731. Baltimore maintained a liberal policy toward the education of blacks, which permitted Banneker to learn to read, write, and do arithmetic at a relatively early age. He became an extremely well educated man. One of his first accomplishments was to manufacture the first clock made in the United States in 1770. After attracting the attention of the scientific world, he turned his attention specifically to astronomy. Without any instruction, but with the help of books borrowed from an encouraging white inventor, Banneker soon could calculate eclipses of the sun and moon. His accuracy far excelled that of any other American. The outstanding works of this inventor aroused the curiosity of Thomas Jefferson. In 1803, Banneker was invited to Jefferson's home in Monticello. The acknowledgement of this black man's achievement by this noted statesman was yet another milestone in the education of the black and in his elevation from a subservient status.

Frederick Douglass, born a slave in Maryland in 1817, ran away from slavery and started talking to abolitionist groups about his slave experiences. He attributed the fluency of his speech to listening to his master talk. Douglass was firmly committed to the view that the black's plight would be considerably bettered if Douglass devoted all his efforts to improving vocational education. Douglass believed that previous attempts by educators to combine a liberal and vocational education had failed, so his emphasis was solely on vocational education.

One of the first Northern schools regularly established for blacks appears to have been that of Elias Neau in New York City in 1704. Neau was an agent of the Society for the Propagation of the Gospel in Foreign Parts.

In 1807, free blacks, including George Bell, Nicholas Franklin, and Moses Liverpool, built the first schoolhouse for blacks in the District of

Columbia. However, it was not until 1824 that there was a black teacher, John Adams, in that district. In 1851, Washington citizens attempted to discourage Myrtilla Miner from establishing an academy for black girls. After much turmoil and harassment, the institution was started by this white schoolmistress from New York and is still functioning today.

Prudence Crandall, a young Quaker lady, established an early boarding school at Canterbury, Connecticut. The trouble she ran into dramatized some of the Northern animosity toward the education of black people. Trouble arose when Sarah Harris, a "colored girl," asked to be admitted to the institution. After much deliberation, Miss Crandall finally consented. White parents objected to the black girl attending the school and withdrew their children. To keep the school open, Miss Crandall resorted to the recruiting of black children. The pupils were threatened with violence, local stores would not trade with her, and the school building was vandalized. The citizens of Canterbury petitioned the state legislature to enact a law that would make it illegal to educate blacks from out of state. Miss Crandall was jailed and tried before the state supreme court in July, 1834. The court never gave a final decision because defects were found in the information prepared by the attorney for the state, and the indictment was eventually dropped.

Finally, Boston, the seat of Northern liberalism, established a separate school for black children in 1798. Elisha Sylvester, a white man, was in charge. The school was founded in the home of Primus Hall, a "Negro in good standing." Two years later, sixty-six free blacks petitioned the school committee for a separate school and were refused. Undaunted, the patrons of Hall's house employed two instructors from Harvard; thirty-five years later, the school was allowed to move to a separate building. The city of Boston opened its first primary school for the education of black children in 1820—yet one more milestone in the history of black education.

Unfortunately, while isolated efforts were made, such as those just mentioned, blacks received pathetically little formal education until the Emancipation Proclamation was issued by President Abraham Lincoln on 1 January 1863. At that time, the literacy rate among blacks was estimated at 5 percent. Sunday school represented about the only opportunity most black people had to learn to read. In the late 1700s and early 1800s, some communities did set up separate schools for blacks; however, only a very small percentage of blacks ever attended such schools. A few colleges such as Oberlin, Bowdoin, Franklin, Rutland, and Harvard admitted black students; but once again, an extremely small number of blacks attended colleges at that time. There were even a few black colleges such as Lincoln University in Pennsylvania (1854) and Wilberforce University in Ohio (1856) in existence; however, the efforts and opportunities for the education of American blacks were pathetically few in view of the size of the black population.

Although there was no great rush to educate black people, the abolishment of slavery in 1861 signaled the beginning of a slow but steady effort to improve their education. By 1890, literacy rose to 40 percent; by 1910, it was estimated that 70 percent of black Americans had learned to read and write. These statistics showing the rapid increase in black literacy are impressive; however, they are dampened by a report of the U.S. Commissioner of Education, which showed that, by 1900, less than seventy out of one thousand public high schools in the South were provided for blacks.

The major and most significant developments in the education of American blacks have occurred during the twentieth century—in fact, since 1950. These developments are thoroughly discussed in Parts I, II, and III.

Private Education in America

Private education has always played an extremely important role in the development of America. In fact, private schools carried on most of the education that existed in colonial America. The first colonial colleges—Harvard, William and Mary, Yale, and Princeton—were private schools. Many of the other early colonial schools were also conducted by churches, missionary societies, or private individuals. These early private schools have already been discussed in some detail earlier in this chapter.

It was not until after the Revolution, when a strong sense of nationalism arose, that certain educators advocated that a strong public school system should be established in the new nation. Such recommendations, however, were not destined to be implemented for many years.

In the meantime, some of the Protestant churches continued to expand the schools they had established during the colonial period. For instance, the Congregational, Quaker, Episcopalian, Baptist, Methodist, Presbyterian, and Reform Churches all at various times and in varying degrees established and operated schools for their youth. It was the Roman Catholics and Lutherans, however, that eventually developed elaborate parochial school systems.

As early as 1820, there were 240 Lutheran parochial schools in Pennsylvania. While the number of Lutheran schools in that particular state eventually dwindled, Henry Muhlenburg and other Lutheran leaders continued to establish parochial schools until the public school system became well established. The Missouri Synod Lutheran Church has continued to maintain a rather well-developed parochial school system right down to the present time. Currently there are approximately 1,700 Lutheran elementary and secondary schools, which enroll about 200,000 pupils in the United States. The bulk of these schools are conducted by the Missouri Synod Lutheran Church.

The Roman Catholic parochial school system grew rapidly beginning in the 1800s. This growth continued into the twentieth century to the point at which the Roman Catholic parochial school system is now the largest private school system in the world. At the present time, the American Roman Catholic school system enrolls about four million elementary students and one million secondary students. This represents about 10 percent of all school children in the country—and approximately 80 percent of all the students attending private schools in the United States.

Federal Involvement in Education

The United States Constitution makes no mention of education and therefore, by virtue of the Tenth Amendment, which states: "The powers not delegated to the United States by the Constitution, nor prohibited by it to the states, are reserved to the states respectively, or to the people," education is a function of each state in the United States. There is some question about whether the makers of the Constitution thoughtfully intended to leave education up to each state or whether they merely forgot to mention it. Some historians believe that our founding fathers wisely realized that local control of education would build a better America. Other historians believe that the framers of the Constitution were so preoccupied with what they felt were more important issues that they never thought to make national provisions for education.

Even though the Constitution makes no mention of education, the federal government has been active in educational affairs from the very beginning; furthermore, the role it has played has been ever-increasing. Highlights of this federal involvement in education are briefly reviewed below.

In 1785 and 1787, the Continental Congress passed the Northwest Ordinance Acts. These acts made provisions for disposition of the Northwest Territory and encouraged the establishment of schools in the territory by stating: "Religion, morality and knowledge being necessary to good government and the happiness of mankind, schools and the means of education shall forever be encouraged." As the various states formed from the Northwest Territory, they were required to set aside the sixteenth section of each township to be used for educational purposes.

In 1862, the federal government passed the Morrill Land Grant Act, when it became apparent that existing colleges were not providing vocational programs needed by a developing country. The Hatch Act of 1887 established agricultural experimental stations across the country; the Smith-Lever Agricultural Extension Act of 1914 carried the services of land-grant colleges to the people through extension services. These early federal acts did much to improve agriculture and industry at a time when improvements in these areas was badly needed by our rapidly developing nation.

In 1917, the federal government passed the first act that provided financial aid to public schools below the college level. This was the

Smith-Hughes Act, which provided for the establishment of high school vocational programs in agriculture, trades, and industry, and home-making. In view of the fact that high schools were very academically oriented, the Smith-Hughes Act served to stimulate the development of badly needed vocational programs.

The 1930s were depression days, and the government was seeking solutions to economic difficulties. Legislation was enacted during these years to encourage economic development, but this legislation indirectly provided financial aid to education. Johns and Morphet list five relief agencies related to education during this time:

1. The Civilian Conservation Corps was established in 1933 and abolished in 1943. This agency carried on organized educational activities for men in CCC camps. Over 2.7 million men participated in these activities.

2. The National Youth Administration was established by the executive order of the President in 1935 and was liquidated in 1944. This organization provided work relief for thousands of secondary and college students and enabled them to continue their education. The NYA also established special schools in some states.

3. The Federal Emergency Relief Administration was established in 1933, superseded by the Works Progress Administration in 1939, and abolished in the early 1940s. These organizations carried on extensive programs of school building construction, maintenance, and repair; paid the salaries of many teachers on a relief basis in a number of states; supported educational projects for adult education, nursery schools, vocational rehabilitation, part-time employment of college students, and literacy and naturalization classes; and provided labor for school lunchrooms.

4. The Public Works Administration was established in 1933 and abolished in the early 1940s. It made grants for school buildings (first on the basis of 30 percent federal funds and 70 percent state and local funds, and later on a 45 to 55 basis) and made loans for school building construction. The matching requirement limited the benefits of the PWA largely to school districts of greatest wealth.

5. The Federal Surplus Commodities Corporation was established in 1935. It purchased and distributed surplus commodities to school lunchrooms operated on a nonprofit basis. Some cash assistance to lunchrooms was also provided primarily for the purchase of surplus foods locally. This organization was administered by the Department of Agriculture. These lunchroom aids were made available for lunchrooms operated by private schools as well as public schools. This was justified on the basis that lunchroom assistance is an aid to the child and not to the school.[5]

5. R. L. Johns and Edgar L. Morphet, *Financing the Public Schools* (Englewood Cliffs, N.J.: Prentice-Hall, 1960), p. 378.

The preceding federal programs, not sponsored primarily for education, benefited education and did so in response to the needs of the time: the child benefit theory was applied to school lunches.

The 1940s saw the nation threatened by war. This need was met categorically by the Vocational Education for National Defense Act, a crash program to prepare workers needed in industry to produce goods needed for national defense. The program operated through state educational agencies and trained over 7,000,000 workers. In 1941, the Lanham Act provided for the construction, maintenance, and operation of community facilities in areas where unusual burdens were placed on local communities because of defense and war activities.

The G.I. Bill of 1944 provided liberally for the education of veterans of World War II. Later, similar bills provided for veterans of the Korean conflict. It is estimated that these bills have provided education for over ten million veterans at a cost of almost $20 billion. Payments from the federal government were made directly to the veteran and also to the college or school where he was in attendance. The government recognized a need to assist young people whose careers were interrupted by military service. In 1966, another G.I. Bill was passed for veterans of the war in Southeast Asia.

The National Science Foundation, established in 1950, emphasized the need for continued support of basic scientific research. It was created to "promote the progress of science; to advance the national health, prosperity, and welfare; to secure the national defense; and for other purposes." The Cooperative Research Program of 1954 authorized the U.S. Commissioner of Education to enter into contracts with universities, colleges, and state education agencies for the conduct of educational research.

Starting in 1957, when the first Russian space vehicle was launched, the federal government increased its participation in education even more. The National Defense Education Act of 1958, the Vocational Education Act of 1963, the Manpower Development and Training Act of

Table 14–2. Federal education acts.

1787	Northwest Ordinance	1950	National Science Foundation
1862	Morrill Land Grant Act	1954	Cooperative Research
1887	Hatch Act		Program
1914	Smith-Lever Agriculture Extension Act	1958	National Defense Education Act
1917	Smith-Hughes Vocational Act	1963	Vocational Education Act
1940	Vocational Education for National Defense Act	1963	Manpower Development and Training Act
1941	Lanham Act	1965	Elementary and Secondary Education Act
1944	G.I. Bill of Rights	1966	International Education Act

1963, the Elementary and Secondary Education Act of 1965, and the International Education Act of 1966—examples of the more recent increased federal participation in educational affairs—are discussed in detail in Parts I and II. Federally supported educational programs such as Project Head Start, National Teacher Corps, and Upward Bound Project were elaborated upon in Part I.

Table 14–2 lists some of the major federal programs that have supported education. All these acts have involved *categorical* federal aid to education—aid that has been provided for a specific use.

Some individuals feel that the federal influence on education is now greater than either the state or the local influence. There can be no denying that through federal legislation, United States Supreme Court decisions, and federal administrative influence, the total federal impact on education is indeed great. Indications are that this impact will become even greater in the future. It will remain for future historians to determine whether or not this is a wise trend in American education.

Summary and Implications

In conclusion, Part IV has presented an overview of the historical development of education in the United States. Beginning with historic antecedents in Europe, a chronology of these highlights is presented in Table 14–3.

Table 14–3. A chronology of important dates in the history of education.

about 4000	B.C.	Written language developed
2000		First schools
1200		Trojan War
479–338		Period of Greek brilliance
445–431		Greek Age of Pericles
404		Fall of Athens
336–323		Ascendancy of Alexander the Great
303		A few private Greek teachers set up schools in Rome
167		First Greek library in Rome
146		Fall of Corinth: Greece falls to Rome
0		Christ born
A.D. 31–476		Empire of Rome
70		Destruction of Jerusalem
476		Fall of Rome in the West
800		Charlemagne crowned Emperor
1100–1300		Crusades
1150	c.	Universities of Paris and Bologna
1209		Cambridge founded
1295		Voyage of Marco Polo
1384		Order of Brethren of the Common Life founded
1400	c.	Thirty-eight universities; 108 by 1600

Table 14–3. (continued)

1423		Printing invented
1456		First book printed
1487		Vasco da Gama discovered African route to India
1500	c.	250 Latin grammar schools in England
1517		Luther nails theses to cathedral door; beginning of Reformation
1519–1521		Magellan first circumnavigates the globe
1534		Founding of Jesuits
1536		Sturm established his Gymnasium in Germany, the first classical secondary school
1601		English Poor Law, established principle of tax-supported schools
1618		Holland had compulsory school law
1620		Plymouth Colony, Massachusetts, settled
1635		Boston Latin Grammar School founded
1636		Harvard founded
1642		Massachusetts law of 1642 compelled inspection
1647		Massachusetts law of 1647 compelled establishment of schools
1662		First newspaper in England
1672		First teacher-training class, Father Demia, France
1684		Brothers of the Christian Schools founded
1685		First normal school, de la Salle, Rheims, France
1697		First teacher training in Germany, Francke's Seminary, Halle
1751		Franklin established first academy in the United States
1762		*Émile* of Rousseau published
1775–1783		Revolution, United States
1789		Adoption of Constitution, United States
1798		Lancaster discovered monitorial plan of education
1799–1815		Ascendancy of Napoleon, Waterloo
1804		Pestalozzi's Institute at Yverdon established
1806		First Lancastrian School in New York
1819		Dartmouth College Decision
1821		First American high school
1821		Troy Seminary for Women, Emma Willard, first higher education for women, United States
1823		Hall, first private normal school in the United States, Concord, Vermont
1825		Labor unions come on the scene
1826		Froebel's *The Education of Man*
1827		Massachusetts law compelled high schools

Table 14–3. (continued)

1837	Massachusetts had first state board, H. Mann first secretary
1839	First public normal school, United States, Lexington, Massachusetts
1855	First kindergarten in United States—after German model; Mrs. Schurz
1861–1865	Civil War
1861	Oswego Normal School (Sheldon)
1862	Morrill Land Grant Act: college of engineering, military science, agriculture in each state
1868	Herbartian Society founded
1872	Kalamazoo Decision, made high schools legal
1888	Teachers College, Columbia, founded
1892	Committee of Ten established
1909–1910	The first junior high schools established at Berkeley, California, and Columbus, Ohio
about 1910	The first junior colleges established at Fresno, California, and Joliet, Illinois
1917	The Smith-Hughes Act, encouraged agriculture, industry, and home-economics education in the United States
1932–1940	The Eight Year Study of thirty high schools completed by the Progressive Education Association; reported favorably on the modern school
1944–1946	Legislation by 78th Congress provided subsistence allowance, tuition fees, and supplies for the education of veterans of World War II
1945	The United Nations Educational, Scientific, and Cultural Organization (UNESCO) initiated efforts to improve educational standards throughout the world
1952	The G.I. Bill's educational benefits extended to Korean veterans
1954	United States Supreme Court decision required eventual racial integration of public schools
1965	Passage of Public Law 89–10.
1966	The G.I. Bill's educational benefits extended to Southeast Asia war veterans
1972	Indian Education Act passed, designed to help native Americans help themselves
1972	Title IX Education Amendment outlawing discrimination on the basis of sex
1975	Education for All Handicapped Children: Public Law 94–142 implemented
1978	Supreme Court rules against reverse discrimination; Bakke case

The history of American education is filled with many messages. Some of these messages tell of successes, some of failures, others of dedicated teachers, of humble beginnings, of the individual's thirst for knowledge—even of those who have been willing to die for the truth. These historical events have implications for the present. Contemporary educators can learn much from our educational history if they will listen carefully to these messages from the past.

Discussion Questions

1. What present educational issues have been issues throughout American education?
2. How did the development of public education differ in the Northern, Middle, and Southern Colonies?
3. What historical conditions led to the development of that uniquely American institution, the comprehensive high school?
4. How has the relative social and economic status of the American teacher changed through the various phases of American history?
5. How has the concept of the nature of humankind changed in the past 300 years? What effect has this change had upon teacher education?
6. What are the highlights of the history of education of black people in America?

Supplemental Activities

1. Invite an elderly retired teacher to your class to discuss his or her early teaching experience.
2. Invite a professor from the history department to discuss the history of education from his or her viewpoint.
3. Create a number of artistic displays, charts, or exhibits—using various materials—depicting significant aspects of the history of education.
4. Make a hornbook, battledore, wax tablet, or quill pen.
5. Collect some old books and other educational artifacts. Study these and then give them to your school so that future students may see and study them.

Bibliography

Buetow, Harold A. *Of Singular Benefit: The Story of U.S. Catholic Education.* New York: Macmillan, 1970.

Carpenter, Charles. *History of American Schoolbooks.* Philadelphia: University of Pennsylvania Press, 1963.

Church, Robert L., and Sedlak, Michael W. *Education in the United States: An Interpretive History.* New York: Macmillan, 1976.

Cohen, Sheldon S. *A History of Colonial Education 1607–1776.* New York: Wiley, 1974.

Cordasco, Francesco, and Cremin, Lawrence. *A History of Education in American Culture.* New York: Holt, Rinehart and Winston, 1953.

French, William M. *America's Educational Tradition.* Boston: D.C. Heath, 1964.

Gartner, Lloyd P. *Jewish Education in the United States: A Documentary History.* New York: Teachers College Press, 1970.

Gross, Carl H., and Chandler, Charles C. *The History of American Education through Readings.* Boston: D.C. Heath, 1964.

Klassen, Frank. "Persistence and Change in Eighteenth-Century Colonial Education." *History of Education Quarterly* 2 (June 1962): 83–99.

Perkinson, Henry J. *Two Hundred Years of American Educational Thought*. New York: McKay, 1976.

Rippa, S. Alexander. *Education in a Free Society: An American History*. New York: McKay, 1976.

PART V

Philosophical Bases of Education

Any attempt to suggest the many facets of even the major philosophical concepts bears the inherent risk of oversimplification. The study of philosophy is an academic and comprehensive discipline. Considerable time-consuming study of the original works of many outstanding thinkers is required of the student who wishes to develop a thorough knowledge of philosophy. No pretense is made that this part of the book might serve as a substitute for an in-depth study of any one of the many original works of philosophy mentioned. Rather, this part is intended merely to set the stage for such in-depth study and reading in the field of philosophy by prospective teachers.

Any implication that the classroom teacher must first be a philosopher is not intended. It is suggested, however, that a degree of philosophical understanding on the part of all teachers with regard to both classical and contemporary philosophical systems could provide the clues that teachers might profitably use in helping to develop the minds of their pupils. The growth of the comprehensive American system of education has obviously been aligned with the growth of the American democratic way of life. American democracy depends upon an educated citizenry functioning within a framework of several systems of thought that exist simultaneously. Teachers working within the framework of American democracy usually develop or select a personal philosophical approach to education that best enables them to work with their pupils. It is argued that most of the current views on education have roots within the classical philosophies of the historical past and that teachers usually draw upon classical systems of philosophy as they develop or select a personal philosophical approach to teaching. One could make a substantial case for future teachers studying philosophy, since such inquiry forces them to reflect on and evaluate their own values and assumptions prior to the acceptance of a teaching role.

Much of what is offered as philosophy of education courses by education departments is usually a definitional method of relating educational philosophy to classical systems of philosophy. Particularly during the past decade, philosophers have increasingly taken issue with the philosophy attempted by educationists. Out of the philosopher-educationist conflict, the study of twentieth-century *existentialism* has become popular as a newer philosophical approach to education. The existentialist questions whether philosophy can be defined as a logical system of thought. Instead, an individual's philosophy is viewed as a way of life within which the individual must discover meaning for his or her existence through experience rather than by attempting to understand a set of predetermined propositions or truths.

The purpose of Part V is to provide the prospective teacher with an overview of classical and educational philosophy. Since no assumptions are made with regard to the number of introductory philosophy courses prospective teachers may or may not have had, this will be an elementary introduction to the terminology of philosophy and to selected types of classical and educational philosophy most prevalent in contemporary American schools. The works of other authors are drawn upon as illustrations and summaries of the educational philosophies adopted from the classical systems of philosophy.

CHAPTER 15

Philosophy

THE PHILOSOPHY OF AN INDIVIDUAL COULD BE DEFINED AS AN organized system of that individual's convictions or beliefs. While such a definition might be acceptable for the lay person, it is also incomplete. The basis for formulation of one's beliefs relates to the culture of the individual, the philosophical problems out of which the beliefs have grown, and the activities engaged in by the individual when beliefs are formulated.

Why is it that several people who are in a common setting will each develop a different set of beliefs? For what reasons do individuals hold their beliefs as true and the beliefs of others as false? Or value something as ugly while others value the same as beautiful? Or judge something morally good or bad? Or accept something as real or not real?

Definition of Philosophy   Extraction of root words from the Greek word *philosophia* yields *phileo* (love) and *sophia* (wisdom). Thus the literal meaning of philosophy is "love of wisdom." If one thinks of wisdom as meaning "a high degree of knowledge," the extended literal meaning of philosophy becomes "love of a high degree of knowledge." On this point Aristotle made a statement that typifies Greek thought: "All men by nature desire to know." Not included in Aristotle's statement is a specification of "what" man desires to know. "What" to know as the essence of wisdom is something upon which different individuals at different times have disagreed. Wisdom as the basic substance of philosophy encompasses religion, science, and art; it engages one's thinking processes and deals with abstract concepts and theory. One who is seeking wisdom is concerned with *observations, values, mental conceptualizations, spiritual beings, knowledge,* and *nature.* There is general agreement that there are three basic questions of philosophy: What is real? How do we know? What is of value? Seeking answers to these questions becomes a most meaningful activity from the perspective of the individual. Many individuals (teachers) borrow from existing systems of thought in an attempt to substantiate beliefs and to seek wisdom. Classical philosophers attempted to answer the basic questions posed, and their speculations have proved of inexhaustible interest to all subsequent thinkers.

Philosophy can also be viewed as the attempt to think in an organized and systematic way. Human life takes on meaning as the varied aspects of experience become systematized into some pattern. George Kneller states: "Philosophy springs from man's need to organize his ideas and to find meaning in the whole realm of thought and action."[1] Thus philosophy attempts to investigate the whole of reality by assessing experiences and then structuring those experiences in an order that is sensible to the individual. From this perspective, philosophy may be considered as an inquiry into the whole human and cultural enterprise.

Analysis, Criticism, and Evaluation of Beliefs

Philosophy functions as the analysis, criticism, and evaluation of existing beliefs held by an individual. An analysis of a system of beliefs may be made for the sole purpose of reviewing and classifying these beliefs into a meaningful order. If the function stops with analysis, the ordered view of the beliefs would constitute no more than a presentation of the dogmatic convictions of the individual. An attendant circumstance of analysis is the application of principles or standards for judging beliefs. Most of us are willing to accept that part of analysis which calls for ordering our beliefs, but we are not so willing to accept that part of analysis which calls for the judging of our prized convictions. Perhaps we tend to be wary for fear that judgment would show that our convictions were not valid over a period of time. It is important for the beginning teacher to realize that, on the contrary, convictions withstanding the stress of analysis and criticism may stand up, over time, far better than convictions based on sentiment. Finally, individuals should evaluate their beliefs in terms of their current needs. Evaluation in this context has to do with arranging one's tested beliefs in order of importance in reference to a given point in time. An underlying assumption is that analysis and criticism have shown the ordered beliefs to be worthy of retention. Evaluation also obligates the individual to discard those beliefs that cannot be substantiated through analysis and criticism.

The Structuring of Thought Processes

Another function of philosophy is that it assists individuals in structuring thought processes so that beliefs may be formulated anew and apart from, or refute or support, existing beliefs. Each of the general questions of philosophy (What is real? How do we know? What is of value?) specifies a branch of philosophy. Consideration of a single one

1. George F. Kneller, *Introduction to the Philosophy of Education* (New York: John Wiley, 1965), p. 2.

Jean Jacques Rousseau. (*Painting by La Tour; The Bettmann Archive*)

of the three general questions causes individual thought to be ordered at least to the extent that that single branch of philosophy is examined in light of its essence. For example, individual thought structured to deal with reality may generate new beliefs regarding reality, or may generate beliefs that refute or support existing beliefs regarding reality. Similar thoughtful examination of either the branch of philosophy dealing with knowledge or the branch of philosophy dealing with values may also generate new beliefs or refute existing beliefs with respect to knowledge and values. Philosophy functioning in this manner provides a sort of introspective examination of the system of beliefs held by an individual.

External Comparisons

In addition to having an introspective function, philosophy also serves a function of externality. The initial consideration of the externals of philosophy would be the relatedness of the branches. It is most difficult to delimit thought to a single branch of philosophy. The first reasonable extension of such thought is to begin a cross-examination of the effects on beliefs when two or more branches of philosophy are considered to be interacting. Up to this point, the thought-influencing function of philosophy has not taken us outside our personal system of beliefs. Obviously, philosophy must also deal with the realm of comparative thought between other individual and academic philosophies. As with the structured introspective thought associated with a single branch of philosophy, external thought may also produce new beliefs, or refute or support existing beliefs cherished as part of one's personal philosophy.

Terminology of Philosophy

Among others, Plato, Aristotle, St. Thomas Aquinas, Hegel, and Dewey are identified with elaborate systems of philosophy. As an expedient for communication, it is understandable that a language of philosophy developed. For the most part, the resultant vocabulary has been a straightforward development of words to identify the nature of activities or positions held within the domain of philosophy.

Since much of the vocabulary of philosophy consists of words that have clear, straightforward meanings, lack of clarity arises when terms from our everyday forms of speech are loosely interpreted or used when solving problems of a philosophical nature. Linguistic analysis, as a part of analytic philosophy, stresses that the clarity and analysis of terms are essential in the approach to all philosophic and educational problems.

The terminology considered necessary here consists of the basic terms that have become commonly accepted as philosophical definitions. Familiarity with such terms permits teachers to be comfortable while examining philosophical systems. It will be of help to the student to recall that the -*ologies* of philosophy result from using the -*logy* suffix—taken from the Greek word *logos*, meaning "speech, discourse on, reason for, theory of." Adding a prefix such as *onto* taken from the Greek *on* (*ont-*), meaning "being," we have one of the important words of philosophy, *ontology*, the theory of being or the meaning of existence. The -*ism* suffix is taken from the Greek -*ismos* and is used as a terminal form of nouns to indicate "action, the process of such action, a condition, quality, or system." For example, using the term *evolution* as a prefix yields *evolutionism*, which is the philosophical theory that accounts for the universe as evolving by the combination of atoms. Analogously, meanings for many of the "ologies" and "isms" of philosophy may be worked out.

Fully developed dictionaries of philosophy may be purchased by those who seek a more complete understanding of the language of philosophy. J. Donald Butler treats the terminology of philosophy in outline form in order "to define terms, and to show, by the outline arrangement, some of the interrelationships between terms and the problems with which they are commonly associated."[2] Consideration is given here to terminology identified with the three general questions of philosophy previously posed: What is real? How do we know? What is of value?

Metaphysics (Ontology)

Metaphysics is considered to be a more inclusive term than *ontology* because it has a *plural* meaning; that is, it is that branch of philosophy which deals with various *theories* of reality. The literal meaning of the Greek phrase *ton meta ta physika*, "that which came after physics," is the systematic study of the first principles of being and of knowledge, *ontology*. Ontology may be considered as the branch of metaphysics that seeks to answer the general question, What is real?

Many persons have been reared according to the traditions of a basically Judeo-Christian culture such as that in the United States. Accordingly, ontology (reality) is conceptualized as being dependent upon an ultimate being in God. Existence and God are identical. God made a perfect spiritual world, and humankind is a part of that world. Ultimate reality has been created from the Absolute Mind. Reality viewed ontologically also gives rise to questions of physical existence. That is, does existence mean merely the occupation of time and space? May we say that existence is no more than matter and physical energy? May we say that ultimate reality is vested in the physical world? Reasoning related to ultimate reality from either the spiritual or physical aspect may be held as not valid philosophically. Why must one subscribe to the belief that existence possesses an ultimate quality? Perhaps a more practical approach to reality would be acceptance of the position that existence constantly changes. If everything constantly changes, nothing would be considered as existing in any ultimate sense. Existence, then, is of the moment and defined by circumstances and conditions of that moment. In the future, as in the past, existence will not be and was not the same as it is for our time.

Anthropology

Anthropology is a theory that holds that the nature of man is one important aspect of reality. Each of us needs to determine an acceptable belief relative to the basic nature of the self. From this viewpoint, similar to the ontological view of existence, the self may be accepted as a spiritual, a physical, or a social phenomenon in a state of flux. Many anthropological questions bear investigation as a means of clarifying beliefs regarding reality. What is the relation of mind and body? Is there interaction between mind and body? Is mind more fundamental than body, with body depending on mind, or vice versa? Consideration must

2. J. Donald Butler, *Four Philosophies and Their Practice in Education and Religion* (New York: Harper & Brothers, 1957), pp. 48–54.

Neo-Thomism has been a strong force in parochial education. (*Photograph by Ellis Herwig, Stock, Boston*)

also be given to the problem of the freedom of human beings. Are actions determined by forces greater than the person? Or does man or woman have the power of choice through a free will? Perhaps a person is neither free nor determined. Teachers are obligated to identify and order their beliefs in light of these philosophical questions for the purpose of developing a more complete understanding of the nature of their pupils.

Theology   *Theology* may be considered as that part of religious theory that has to do with conceptions of and about God. Is there a God? One God? More than one God? What are the attributes of God? Most who assume that God does exist also assume that God is all good. This does not mean that God is all-powerful—or does it? If you believe that God is all-powerful, how is it that God permits so much bad to exist? *Atheism* suggests there is no ultimate reality or God behind the universe. *Deism* views God as the maker of nature and moral laws, but asserts that God exists apart from, and is disinterested in, the physical universe and human beings. *Pantheism* poses that God and the universe are identical—all is God and God is all. Beliefs about ultimate reality and God are of no concern to the atheist in assessing the ontological branch of his or her philosophy.

Epistemology   *Epistemology* is a branch of philosophy that is concerned with theories of the nature of knowledge. Epistemology seeks an answer to the general philosophical question, How do we know? One of the functions of teachers is to seek knowledge and transmit that knowledge to their students. One of the functions of epistemology specifies the instruments or the means by which knowledge is acquired. The instruments of knowledge vary according to the beliefs of the several schools of philosophy. Some of the philosophically determined instruments of knowledge are: (1) knowledge is gained empirically through sense-perceptual experience; (2) knowledge is gained chiefly through reason; (3) knowledge is gained in some instances by intuition; and (4) knowledge is certified by an indisputable authority.

It may be contended that knowledge is based upon experience and observation. On the other hand, some knowledge is self-evident. Certain truths have long been understood and do not require proof through observation and experimentation. Another viewpoint is that conclusive knowledge of ultimate reality is an impossibility; *agnosticism* holds to this notion. *Skepticism* holds a questioning attitude toward the possibility of gaining knowledge. You may believe that true knowledge of ultimate reality is possible. Or you may believe that knowledge functions in situations where it is needed. Future teachers need to be concerned with those theories regarding the nature of knowledge that they can accept as a part of their personal philosophies.

Axiology   *Axiology* is a branch of philosophy that specifies the nature of values, the kinds of value, and the values worthy of possession. Axiology seeks to answer the third general philosophical question, What is of value? What we desire, we value. An interest theory of value suggests that values exist only to the extent that they are supported by the interest of the valuer. A value of interest to one person may not exist at all for a second person. In contrast, an opposing theory holds that values have an existence independent of the valuer and his or her interest. In this context, values are universal and exist for anyone to possess.

Ethics is the realm of value related to the nature of good and bad. Concerning the question "Is life worth living?" *optimism* tells us that existence is good; *pessimism* tells us that existence is bad. Ethics considers ends, aims, and objectives of living; criteria of conduct in our lives; and motivation of conduct.

Aesthetics is the realm of value that searches for the principles governing the creation and appreciation of beautiful things. Other realms of value deal with religion, education, society, and utility.

Summary and Implications

In our pluralistic social world, frustration and anxiety may be induced when one behaves according to the value structure of a group rather than as one would individually prefer to behave. By focusing upon the values of philosophy, one may gain a conscious awareness of personally cherished values on which to base personal behavior. Lack of clarity about one's individual values leads to conforming behavior determined by group values for given situations. Behavior of this sort may be frustrating when the group behavior is contradictory to one's personally held—but not consciously identified—behavior values.

In order for teachers to sustain meaningful actions with their students and in order to avoid hypocritical pedagogy, teachers clearly need to systematize their personal beliefs regarding a philosophy of education. Prospective teachers should be acquainted with the traditional philosophical concepts that may provide the basis for educational views applicable to the present. The effectiveness of the classroom teacher is maximized when his or her personal beliefs about education are specifically clarified, developed, and understood in terms of philosophic concepts and terminology. In this way, teachers will understand why they act the way they do pedagogically, as they work to meet the needs of their pupils. Likewise, teachers usually respond to management problems associated with the classroom according to an underlying value system that frames their particular philosophy of education.

Discussion Questions

1. Define philosophy. Illustrate the extent to which individual beliefs are accounted for in your definition.
2. How does philosophy function in the evaluation of one's existing beliefs?
3. How does philosophy assist an individual in structuring his or her thought processes in order to refute or to support his or her existing beliefs?

4. Ethics is the realm of values, related to the nature of good and bad. What has contributed to your personal ethics? What do you rely on to help you judge what is good from what is bad?
5. What is your understanding of epistemology? How is knowledge important to philosophy?

Supplemental Activities

1. Assemble class panels to study and report on these branches of philosophy: metaphysics, epistemology, and axiology.
2. Invite a professor of philosophy to class to discuss philosophy as an academic discipline.
3. Invite a minister or priest to class to discuss his or her particular theology. Include in the discussion comments on atheism, deism, and pantheism.

4. Assemble a panel to research and report on the written literature and court decisions related to atheism.
5. Develop a questionnaire that may be used to poll the understanding of the meanings of the terms *metaphysics, epistemology,* and *axiology* among classroom teachers. Administer the instrument and report the results of your study.

Bibliography

Daley, Leo Charles. *College Level Philosophy.* New York: Monarch, 1965.

Demiashkevich, M. *An Introduction to the Philosophy of Education.* New York: American Book, 1935.

Kneller, George F. *Introduction to the Philosophy of Education.* New York: John Wiley, 1965.

Kohlberg, Lawrence. "From Is to Ought: How to Commit the Naturalistic Fallacy and Get Away with It in the Study of Moral Development." In *Cognitive Development and Epistemology,* edited by Theodore Mischel. New York: Academic Press, 1971, pp. 181–85.

Morris, Van Cleve, and Pai, Young. *Philosophy and the American School.* 2nd ed. Boston: Houghton Mifflin, 1976.

Park, Joe. *Selected Readings in the Philosophy of Education.* New York: Macmillan, 1963.

Randall, John H., Jr., and Buchler, Justus. *Philosophy: An Introduction.* New York: Barnes and Noble, 1942.

Rokeach, Milton. *Beliefs, Attitudes, and Values.* San Francisco: Jossey-Bass, 1968.

Runes, Dagobert D., ed. *Dictionary of Philosophy.* Totowa, N.J.: Littlefield, Adams, 1964.

Simon, Sidney, and Goodman, Joel. "Values Shock." *Adult Leader* 6 (September 1973): 16–17.

CHAPTER 16

Classical Philosophical Concepts: Traditional and Contemporary Educational Views

SINCE PHILOSOPHERS HAVE NOT BEEN ABLE TO AGREE UPON THE number of philosophies that exist, attempts to group schools of philosophy by classification schemes have only limited usefulness. As an example, if one desired to investigate *idealism* as a school of philosophy, related readings would lead to headings such as spiritualism, mentalism, personalistic idealism, monistic idealism, pluralistic idealism, and even realistic idealism. Further confusion arises when classifications are made under the headings of traditional philosophies and contemporary philosophies. The selected classical philosophical concepts discussed in this chapter are those basic to traditional educational views and those basic to contemporary educational views.

Traditional Bases   Idealism, realism, and Neo-Thomism are the selected philosophical concepts that will be considered as formulating the bases for the traditional view. It is well to keep in mind that several other philosophical concepts not included in our discussion could also be considered as a part of the bases for the traditional view.

Idealism   From a standpoint of including various philosophical tenets, perhaps *ideaism* should be substituted for the term *idealism*. Popular confusion arises from the fact that idealism is related to both ideas and ideals. Historically the term *idea* has been used to mean many things: form, semblance, universal, class concepts in the human mind, subsistent in the mind of God, sense perception, faint image, and absolute. When the notion of idea is presently considered, we assume that activity of the mind is involved. Ideas are mental, of the mind.

　　　Ideals are also mental, of the mind, and pertaining to ideas. An ideal "something or other" is judged as possessing the character of perfection with respect to a standard. It may be argued that such standards are external to the mind; but when an individual makes his judgment related to the standards, activity of the mind is involved. Idealism includes the extension of such words as idea, mind, spirit, and thought.

Therefore one's "ideaism" is a function of one's mind. This function of one's mind may be thought of as a conceptual process of a miniature Ultimate Mind seeking reality, knowledge, and values. Idealism involves one's mind perceiving reality, knowledge, and values according to the ideal standards of perfection of an Ultimate Mind. Modern idealism strives to associate men and women and the spiritual existence to which they belong.

Metaphysics of Idealism

How does *idealism* seek to answer the question, What is real? What is the metaphysics of idealism? To the idealist, reality is constituted by ideas, by the mind, by the self. Reality is a world of mind; it is spiritual rather than physical. Material things are not regarded as reality because the idealist believes nature is dependent upon a Universal Mind or God. Ontological reality may be identified essentially with subconscious spiritual principles. One of the timeworn discussion topics of subconscious concepts of reality is that of the explanation of first events of nature. The discussion almost always reaches the point at which an assertion is made that indicates that nature could not have brought itself into being. Consideration must then be given to what could have caused the first events of nature. Regression along a line of causes culminates with the presentation of the *first cause* as God. Certain theories of nature that include cause-and-effect relationships suggest that the universe came to exist through the working of a *creative cause*. The pure idealist subscribes to such ontological theories and maintains that God created the universe.

Along with the premise of creationism, idealists hold basic conceptions of and about God. While it may be generally stated that God and the universe have some relationship, the manner in which the relationship is identified may be a bit perplexing. Is God a personal God? Is God one or more than one? Are God and the universe identical? Is God all-good and all-powerful? Or is God all-good but not necessarily all-powerful? Is God interested in or disinterested in the physical universe and in human beings? Pure idealism accepts the view of Christian theism that suggests that ultimate reality is a personal God who is more than the universe. The universe exists within and through God. The polytheistic doctrine that spiritual reality is plural (more than one God) could be contained within idealism. The distinguishing note is that idealism holds God or Gods to be an ultimate reality that is more than the universe.

What about the nature of man or woman in relation to reality? A

Martin Luther.
(*An engraving
from a painting by
Holbein; The
Bettmann Archive*)

principle of idealism states one has a self in the form of a soul. One's soul is a spiritual being. When one equates spiritual being with mind, the problem of the relation of body and mind is introduced. Idealists most commonly resolve this problem by purporting mind to be more fundamental than body, i.e., body depends upon mind. What does this mean? If one considers the mind as a miniature model of a Supreme Mind, idealism becomes somewhat deterministic. As one's body depends upon one's mind and as one's mind is a working replica of a Supreme Mind, then actions are determined by forces greater than the individual. Such an analogy might be immediately countered with the suggestion that one's mind, whether or not it be considered a miniature of a Supreme Mind, works independently and makes interpretations of reality in its own right. The deterministic quality of idealism is thus qualified to the extent that each one's actions are determined by God. According to George Kneller, "We see that Idealists are united in their acceptance of man's spiritual essence, but they disagree as to how exactly he is related to the ultimate spiritual reality from which he springs."[1]

Epistemology of Idealism

What is the epistemology of idealism? What is knowledge? How do we know? Various theories of knowledge have been held at different times by idealists. Contemporary idealists believe that there are instruments of knowledge other than the scientific methods. Idealism also considers faith, authoritarianism, and intuition as instruments of knowledge. It may be said that faith is a way we come to know certain things. Faith suggests that a person firmly believes and accepts what he or she believes as knowledge despite any arguments against this belief. Idealists often accept knowledge on the basis of faith. Such knowledge based on faith is more than a mere belief. For example, a person believes that God exists because faith as an instrument of knowledge has enabled the person to *know* God. Whether it be called immaterialism, mysticism, spiritualism, or whatever, such a belief in a Supreme Mind is a significant aspect of the epistemology of idealism. Perhaps authoritarianism and faith in God become synonymous relative to knowledge certified to us by such authorities as the Bible and the church. In this case, the indisputable authority of the Bible and the church may actually be tools for formulating faith. However, in the absence of faith, important knowledge may be certified to us directly from the Bible and the church, or from any other authority, such as the state.

Intuition means to know in a direct fashion. Idealists believe that there are some things we can know directly without reasoning. Knowledge may come to us intuitively. One who takes an extended position on intuition as a source of knowledge would claim that all knowledge is based on intuition. Idealism includes intuition among the instruments of knowledge. Historically, in the realm of knowledge, idealists have conceived of truth as ideas. George Berkeley (1685–1753), an Anglican bishop and philosopher, is called an *idealist* because he believed that existence was mind-dependent. In order for anything to exist it must be perceived by mind, but not necessarily our human minds. Berkeley argued that things exist even when a human mind is not perceiving them because the Ultimate Mind of God is perceiving all things. Idealism is not entirely Christian thought; but as a philosophy, it does concur with

1. George F. Kneller, *Introduction to the Philosophy of Education* (New York: John Wiley, 1965), p. 34.

the philosophy of the deeply religious Christian Berkeley in holding that ultimate existence and knowledge are perceived by a Supreme Mind.

Axiology of
Idealism

What does idealism have to suggest regarding the most personal question of philosophy: What is of value? What are the *ethics* and *aesthetics* of idealism? As presented in the context of supernaturalism, idealism has God as the standard of goodness. Moral persons are those who live according to the will of God. The inherent problem is that of mortals knowing the will of God. It follows that evil may be expressed as acting against the will of God. The assumption that morality is based upon the will of God is widespread. Idealists, perhaps on the basis of faith, accept the will of God as expressed in the Bible, in the teaching of Christ, and in the interpretations of the church. The problem of evil has been troublesome to supernaturalism since ancient times. Discussion of the problem of evil causes attention to be directed toward the attributes of benevolence and omnipotence of God. An omnipotent God is all-powerful and could abolish evil, but in so doing could not be benevolent. In abolishing evil, God may not be able to be benevolent to evildoers; thus a benevolent God could be lacking in power. God as the absolute perfection is both omnipotent and benevolent. A denial of either attribute would be a denial of the divineness of God. Since moral goodness is one's imitation of a perfect and divine God who is both omnipotent and benevolent, one can see why the problem of evil has been most perplexing to idealism.

Aesthetics in idealism becomes the logical outgrowth of the ethics in idealism. Beauty is ascribed as the reflection of God. In other words, as people continually strive to become morally good by imitating God, they reflect the ideal God more and more. Such reflection of God becomes the aesthetics, the beauty of idealism.

Realism

Like naturalism, *realism* regards the world of nature as all there is. Realism holds that objects of the external world are real in and of themselves. It is an antithetical view of idealism. Realism is not the sole antithesis to idealism: *materialism* and *naturalism* are terms that have been used interchangeably or synonymously as antitheses of idealism. Realism, as sketched in this presentation, has as its essence an interchange of materialism and naturalism. However, realism does denote the physical world as the sum total of reality. There is no dependence upon a mind—human's or God's—to comprehend concepts. A realist rejects the existence of anything beyond nature. Everything comes from nature and is subject to scientific laws. *Naturalism* has been aligned with natural science: the physical world includes only that which can be scientifically investigated. Objects that science can investigate are the physical or material. Matter is a fundamental constituent of the universe. The universe is not governed by mind, spirits, mental ideas, sense perceptions, or God as a first cause. Plato's dualism gave reference to an actual world of particulars and an ideal world of pure essences. Realism as naturalism suggests that human life—physical, mental, moral, and spiritual—is an ordinary natural event attributable in all respects to the ordinary operations of nature.

Metaphysics of Realism

Realism specifies reality in things or objects. Natural things have always existed. The universe as a physical world evolved of itself naturally—as opposed to having been created by a supernatural force beyond nature. In a discussion of the concept of reality and events of nature, realists hold to the theory that the universe did evolve of itself. Realists consider causes of the events of nature but do not believe, as does an idealist, that the first cause is a God. A realist may hold that no ultimate reality exists behind the universe. God also may be conceived by realists as emerging or evolving with the universe. Cause-and-effect relations are viewed as being governed by natural law. A realist feels that when a cause question cannot presently be answered, it is because we have not learned to understand all of nature. When we know all of nature, we will know answers to all questions of causes.

What of the essential nature of man and woman as seen by realism? A principle of naturalism views the self as essentially the same as the body. So far as the relation of body and mind, a realist believes mind to be something new and produced by nature in the evolutionary process, neither identical with body nor wholly dependent upon it. Another realist concept suggests that mind is merely a function of the brain. In this context, mind does not influence bodily activity but merely accompanies bodily activity. The stage for one's physical activity is and has been an orderly, purposeful universe. To exist in the universe is to occupy time and space and to be physical matter. Nature is identical with existence.

Epistemology of Realism

What are the instruments of knowledge in realism (naturalism)? What is knowledge? Realism affirms the possibility of knowledge. Truth is viewed as observable fact. Sense-perceptual experience is the medium for gaining knowledge. Realists observe the data obtained on the physical nature of the universe. On the basis of these observations, general principles are formulated to assist in making the universe intelligible. Realism utilizes the inductive method of the investigation of nature in detecting general principles from observations. Contemporary naturalism adheres to the scientific method for formulating general principles of knowledge. The essence of the epistemology of realism is that knowledge is based upon experience and observation. Nature contains truth, and that truth is obtainable by the scientific investigation of nature.

Axiology of Realism

Regarding the axiology of realism, values are also obtained from nature. As a result of observing nature, one comes to know natural laws that provide the basis for ethical and aesthetical value judgments. Values so derived from nature are permanent. Values will have a natural quality rather than a supernatural quality. Assuming the universe is thus the standard of goodness, those who live in accordance with the general principles of nature are moral persons. This universe as the standard of goodness for one's ethical structure may also be considered as the standard for the determination of evil; that is, evil becomes that which violates one's ethical structure. Moral people are responsible for selecting the laws of nature that denote good and then for conducting themselves by such laws. Nature provides the principles that govern appreciation of beauty: aesthetics is the reflection of nature.

Neo-Thomism

Neo means "new"; *Thomism* is the branch of Christian Scholasticism associated with the work of St. Thomas Aquinas (1225–1274). Until the time of Aquinas, the dualism of *idealism* and *realism* dominated philosophy. Divergent thinking regarding supernatural and natural causes, mind and body, and physical objects and mental conceptions set the two philosophical camps apart, as shown in Figure 16–1. By the 1200s, Christian philosophers wanted to inject basic Christian doctrines into their systems of thought. Christian discussions were concerned with such topics as the existence of God, the nature of man, and faith and reason. At this time, the views of Aristotle were little known. Thomas Aquinas was instrumental in getting Aristotle's works translated from Greek into Latin. The works of Thomas Aquinas were a combination of Aristotle's thought and the Christian thought of the time. Aquinas suggested that reason was the basis for universal organization: he contended that there is no conflict between faith and reason. St. Thomas, however, did assign first priority to God, in stating that, since God cannot be at fault, any differences between conclusions based on reason and on faith must come from faulty reasoning. Although St. Thomas had

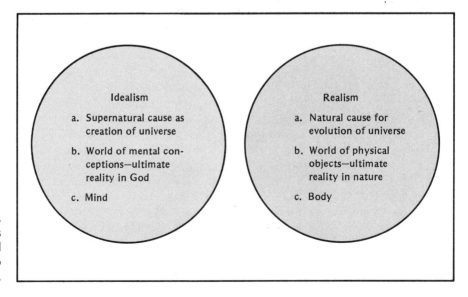

Figure 16–1. Dualistic positions of idealism and realism prior to the Middle Ages.

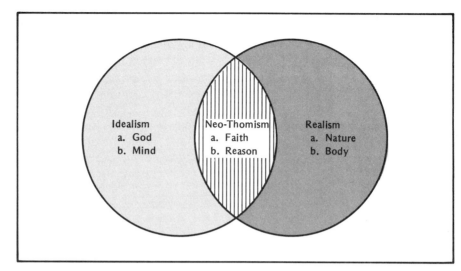

Figure 16–2.
Relationship between idealism, realism, and Neo-Thomism after the Middle Ages.

little success in solving the idealism-realism dualism, his views added new perspectives to the traditional Christian doctrines and consequently generated much interest in philosophical thought. The scholarship of the Christian philosophers is referred to as *Scholasticism*; Thomism is but one facet of Scholasticism. Scholasticism declined as a movement by the 1400s, rose again in the early 1600s, only to decline a second time before 1700. Pope Leo III (late 1800s) adopted Thomism as the official position of the Roman Catholic church. The version of Thomism being revived today has come to be known as Neo-Thomism. Neo-Thomism is divided into lay groups and ecclesiastical groups (Roman Catholic). The works of Thomas Aquinas and others have brought the philosophical positions of idealism and realism into contact with each other. Figure 16–2 demonstrates the contemporary relationship between idealism and realism and also shows the related position of Neo-Thomism. This schema also illustrates the contention of Aquinas that faith from *idealism* and reason from *realism* are not in conflict with each other.

Metaphysics of Neo-Thomism

The nature of reality in Neo-Thomism is that of the harmony of faith and reason. Reality is proposed to be a world of reason. Existence may be viewed as residing in the reasoning powers of the human mind. Ideas are real in and of themselves. Physical objects exist whether or not they are perceived by humans. The universe exists independent of people. However, Thomists argue that man, his ideas, his mind, and his spirit, as well as the physical objects in the world, have been created by God. Reality is dualistic to the Roman Catholic Neo-Thomists; however, the apparent antithesis of God and physical matter is not one of equal balance. While Neo-Thomists consider both God and physical matter real, God as a perfect being is considered more important.

Epistemology of
Neo-Thomism

Neo-Thomists seek knowledge through both faith and reason. The ecclesiastical group added revelation to intuition as the basis of their epistemology. Faith by which knowledge is affirmed is held as developing from history, the Bible, and God's word as taught by Jesus Christ. Knowledge is also gained through reason and experience. Basic knowledge, in this context, is in the realm of human thoughts. Empiricism serves as an instrument of knowledge whereby experience becomes the medium for gaining knowledge. On the basis of knowledge gained, people reason toward truth. The fundamental truths arrived at by reason and faith are unchangeable and dependable.

Axiology of
Neo-Thomism

What is of value to the lay and ecclesiastical Neo-Thomists? As with knowledge, values are permanent. Lay Neo-Thomists value moral law discerned by reason. People should live by these rational moral standards. The rational acts of men and women, their moral conduct, and their relations with others constitute their ethics. The ecclesiastical Neo-Thomists go beyond reasoning to insist that God has established the moral law and provided us with the power of reason for the purpose of finding God's moral law. Thus we are bound to conduct our lives according to God's moral laws because that is God's will.

**Contemporary
Bases**

Experimentalism, reconstructionism, and existentialism are the selected philosophical concepts that we will use to formulate the bases for the contemporary view of educational thought. Several other philosophical concepts, not discussed, could also be considered as a part of the bases for the contemporary view of education.

Experimentalism

By the beginning of the seventeenth century, England was rapidly growing in power and territory. As a consequence of this growth, a more practical approach to reality and knowledge was needed. A vast amount of new information that was being brought to England by merchants and scholars had to be combined with existing knowledge. The traditional beliefs and systems of thought regarding reality and knowledge seemed inadequate. Because of these conditions, a philosophical movement known as *empiricism* developed in England. Empiricism postulated experience to be the basis of reality and knowledge. Through the years, the term *empiricism* has been ambiguously associated with numerous positions and practices. The term *experimentalism* includes the appeal to experience related to the English empiricists as well as other experience-oriented thinkers. Although early Greek philosophers first suggested that experience was the basis of reality, experimentalism grew largely out of English empiricism and therefore is classified as a contemporary view. The philosophical speculations at the beginning of the seventeenth century centered around questions of one's acquisition of knowledge (epistemology) rather than questions of reality (metaphysics). A general premise of experimentalism, as well as empiricism, is that reality and knowledge are dependent upon one's observations and experiences.

Metaphysics of Experimentalism

What does reality become in this system of thought? What of the causality of the universe? The metaphysics of *experimentalism* appears to be flexible and capable of change—compared to the rigidly fixed metaphysical positions of the traditional philosophical concepts previously discussed. Each of us becomes the determiner of reality through individual conceptualizations. We may choose our beliefs regarding the origin and development of the universe. We may consider the universe as coming into existence as an act of God or as a natural process of evolution. Experimentalists consider the self as an occurrence in consciousness in contrast to an existence in itself. Each of us exists as a social part of the universe. Our self then becomes directly observable as an appearance or action. Our mind exists as a function of the brain so that observations of activities may be conceptualized. From responses to all such conceptualizations, we draw out those responses which give direction and meaning to reality. Thus one's actions are not determined by forces greater than oneself, nor is one capable of genuine initiative with free will or power of choice. Functioning in this manner, one becomes the determiner, or interpreter if you prefer, of numerous considerations of reality. Experimentalists see purpose in the universe as emerging from one's purposeful activity rather than purpose being inherent in existence or coming from accident. Reality is a changing quantity consisting of numerous activities, materials, and processes: everything is in a changing state. Nothing exists in any ultimate state, that is, immune from the possibility of change.

Epistemology of Experimentalism

In what way do we come to know truth? What is knowledge? Is it possible to have ultimate knowledge when *experimentalism* does not allow for ultimate reality? What is the source of knowledge for the experimentalists? Questions regarding the ways in which we acquire knowledge are of primary concern to experimentalism. Experimentalists believe truth to be that which is functional. What is necessary to solve our problems becomes the essence of our knowledge. Knowledge, while based on observations and experience, is not concluded to be final by experimentalists. Rather, knowledge is considered to be functional insofar as it may be used to solve one's problems. Knowledge is continually additive from the observations and experiences of the individual. *Agnosticism*, defined as the conclusive knowledge that ultimate reality is an impossibility, appears to be the credo of the experimentalists. Thus, experimentalism does not accept reality as ultimate, nor does it accept knowledge as conclusive. It is reasonable to assume that rationalism is a part of the experimentalist system of acquiring knowledge. The epistemological view of experimentalism suggests that knowledge (truth) is that which we know to solve our problems.

Self-knowledge is one of the valuable outcomes of a study of philosophy. (*Photograph by Ellis Herwig, Stock, Boston*)

Axiology of Experimentalism

What of values? What is the axiology of this system of thought? Experimentalists' values are relative. From what we know of the epistemology of experimentalists, it seems logical to consider their ethics as tentative. What is good or evil today may not be valued in a like manner in the future. One's moral status is largely determined by the public acceptance of one's conduct. The older members of society often judge the younger members to be "going to pot," which implies that a less moral system of values exists for the younger members. Experimentalism points to such judgments as evidence that moral standards change from generation to generation. The judgments of the members of the older generations are made from a pattern of ethics that has changed to a different pattern of ethics for younger generations. Aesthetics are determined by the public taste. Democracy as a way of life becomes a necessary ingredient of experimentalism's value structure. Only in a democracy is it possible for the nature of good and evil and the creation and appreciation of beautiful things to be assessed by all points of view in the public. Ethical and aesthetical values are those of continuous process. Values exist in a state of flux and are relative.

Figure 16–3 shows experimentalism in relation to the traditional philosophical concepts previously discussed. As indicated, experimentalism shares areas of conceptual overlap with idealism, neo-Thomism, and realism.

Existentialism *Existentialism* is a relatively recent philosophy spawned in Europe after World War I. Actually a Danish philosopher, Sören Kierkegaard (1813–1853), laid the foundation for existentialism when he wrote and taught of man's inner freedom to direct his own life. It was not until early in

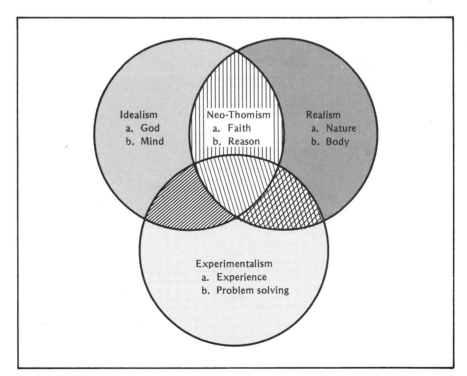

Figure 16–3. Relationship between realism, idealism, Neo-Thomism, and experimentalism.

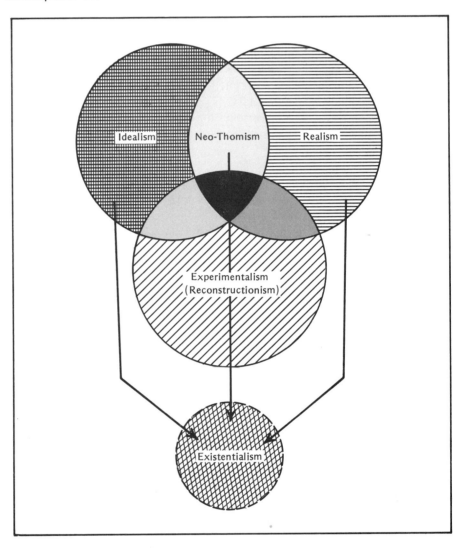

Figure 16–4.
Existentialism apart
from yet depend-
ent upon other
philosophies.

the 1900s that the works of Kierkegaard began to be translated into German; it was not until the 1930s that English translations appeared. As a consequence of both delayed translations of Kierkegaard and World War II, most of the development of existential philosophies has been of recent origin. To a degree, existentialism emphasizes casting off traditional and contemporary philosophies. Emphasis is placed on one's responsibility to set goals and to make decisions free from group norms. The individualistic character of existentialism has, in many instances, caused group-oriented societies to label existentialism as a faddish philosophy that is disinterested in morals. Such misinterpreted castigations of existentialism may be related to the popularity of the French playwright Jean-Paul Sartre, labeled as the leader of the atheistic camp within the existentialist movement. In practice, many existentialists are strongly theistic and hold that one's desires lead to knowledge of God. Of this group, the German Karl Jaspers and the French Gabriel Marcel, who are both Roman Catholics, represent the theistic segment of existentialism. George F. Kneller states that one of the obstacles in attempting to comprehend the general nature of existentialism is that it "cannot be studied objectively from without, but requires the student to identify himself with its doctrines from within."[2] Others say that existentialism is not a wholly new orientation of thought but rather an individualistic way of looking at other systems of thought. With the inner freedom of man or woman to determine existence, reality to the existentialist becomes one's subjective existence. There is no difference between one's external and internal world. What is true is represented by one's personal choice. We know ourselves as actors on life's scene and act according to individual choice. Existential values consist of the morality of people choosing freely. The existentialist finds beauty in one's capacity to function apart from the public norms. Nevertheless, existentialism stresses *responsibility*. While personal choice is important, once the choice is exercised, the existentialist accepts the responsibility accompanying that choice. Figure 16–4 shows existentialism to be apart from yet dependent upon other philosophies. Figure 16–4 also illustrates the notion that the various philosophical concepts overlap each other to some degree—whether generally categorized as traditional or contemporary. The contemporary educational view known as *reconstructionism* is discussed in the next chapter.

Summary and Implications   We hope that this brief overview has provided a basic introduction to some of the traditional and contemporary educational views held by American educators. At some point in their career development, most successful educators must come to grips with determining how learners —regardless of age or grade level—conceive of reality (metaphysics), knowledge (epistemology), and values (axiology). In this manner, the educator clarifies his or her personal belief system regarding learning and teaching. Practicing educators often find themselves compelled to pursue the study of philosophy as an academic and comprehensive discipline to clarify their personal beliefs about learning and teaching.

Discussion Questions

1. What effect did the modern emphasis on science have on problems of metaphysics?
2. In your opinion, why are educational psychologists so interested in epistemology?

3. What do you deduce from the fact that existentialism became popular in Europe shortly after World War I?

2. Ibid., p. 56.

4. What are your views concerning moral and spiritual values? Can moral values and spiritual values be considered separately—or must they be considered together?

5. Is intelligence in any way associated with the sensitivity an individual possesses in the field of aesthetics? How is education associated with aesthetics?

Supplemental Activities

1. Research and report on the life and work of St. Thomas Aquinas (1225–1274).
2. Research and report on a philosophical movement known as *empiricism,* which developed in England at the beginning of the seventeenth century.
3. Assign three class panels to discuss the (1) metaphysics, (2) epistemology, and (3) axiology of the traditional views of idealism and realism.
4. Assign three class panels to discuss the (1) metaphysics, (2) epistemology, and (3) axiology of the contemporary views of experimentalism.
5. Invite a professor of philosophy to class to discuss existentialism.

Bibliography

Burnett, Joe R. "Observations on the Logical Implications of Philosophic Theory for Educational Theory and Practice." *Educational Theory* 11 (April 1961): 65–70.

Dewey, John. *Democracy and Education.* New York: Macmillan, 1916.

Dewey, John. *The Quest for Certainty: A Study of the Relation of Knowledge and Action.* New York: Minton, Balch, 1929.

Kattsoff, L. O. "Observation and Interpretation in Science." *Philosophical Review* 56 (1947): 682–689.

Naumann, St. Elmo, Jr., ed. *The New Dictionary of Existentialism.* New York: Philosophical Library, 1971.

Sartre, Jean-Paul. *Existentialism and Human Emotions.* New York: Philosophical Library, 1957.

Scheffler, Israel. *Conditions of Knowledge: An Introduction to Epistemology and Education.* Chicago: Scott, Foresman, 1965.

Taylor, A. E. *Elements of Metaphysics.* 12th ed. London: Methuen, 1946.

Whitehead, Alfred North. *The Aims of Education.* New York: New American Library, 1929.

Wingo, G. Max. *The Philosophy of American Education.* Boston: D.C. Heath, 1965.

CHAPTER 17

Traditional and Contemporary Educational Views

EACH OF THE EDUCATIONAL VIEWS CONSIDERED IN THE FOLLOW-
ing discussion, particularly essentialism, perennialism, progressivism,
and reconstructionism, is reflected with varying degrees of emphasis
in today's schools. With regard to their present-day application, each
of the educational views might be thought of as contemporary. Generally, the basic traditional philosophical concepts are contained in the
educational views of *essentialism* and *perennialism*, whereas the basic
contemporary philosophical concepts are contained in the educational
views of *progressivism* and *reconstructionism*. The philosophical concepts of both idealism and realism as related to metaphysics (reality),
epistemology (knowledge), and axiology (values) are contained in essentialism. The philosophical concepts of Neo-Thomism are carried into
perennialism. Of these two traditional views, essentialism is the leading educational philosophy.

The philosophical concepts of experimentalism are related directly
to progressivism. Progressivism, which is considered by most educational philosophers to also contain reconstructionism, is regarded as
the major contemporary educational view. As a philosophy of education, progressivism is uniquely American. It has grown to a position of
dominant influence upon public education in the United States during
the short span of the past sixty years. On the one hand, *progressivism*
is generally credited as the prime mover in bringing about considerable
change in educational theory and practice; on the other hand, progressivism—with its close relationship to *experimentalism*—is the target of
considerable philosophical opposition, which calls for alternative and
different views.

Since the school in the United States is a social organization, it is
very difficult to define an educational view of *existentialism*. Existen-

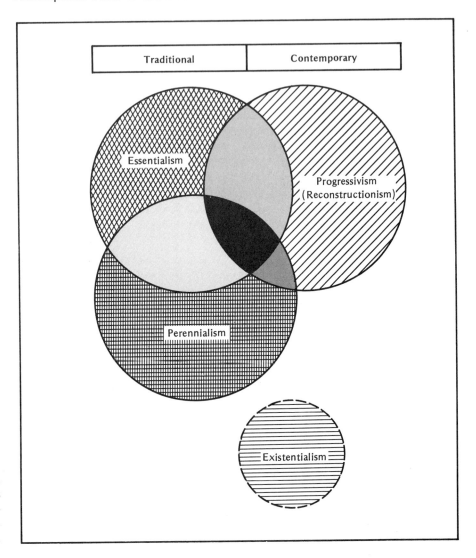

Figure 17–1.
Relationships
among educa-
tional philoso-
phies.

tialism is oriented toward the individual and, therefore, cannot be wholly adapted for use in a social institution. Existentialism has been described as "a name for a philosophical tendency rather than a philosophy."[1] Nonetheless, several attempts have been made to relate existentialism to education. Currently many educators are repudiating the overly social, group-oriented activities of schools and favoring programs that stress the individuality and personal integrity of the learners. Thus a central theme of existentialism, which places considerable emphasis on the interests of the existing individual, may be manifested

1. Joe Park, *Selected Readings in the Philosophy of Education* (New York: Macmillan, 1963), p. 530.

to a large degree in contemporary curriculum trends. Figure 17–1 shows the relationship of the educational views as systems for educating groups of students in our schools. Since existentialism is more a philosophical tendency than an educational system, it is shown apart from the interrelatedness of the other educational views.

Figure 17–2, developed by Van Cleve Morris and Young Pai, illustrates traditional and contemporary relationships between the basic philosophical concepts and respective educational views.[2] Since 1961, several educational practices, which have specific terminology associated with them, have earned varying degrees of popularity. Some of the newer methodologies, such as *behavior modification,* may be considered as traditional in practice. Others, such as *free schools,* may be considered as basically contemporary in practice. The point is the adapted schema in Figure 17–2 are not meant to be all inclusive.

Essentialism   As a clearly defined educational philosophy, *essentialism* was formulated in a paper presented to a group of educators in 1938 by William C. Bagley.[3] It has been a dominant practice of schools considered on a worldwide basis, past and present. Although *progressivism* has been extremely popular in America, essentialism appears destined to continue to be the dominant worldwide educational view. The Essentialist Committee for the Advancement of Education, led by Bagley, launched an attack upon progressivism, which had gained considerable support in the 1920s. At present, the influence of essentialism continues to be felt more and more strongly even though the Essentialist Committee has been inactive since Bagley's death in 1946.

Essentialism holds that the *essential* elements of education be selected from historical and contemporary knowledge. The function of the schools becomes that of teaching such *essentials* of education. Essentialism includes the philosophical tenets of idealism and realism. From idealism, the idea of viewing the mind as the central element of reality becomes a significant factor in determining the essentials of essentialism. Realism contributes the basic view that reality is in things or physical objects and leads to an emphasis on the quantitative aspects of education. Organization and factual mastery of content are imperative if one is to learn through observation and nature. Essentialism advocates the return to the fundamentals of learning—the three Rs.

Since essentialism has advocates who may be either idealists or realists, it does not constitute a united front. When considering theories of learning in essentialism, it becomes necessary to examine the idealist theories and the realist theories. Idealism depicts the learner as a miniature mind of the absolute mind of God. Knowledge is gained by

2.   Van Cleve Morris and Young Pai, *Philosophy and the American School,* 2nd ed. (Boston: Houghton Mifflin, 1976), pp. 294–295.
3.   William C. Bagley, "An Essentialist's Platform for the Advancement of American Education," *Educational Administration and Supervision* (April 1938): 241–256.

Figure 17–2. Schematic summary of views.

Comparative Philosophies

	Definition	Idealism	Realism	Neo-Thomism	Experimentalism	Existentialism
Metaphysics	The study of reality: What is real?	A world of mind	A world of things	A world of Reason and Being/God	A world of experience	A world of existing
Epistemology	The study of knowing and knowledge: What is true?	Seeing with the "mind's eye"—consistency of ideas	Spectator Theory: sensation and correspondence	Intuition, logical reasoning, and revelation	Testing to see what works	Subjective choice, personal appropriation
Axiology — **Ethics**	The study of valuing and values: What is good?	The imitation of the Absolute Self	The law of nature	The rational act	The public test	The anguish of freedom
Axiology — **Aesthetics**	What is beautiful?	Reflection of the Ideal	Reflection of nature	Creative intuition	The public taste	Revolt from the public norm

Source: Van Cleve Morris and Young Pai, *Philosophy and the American School,* 2nd ed. (Boston: Houghton Mifflin, 1976), pp. 294–295. Reprinted by permission.

Educational Implications

	Idealism	Realism	Neo-Thomism	Experimentalism	Existentialism
Curricular Emphasis	Subject matter of the mind: literature, intellectual history, philosophy, religion	Subject matter of the physical world: mathematics and science	Subject matter of intellect and spirit; disciplinary subjects: mathematics and language and doctrine	Subject matter of social experience: the social studies	Subject matter of choice: art, ethics, moral philosophy, religion
Preferred Method	Teaching for the handling of ideas: lecture, discussion	Teaching for mastery of factual information and basic skills: demonstration, recitation	Disciplining the mind: formal drill—readying the spirit: catechism	Problem solving: project method	Arousing personal response: Socratic questioning
Character Education	Imitating exemplars, heroes	Training in rules of conduct	Disciplining behavior to reason	Making group decisions in light of consequences	Awakening the self to responsibility
Developing Taste	Studying the masterworks	Studying design in nature	Finding beauty in reason	Participating in art projects	Composing a personal art work

intuition, revelation, and authoritarianism. The mind of the learner must be actively involved: any form of education that lends to the training of the mind is supported by essentialism. Development of abilities for remembering, reasoning, and comprehending is important. Such learning activities are thought to contribute to the spiritual outreaching of idealism. As the individual mind develops, the learner becomes more like the Spiritual Being. The learner is closer to ultimate knowledge when he or she gradually assumes the mind qualities of God. Idealism also includes some of the more recent findings that stress the psychology of learning. In this realm, the mind is believed to have the capability of combining pieces of learning into more meaningful whole concepts.

Aspects of learning theory related to realism have received greater attention in educational psychology than the views of idealism. In the realist school, the theory is that the learner adjusts to or becomes aware of his or her relation to the physical world. Realists' educational philosophies are closely associated with reality as a natural world of things. The observable facts of the external world of nature constitute knowledge. The learner is considered a sense mechanism who becomes aware of the scientific facts and laws of nature as the foundation of ultimate knowledge.

The essentialist curriculum, as developed from the idealist point of view, contains subject matter of symbol and content. Such subject matter includes literature, history, foreign languages, and religion. Methodology requires formal discipline through emphasis on required reading, lectures, memorization, repetition, and examinations.

Realist philosophers of education differ in their views on curriculum, but generally they agree regarding the inclusion of subject matter of the physical world. Mathematics and the natural sciences are examples of subjects that contribute to the learner's knowledge of natural law. Activities that require mastering facts and information on the physical world are significant aspects of realist methodology. With truth defined as observable fact, field trips, laboratories, audiovisual materials, and nature are ingredients of methodology. Habits of intellectual discipline are held to be ends in themselves. Realism advocates the study of the laws of nature and the accompanying universal truths of the physical world.

Essentialism envisions subject matter as the core of the educational process. Severe criticism has been leveled at American education by those who advocate an emphasis on basic education. Essentialism assigns to the schools the task of conserving the heritage and transmitting knowledge of the physical world. In a sense, the school is a curator of knowledge. Herein lies the major criticism of essentialism: with the burgeoning of new knowledge, essentialism as the curator of past knowledge may contribute to the slow manner in which our schools change.

The open class-
room with flexible
arrangements of
desks is a marked
change from the
traditional class-
room. (*Photograph
by Talbot Lovering*)

Summary of
Essentialism

Today essentialism (often identified by other terms) is experiencing a strong resurgence not only in education but even more in scholarship and among intellectuals. Indeed, among many of the latter it is now more fashionable to repudiate than to defend progressivist-liberal ideals and to express a sophisticated conservatism that is not necessarily identified with any formal philosophy.

If its contemporary import is to be understood, essentialism . . . must be observed in its historic context. Most of its leading exponents are still strikingly devoted disciples of the two major systems of philosophic thought —idealism and realism—that emerged in the Renaissance and attained their mature formulations between the early part of the eighteenth and the latter part of the nineteenth centuries. The expressions into which each system matured are extremely diverse and not always internally consistent, with the consequence that essentialism, which includes both idealism and realism, abounds with eclectic elements.

Despite their differences, however, idealist and realist philosophies alike are deeply concerned with the three chief areas of belief: reality, knowledge, and value. And all three, after many qualifications are taken into account, converge around one common belief—namely, that reality in both its more personal and its more objective expressions is governed by uniform, permanent, and antecedently determined regularities, procedures, principles, and axioms of all truth, all goodness, and all beauty. Idealists find in this belief the "reason for being" of a spiritual universe, while realists usually associate it with a more material, machine-like universe. Although, in certain writings, some exponents of both positions find the individual more important than the law-abiding universe of which he is an integral part, they most often seek to integrate him, his knowledge and his conduct, within the whole of that universe.

Philosophers of education in every modern century beginning with the fifteenth-century Erasmus may be broadly identified with the essentialist movement. Today, however, they cannot, even if they wish to do so, disregard the influence of recent developments in philosophy and psychology. Their theories of learning, for example, often incorporate functional, organismic tendencies with strong democratic implications. At the same time, despite such modernizing and the attractions of "later liberalism" for some of them, they remain admirably loyal to the idealist and realist belief that truth must be measured by the exactitude of correspondence with prior structures, facts, events, and causes, that is, with spiritual or physical relations and laws. Thus, when appraised in terms of their total impact their curriculum proposals, for example, are found to be based primarily on inherited subject matters in content and sequence and to be tested by quantitative techniques borrowed from the exact sciences. Finally, their conception of the school's role in society, although influenced by recent developments of democratic tendency, is to emulate patterns of control of the wider cultural environment—line-staff administration, local school autonomy, training of skilled and obedient workers, discipline by the mature over the immature, and a dominant leadership to formulate and carry out policy.

The significance of essentialism in our own culture can be fully appraised, however, only as the great systems of modern philosophy are placed in the setting of more than four centuries of history—centuries marked by both destructive turbulence and momentous accomplishments, of which by far the most destructive and momentous is the rise of a new type of economy. This gigantic and powerful economy, which came to be called capitalism, has required new political institutions to support its expansion and to sanction the authority of its promoters. Equally, if less obviously, capitalism requires the continuous cooperation of the economy with science, religion, morality, and education. The school thus comes to serve, both theoretically and practically, as one of the key underpinnings of modern culture. For not only does it train leaders to control and workers to function under its socioeconomic institutions but—of even more importance—it cultivates habits of devotion to and compliance with those institutions. Viewed in this historical perspective essentialist education may be seen to have served the culture well. Indeed, on the basis of its own premises it was and still is "good" education, having made permanent and constructive contributions to society and to the development of education. The success of realism in analyzing educational processes in terms of scientific canons, for example, has advanced such fields as educational psychology, and the idealist stress upon selfhood has helped to provide a more friendly school atmosphere for individual child development.

But essentialism, although a dynamic force in the earlier stages of modern history, becomes a conserving force as the culture that formerly nourished it and to which it has since been loyal and grateful strains toward further sweeping change. In a crisis-culture such as our own, therefore, essentialism performs primarily the role of protecting the culture against the encroachments typified by progressivism. The performance of such a role is an educational symptom of a great cultural lag—the results of which are various concealments frequently not recognized as such even by essentialism's sincere proponents. Thus, the social heritage is often glorified for its own sake and without discrimination. Learning becomes largely an acquiescent process of corresponding with, by responding to and representing, the selective stimuli of those who control the schools in the interests of their own entrenched patterns of authority. And the belief that both individual self and objective world are governed by predetermined uniformities and mandates becomes a subtle, sometimes inadvertent, but still potent means to instill habits of conformity with what has been and hence is assumed still to be both inevitable and right.[4]

Perennialism   The basic educational view of *perennialism* is that the principles of knowledge in this system are truly perennial. Perennialism is the parent philosophy of essentialism. The foundation of the perennialist educational view is vested in the work of Thomas Aquinas, who stressed that the rational powers of humans along with faith were the instruments of knowledge. Thomism recognized the importance of human daily life as well as the supernatural virtues not derived from experience; consequently, it has probably had as large a following as any Western philosophy. Nevertheless, Thomism declined when knowledge expanded so rapidly that the academic disciplines found it difficult to fit the expanding knowledge into the confines of such a closed system of thought.

In the past few decades, perennialist philosophy has been revived under the heading of Neo-Thomism. Growing numbers of intellectuals adhere to the thinking that the basic beliefs and knowledge of ancient cultures can be successfully applied to our lives today. Historically Thomism has been associated with the Roman Catholic church, but the revival of perennialism in America is associated mainly with lay educators. Differences between the views of lay and ecclesiastical Neo-Thomists, if judged by religious standards, would be considered vast. Yet Roman Catholic educators have welcomed the revival of the Scholasticism of Thomas Aquinas and share many common educational views with lay perennialists.

The focus of learning in perennialism lies in activities designed to discipline the mind. Subject matter of a disciplinary and spiritual nature such as the content of mathematics, languages, logic, great books, and

4.   From *Philosophies of Education in Cultural Perspective* by Theodore Brameld, pp. 281–284. Copyright © 1955 by Holt, Rinehart and Winston, Inc. Reprinted by permission of Holt, Rinehart and Winston.

doctrines must be studied. The point is that the study of such subjects disciplines the mind. The learner is assumed to be a rational and spiritual person. The methods of teaching are cut-and-dried. Difficult mental calisthenics such as reading, writing, drill, rote memory, and computations are important in training the intellect. Perennialism holds that learning to reason is also very important and is attainable only by additional mental exercises in grammar, logic, and rhetoric.

With regard to school curriculum, the perennialist believes that schooling in the early years is best directed toward preparation for maturity and emphasizes the three Rs in the elementary schools. In this view, perennialism and essentialism share some common thoughts. Some lay and ecclesiastical perennialists consider character training, enhanced through Bible study, as equally important at the elementary level. At the secondary level, the perennialist's program of education becomes more directed toward the education of the intellectually elite. Perennialism favors trade and skill training for those students who are not engaged in the rigors of the general education program. Perennialists generally agree that the curriculum at the secondary level should provide a general education program for the intellectually gifted and vocational training for the less gifted. All perennialists are not in agreement about the curriculum design for general education. While it is true that the Great Books Program associated with Robert M. Hutchins and Mortimer Adler has brought the most attention to perennialism, other leaders in this movement do not support such a program. Those who endorse the Great Books Program maintain that studying the works of the leading scholars of history is the best means to general education. Perennialists who do not favor the Great Books Program maintain that contemporary sources may be used to acquire knowledge. The ecclesiastical perennialists insist that all programs give priority to the study of theology.

Perennialism and essentialism are criticized as being obsolete. Such criticism implies that neither perennialism nor essentialism satisfies the twentieth-century needs of our youth. The philosophers within the movement deny such criticism and claim to have incorporated modern influences into the system. Perennialism is also criticized as being in opposition to democracy: the system calls for the education of the intellectually elite. Leaders of society would be drawn from the carefully developed intelligentsia. Within the educational system, any allegiance to democratic processes is disregarded: the process of perennialism is almost entirely authoritative. In spite of the fact that perennialists have a general concern for educating all youth, the manner in which the educational programs operate is not democratic. This has led some to suggest that perennialism, as an educational system, would contribute to the development of undemocratic attitudes in the minds of its students.

Summary of Perennialism

Perennialism, as a philosophy of education, is rooted in a philosophy of culture. Its central position is regressive in the precise sense that it reacts against such characteristic beliefs of our present democratic culture as science and majority control in favor of a constellation of beliefs characterizing great cultures of past ages. In this regression, it draws most heavily upon three thinkers—Plato, Aristotle, and Aquinas—revising their principles only superficially, often merely by expressing them in terminology more appropriate to the twentieth century. Differences between clerical and secular perennialists arise in the area of theology—the former upholding the supremacy of the Roman Catholic church and its interpretations of perennialist doctrine. Nevertheless, the two wings of perennialist philosophy recognize at least as many common principles, if judged by cultural and hence educational consequences, as do the realist and the idealist wings of essentialist philosophy.

Perennialist beliefs about reality pivot around the doctrine of hylomorphism: the unfolding of everlasting or perennial forms which lie potentially within matter. This doctrine is developed with great complexity through many related principles, among the most important of which are teleology (belief in the inherently purposeful character of all beings) and supernaturalism (belief in the existence of a realm of absolute spirit, which finally controls all lower realms).

Beliefs about knowledge are strictly consistent with these principles of reality. Knowledge arises in ascending levels of purity, from the sheer ignorance of material passion through intermediate levels of empirical method and opinion to that level of rare achievement of reason and spirit where self-evident first principles and, still higher, revelation stand as the supreme accomplishments of man.

Beliefs about value rise also in an increasingly more nearly perfect series—the "moral" virtues being subordinate to the "intellectual." Art and prudence are characterized by both the moral and the intellectual virtues. Politics, although concerned primarily with the moral virtues, is nevertheless also inspired by the intellectual-spiritual fountainhead of metaphysics and extranatural intuition.

Perennialist education is a unified development of its own deepest philosophy. Even the particular educational proposals of contemporary thinkers are often astonishingly similar to ancient-medieval proposals. Learning, for example, is typified by the kind of mental discipline that guarantees the maximum unfolding of man's more or less latent rationality, while teaching is best characterized by the assistance it gives man in this developing. This does not mean that perennialist educators are always unconcerned about emotional or other kinds of experience; rather, quite consistently with their belief in man's many-sided nature, they may borrow from progressivist and other modern practices. They are careful, however, to point out the signal limitations of this kind of education. They return always, therefore, to the key principle—learning is ultimately not *doing* but *reasoning*—and hence to the supreme importance of education of the mind and spirit.

We may understand from this doctrine why perennialist curriculums often closely resemble essentialist emphases upon learning by correspondence, upon mental substances, and upon similar beliefs. But in the perennialist programs for junior colleges, adult education, and higher learning (great books are central to the first two, training of intellectual leaders to the third) its proposals are more original.

In their approach to social and educational control, perennialist educators are concerned chiefly with fomenting a "spiritual and intellectual revolution." With rare exceptions, programs of control, processes, and means might seem ambiguous or innocuous were we to forget that they are held to be relatively unimportant by comparison with the need for "rational" training of the many and philosophic-religious leadership by the few.

In evaluating this profound and influential philosophy of education, we must recall primarily not only that it is derived directly from aristocratic, hierarchical patterns of culture but also that it proves to be both interpreter and archapologist for just such patterns. In final analysis, the crisis that contemporary perennialists find so threatening to our own civilization is to be met by restoring the kind of beliefs most characteristic of and fundamental to both ancient and medieval cultures, adapted to modern conditions.[5]

Progressivism   *Progressivism* is a contemporary American educational philosophy. Since its establishment in the mid-1920s, progressivism has been the most influential educational view in America. Progressivists are basically opposed to authoritarianism and favor human experiences as a basis for knowledge. The progressivist believes that all things are in a state of flux; therefore, no stress is given to absolute knowledge. Progressivism favors the scientific method of teaching and learning, allows for the beliefs of individuals, and stresses programs of student involvement that help teach students how to think. With the rise of democracy in America, the expansion of modern science and technology, and the need for all people to be able to adjust to change, contemporary America needed a new and different approach to the acquisition of knowledge to solve problems. Although the beginning of the progressivist movement had its origin in the pragmatism of Charles S. Peirce and William James, the underlying principles of progressivism as the contemporary educational philosophy stem from the writings and works of John Dewey.

Progressivists feel that the school should actively prepare its students for change. A major emphasis of the progressive schools is placed on learning how to think rather than what to think. Flexibility is an important term in the curriculum design. Emphasis is placed on experimentation, with no single body of content stressed more than any other. Since the experiences of life determine curriculum content, all types of content must be permitted for study. Certain learning areas regarded as traditional subjects are recognized by progressivists as desirable areas for study. Progressivist educators would organize scientific method-oriented learning activities around the traditional subject areas. Such

5.   Ibid., pp. 378–380.

Classroom management often reflects the educational direction of the local school board. (*Photograph by Talbot Lovering*)

curriculum approaches are called *experience-centered* or *student-centered*, whereas the essentialist and perennialist curriculum is *subject-centered*. Progressivism calls for bringing pupils together in heterogeneous, integrated groups so that the benefits of socialization are incorporated in the learning activity. Considerable stress is placed on the processes of learning rather than on the end results of learning. The "problem approach" to learning functions less well when school authorities routinely define the problem areas and then form a curriculum of specific courses for each student to study. Progressivism is **more** compatible with a core of problem areas across all academic disciplines than with a subject-centered approach. It would be naive to suggest that memorization and rote practice are ruled out of the progressive approach to education. However, it is valid to suggest that progressivism does not stress memorization of facts and rote practice as primary learning techniques. The assertion is that interest in an intellectual activity will generate all the practice needed for learning.

A tenet of progressivism is that the schools become major societal institutions assigned the task of improving the way of life in society. To this end, the progressive school is deemed a working model of democracy. Freedom is explicit in a democracy, so freedom must be explicit in our schools. Certainly freedom—rather than being a haphazard release of free will—must be organized to have meaning. Organized freedom permits each member of the school society to share in the making of decisions. Experiences must be shared by all in order to assure meaningful decision making.

The learner is viewed as an experiencing, thinking, exploring individual. Progressivism exposes the learner to the subject matter of social experiences, social studies, projects, problems, and experiments that, when studied by the scientific method, will result in functional knowledge from all subject matter areas. Books are regarded as tools to be used in the learning process rather than as sources of indisputable knowledge. Progressivism can be viewed as liberal in all respects pertaining to books, pupils, teachers, discipline, learning devices, and teaching methods.

Many believe that the socialization aspects of progressive education are the most valuable aspects of the movement. Progressivism, in this way, represents the growing edge of our heritage and teaches our members how to manage change. Progressivism is criticized for placing so much stress on the processes of education that the ends of education are neglected. Progressive schools have been labeled "uncommitted" as an outgrowth of their curriculum philosophy. Their severe critics contend that there is little personal commitment to anything—the result producing many graduates who are likewise uncommitted and who are content to drift through life. Progressivism as an educational view is young and, by its basic principle of the scientific method, is willing to make trial-and-error mistakes. Whether or not progressivism withstands the stresses of time, one cannot deny that its advent has given considerable excitement and impetus to the total educational movement.

Summary of Progressivism

Progressivism is the educational expression of the "liberal road to culture." Influenced deeply by the fertile and eager American environment, it is grounded philosophically in pragmatism—instrumentalism—experimentalism as developed primarily by three emancipating thinkers: Peirce, James, and Dewey. Its beliefs about reality focus on the concept that natural experience is dynamic, temporal, spatial, pluralistic. Its beliefs about knowledge revolve around intelligence as the scientific method operating in every area of experience. (Thus, the act of thought—awareness of obstacles, analysis, suggestions, inference, and active testing—becomes central to logic as a theory of inquiry into problems significant for living.) Pragmatic beliefs about value, related always to nature and intelligence, crystallize in: (1) such interactive principles of conduct as intrinsic and instrumental and personal and social values; (2) a philosophy of art that stresses the rhythm of esthetic expression between the doing or mediate phase of experience and the undergoing or immediate phase; (3) the supreme value of democracy both as critique of the shortcomings of our culture and as norm of the possibilities for growing and sharing richly in the creative opportunities of natural and cultural life.

As educational theory and practice, progressivism, like pragmatism, derives from many thinkers and cultural influences and commands great prestige through organizations as well as experimental schools. Its doctrine of learning rests upon its ontology, epistemology, and axiology. Therefore, it stresses the fullness of experience and the "whole child" as the proper subject matter of education, and it refines its psychology through such operational concepts as interest, effort, habit, growth, organism, culture, and, above all, intelligence. Its curriculum proposals, typically experimental, are perhaps most advanced in the "experience-centered curriculum," which discards fixed contents and routines in favor of units built cooperatively upon needs and interests of the learners. In developing its educational methodology, progressivism aims to substitute "real problems" for the "cookbook problems" of traditional courses; it admits drill only as a subordinate technique; it rejects indoctrination and the dichotomy between work and play; it supports both child-centered and community-centered schools but would prefer that one school should be both; and it favors greatly widened adult education. In its approach to the problem of education and social control, progressivism insists that freedom is a positive correlate of order. Hence, it approves the kind of discipline that emerges from freely associated living and participating, just as it disapproves line-staff school administrations. Progressivists are not equally agreed, however, in translating into concrete practice their generalizations about social control. For example, some favor and some disfavor affiliation of teachers with organized labor. They are also not agreed or clear on how much or what kinds of social controls they favor in the "planning society," which they endorse in opposition to both *laissez faire* individualism and a "planned society."

In evaluating progressivism it is necessary to bear in mind that its strengths and weaknesses are those of Western culture, in general, and American culture, in particular. It is from these cultures that progressivism emerges and to which it renders loyal service. In essence, Western culture developed to its present stage of acute instability after breaking away from medievalism and evolving through two overlapping stages, which we have called early and later liberalism. Early liberalism was characterized by the virtues of private competition, agrarian self-sufficiency, and frontier independence.

Later liberalism, while incorporating strong qualities of its precursor, is more fully industrialized, integrated, and dynamic. Progressivism is the epitome of later liberalism in that it attempts to maintain a steady growth of relations between individual-social responsibilities and activities. In contradistinction to the three-R's school of agrarian culture, it wishes to widen the sphere of learning interests so as to embrace the entire communal experience of children and adults while at the same time paying close attention to the interests of the individual. Its greater concern with the continuous *process* of interaction between self and society than with the determination of the normative and descriptive *products* of that interaction gives it a peculiarly pendulum-like quality.

In recent years the flexibility and cultural continuity that characterize liberalism, although extremely popular in progressive education and in liberal politics, law, and economics, have faced determined opposition. Progressive education has become a term of repugnance to great numbers of educators and laymen who have been influenced by well-organized, widely publicized, heavily financed attacks. Although progressivism meets many of its critics effectively, they continue to be articulate and often influential. Ultimate reasons for the strength of the attackers, however, are not to be discovered merely in critical evaluation of educational beliefs and practices. And they are not to be found only in the fact that some progressivist leaders fail, because of their own eclectic tendencies, to recognize the actual unity between their educational methods and the philosophic principles that underlie these methods. They are found still more fundamentally in the roots of a culture that suffers acutely from crisis—from the fears and intimidations spawned by the Cold War and other insecurities—a culture that tends, therefore, to become restless, dissatisfied with the optimistic and compromising spirit of gradual progress so excellently typified by later liberalism.

If we are not to turn back from liberalism-progressivism to either the conservative-essentialist or the regressivist-perennialist alternative (both of which have strong appeal for some individuals and some powerful groups, both of which deserve to be heard with the care and respect . . .), our task is not to reject but to re-examine, correct, and supplement liberalism-progressivism as fully and forthrightly as possible. Basic to our task is the diagnosis of two spheres of tension that are, we believe, chronic to this theory and program: one, the tension between means and ends; the other, the tension between individuality and sociality. The great opportunity that now rises before citizens and teachers in search of philosophy of life and education appropriate to our revolutionary age is to consider how each of these tensions can be at once utilized and constructively released: the tension between means and ends, through courageous commitments, convictions, and future-centered purposes, which, in the course of their attainment, strengthen and refine scientific methodology; the tension between individuality and sociality, through relentless analysis of cultural obstacles, through aggressive social strategies, and through enhancement of the values of the individual in the normative matrix of a designed world order and a *planned* democratic culture.

The task is supremely difficult, and we may fail. But it must be undertaken if we are to maintain and advance the richest single contribution thus far made by American philosophy and education to the welfare of mankind.[6]

Reconstructionism Theodore Brameld, a leading American philosopher of education, is regarded as the father of *reconstructionism*. While reconstructionism is sometimes regarded as a part of progressivism, Brameld presents reconstructionism as a separate organizing category having something in common with essentialism, perennialism, and progressivism. He states that "Essentialism and Perennialism, especially, will be found to share a good deal of the same philosophic, educational, and cultural outlook, as do Reconstructionism and Progressivism share theirs."[7] Figure 17–3 illustrates the position of reconstructionism in relation to the other educational views.

A persistent reconstructionist thesis is that public education should be the direct instrument of world reformation. Hobert W. Burns reviewed reconstructionism and the many books and articles written by

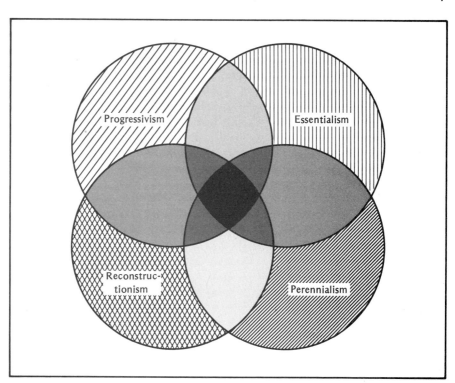

Figure 17–3. Brameld's view of reconstruction as an educational philosophy.

Source: From *Philosophies of Education in Cultural Perspective* by Theodore Brameld, p. 77. Copyright © 1955 by Holt, Rinehart and Winston, Inc. Reprinted by permission of Holt, Rinehart and Winston.

6. Ibid., pp. 197–200.
7. Theodore Brameld, *Patterns of Educational Philosophy* (New York: Holt, Rinehart and Winston, 1971), pp. 63–64.

Theodore Brameld. Burns identified the central concern of reconstructionism as this: "We are in the midst of a worldwide crisis, the only effective solution to which is the creation of a planetary social order, and the schools of the world should be the engines powering the reconstruction of earth men and their cultures."[8] Burns further suggested:

> the raison d'être of [Brameld's] concern and anxiety lies implicit in the basic premise that we are facing the very end of civilization as we know it (the crisis-culture thesis), upon the analysis that salvation can come only through a reconstructed world order (the end), which would be the consequence of a dramatic, radical alteration in the structure, function, and purpose of education throughout the world (the means). This is no gentle thesis, for the philosophic concepts and practical suggestions of Reconstructionism entail social, political, and economic revolutions on such a scale and in such a depth as to be more reminiscent of Marx than Dewey, even though Brameld's technical philosophic thought evidences a heavier dependence upon Dewey than Marx. Indeed, some have said and Brameld has implied that reconstructionism should be treated as the logical extension and chronological updating of Dewey's social and educational thought.[9]

Existentialism Generally the American system of education has been dependent upon group processes and group norms. In such a group-oriented system, *existentialism* does not serve as a functional philosophy of American public education, since existentialism directs its attention to individual self-fulfillment. Currently American educators are giving considerable attention to problems and processes concerned with individual differences. Much of this effort has been aimed at minimizing the individual difference variables by such tactics as forming homogeneous groupings for particular subject matter instruction. The rationale for these practices is that the group instruction can proceed more smoothly since the individuals involved are better adjusted to the group. With reference to helping adjust the individual to the group, an existentialist would argue: "this we now know to be a lost cause, for studies in many fields lead us to the same conclusion, that the extent of these differences is far greater than we thought. Much injustice has been done in the process of ironing them out and many a personality violated."[10]

From the sixties to the present, the influence of existentialism may be identified with various innovative programs and with various written materials. A. S. Neill proposes a "radical approach to child rearing" in his book *Summerhill*. Charles E. Silberman, in his *Crisis in the Classroom*, calls for "the remaking of American education" to provide for greater consideration of the individual. Various textbooks discuss such themes

8. Hobert W. Burns, "Brameld's Reconstructionism Reviewed," *Phi Delta Kappan* (November 1965): 147.
9. Ibid., p. 148.
10. George F. Kneller, "Education, Knowledge, and the Problem of Existence," *Harvard Educational Review* 31 (fall 1961): 430.

as the open access curriculum, humanism in education, nongraded instruction, and multiage grouping, each of which attends to the uniqueness of the learner. In their school programs, educators are now making various attempts to individualize education. Modular scheduling permits greater flexibility for students to arrange classes of their choice. Free schools, storefront schools, schools without walls, and area vocational centers provide alternatives to attendance within the traditional schools. Educational programs that maximize the needs of the individual are usually more costly per pupil than the traditional group-centered programs. Consequently, as taxpayer demands for accountability mount, individualized programs often are brought under unit cost scrutiny. Nonetheless, increasing numbers of educators are willing to defend increased expenditures to meet the needs of the individual learner within the instructional programs of the schools.

Existentialism advocates complete sensitivity to the specifics of individual uniqueness. This does not necessarily imply that emphasis given to the development of the individual has no place in the public schools merely because such activity would be contrary to the group orientation of the public educational system. The classroom teacher would need to function from a conceptual base that rules out time-honored conventional notions. With regard to the existentialist view of the individual as unique and the commensurate effects upon the teacher's conception of education, George Kneller writes: "To begin, it rules out three conventional notions: that education is primarily an agency of society, set up to perpetuate a cultural heritage; that it is a pipeline of perennial truths; and that it is a means for adjusting the young to life in a democratic community. In place of these, let education exist for the individual. Let it teach him to live as his own nature bids him, spontaneously and authentically."[11]

The most significant writings of the existential philosophers are concerned with university education (e.g. Jasper's *The Idea of the University*). General speaking, existential philosophers have not been concerned with philosophical discussions of the issues of mass education; however, the writings of educational philosophers do provide descriptive commentaries about certain existential views related to education. William F. O'Neil, professor of social and philosophical foundations of education at the University of Southern California, provides some insight regarding the existentialist's advocacy of education for moral choice:

> In the last ten or fifteen years educators have become increasingly aware of just how little they know, not only about ethics in general, but about the whole process of education for the development of moral character. It is probably true that to some degree this discomfiting sense of disorientation stems from a radical new sense of urgency with respect to the whole ques-

11. Ibid., p. 428.

tion of human values which has in part grown out of the activities of a relatively small group of intellectuals who are frequently referred to as "the existentialists."

Existentialism is a difficult term to define. In perhaps the most basic sense, it is a sort of metaphysical first principle which holds that all meaning is a product of direct personal experience. Existentialism at its broadest does not necessarily imply any particular concepts of value. On the other hand, most existentialist philosophers have clearly developed their theories beyond the bare assertion that "existence precedes essence" and most are in fundamental agreement of what might be termed a sort of minimum existentialist theory of value. In a very general sense, this theory can be reduced to three basic principles:

1. Man exists—experiences the world—through the medium of choice.
2. His moral standards are also choices, by means of which he regulates his responsibility with respect to others.
3. A good choice (including a good moral choice), is one which has been derived "authentically"—that is, on the basis of active, conscious, and self-determined experience.

Virtually all of the existentialist philosophers have developed some ethical point of view which encompasses these basic assumptions. The fundamental differences between these theories are those which exist between the *theistic* (religious) existentialists, who are perhaps best represented by such individuals as Kierkegaard and, more recently, Jaspers, Tillich, Marcel, and Buber, and the *nontheistic* (agnostic and/or atheistic) existentialists such as Heidegger and Sartre. . . . The aim of existentialist education is not simply to help the individual *cope* with his existence. Its primary purpose is to help him to *experience his existence* by confronting it with a sense of defined purpose. For the existentialist, the proper outcome of education is a certain sort of attitude toward life. Such an attitude includes a more than "openness," however; it also implies an "eagerness." The educated man is characterized not only by what he *knows* but also, and perhaps even more, by what he is *capable of knowing and experiencing*. In a basic sense, then, the hallmark of an existentialist education is not knowledge as such but rather "educability."

The existentialist advocates "education for choice" because he has a clear awareness that the most basic educational problem pertains to the criteria for selecting appropriate knowledge and not with the techniques for disseminating knowledge as such. The existentialist is concerned, above all, with "the habit of growth." He focuses on values precisely because he recognizes that values are directive and, therefore, determinative of most subsequent knowledge.[12]

Summary and Implications The curricular emphases and preferred methods suggested within traditional idealism, realism, and Neo-Thomism are reflected in the educational philosophies of essentialism and perennialism. Similarly, the curricular emphases and preferred methods suggested within classical

12. William F. O'Neil, "Existentialism and Education for Moral Choice," *Phi Delta Kappan* (October 1964): 48–53.

experimentalism are reflected in the educational philosophies of progressivism and reconstructionism. Existentialism is a contemporary educational philosophy stressing subject matter of personal choice.

If each prospective teacher were to begin to consider the many facets of both the traditional and contemporary educational philosophies, the result might be an *eclecticism*—that is, each teacher might select what appears to be the most promising directions from each philosophy. In this eclecticism, there is the inherent risk of internal inconsistency, which could detract from the teacher's developing the best possible and most consistent educational view for classroom practice. If one's beliefs do influence one's actions, perhaps a more orderly development of one's educational philosophy—other than an eclectic approach—would contribute to more consistent classroom practices.

Discussion Questions

1. What specific evidence is there for the contention that essentialism has always been the predominant American philosophy of education? Are there any recent indications that this is particularly so today?
2. What evidence is there that progressivism in education is on the decline?
3. What is meant by the expression "education of the whole child"? Do you accept this position as a legitimate goal of the American school?

4. How would an existentialist react to the aim of the American public schools—to give each student the chance to develop his or her talents to the fullest extent? How do you view such an aim?
5. Should "democracy as a way of life" necessarily be an operating principle for our schools? Is American public education democratic? Do you agree that, at times, teachers must be dictatorial?

Supplemental Activities

1. Engage in debates related to traditional versus contemporary educational views and practices.
2. Argue the case for and against the inclusion of the following offerings in the high school curriculum: driver training, home economics, vocational agriculture, welding, physical education, athletics, electronics, aeronautics, space sciences, and typing.
3. Search the audiovisual library for audiotapes and films that deal with the *traditional* educational philosophies. Utilize such materials as a basis for class discussion.
4. Search the audiovisual library for audiotapes and films that deal with the *contemporary* educational philosophies. Utilize such materials as a basis for class discussion.
5. Visit a so-called open school and report to class on the educational practices in that school.

Bibliography

Bagley, William C. "An Essentialist's Platform for the Advancement of American Education." *Educational Administration and Supervision* (April 1938).

Brameld, Theodore. *Patterns of Educational Philosophy*. New York: Holt, Rinehart and Winston, 1971.

Kirk, Russell. *A Program for Conservatives*. Rev. ed. Chicago: Henry Regnery, 1962.

Maritain, Jacques. *Education at the Crossroads*. New Haven: Yale University Press, 1953.

McCarthy, Eugene J. *A Liberal Answer to the Conservative Challenge*. New York: Macfadden-Bartell, 1964.

Morris, Van Cleve, and Pai, Young. *Philosophy and the American School*. 2nd ed. Boston: Houghton Mifflin, 1976.

Ozmon, Howard. *Dialogue in the Philosophy of Education*. Columbus, Ohio: Charles E. Merrill, 1972.

Sayers, Ephraim Vern, and Madden, Ward. *Education and the Democratic Faith: An Introduction to the Philosophy of Education*. New York: Appleton-Century-Crofts, 1959.

Scheffler, Israel. *Philosophy and Education*. Boston: Allyn and Bacon, 1966.

Wingo, G. Max. *The Philosophy of American Education*. Boston: D.C. Heath, 1965.

CHAPTER 18

Philosophical Influence on Pedagogy

TEACHER BEHAVIOR IS BASED UPON THE SUM TOTAL OF THE teacher's beliefs—the philosophy of the teacher. It is hoped that, from what has been presented so far, the prospective teacher will be able to work out a personal philosophy in terms of the concepts of reality, knowledge, and value. It should also be possible to envision the way in which these philosophical concepts carry over and influence the educational views functioning in our schools. This is the theoretical, rational part of developing a personal philosophy of education. Such mental perception of a philosophy of education is one thing; to teach according to the mentally perceived philosophy is yet another thing. In the act of teaching, one exhibits behavior that is compatible with a personal educational view. In reality, most teachers find it advantageous to pick and choose from the various educational views. So long as this kind of eclecticism serves the pedagogical purposes of the teacher and serves as the basis for consistent behavior by the teacher in the classroom, learning will occur. If, however, this kind of eclecticism results in frequently changing behavior exhibited by the teacher that distracts from the learning process, the teacher could profit from subscribing to the principles of one specific educational view. Nonetheless, most teachers adopt philosophical principles that have been drawn from more than one educational philosophy.

Teachers' Needs   Unquestionably, teachers face many practical problems in the classroom. If one's beliefs influence one's actions, it is reasonable to suggest that an individual teacher's philosophy will help determine the manner in which he or she handles everyday problems.

A well-developed theoretical set of beliefs also provides one with a test of one's actual practices. Philosophical constructs within theories serve as a check on practice—and vice versa. For example, if a teacher believes in a theory of social justice and is teaching in a school that practices racial segregation, the theory adhered to by the teacher is incompatible with the segregation practice. Another example might be a teacher who claims to emphasize the human dignity of his or her pupils, but in practice uses corporal punishment in the classroom. Too often teachers operate from similar hypocritical positions of professing to believe in one thing but practicing something else.

Current Views in American Schools

Some classroom teachers continue to be skeptical of educational theory and skeptical of those who espouse theory as a basis for practice. Yet new theories about educating children continue to proliferate, while the older, traditional beliefs remain strong in today's schools. Traditionalist educators continue to hold that the purpose of education is to train the minds of pupils so they may better deal with the intellectual concepts of life; in addition, they emphasize the mastery of facts and information. The general notion that any child can learn any subject at any level if the subject matter is properly presented remains strong as a challenge to teachers to arouse motivation for subject-matter mastery among pupils. The concept of *mastery learning* suggests that with the exception of the few youngsters who are mentally, emotionally, or physically impaired, every other youngster can master the entire curriculum of the school when adequate time is given for the slower learners to master the content. Continued attention to test scores, grade level achievement, and other measures of subject matter competency reflect the importance still attached to the more traditional views of education. School boards, parents, and the general public demand more and more often that teachers provide concrete evidence that their pupils have made progress in the mastery of subject matter.

On the other hand, many American teachers uphold John Dewey's view that the mind is not merely a muscle to be developed. They consider as basic to teaching the notion that human beings are problem solvers who profit from experience—and that experience is the best teacher. These educators also take into consideration the existential position that emphasizes the importance of the individual and of personal awareness. Since Dewey's philosophical views have prevailed in American teachers' colleges for the past half century, it is not surprising to find that American schools reflect this view more than other schools throughout the world. Like the traditional view, this increasingly important progressive view also presents a motivational challenge to the classroom teachers. While subject matter is forgotten in favor of an interesting project for initiating learning, some teachers find that many pupils are not interested in much of anything. In such instances,

The underlying principles of *progressivism* stem from the work of John Dewey. (*Photograph: Keystone View Co.*)

teachers are challenged to arouse student interest in inquiry in much the same fashion as traditionalist teachers are challenged to arouse interest in the mastery of subject matter.

Extended surveys of contemporary views of learning—as expressed in philosophy, psychology, and education journals and studies—reveal a seemingly endless and divergent range of topics. Although a taxonomy for classifying the various approaches to educational practice does not exist, curriculum specialists generally refer to the approaches that stress subject matter as traditional approaches and to those that stress the learner as contemporary approaches. Contemporary classroom teachers are faced with the task of identifying the belief that they choose to espouse and, guided by it, of helping to educate the young who frequent our schools.

Models for Educational Design

As a means of illustrating how the traditional and contemporary philosophical concepts and ideas eventually find their way into the classrooms, Morris and Pai propose three philosophical models for educational design:[1]

- Education as Behavior Engineering: The Technological Model
- Education as Self-Actualization: The Humanistic Model
- Education and Cultural Pluralism: The Social Dimension

Technological Model

This model draws heavily on what the noted contemporary psychologist B. F. Skinner calls the technology of behavior. This approach holds that educational practice should deal primarily with the behaviors that are controllable and measurable. Morris and Pai suggest:

> In spite of its radical departure from traditional education emphasizing the intellect, the self, the mind, and the will, this approach to education is drawing increased national attention, producing a profound impact on the development and implementation of educational policies and programs in this country. For example, the rapidly growing professional interest in behavioral objectives, teacher accountability, performance-based teacher education, and programed instruction can be traced directly to this educational theory.[2]

Humanistic Model

The so-called humanistic educators criticize the American schools as "not only repressive but mindless and inhumane." The critics contend that the traditional schools have destroyed most children's joy of learning:

> If the traditional schools have caused this damage, the new technology of education has not brought much new hope, for behavior engineers see children as raw materials to be processed through impersonal and mechanical procedures, to be molded according to predetermined specifications over which neither the children nor their parents have any choice. Humanistic educators go on to point out that this efficiency-oriented view of education not only neglects human dignity but denies our personal freedom. In other words, the traditional approach to education is demeaning to children, while the recent technological movement in education has taken away their worth as unique individuals by objectifying them and treating them as objects.
>
> Though there are some differences in their strategies, humanistic educators generally agree that education can be made more meaningful to the learner's life if it is "humanized." That is, we should make our schools direct their efforts to "the development within each human being of intelligence, self-esteem, and personal dignity." All children must be helped to become the best of what they are able to become through both cognitive

1. Van Cleve Morris and Young Pài, *Philosophy and the American School*, 2nd ed. (Boston: Houghton Mifflin, 1976) p. 300.
2. Ibid., p. 303.

(intellectual) and affective (emotional) growth. Hence, in humanistic education, fostering good attitudes and feelings is as important as imparting intellectual skills and knowledge.[3]

Social Dimension Model   Most teachers realize that education is more than the modification of the learner's behavior and more than the "humanization" of the learning environment. Much has been written about the importance of education in the development of productive and worthy citizens. In this sense, the "social dimension" model of education is viewed as a means for the transmission of culture—a means of realizing social, economic, political, and moral ends:

> Cultural pluralism as a social ideal cannot be accomplished by improving the school alone. Nor can multicultural education be achieved through changes in school curriculum and reassignment of teaching personnel, because fundamental changes in the sociopolitical and economic systems of the country are essential to any major social reform, such as cultural pluralism. But the American school could contribute to significant social change in the long run if our students are made to see the contradictions between the supposed ideals of American democracy and social reality. We must make sure that educational reforms are not adopted simply as more effective means of transmitting the long-established and traditional values. In other words, our schools as instruments of a free society "must serve as the principal medium for developing in youth the attitude and skills of social, political, and cultural criticisms."[4]

Classroom Practices   It is indeed risky to engage in overly simplistic labeling of the classroom practices of teachers. The following brief paragraphs describe traditional and contemporary forms of classroom management, methodology, discipline, grading, and community. Our recommendation to the prospective teacher is that he or she carefully identify a personal set of operational principles with regard to these five factors. Whether the operational principles are drawn from the following brief descriptions or elsewhere, the classroom teacher should strive for consistent behavior within the framework provided by the principles adopted.

Classroom Management   Traditional classrooms are conducted in a highly organized, systematic manner. Preference is given to permanent desks placed in rows equally spaced. Materials and equipment are indexed and stored, to be used at given times for specific learning activities. Attention is given to orderliness throughout, and the classroom is managed in an efficient, businesslike manner.

3.   Ibid., pp. 351–352.
4.   Ibid., pp. 461–462. Prospective teachers would find the study of chapters 11, 12, and 13 in the Morris and Pai text very helpful for further study of these philosophical models for educational practice.

Contemporary classrooms are managed in a much less formal manner. The classroom is now considered as a laboratory. Movable furniture is preferred. Materials and equipment are accessible to students most of the time for use at their own discretion. Less concern is given to order, efficiency, and the businesslike atmosphere within the contemporary classroom.

Methodology

Traditional methodology is old-fashioned, routine, dogmatic, precise, and formal. Students are assigned seats, and detailed records are kept of students' abilities and achievements. Stress is placed on rote practice, memorization of facts and information, book reports, written exercises, and recitation. Important teacher activities include lectures, demonstrations, and continuing study. Much importance is placed on extensive examinations and on other qualitative activities such as assigned problems and homework. The traditional teacher, who plans the learning activities for the class in advance, is businesslike and formal in his or her teaching.

Contemporary methodology is less routine, less dogmatic, and more informal. While specific educational objectives are identified, the means of reaching these objectives are informally obtained. Students are less likely to be assigned a particular seat. The teacher views herself or himself as a learning guide who shares, rather than prescribes, learning activities with his or her students. Major emphasis is placed upon problem-solving activities, demonstrations, and projects; less emphasis is given to memory drill and mental discipline. The contemporary teacher plans activities well in advance but is not concerned with the structure of a lesson plan. Students are engaged in actively carrying out projects rather than in passively observing. The teacher conducts classes in an informal, nondirective manner.

Discipline

Classroom discipline is handled in an autocratic, authoritative way in the traditional setting. The teacher is in charge of the room and insists upon having the final voice in all matters. Student-teacher relationships are impersonal and may lack cordiality. The teacher holds himself or herself as the model of conduct to be imitated. There is little room for exchange of opinions. Specified rules and regulations outline operations within the room. No implication of harshness is intended; rather, consistent, authoritative control of events and conduct is vested with the teacher.

In the contemporary classroom, discipline is managed as a function of the democratic process. The students participate with the teacher in formulating rules and regulations to govern class activities and conduct. Student-teacher relationships are personal and cordial. In handling discipline situations, the teacher makes allowances for the students' views and attitudes.

Grading   The traditional teacher attempts to quantify and measure the achievement of the students. Test scores are considered to be very important measures of success. This teacher carefully constructs tests, assuming they will yield a numerical term that is an accurate measure of achievement. Scores attained on tests are given letter grade values by mathematically determined grade distributions. The traditional teacher is very much concerned with standards as the external criterion of achievement in the subject area taught.

The contemporary teacher views the central task of education to be the development of the problem-solving capabilities of his or her students. Paper-and-pencil tests of any kind are considered to be inadequate for testing those capabilities. However, since there is no truly reliable technique available for measuring problem-solving skills, the contemporary teacher is usually faced with the dilemma of using the traditional types of tests. Although written tests are used by the teacher, he or she is not satisfied with or interested in what such tests measure. Consequently the contemporary teacher is often viewed as doing a poor job of evaluating the learner because a workable plan for evaluating problem-solving ability has not been developed.

Community   The traditional philosophies do not infer that the school is a social institution of reconstruction. Thus traditional teachers have little to do with forces directed toward bringing about social change. Nor do traditional teachers believe that community influences should affect the curriculum or the operations of the school. They hold the view that schools exist to provide for the students' needs and interests through intellectual discipline. Traditional teachers generally feel that students are not overworked and that intellectual discipline is on the wane. These teachers generally participate only in those programs of community interaction involving the school's intellectual activities, such as science and mathematics.

Contemporary teachers view the school as providing for individual needs while placing great stress on social interaction. Progressive educators are inclined to assume a leading role in programs of social change because a premise of contemporary educational systems is to prepare students for meaningful roles in society. Contemporary teachers take active roles in working with lay groups in bringing about new educational programs in the schools and in reconstructing traditional programs in the schools. These teachers desire to interact with their community to a much greater extent than traditional teachers. While contemporary teachers have awakened public interest in the schools through emphasis on problem-solving approaches to education, this approach has resulted in a loss of interest among some of the intellectually gifted citizens in several communities. Such citizens, who concur with traditional views, have become critical of the progressive orientation of public schools.

Student-teacher interaction reflects the greater informality of present-day society. (*Photograph by Eric Roth, The Picture Cube*)

Thus the prospective teacher should sense that his or her future career would benefit from a soundly developed philosophy of education.

Summary and Implications

From all this, prospective educator, where do you identify yourself? Can you begin to group your former teachers according to what seemed to be their particular educational views? While your views are probably not yet completely committed to essentialism, perennialism, progressivism, reconstructionism, or existentialism, you probably do hold both certain traditional views and certain contemporary views as you approach the teaching task.

1. Do you identify with the educational theory and practice that hold as significant the transmission of knowledge in the form of mastery of facts and information? This would be suggestive of the essentialist orientation—a traditional tendency.
2. Do you see yourself as a teacher identified as a mental disciplinarian interested in training the intellect of the learner? Perhaps yours would be closer to the perennialist orientation—a traditional tendency.
3. Do you see your students as problem solvers? The progressive orientation uses our experiences in daily living and learning as the foundation for each of us to manage change within the present culture—a contemporary tendency.
4. The reconstructionist orientation, while progressive, has a bent toward reconstructing the social order—a contemporary tendency.

5. Are you contemporary in the sense of wanting to develop a learning environment that fosters individual choice? Do you see your student group working on several tasks that may or may not be dealing with the same topic? You might be moving toward an existential orientation.

Too often the beginning teacher jumps from one classroom-management strategy to another—hoping to find a satisfactory behavior for dealing with learners. A far better procedure would be to try to formulate a specific approach—or educational philosophy—prior to job entry and to refine one's educational philosophy gradually, as one gathers experience.

Discussion Questions

1. What do you propose to do about developing a personal philosophy of education? (a) What is your conception of your role as a teacher? (b) What is your conception of the role of the pupils? (c) In what way will your philosophy help to determine your methodology as a teacher? (d) How do you intend to relate your philosophy of education to your particular specialization?

2. In what ways do traditional educational views and contemporary views disagree regarding tests and assignments of grades?

3. Describe the extent to which American public school teachers should encourage their pupils to adopt democratic values.

4. Conditioning theory holds that any verbal or physical behavior can be turned into habituated response. What do you think about this?

5. Compare the ways in which a traditional teacher and a contemporary teacher would manage the classroom. What discipline techniques would be utilized by each teacher?

Supplemental Activities

1. Visit some elementary and secondary school classes for the purpose of determining the prevalent philosophy of education. Report on the traditional practices observed and on the contemporary practices observed.

2. Invite a school superintendent to class to outline what is generally considered to be the educational philosophy of his or her school system.

3. Invite a school board member to class to outline what is considered to be the educational philosophy of his or her school system.

4. Many application forms for teaching positions ask the candidate to state briefly a philosophy of education. Write your own philosophy of education, discussing classroom management, teaching methods, discipline, and evaluation of the learner, the teacher, and the school community.

5. Read from two of the following books and compare the content:

- Boyd H. Bode, *How We Learn*.
- George S. Counts, *Education and American Civilization*.
- John Dewey, *Democracy and Education*.
- William H. Kilpatrick, *Philosophy of Education* and *Selfhood and Civilization*.
- Harold Rugg, *American Life and the School Curriculum*.
- Harold Taylor, *On Education and Freedom*.
- V. T. Thayer, *Public Education and Its Critics*.

Bibliography

Evans, W. Keith, and Applegate, Terry P. "Value Decisions and the Acceptability of Value Principles." *National Education Association* (1976).

Gibbs, John C. "Kohlberg's Stages of Moral Judgment: A Constructive Critique." *Harvard Educational Review* 47 (February 1977).

Hutchins, R. M. *The Conflict in Education in a Democratic Society*. New York: Harper & Brothers, 1953.

Kattef, Esther, and Manzelli, Jane. *Multiple Choice: A Handbook for Informalizing the Classroom*. Newton, Mass.: New England School Development Council, 1974.

Kneller, George F. "Education, Knowledge, and the Problem of Existence." *Harvard Educational Review* 31 (fall 1961): 427–436.

Leeper, Robert R., ed. *Emerging Moral Dimensions in Society: Implications for Schooling*. Washington, D.C.: Association for Supervision and Curriculum Development, 1975.

Marler, Charles Dennis. *Philosophy and Schooling*. Boston: Allyn and Bacon, 1975.

Morris, Van Cleve, and Pai, Young. *Philosophy and the American School*, 2nd ed. Boston: Houghton Mifflin, 1976.

Pine, Gerald John. "Existential Teaching and Learning." *Education* 95 (fall 1974): 18–24.

Shiflett, John M. "Beyond Vibration Teaching: Research and Curriculum Development in Confluent Education" in *The Live Classroom*, edited by George Isaac Brown, pp. 127–128. New York: Viking, 1975.

PART VI

The Structuring of Educational Programs

As we have already indicated, the present-day educational program of the United States is a complex, diverse image of the society it seeks to serve. At the heart of all educational issues are the learners who should, in the course of their education, encounter positive experiences that will prepare them for the future. What this future holds for learners has become extremely complex: the continuing advance of science and technology has made the future extremely difficult to predict. It has become commonplace for young learners to question the importance of planning for the future because of the contradictions created by an infinitely complex society. The contradictions abound. Science and technology have helped us send men to outer space, but experts haven't found a way to keep our own environment free of pollution. Scientists are virtually capable of reproducing life on a microscopic scale; but cancer, heart disease, and other medical problems continue to baffle the scientific community. Technology has given us comforts and goods never before experienced; yet we cannot handle the pollution from these products safely. The acquisition of the materials of learning is now quicker and easier than ever before, but we haven't found a way in which to handle leisure. And finally—and critically important to young learners—we have not learned to live with one another despite all that we have enjoyed in the closing decades of the twentieth century. Fear, tension, and competition continue to plague the quest for peace and harmony among people.

Where does the teacher fit into this picture? In helping to create and provide an educational program for the future, the teacher is charged by society, on the one hand, with preserving the American traditions and, on the other hand, with initiating changes desired by that same society. What does this mean for the structuring of educational programs? As the principal implementer of the school's curriculum, the teacher must muster all necessary professional skills to develop teaching materials, lesson plans, evaluation devices, and humanistic learning environments that will effect positive interaction between the student and the educational program. Today's school programs are preparing youth for the twenty-first century.

It is the major purpose of Part VI to examine, for the prospective teacher, the key issues that affect curriculum development and operation in American public education. It is not expected that the teacher in training become a curriculum expert but rather that he or she become familiar with the key issues that have immediate relevance to the young professional. Specifically Part VI examines aims and objectives of education and how they relate to the host of programs offered by the school system.

One of the key issues in curriculum development is the scheme of curriculum organization. Teachers need to familiarize themselves with the difference between *student-centered* and *subject-centered* curricula, both in a philosophical and practical sense. The differences here are usually found in traditional and contemporary programs. Another issue centers on the various types of administrative organizations that promote different types of school programming. Why and in what way innovative experiences are to be incorporated into school programming is vital to a teacher's

repertoire if the teacher wishes to maximize learning opportunities for students of the future. The need for teachers to be creative and innovative is vital in a period where technology has made it possible for the teacher to be programmed. A teacher, beginning or experienced, needs to be aware: to know how to cull the poor and to adapt the good where it can be used profitably by the learner.

In conclusion, the authors wish to stress for the beginning teacher the need for and value of program evaluation. Successful teaching and learning take place when continuous planned evaluation gives direction to objectives, programs, and adjustments needed for societal change. Society now demands to know precisely what education learners are acquiring and how well they are acquiring it. The demands for accountability should spur educators to plan and to deliver program evaluation—rather than have it forced upon them from the outside. Evaluation has purpose; from it should come the planning and development of future curricula.

CHAPTER 19

The Purposes of Education in American Society

THERE ARE TWO GENERAL, CONFLICTING PHILOSOPHICAL POSI-tions that influence the direction of education today. These positions are found in the practices of traditional and progressive education. During periods of societal stress or national crisis, advocates of both extreme positions come in conflict with one another and rise to praise or fault whatever appears to be current practice.

The traditional purpose of education, which may be traced to the ancient *liberal arts,* stresses that students acquire a selected set of learning skills and a vast store of selected information. It is assumed that as the student acquires the necessary skills and facts, he or she is "educated," and thus will behave intelligently in adulthood. The student is not expected or directed to exercise any creative use of his intelligence during the learning process; learning is to be received passively and stored for future use. Learning is the same for all; and knowledge that was relevant yesterday remains so today.

A contrasting purpose of education, to encourage active student involvement in learning, evolved from the work of John Dewey and his associates after the turn of the century. Referred to as *progressivism* in education, this contemporary position has not been universally accepted in practice. It is, however, still examined and studied as a "school of thought" and has enjoyed considerable acceptance along theoretical lines. Ideally, progressivism, expressed vividly as "expected learner behavior," calls for an exercise of intelligence during the learning period and for increased use of experience as a means to new learning. It urges that intelligent adult behavior is not mystically granted at some accepted level of maturity but, rather, is acquired en route. Learning is relevant; learning is life; a student learns best by actively participating in the learning experience.

By the 1940s, the great American experiment—mass education—was virtually achieved; but in rapid succession, World War II, the "cold war," Korea, and the Russian sputnik spawned alarm concerning the effectiveness of American education. American society responded by calling for an overhaul of the educational program. During the decades of the fifties and sixties, American education shouldered the criticism of poor mental, physical, and psychological preparation of its students. Even though the system had reacted internally and curricular reform had begun in earnest during the late forties and early fifties, it appears that sputnik acted as the catalyst for increased public attention and action. Despite the questionable validity of the criticism heaped upon the educational system, one fact became apparent: as American society approached the midpoint of the twentieth century, education had assumed a new, important role—education for national and international survival. As seen in the 1960s, science and technology were able to take the world to outer space; what remains as an overriding problem is the survival of humankind on inner space, earth. There is little doubt that as geography continues to shrink, as population masses move closer together, and as food and energy supplies become scarcer, fears, tensions, and aggressions among people mount. Education has now become the instrument for survival in this new kind of world.

The Back-to-Basics Movement

Having responded quickly to the pressures for change in the fifties and sixties, the school had to deal with the pressures of the *back-to-basics* movement in the late 1970s. Where this pressure will take the schools in the 1980s has yet to be seen. Poor reading and writing practices, declining college entrance scores, and learners poorly prepared for the work world are all cited as evidence of failure on the part of the schools. The most significant aspect of this new pressure is the lack of commonality in the definition of what constitutes the "basics." There is little doubt, however, that the movement is directed at many of the innovative practices adopted by the schools during the 1960s. The supporters of the movement charge that the use of innovative programs in substance and instruction that were begun in the 1950s and 1960s has led to the decrease in basic skills needed by all learners. Despite the implicit criticisms of education associated with this movement, there is nothing wrong with a national reaffirmation of the importance of the three Rs for all children.

The basics problem lies with balancing the emphasis on the three Rs with the many other significant skills, competencies, and appreciations needed by learners. With rising school costs bringing greater financial stress to education, it may become too easy to eliminate the "frills" in the school in order to concentrate on the basics. Examples of what are considered frills, by some, are usually art, music, foreign language, improved technology, (computer-assisted instruction, computer-managed instruction) and a whole host of cocurricular and extra-

The back-to-basics movement reflects public opinion. (*Photograph by Talbot Lovering*)

curricular activities. If there is anything that learners need for the twenty-first century, it's not only the basics but also all the life-enriching subjects in which the learner can apply these basic skills to creative, artistic, and vocational pursuits.

Minimal Competencies

One of the outgrowths of the back-to-basics movement is the increased attention to *minimal competency standards*. By the end of 1977, some thirty-one states had taken legislative or state board initiatives to institute minimal competency requirements into the schools. One of the problems that has emerged with this competency requirement is that no two states have taken the same approach to the problem. Some of the difficulties lie with the lack of nationwide agreement on the identification of basic skill areas, on the kind of state or local control, on the types of tests to be used, on graduation requirements, and on grade promotions.

As one of the responses to the basics movement, minimal competency standards have now created new problems in areas of school finance, mainstreaming, teacher load, teacher governance, and overall school accountability. If minimal competency programs attest to the competence of a learner and if that learner fails on the job or in advanced schooling, who is to be held accountable for that failure? Despite all of the problems associated with the back-to-basics movement and with minimal competency standards, this new pressure on the schools has made it clear that the nation is awake to the importance of education.

Forces for Change

It seems evident that any planning for future change in school programs should take into account the following:

1. The purposes of education should be clearly defined and should take into account all learners who will enter the system.
2. Objectives, as they relate to purpose, should be developed in behavioral terms that are subject to quality measurement.
3. Curriculum planning should involve teachers, students, administrative and supervisory personnel, lay citizens, and specialists outside the school.
4. Curriculum development should encompass evaluation and continuous cycling procedures for change.
5. Curriculum development should become training in excellence for all participants. Planners should become skilled in their performance of formulating problems, gathering and evaluating data, and projecting and testing hypotheses.

A particular leadership role is apparent for the teacher. In helping to plan the curriculum, teachers must know and understand the differing purposes of education, be knowledgeable about the various ways in which learners learn, comprehend the structure of the disciplines they teach, be able to demonstrate the methodologies appropriate for the objectives they seek to accomplish and, finally, become actively involved in the change process.

Curricular Role

When formulating a general role for the school, those engaged in curriculum planning frequently find that role relatively easy to define but quite difficult to put into practice. There have been many ascribed national roles for education voiced by national, regional, and state commissions. The school may perceive its role as one of reproduction, of readjustment, or of reconstruction—or a combination thereof. These roles were discussed briefly in Part II as they related to school as a social institution; they are discussed here as they relate to the philosophic concepts that prescribe the curricular programs of the school.

Reproduction

If the school elects to serve an exclusive role of *reproduction*, then its task is to transmit simply and unquestioningly our cultural heritage to the nation's youth. Subject matter selected to accomplish this goal would be that which has survived through the ages. In deciding whether or not the school should serve only in a reproductive role, the teacher must consider if the "age" of subject matter is an adequate criterion for its inclusion in the curriculum or if it might be possible for the bad to survive with the good. The teacher must also decide if the good subject matter of yesterday is adequate in terms of the problems and needs of today's youth. The problems associated with this type of decision making are increased by the knowledge explosion. In addition to the "old" that must be passed on, there is the new knowledge that continues to press for its rightful place in the curriculum. How does a teacher cull the curriculum to make room for new knowledge when the *reproduction* role is dominant? It is obvious that a curriculum designed solely to pass on the cultural heritage is fundamentally inadequate in an age when society is constantly confronted with social change.

Readjustment An exclusive role of *readjustment* calls for the school to utilize a curriculum geared to social utility and efficiency. A curriculum of this type is concerned with the student's preparation for present-day adult life; it stresses civic training and social responsibility. The role of readjustment demands that the school retain parts of the past but also suggests that the school must do a certain amount of "readjusting" to meet contemporary needs. Pure application of this role may tend to ignore some of the principles of child development and currently accepted psychologies of learning. The child's need to understand and direct his or her own actions, the child's need to be able to adopt and organize in the light of prior experience, and the crucial need to receive individual attention may be neglected when the utility theme of the adult world is forced upon the school. The role of readjustment, if it is the sole role of the school, may be criticized in that it tends to prohibit changes that are deemed necessary for adults of the future.

Reconstruction The school that adopts the educational role of *reconstruction* favors a curriculum that moves to the forefront of current thought and practice in the society—and strives to change the status quo. The school then assumes a role not only of preparing young people for the future but also of preparing the future for young people. A persistent advocate of the reconstruction role for American schools, George S. Counts, offered this challenge to education in 1932 when he introduced his controversial proposal, *Dare the School Build a New Social Order?* To date, this challenge has not been completely accepted by society. In designing the curriculum, the teacher must be aware of the pitfalls of this extreme approach: the hidden dangers that past and current interests, traditions, and values may be sacrificed for the sake of change.

It is readily apparent that an overemphasis on any one of the three roles for schooling—reproduction, readjustment, or reconstruction—produces an operational and philosophical concept that is inconsistent with the eclectic role that schools should provide. It is the continual *blending* of these three roles that produces a curriculum that affords students the optimal opportunity to become self-supporting, self-respecting, and self-directing participants in American and world society.

This type of blend for a general role of the American school is seen by the authors as:

1. A systematic evaluation and reconstruction of the content of the disciplines used for instruction. A value judgment is made for the heritage to be preserved and for a selection of content considered necessary for existence in the future.
2. A reorganization of materials for instruction to produce not only knowledge in a variety of subject matters but also a sense of direction for creating desirable attitudes and appreciations.
3. A plan for meeting the needs not only of the gifted and slow learners but also of the all-too-often neglected other learners—the average child and the mentally, emotionally, and physically handicapped learner.
4. A plan for encouraging accelerated levels of personal aspiration—not only excellence in space travel, computers, and gross national product but also excellence in the quality of personal and social life for all.

Aims and Goals   In attempting to plan and state aims and objectives of American education, curriculum workers must be cognizant of at least five types of students who have to be accommodated during the process of education:

1. *Terminal group*—students who for various reasons drop out along the way and have to be absorbed by society. Current estimates show the national dropout rate to be 30 to 35 percent, with 60 percent not uncommon in the large urban areas.
2. *College-bound*—students preparing for some form of higher education. Nationally, approximately 50 percent of the high school graduates are pursuing advanced study beyond high school. This figure is somewhat misleading, however, in that it does not take into account those students who have dropped out before graduating from high school. In addition, the preparatory program for the 50 percent must be varied because of the range of post-high school educational desires and opportunities. These numbers, although expected to increase in the decade of the eighties, may be reduced as youth begin to find increasingly lower correlations between college education and job placement.
3. *Vocational-bound*—students who are primarily prepared for jobs while in a comprehensive or vocational high school; however, some of these may further their education at a later date on a formal or informal basis. Although the percentage of students who fall into this category varies by the criteria used, it appears to be on the increase as data for college-trained students suggest a job shortage and as vocational education begins to become an accepted social phenomenon.

4. *Destination unknown*—the so-called late bloomer or "latent student" who has the native ability but does not realize his or her expected level of achievement during the high school period.

5. *Special education*—students who are identified as emotionally, mentally, or physically handicapped. Recent court decisions have ordered that these special students are to be included as regular school students and to be accommodated by the regular school curriculum. As was explained earlier in the discussion of Public Law 94–142, federal law now mandates regular school programs for all exceptional children.

The best analysis of what currently exists as the average school curriculum suggests that the needs of college-bound students continue to receive primary attention. If this were not the case, the national dropout rate—and especially the rate for urban areas—would not be as alarmingly high as it is. Curriculum development should proceed from some special diagnostic attempts to identify the various kinds of students the curriculum is intended to serve.

As one attempts to analyze aims and objectives, it is necessary to distinguish between the two as they relate to a total school program. For purposes of curriculum development, *aims* are considered to be those broad goals for the system as a whole. They are usually formulated by national groups who try to demonstrate an awareness of the pluralistic needs of the society. On the other hand, *objectives* are those expected learner behaviors that the curriculum is intended to produce.

General and Specific Objectives

The broad aims that have been developed by the many national committees and commissions are only as valuable as the success of planned learning outcomes. A presentation of these aims appeared earlier in Chapter 14. Figure 19–1 offers a hierarchy of educational aims and objectives ranging from the specific to the general. It is the successful accomplishment of specific expected learning behaviors that indicates whether or not the school is achieving broad educational aims.

The teacher preparing to participate in curriculum planning, imple-

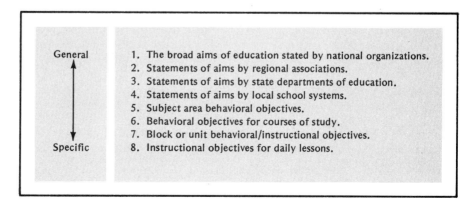

General

Specific

1. The broad aims of education stated by national organizations.
2. Statements of aims by regional associations.
3. Statements of aims by state departments of education.
4. Statements of aims by local school systems.
5. Subject area behavioral objectives.
6. Behavioral objectives for courses of study.
7. Block or unit behavioral/instructional objectives.
8. Instructional objectives for daily lessons.

Figure 19–1.
Hierarchy of educational aims and objectives.

mentation, and evaluation should be thoroughly knowledgeable about the derivation of aims and special objectives. Further, his or her particular role in the process of curricuum development should be addressed to the task of seeking means by which specific objectives can be made operational. Educational goals change as the school grows in a rapidly changing world community, and so the job of defining objectives and implementing curricular change is never finished.

During the 1970s, a monumental effort was mounted aimed at the development of criteria by which instructional objectives could be stated operationally. One has only to engage in a cursory examination of the literature to see the increasing influence that educators such as Bloom, Mager, Popham, Glazer, Esbensen, Gagné, and many others have had on curriculum evaluation. Their work has been directed toward the pursuit of precise descriptions of desired terminal learner behavior as it is effected by instruction. This effort has focused on the notion that if desired learner outcomes can be described in some measurable fashion, then the goals (outcomes) of the curriculum can be measured and evaluated. These outcomes might be assessed on a pass/fail basis or on some percentage of success on cognitive tasks associated with specific goals. However, the case has not been conclusively decided for criterion-referenced evaluation in preference to norm-reference evaluation. Norm-referenced and criterion-referenced evaluations are discussed later in connection with curriculum evaluation.

Specific operational objectives, that is, specific learning outcomes, consist of three explicit criteria: (1) the task confronting the learner; (2) the expected observable behavior; and (3) the minimum level of expected performance. In Table 19–1, an example of a given task leading to specific learning outcome is illustrated.

Table 19–1.   Criteria of a behavioral objective.

(1)	The task confronting the learner:	Given the task of matching fifteen chronological events of the Vietnam War with identified incidents of social stress on the American government,
(2)	The expected observable behavior:	the student will identify these common events
(3)	The minimum level of expected performance:	with 80 percent accuracy.

Increasing numbers of preservice and inservice teachers are being taught to use effectively the criteria advocated by Mager, Esbensen, and others in preparing written operational objectives. Success in this effort provides the first step in meaningful curriculum development. Objectives that are stated operationally and leveled on some cognitive hierarchy remain rather descriptive in nature. Ideally they are operational goals derived from a stated ideological mission or thrust of a school district, a state program, or a national purpose. However, when leveled operational objectives are made applicable to instruction, procedures that began as descriptive in nature tend to become prescriptive for change in learner behavior.

The Domains of Learning   A number of attempts have been made to clarify and develop the concept of educational objectives. Among the many efforts is the comprehensive approach of Bloom and others in *The Taxonomy of Educational Objectives,* in which the desired learning outcomes resulting from specific objectives have been classified into three groups or domains—cognitive, affective, and psychomotor.[1]

1. *Cognitive*—those objectives that are concerned with remembering, recognizing knowledge, and the development of intellectual abilities and skills.
2. *Affective*—those objectives that are concerned with interests, attitudes, opinions, appreciations, values, and emotional sets.
3. *Psychomotor*—those objectives that are concerned with the development of muscular and motor skills.

Ranging from the most superficial to the most advanced, the levels of cognitive learning are numerically ordered to establish a hierarchal arrangement for evaluation of depth in learning. The order is as follows:[2]

    1.00 Knowledge
          1.10 Knowledge of specifics
          1.20 Knowledge of ways and means of dealing with specifics
          1.30 Knowledge of the universals and abstractions in a field
    2.00 Comprehension
          2.10 Translation
          2.20 Interpretation
          2.30 Extrapolation
    3.00 Application
    4.00 Analysis
          4.10 Analysis of elements
          4.20 Analysis of relationships
          4.30 Analysis of organizational principles

1. Benjamin S. Bloom, ed., *Taxonomy of Educational Objectives* (New York: Longmans, Green, 1956), pp. 6–8.
2. Ibid., pp. 201–207.

5.00 Synthesis
    5.10 Production of a unique communication
    5.20 Production of a plan or proposed set of operations
    5.30 Derivation of a set of abstract relations
6.00 Evaluation
    6.10 Judgments in terms of internal evidence
    6.20 Judgments in terms of external criteria

The taxonomy also presents the following scheme for the classification of different levels of affective learning:[3]

1.00 Receiving (attending)
    1.10 Awareness
    1.20 Willingness to receive
    1.30 Controlled or selected attention
2.00 Responding
    2.10 Acquiescence in responding
    2.20 Willingness to respond
    2.30 Satisfaction in response
3.00 Valuing
    3.10 Acceptance of a value
    3.20 Preference for a value
    3.30 Commitment
4.00 Organization
    4.10 Conceptualization of a value
    4.20 Organization of a value system
5.00 Characterization by a value or value complex
    5.10 Generalized set
    5.20 Characterization

The taxonomy for the psychomotor domain was presented by Anita J. Harrow in 1972. Her levels of learning for this taxonomy are as follows:[4]

1.00 Reflex movements
    1.10 Segmental reflexes
    1.20 Intersegmental reflexes
    1.30 Suprasegmental reflexes
2.00 Basic-fundamental movements
    2.10 Locomotor movements
    2.20 Nonlocomotor movements
    2.30 Manipulative movements
3.00 Perceptual abilities
    3.10 Kinesthetic discrimination

3. David R. Krathwohl, Benjamin S. Bloom, and Bertram B. Masia, *Taxonomy of Educational Objectives* (New York: David McKay, 1964), pp. 176–193.
4. Anita J. Harrow, *A Taxonomy of the Psychomotor Domain* (New York: David McKay, 1972), pp. 1–2.

3.20 Visual discrimination
3.30 Auditory discrimination
3.40 Tactile discrimination
3.50 Coordinated abilities
4.00 Physical abilities
4.10 Endurance
4.20 Strength
4.30 Flexibility
4.40 Agility
5.00 Skilled movements
5.10 Simple adaptive skill
5.20 Compound adaptive skill
5.30 Complex adaptive skill
6.00 Nondiscursive communication
6.10 Expressive movement
6.20 Interpretive movement

Although the psychomotor domain has not had the benefit of extensive use for curriculum development, its use may be suggested for speech development, reading readiness, handwriting, and physical education. It certainly has implications for manipulative skills required of business training, broad areas of vocational education, industrial arts education, performance areas in science, art, and music, and is particularly important for early childhood training. It is in the affective and psychomotor domains of educational objectives that curriculum developers of today and of the future must give seriously needed attention. It is accurate to state that American education has been guilty of over-emphasizing cognitive objectives at the expense of those in the areas of affective and psychomotor learning. In Chapter 23, "Curriculum Evaluation," the use of behavioral objectives with the three domains of learning will be discussed.

Summary and Implications

Although the expression "as the blueprint is drawn, the house shall be constructed" may have the ring of a cliché, it also has the ring of truth. Without a stated purpose, without clearly stated objectives, and without specific intended learning outcomes for children, the school program wanders aimlessly and without direction. The pressures of the back-to-basics movement will bring about considerable change in the school programs of the future. If the school responds, however, with planned programs and with systems of accountability, the expected changes will benefit everyone. Teachers need to know and understand why they do what they do to learners. The mandate to prepare specific programs for all types of learners suggests that a deeper understanding on the part of educators of the aims and objectives of education will be forthcoming.

One of the domains of learning is the psychomotor. (*Photograph by Tania D'Avignon*)

Discussion Questions

1. Why have the schools resisted putting into practice the contemporary philosophy of John Dewey?

2. Identify what you believe the back-to-basics movement means.

3. How does a local school system identify the role for its schools in a given community?

4. What is the relationship between instructional objectives and criterion-referenced measurement?

5. What is the value of promoting all three domains of learning as necessary for all students?

Supplemental Activities

1. Write a set of general aims for a school district wishing to promote the role of readjustment for its schools.

2. Visit a local school and identify the makeup of the student body in terms of its career goals.

3. Write an instructional objective for each of the three domains of learning.

4. Prepare a collage that shows the general expectations of society for the educational program of the schools.

5. Interview a parent and a teacher and compare their feelings on the back-to-basics movement.

Bibliography

Gardner, Leonard. "Humanistic Education and Behavioral Objectives: Opposing Theories of Educational Science." *School Review* 85 (May 1977).

Kibler, Robert J.; Cegala, Donald J.; Barker, Larry L.; and Miles, David T. *Objectives for Instruction and Evaluation*. Boston: Allyn and Bacon, 1974.

Koerner, James D. *The Case for Basic Education*. Boston: Little, Brown, 1959.

McNeil, John D. *Curriculum: A Comprehensive Introduction*. Boston: Little, Brown, 1977.

Schaffarzick, Jon. "How Can We Know What Is Best? Procedural Alternatives in Curriculum Development." *Educational Leadership* 33 (May 1976).

Venable, Tom C. *Philosophical Foundations of the Curriculum*. Chicago: Rand McNally, 1967.

CHAPTER 20

The Function of the Educational Program

EMBEDDED IN THE OPERATIONAL PROGRAM OF THE SCHOOL ARE three broad academic components that comprise the function of the educational program. These are general education, exploratory education, and personal education. Placement and emphasis of these components are wholly dependent upon the needs of the learner as these needs relate to growth and development, psychologies of learning, instructional strategies, and the various types of administrative arrangements discussed earlier.

General Education

General education is that broad area of the school program that primarily concerns itself with the development of *common learnings*. Its central purpose is one of helping students to become participating citizens and well-adjusted individuals. Although it is most concentrated in the elementary school, there are some elements of general education throughout the entire period of formal education. It is important to note, however, that the other two broad areas of the school program, *exploratory* and *personal education*, contain general education outcomes but are not organized primarily for that purpose.

The general education program concentrates upon the development of basic skills and introduces the student to basic study areas, including reading, composition, listening, speaking, and computing. The learner is expected to acquire creative and disciplined thinking that includes the use of different methods of inquiry and the application of knowledge. General education also encompasses the humanities—an appreciation for literature, music, and the visual arts—and the social and natural sciences. Within the context of a general education program, the learner is expected to acquire the essential, adult basic-performance skills that are needed to function successfully in society. However, how all of these general education priorities are met varies from school district to school district.

Elementary Program

These identified areas of common learning provide the basic core of general education in the elementary school and are improved and developed further throughout the total formal program of education. Figure 20–1 illustrates the general education emphasis for the formal N–12 structure.

One of the most perplexing problems facing the general education planners is maintaining the placement sequence in the total scheme of education. As we have seen in the recent past, the number of years of schooling that are devoted to general education is determined by changing economic factors and by society's concern with efficiency and productivity. Those who demand accountability from today's schools have joined with those who call for more general education. In the very recent past, the need for specialization has caused a slackening of interest in general education and an increase of emphasis on specialized studies and the applied fields. It seems evident that the next decade will show increased attention to general education as a response to the pressures of accountability.

Pressures on General Education

During the past two decades, increasing pressures have brought about a downward movement of learning experiences in the curriculum. More advanced skills and some special training, previously reserved for the secondary school, have been introduced into the elementary time block of common learnings. It has become common practice to introduce at earlier grade levels the formal teaching of foreign language, principles

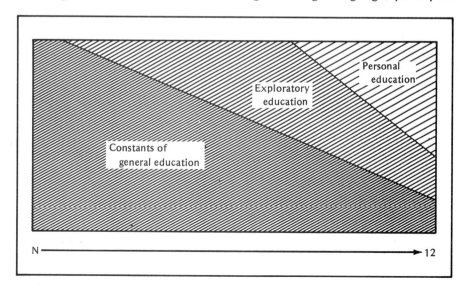

Figure 20–1. Educational emphases in the N–12 program.

of economics, drug and sex education, advanced principles of mathematics, and introductory programs of vocational career choices. Although there are justifiable reasons for the movement, it does not change the nature or purpose of common learnings in the elementary program. With this increased emphasis on the expansion of common learnings for the elementary school, it is evident that a reassessment of the general education program is necessary. This may even require a new definition of common learnings. As preschool and early childhood education receives increased philosophical and financial support, the general education program, identified as common learnings for all, should be redistributed over a broader continuum, nursery school through grade 14.

Exploratory Education

The *exploratory education* program has been designed primarily for a unique American organization of education, the junior high school. Depending upon school district organization, the junior high school or intermediate school continues the development of general education and introduces the student, on a limited basis, to a variety of specialized educational areas. There are many reasons for its existence:

1. The junior high school provides a transitional period to ease the student's transfer from the elementary school to the high school. The junior high school is designed for students who are entering the early adolescent period, a trying period of growth and development. Since the transition from childhood to adulthood is such a crucial period of development, the junior high school is planned to accommodate the special physical, emotional, and social problems of this age group. In general, these students have come from an administrative unit that is child-centered and are preparing to enter one that is subject-centered. It is hoped that the junior high school introduces the student to a program that allows for the gradual development of independence in learning and self-discipline. To provide the student with a "home base," block scheduling is sometimes used for the language arts–social studies program, and the teacher for this block has a better chance to know and help the student. The junior high school student also takes a number of courses taught by specialist teachers and in this way is gradually introduced to the departmentalized, more subject-centered senior high school. (See Figure 20–2.)

2. The junior high school allows for the exploration of interests, aptitudes, and abilities, thus aiding the student in planning future vocational areas and educational pursuits. The program introduces, in concentrated periods of time, such subjects as art, music, home economics, vocational education, and speech. The intention is that, as the students progress toward senior high school, they will explore areas of learning in which they later may specialize. These

Figure 20–2.   A junior high school exploratory program.

7th Grade		8th Grade		9th Grade	
Subjects (Required)	Periods per week	Subjects (Required)	Periods per week	Subjects (Required)	Periods per week
Core	10	Core	10	Core	10
Physical Education	3	Physical Education	3	Physical Education	3
Science	5	Science	5	General Science	5
Mathematics	5	Mathematics	5	Electives	17
Practical Arts	5	Electives	12		
Band or Chorus	5				
Art	2				

	Electives	
Art	General Business	Algebra
Creative Writing	Home Economics	Mechanical Drawing
Drama	Industrial Arts	Music
Foreign Language	General Mathematics	Industrial Arts

exploratory programs may be of nine-week or one-semester duration and offered on a rotating basis.

3. The junior high school student is introduced to a more elaborate program of guidance and counseling that will continue through the senior high school. This program is intended to assist students in intelligent decision making essential for adult life. With the use of specially trained guidance personnel, the junior high school gives intensive emphasis to the development of wholesome attitudes for mental, emotional, and social growth among its student body.

4. Providing for variety in the junior high school program helps to lower the school dropout rate. This type of programming considers the differing and special abilities of youth and is based on a rationale stressing the important effect of socioeconomic background upon the interests, aptitudes, personalities, and needs of pupils.

5. Articulation of the total twelve-year school program may be stimulated by the junior high school. This administrative unit has the advantage of examining the elementary program and planning for articulation with the senior high school. It should be noted that successful articulation is accomplished when all the teachers within the school system work together to understand and appreciate the special tasks each must perform.

Junior High School or Middle School

Like the elementary school, the junior high school has had to find ways to accommodate to the continuing downward movement in the curriculum. There is little doubt that the pressure of content requirements from the senior high school and the accompanying problems associated with Carnegie Units of credits has caused the junior high school to become "a senior high school in short pants." In an attempt to return to the initial philosophy that guided the early development of the junior high school, school districts have begun to place the ninth grade back in the senior high school and to create a new administrative organization of grades 6–8, labeled an *intermediate* or *middle* school. This newly emerging middle school concept is intended to provide for exploratory learning experiences that the junior school never quite achieved. As Doll indicates:

> The middle school, originally designed in many communities as an expedient for accommodating rapidly increasing school population, is beginning to have its own purposes and programs. A search is being made for relevant content, with the thought that the middle school can, without due care, go the way of the junior high school by becoming a miniature high school. Presumably, the middle school, if it provides appropriate experiences for children, can meet the needs of earlier-developing adolescents, whose physical maturation and peer interaction patterns have moved downward in the age scale. Programs which emphasize individualization, varied group activities, inquiry, helpful guidance, and subject matter that permits pupil action give promise of helping the middle school succeed.[1]

In discussing individualized learning in the middle school, Kohut suggests:

> An integral curricular component in the middle school is the unipac. Although it is called by many names, basically the unipac is an individualized learning package for student self-directed study requiring the use of a multi-media resource center or laboratory. The unipac, with many organizational formats is a teacher-constructed, subject-oriented, self-instructional unit containing an overview or introduction, general and specific learning objectives, content outline, student activities section, pre- and post-unit evaluation instruments, and additional requirements dictated by a particular discipline or the interests and abilities of the student."[2]

Personal Education

The senior high school assumes the special task of bringing together the foundations of *general education* and the introductions to *exploratory education* to provide a culminating educational program that meets

1. Ronald C. Doll, *Curriculum Improvement: Decision Making and Process*, 3rd ed. (Boston: Allyn and Bacon, 1974), p. 348.
2. Sylvester Kohut, Jr., *The Middle School: A Bridge between Elementary and Secondary Schools* (Washington, D.C.: National Education Association, 1976), p. 8.

Vocational education provides training in marketable skills. (*Photograph by Talbot Lovering*)

the needs for *personal education*. For some students, the senior high school will terminate their formal education; for others it will prepare them for a more advanced and specialized college education or for special post-high school training. Because increasing numbers of high school graduates go on to college, it is tempting to overemphasize the college preparatory program. However, high school should offer programs designed to meet the needs of all students.

In the secondary school, attention is given to individual choices by the establishment of various programs. In schools, these programs are referred to as "program of study in each area of curriculum specialization—professional, business, industrial, and general. Although each student is asked to register in a certain program, he may take subjects in another curriculum."

Presumably each of these designations has in mind special-interest education.[3]

As the learner progresses through the educational system, the increase of personalized education should encourage the development of an individual's intellectual curiosity and passion for knowledge. It should also provide good habits for a particular kind of inquiry. Personalized education should develop higher levels of learning within the cognitive domain.

College Preparatory Program

In continuing the program for general education (Figure 20–1), the high school has established a core of general education courses required of all students. These general education requirements usually account for seven to nine of the sixteen to twenty Carnegie Units required for graduation. However, this varies from state to state. Included in the general education requirements (by state law) are English—three units; mathematics—one unit; science—one unit; social studies (American history and government)—two units; and physical education and health—one unit. One Carnegie Unit of credit is awarded for each class that meets for 200 minutes of formal instruction per week for thirty-six weeks per school year. The remainder of the units required for graduation are satisfied by the elective programs for specialization and enrichment. The special programs vary in name, sequence, and scope but often are referred to as a *track* or *constants-variable* program within the comprehensive senior high school, as shown in Figure 20–3.

The comprehensive high school has been advocated by professional educators for over thirty years but has not yet been achieved as desired. A persistent vocal supporter of the comprehensive high school has been James B. Conant. The school he advocated would provide a secondary program for all learners, whether academic or vocational, and would maintain a continuing emphasis on general education for all except the slow and gifted students. Unfortunately the secondary school has remained primarily a post-secondary preparatory school—usually emphasizing college preparation.

Constants-Variable Program

Figure 20–3 suggests a type of constants-variable program advocated by the many proponents of the comprehensive senior high school. Adoption of this type of program promises more flexibility in career choices for the student and tends to thwart the rigidity that accompanies tracking programs. Although the constants-variable program depicted in the figure is not all-inclusive, it suggests various elective studies that students might pursue. With more freedom for course selection, students may work out individualized programs according to their needs and interests. Some form of flexible scheduling, differentiated

3. Albert I. Oliver, *Curriculum Improvement*, 2nd ed. (New York: Harper & Row, 1977), p. 233.

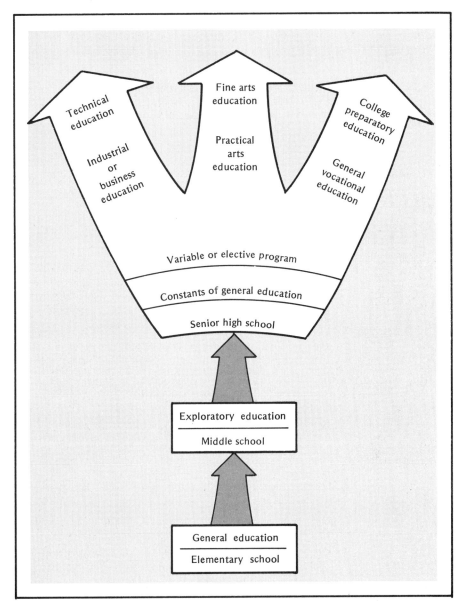

staffing arrangements, and an operational challenge to the Carnegie Unit system will offer to teacher and learner even greater program flexibility.

The basic high school course requirements, more commonly referred to as *constants*, are required of all students, and many of the electives become required course work for a particular avenue of learning. Within the area of the constants, however, additional provisions are made to take into account the special needs, interests, and abilities of students: for example, a high school requiring three years of English may allow its students a relative degree of freedom in meeting this requirement. Mini-courses have, until recent years, provided this flexibility. Levels and degree of intensity are established by the English department to meet the varying levels of ability, and students may satisfy the requirements by pursuing course work in creative writing, journalism, speech, drama, or literature. As the student progresses through the program of constants, he or she subsequently branches into areas of specialization and takes elective programs aimed at vocational competence and enrichment.

Carnegie Units —Tracking

In recent years, any teaching program that follows the Carnegie Unit system of secondary education has come under serious attack. As was indicated earlier, the rigid tracking program of the Washington, D.C., public school system was declared illegal on the grounds that the tracking system used denied individual rights. Although tracking was thought to have provided for individual differences, it appears that it introduces a more rigid program of constants, with little elective participation on the part of the student. For instance, one of the common tracks, the college preparatory program, becomes a rather rigorous intellectual curriculum designed to prepare the student for more advanced learning. In so doing, it tends to limit the student's participation in the areas of aesthetics and appreciation—such as art and music. The typical college preparatory program requires the student to satisfy requirements of four units in English, three units in social studies, three to four units in science and mathematics, three units in foreign language, and at least two units in physical education and health. These requirements total eighteen Carnegie Units; very little time is therefore available for courses in art, music, or drama, and even less for courses in home economics, practical arts—or such skills as typing or driver education. Examination of the back-to-basics movement and its applicability to the rigid offerings in tracking programs suggests that there is little room in the curriculum for basics other than the three Rs. An even broader definition of the back-to-basics movement would suggest that coping skills needed to survive in a technological society cannot be found in tracking programs.

The major difficulty associated with the Carnegie Unit system is that it does not take into account well-respected research on student learning. All students do not learn at the same rate; nor do they maintain a learning rate that is constant during the learning process. Yet the majority of American secondary schools continue to schedule students into established time modules consistent with the definition of a Carnegie Unit, given for time devoted to a particular experience. School systems simply do not apply sound reasoning supported by research when they conclude that all students need two hundred minutes per week of varied instruction for thirty-six weeks in order to accomplish, successfully, one Carnegie Unit. If learning objectives are clearly specified operationally, some students are capable of meeting them in less time than others. The criterion for success should not be time or attendance; rather, it should focus on successful attainment of objectives and of minimum criterion levels previously established. If students meet the objectives, they should be awarded the credit previously determined for these objectives.

Vocational Education

The narrowness of the typical track program in senior high schools has undoubtedly contributed to the continuing shortage of high school graduates who are well prepared in the vocational-technical fields. All too often, these students drift into the vocational track because they "can't make it academically." What appears to be forgotten is that this type of training requires a student who is capable of both academic and vocational-technical work. More specifically, the constants-variable program should include meaningful training for students that will enable them to adapt to the new industry and new skills required for the changing economy. Too often in the past, and even more so in the present, this training has tended to be obsolescent. The constants-variable program should stress work experience and on-the-job training that relates to school experience. A well-conceived vocational-technical program meets the following criteria:

1. The program is directly related to employment opportunities, determined by school officials in cooperation with occupational experts and competent individuals and groups.
2. The course content is confirmed or changed by periodic analyses of the occupations for which the training is being given.
3. The courses for a specific occupation are set up and maintained with the advice and cooperation of the various occupational groups concerned.
4. The facilities and equipment used in instruction are comparable to those found in the particular occupation.
5. The conditions under which instruction is given duplicate as nearly as possible desirable conditions in the occupation itself and at the same time provide effective learning situations.
6. The length of teaching periods and total hours of instruction are determined by the requirements of the occupation and the needs of the students.
7. Training in a particular occupation develops marketable skills, abilities, attitudes, work habits, and appreciations to the point that enables the trainee to get and hold a job in that occupation.
8. Day and evening classes are scheduled at hours and during seasons convenient to enrollees.
9. Instruction is offered only to persons who need, desire, and can profit from it occupationally.

10. The teachers are competent in the occupation for which they are giving instruction and possess adequate professional qualifications for teaching.
11. Vocational guidance, including effective follow-up of all students who finish or drop out of a course, is an integral and continuing part of the program.
12. Continuous research is an integral part of the program.

This is not to suggest that vocational programs be abandoned in the senior high school but, rather, that they be reorganized. Federal funds in recent years have added new dimensions to the early Vocational Acts of 1917. The Manpower Development and Training Act and the Vocational Act of 1963 have provided funding for a changing economy requiring new technologies, markets, materials, and occupations. These acts were strengthened by amendments in 1968 that afforded financial benefits to states that would provide leadership responsibility for vocational education for the disadvantaged and physically handicapped. The whole vocational education movement now encompasses middle school and post-secondary school programs. There is little doubt that federal support of vocational education and the continuing emphasis on career development will continue through the decade of the eighties. The amended acts of 1968 are scheduled to continue into fiscal year 1979. Parts of these vocational bills—state grants for research and training—are permanently authorized for federal funding.

One of the major changes associated with vocational education in the 1970s has been the development of a comprehensive vocational curriculum. Learners are exposed to and trained in a program developed around a *career cluster* concept that allows the young learner to move horizontally and vertically within the career cluster as needs and future opportunities suggest. For example, a career cluster in agriculture would encompass not only courses in farm production but also in agribusiness, agricultural mechanics, food processing, horticulture, and landscaping. The young learner can prepare for a variety of careers within a cluster; these clusters are developed around specific job titles.

This type of vocational training has brought about significant changes in the comprehensive high school. Since it has been extremely difficult and costly for a local school district to provide adequate vocational training in the regular high school, area vocational-technical schools have been created. These schools, training students from several participating school districts, provide a great variety of career clusters for vocational curricula. The area vocational-technical school can provide a far more comprehensive program than a local high school, attempting by itself to serve the needs of all of its students. Federal funding has assisted in this type of vocational training—but not to the degree needed. Although estimates for the 1970s suggest that 25 percent of all high school students received some form of vocational training, this percentage is far below what it should be.

Education is for all youth in a democratic state, and if personal and group goals are to be achieved, then the educational program must be tailored to accommodate everyone.

Special Needs of Learners

In addition to the regular school programs, there has emerged a renewed emphasis on special needs beyond those associated with the formal classroom settings, N–12. These areas of special needs are (1) education for handicapped or exceptional children, (2) early childhood education, and (3) cocurricular activities. Although these areas are not new to the curricula of American education, they are now receiving increased attention.

Exceptional Children

In 1968, the Handicapped Children's Early Education Assistance Act was passed by Congress. Although the long-range impact of this legislation remains to be seen, there appears to be little doubt of its effect on the total school program. The Bureau of Education for the Handicapped (BEH) has estimated that 7,000,000 youngsters in the United States suffer from physical and mental handicaps. About 1,000,000 of these are pre-school children. The list of handicapped children includes those with mental retardation, speech problems, emotional disorders, deafness, blindness, crippling conditions, and other health impairments. Many children suffer combinations of these problems. Despite the identification of such large numbers of children needing special programs of education, BEH estimates that less than 50 percent of these children are receiving the type of special programs they need. Many of these exceptional learners are now being accommodated in regular school programs. A landmark U.S. District Court decision in 1971 held that all mentally retarded children in Pennsylvania had to be provided with an education at public expense. A follow-up decision in the District of Columbia extended that interpretation to all handicapped children.

In 1975, Public Law 94–142 mandated individualized programs for handicapped learners to be implemented in all schools by 1 October 1976. The due process problems associated with this legislation remain to be solved; however, the new legislation has generated many new programs geared toward earlier identification of exceptional children and has provided for special training for parents and teachers who work with these youngsters. Whenever possible, these youngsters are now being considered for mainstreaming programs rather than remedial programs. The tendency is to reduce the negative labeling effects and to afford the learner an atmosphere in which he or she can gain positive emotional strength despite the handicap—rather than to compound the handicap with secondary emotional disturbances.

The special needs of handicapped learners require a merger of roles such as the formal institution of education has never witnessed. Teachers, clinicians, parents, and special agencies all become crucial elements in a program for handicapped youth. The school system must now de-

With more American women working, early childhood education is an expanding area in education. (*Photograph courtesy of HUD*)

velop resources within the regular school setting to provide services that support the regular learning activities of the classroom. Rather than parents being shielded from active roles in the process of schooling, they are now encouraged to assist in the planning of policy and programs, evaluation, and dissemination of programs. The handicapped learner is no longer viewed as "aside" from the regular program, but as one who takes his or her regular place in the usual school setting.

Early Childhood Education— Nursery and Day Care   Closely associated with the increased attention to the education of exceptional children is the thrust toward providing improved early childhood education. This thrust has been directed toward the increased use of nursery schools for three- and four-year-olds, educational programs for parents of young children, day-care centers for young children whose parents cannot or will not provide the early developmental experiences for them, and planned formal educational programs for young children through grade five. In 1956, it was estimated that one out of every ten three- and four-year-old children was enrolled in a preschool program; by 1970, this rate had doubled.

Early childhood programs received increased attention during the 1960s with the War on Poverty and early Head Start programs. Some of the early work of Bloom, Hunt, and Piaget had suggested the importance of early environmental development as a crucial variable that influenced the intellectual growth of children. Early work with disadvantaged children suggested that the usual compensatory program for five- and six-year-old children was too late to make any marked effect on their cognitive and affective development. In a changing labor market, the demand for day-care centers has increased, as more and more mothers enter the labor force. It is estimated by the Department of Labor that, in the future, over five million mothers with preschool-age children will be working. The demand for early childhood education casts a new role on the elementary teacher who also now functions as an early childhood educator. Teachers need to be able to function as home visitors, staff trainers, and resource specialists. They need to have a greater understanding of human behavior and child development. Most of all, they need to comprehend the implications of curriculum change as it affects the total school program, N–12.

Summary and Implications

The formal structure of the school program is affected by both the types of learners it encounters and the societal expectation for the program. In the broadest terms, the components of the school's curriculum are divided into general, exploratory, and personal education. With increased attention being given to the education of young children, exceptional learners, and vocational learners, the function of the school program will undoubtedly change. The traditional Carnegie Unit and tracking systems of the secondary school will also be altered to satisfy current demands that the schools provide for individual needs within the school program. Teachers of the future will be expected to provide program clusters of learning, where all types of learners will share general and personal educational opportunities. As diagnosticians, teachers will be responsible for giving greater attention to the constants-variable type of program from elementary through secondary school. In addition, the community will play a greater role in the formal education of its youth.

Discussion Questions

1. Of what value is the Carnegie Unit? Explain.

2. How does the middle school differ from the junior high school?

3   Contrast the purposes of general and of exploratory education.

4.   Why should the elementary school provide the bulk of general education?

5.   What implications do the schools' increased efforts in early childhood education have for elementary education?

Supplemental Activities

1.   Examine the curriculum guide of a local school district and identify the general education component.

2.   Study your state's curriculum regulations to see how general, exploratory, and personal educational goals are to be met.

3.   List an exploratory program of study for a middle school.

4.   Have a senior high school guidance counselor visit your class and explain how the high school meets the personal education needs of the students.

5.   Debate the question: "Is general education merely the 'basics'?"

Bibliography

Apple, Michael W., and King, Nancy R. "What Do Schools Teach?" *Curriculum Inquiry* 6 (1977).

Hass, Glen. *Curriculum Planning: A New Approach*. 2nd ed. Boston: Allyn and Bacon, 1977.

Kohut, Sylvester, Jr. *The Middle School: A Bridge Between Elementary and Secondary Schools*. Washington, D.C.: National Education Association, 1976.

Tanner, Daniel, and Tanner, Laurel. *Curriculum Development: Theory into Practice*. New York: Macmillan, 1975.

Zais, Robert S. *Curriculum: Principles and Foundations*. New York: Crowell, 1976.

CHAPTER 21

Patterns of Curriculum Organization

ANY SCHOOL SYSTEM HAS ALTERNATIVE PATTERNS FOR CURRICU-lum organization from which to choose its own pattern. These patterns tend to range between a subject-centered and a student-centered organization. Within the two extremes, subject-centered and student-centered, a continuum of curricular organization exists—with schools that employ various elements from either or both extremes. In general, curricular organization that tends to be subject-centered is more *content oriented*; curricular organization that employs a student-centered pattern is *learner oriented*.

This chapter presents an analysis of the curriculum continuum as it ranges from content-oriented curricula to learner-oriented curricula. Those patterns that employ separate courses for the various academic disciplines and those that provide some fusion of the disciplines are discussed under the broad heading of *subject-centered* patterns of curriculum organization. Correlated programs and activity programs will be classified as *student-centered* patterns of curriculum organization. The reader should recognize that often the patterns of curricular organization used by various schools tend to be eclectic—and thus are borrowed from many sources. How a school district organizes its curriculum is related strongly to the philosophical position it takes toward the purposes of education.

Subject-centered Curriculum The *subject-centered curriculum* is the oldest and still one of the most widely used organizations in the schools of the United States. Its history can be traced to the *liberal arts* of the ancient world. The ancient *Trivium* was composed of grammar, rhetoric, and logic; the *Quadrivium* included the study of arithmetic, geometry, astronomy, and music. As time progressed, the Trivium also came to include history and literature; whereas the Quadrivium was expanded to include algebra, trigonometry, geography, botany, zoology, physics, and chemistry.

The modern subject-centered curriculum is distinctive in that all the subjects for instruction are compartmentalized. In the extreme use of this approach, the separate disciplines of knowledge are taught in isolation from one another with no attempt at *integration*. The intent is to provide a discipline for students that alerts them to set classifications and to arrangements of facts and ideas. The important criteria for the selection of ideas are to choose those that have proved beneficial for the problems of investigation in research. These are the facts and ideas that have withstood the test of time.

The use of this curriculum calls for extensive techniques of explanation and oral discourse. The subject-centered curriculum utilizes formal step-by-step study of ideas and facts; rarely is the student expected or encouraged to explore or experiment on his or her own. The teaching methods employ extensive use of verbal activities including lectures, discussions, questions and answers, and written exercises such as term papers and other evaluations.

Often this curriculum has come under criticism for failure to develop critical or creative thinking. Those who decry this approach suggest that its focal point of instruction becomes absorption and memorization of the presented facts and ideas.

Compartmental-   In his discussion of the limitations of the subject-centered curriculum,
ized Learning   Daniel Tanner states:

> The subject-centered curriculum is not consistent with our knowledge concerning the psychology of learning. Under this system, the primary focus is on the logical organization of the subject matter, and the problems and interests of the learners may be ignored or treated as of secondary importance. Students may learn facts and information from the textbook only to pass examinations, but they may retain very little of this type of learning once the examinations have been passed and the course is completed. The motivation for learning it too often geared to the extrinsic reward of receiving a passing grade. And what has been learned may soon be conveniently forgotten simply because it was artificial to the student in the first place.[1]

This criticism may not be altogether valid, in that a teacher properly schooled in this organization, utilizing the scientific approach to instruction, might well foster the development of critical thinking. Those who endorse the subject-matter curriculum point out that much of the failure of this approach may be the fault of the teacher and not of the curricular design.

1.   Daniel Tanner, *Schools for Youth* (New York: Macmillan, 1965), p. 233.

Core of Subjects   The subject-centered curriculum outlines in advance all the subjects that everyone must take. The constant subjects (general education) usually make up the majority of the program, and the student is not given much choice in selecting courses. Some authorities say that this curriculum facilitates the tracking system because it provides the elective area of learning desired by students in various tracks. As has been mentioned previously, the rigid track tends to make the elective program become required and constant. Within the subject-centered curriculum, there is some provision for individual interests and abilities. A few electives are provided for the students, and the teacher can also adjust for student differences within the required core of subjects. This adjustment may be achieved by the use of ability grouping within the subject or by varying special assignments designed for the many levels of ability the teacher must accommodate.

The elementary teacher operating within the framework of a subject-centered curriculum may group and subgroup the students by subject in the self-contained classroom in an attempt to provide for individual differences. Perhaps a fair criticism of the subject-centered curriculum is that it tends to neglect individual differences and to establish a system of common hurdles over which all students must pass.

One of the most persistent criticisms of the subject-centered curriculum has been its failure to lead the student toward an awareness and an understanding of current social problems. Much of what is taught tends to be centered on the past rather than the present and future. For instance, students studying American history are not likely to study in depth beyond the Korean conflict, and yet they were all born after that period. In addition, they may be studying and memorizing facts that probably could be stored and retrieved for better use by a computer. Although he made the following statement in 1929, Alfred N. Whitehead's summation is appropriate today.

> There is only one subject-matter for education, and that is Life in all its manifestations. Instead of this single unity, we offer children—Algebra, from which nothing follows; Geometry, from which nothing follows; Science from which nothing follows; History, from which nothing follows; a Couple of Languages, never mastered; and lastly, most dreary of all, Literature, represented by plays of Shakespeare, with philological notes and short analyses of plot and character to be in substance committed to memory. Can such a list be said to represent Life, as it is known in the midst of the living of it? The best that can be said of it is, that it is a rapid table of contents which a deity might run over in his mind while he was thinking of creating a world, and had not yet determined how to put it together.[2]

2.   Alfred N. Whitehead, *The Aims of Education* (New York: New American Library, 1957), pp. 18, 19. Copyright by The Macmillan Company.

Knowledge
Explosion

The world in which students now live and must face the future is very different and more complex than the world of the past. In the teaching of literature in a subject-centered curriculum, contemporary writings are often neglected. Principles of current economics and government also seem to escape this type of curriculum, and the student is passed into the adult society with little or no knowledge or appreciation of these important areas.

Those who support and defend the subject-centered curriculum argue that subjects that have withstood the test of time are most worthy. They also argue that, just because some children do not learn well in such a curriculum, this does not necessarily imply an inherent weakness in the curriculum organization. Among the many supporters of this type of curriculum are Arthur Bestor, William Bagley, James Koerner, Clifton Fadiman, and Hyman Rickover. In his studies of American and European education, Admiral Rickover has consistently concluded that the principal task of the school is to develop the intellect of its students. Called to testify before various House of Representatives' committees in 1962, he elaborated on three tasks he felt the schools should accomplish. In the hearings of the Eighty-seventh Congress, he stated that the school should: (1) pass on to the pupil a significant body of knowledge; (2) develop within the pupil the skill to use this knowledge intelligently in solving problems to be met during adult life; and (3) instill within the student the habit of assessing critical issues on the basis of fact and logical thinking.

The advocates of the subject-centered curriculum point out that everything cannot be studied at once nor can any study be all-inclusive. With the rapid explosion of knowledge, there simply has to be an ordered, segmented approach to study a subject effectively. The subjects, therefore, just become a convenient way for clarifying all this knowledge so it can be comprehended by students. It seems evident that the subject-centered approach to curriculum is not totally unworthy. Despite many attempts at curricular reform, the subject-centered curriculum has remained one of the most widely used curricular designs. Those who defend this curriculum point out that, while many schools were employing the subject-centered curriculum, our nation has produced a great many goods and services, provided a high standard of living for the total population, successfully brought about mass education, and contributed much to the entire world.

The advance of science and technology has changed the world of today and will bring greater changes tomorrow. A current assessment of social, political, economic, and technical needs suggests that the continuation of a strictly subject-centered curriculum will not adequately prepare youth for the adult world in which they must live.

Fused Curriculum

The *fused curriculum* has come about in an attempt to decrease the many separate subjects that gradually were brought into the subject-

Concern for students' needs has led to the development of the student-centered curriculum. (*Photograph by Elizabeth Hamlin, Stock, Boston*)

centered curriculum. In the place of separate and isolated classes in reading, writing, spelling, grammar, speech, and literature, the fused curriculum combines these subjects under English or language arts. The subject-centered curriculum remains almost intact, but students are introduced to the field as a whole rather than to bits and pieces. Subject matter goals are left whole, but the fused approach provides the teacher and student more latitude within the broad subject area. The fused social studies course encompasses history, geography, economics, political science, sociology, and anthropology. Fused science programs combine botany, zoology, and geology. Mathematics fuses arithmetic, geometry, and algebra. This fusion can also take place with physical education, home economics, industrial arts, art, and music.

As an illustration of how fusion operates within the language arts, the student may begin his study with a typical reading assignment. The teacher uses this basic assignment to explore principles of writing, discussion, vocabulary, and speech. The process may be reversed or arranged in any order, but the principle remains the same. Fusion attempts to show the interrelatedness of a core of common subject areas. This process is frequently called *integration* of subject matter. The teacher of social studies may use a historical event to introduce principles of economics and civics. He may, at the same time, focus attention on the geographical, sociological, and political implications of this particular historical event.

Instructional Units

Many teachers feel that the most successful way to fuse separate subjects into broad fields is through the unit approach. Three such potential units are fact-centered units, project-centered units, and idea-centered units. The *fact-centered unit* may center around the nature, history, and operation of language or become more specific in the study of a novel, a play, or even a particular author. The *project-centered unit*, taking into account individual differences, may be developed around a research paper, an autobiography, a field trip, or a community activity. The *idea-centered unit* focuses on expression and feelings. These units, if properly developed and nurtured, may offer promise and stimulation in the area of *affective* learning.

Subject Matter Integration

The fused or broad-field curriculum has enjoyed its greatest success at the elementary level. Separate subjects, once each taught for short periods during the day, are now more apt to be taught in a fused fashion over longer periods of time. Common fused study areas found in the elementary school are centered around language arts, social studies, general science, mathematics, art, music, and physical education and health.

In the past, the American junior high school has developed a number of variations on the fused program. Some schools have combined language arts and social studies with *block-type scheduling*, thus providing a longer time period in which these two broad areas can be taught; however, in more recent years, the downward movement of subject matter has resulted in many junior high schools taking on the predominantly subject-centered approach of the senior high school.

In the senior high school, the fused curriculum has met with relatively little success. Examples of the few high school courses that are patterned after this approach are general science, problems of democracy in the social studies, and family living. Perhaps the most significant impact that the fused curriculum has had upon the senior high school has been the integration of unified areas into subject-centered courses. Many high school teachers of American history now make an attempt to interlace a certain amount of geography and political science with their history courses. Those who favor the fused curriculum offer the following advantages:

1. Subject matter may be integrated more readily.
2. This approach establishes a more logical and useful organization for the presentation of knowledge.

3. This approach enables the student to learn with greater understanding and appreciation.
4. Basic principles and generalizations necessary for the development of critical thinking are given greater emphasis than isolated facts.

In reality, the fused curriculum has many of the same advantages and disadvantages of the subject-centered curriculum. Some of the criticisms voiced against the fused curriculum are (1) the compression of several courses into one does not guarantee integration; (2) fusion tends to result in a sketchy knowledge and a "watering down" of a specific discipline; and (3) with the emphasis on generalizations rather than specifics, learning tends to be more abstract than desirable.

Student-centered Curriculum

The concern for students' needs and interests has aided in the development of the *student-centered curriculum*. In the past and to some extent in the present, these needs have had both social and psychological interpretations. It appears that needs of youth today are considered those requirements the society expects of maturing young adults. Although an extreme interpretation of the subject-centered curriculum has stressed that learning is most effective if it is rigorous and difficult, the student-centered curriculum has placed emphasis on encouraging the students' interests in and appreciation for learning. When the interests and needs of learners are incorporated within the curriculum, motivation tends to become intrinsic rather than extrinsic. This is not to imply that the student-centered curriculum is directed by the whims of the learner but rather that learning is more successfully achieved if it builds upon the interests the learner has developed prior to a formal learning process. In the following discussion of core and activity programs, the reader is challenged to compare and contrast the student-centered curriculum with the subject-centered curriculum.

Core Curriculum

The *core curriculum* grew out of a general dissatisfaction with the piecemeal learning promoted by the subject-centered curriculum. In an attempt to offer a more enriching educational experience for students, proponents of the core curriculum felt that a unification of subjects and a new methodology were needed. Since society had become increasingly fragmented, with the increased emphasis on science and technology, they felt that the only logical approach for developing societal values and social vision was through a core pattern of organization. The core curriculum may be structured or unstructured in emphasis and may cross broader subject-area lines; it places even greater stress than the fused curriculum upon the need to integrate subject matter.

The core curriculum stresses social values: considerable time is given to the study of the culture and its moral content. This curriculum utilizes the problem-solving approach to learning; within this approach, stress is given to factual content, descriptive principles, socio-economic conditions, and moral rules of conduct and behavior. In its purest form, the core is basically "normative" in its presentation to students. Concern centers around such topics as "What are the social needs of today?"

Social Values A typical application of the core curriculum would be a study of the persistent themes of social living. The subject matter is not an isolated block of content; but rather it is used as a means to define and solve problems common to many or all students. The core curriculum takes into account the interests of students; however, student interest is not the sole criterion for selection and organization of learning experiences. Group processes and dynamics become the center of planned activity, and often the community becomes a resource for study.

Another special and distinguishing characteristic of the core program is the cooperative planning of learning activities by the students and teacher. This planning tends to be concerned more with the "how" rather than "what" to study. All students, regardless of their individual abilities, concentrate upon those areas of learning that are essential to all members of society. This should not imply that all learn the same thing with the same degree of skill or proficiency; it does imply that all are exposed to the common problems, and each is allowed to visualize himself or herself accepting or rejecting a particular vocational role within society.

Block Programs There is maximum provision in the core program for special needs and interests as they arise. Since one feature of the core curriculum is a longer block of instructional time, the classroom program is quite flexible and includes remedial, developmental, and accelerated activities as they fit into the study at hand. There is ample time available for much needed guidance and counseling, both individual and group. Skills are taught as needed to solve problems, and these problems are used to increase student motivation. The core program, although it continues to decline in popular use, still tends to be found most commonly at the junior high school level.

Teacher Preparation A core program demands many special considerations if it is to meet with any reasonable degree of success. The foremost consideration is the teacher in the program. In addition to a broad preparation in the liberal arts, core teachers need a keen understanding of social foundations, of child and adolescent psychology, of the structure and dynamics of group processes, of guidance, and of the problems approach to learning. The lack of adequately prepared teachers has hindered the growth and acceptance of the core curriculum. Classrooms and buildings must be large and flexible to provide for the variety of group activities used in the core; an abundance of supplementary teaching materials is essential. Schedules must include large and flexible time blocks, and flexible grouping of students by age and grade is necessary. Last but not least, an effective public relations program for parents and community is vital if the core curriculum is to be understood and accepted.

Activity Program
To the extreme right of a curriculum continuum is the *activity curriculum* (Figure 21–1). In its purest form, it operates with the child as the sole center of learning. Since education is life and life is ever changing, the activity curriculum expects to change continually. Students' needs and interests are assessed, and the curriculum is built upon that basis. The psychology of learning practiced in this approach is one based upon the emotional involvement of the learner. If a child develops an interest in something and becomes emotionally involved with it, the learning process is enhanced—according to the proponents of the activity curriculum. This curriculum, never fixed, completely crosses subject matter lines. Completely unstructured, the activity for the early learner may be centered on such topics as pets, toys, boats, letter carriers, or police officers. Emphasis is placed upon observation, play, stories, and handiwork.

The activity curriculum has not been as acceptable to the public as the subject-centered curriculum. When used, it has been most successful at the elementary level. Although it has never secured a foothold in the secondary curriculum, the activity curriculum has had some influence on the high school program. The lack of acceptance at the high school level may be due in part to the subject orientation that secondary teachers and administrators have had. Also, the public seems

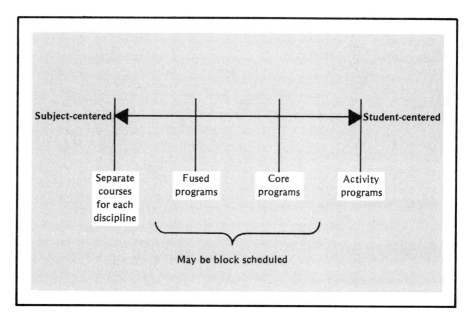

Figure 21–1.
A curriculum continuum.

In its purest form, the activity curriculum operates with the child as the sole center of learning. (*Photograph by Glenna Collett*)

to prefer the traditional organization and methodology of the subject-centered high school.

The activity curriculum is quite different from all other patterns of curricular organization in a number of characteristic ways. First, the interests and purposes of children determine the educational program. Second, common learnings (general education) come about as a result of individual interests. Third, this curriculum is not planned in advance, but guidelines are established to help the students choose alternatives intelligently as they proceed through the program. Activities are planned cooperatively by students and teachers; what they plan and pursue may or may not have any deliberate social direction. In the pursuit of planned goals, problem solving becomes the major method for teaching. Little or no need for extracurricular activities develops because all interests are accommodated within the regular program.

The teacher, in preparing to teach in the activity curriculum, needs all the prerequisites of the core teacher—and even more. Because of the unstructured nature of the activity curriculum, the need for space and flexible scheduling is paramount. Schedules utilizing large blocks of time are necessary to afford the maximum potential of the program.

Curriculum Contrasts   The subject-centered curriculum and the student-centered curriculum represent the two extremities of a curriculum continuum. The two curricula are contrasted in the following list.[3]

Subject-centered Curriculum	Student-centered Curriculum
1. Centered in *subjects*.	1. Centered in *learners*.
2. Emphasis upon teaching subject matter.	2. Emphasis upon promoting the all-around growth of the learners.
3. Subject matter selected and organized *before* the teaching situation.	3. Subject matter selected and organized cooperatively by all learners *during* the learning situation.
4. Controlled by the teacher or someone representing authority external to the learning situation.	4. Controlled and directed cooperatively by learners (pupils, teachers, parents, supervisors, principals, and others) in the learning situation.
5. Emphasis upon teaching facts, imparting information, requiring knowledge for its own sake or for possible future use.	5. Emphasis upon meanings which will function immediately in improving living.
6. Emphasis upon teaching specific habits and skills as separate and isolated aspects of learning.	6. Emphasis upon building habits and skills as integral parts of larger experiences.
7. Emphasis upon improving methods of teaching subject matter of specific subjects.	7. Emphasis upon understanding and improving through use of the process of learning.
8. Emphasis upon uniformity of exposures to learning situations and, insofar as possible, uniformity of learning results.	8. Emphasis upon variability in exposures to learning situations and variability in the results expected and achieved.
9. Education as conforming to the patterns set by the curriculum and its various associated instruments.	9. Education as aiding each child to build a socially creative individuality.
10. Education considered as schooling.	10. Education considered as a continuous intelligent process of growth.

3. L. Thomas Hopkins, *Interaction: A Democratic Process* (Boston: D. C. Heath, 1941).

Grouping Practices

The special problems of ability grouping are closely related to any discussion of patterns for curriculum organization. Generally ability grouping has been defended as a means whereby the teacher could more adequately provide for individual differences. Whereas the elementary school tends to group pupils by subject areas within the self-contained classroom, the secondary school tends to group students by subjects, as learners develop and pursue special interests. The usual effects of grouping have caused a particular problem to emerge: special and separate classes are established for the academically talented, the slow learners, and the average learners.

Homogeneous— Heterogeneous

The position that school systems take with regard to ability grouping depends to a large degree on their basic conceptions of the individual and of the general purposes of education. If the philosophical position of the school is focused upon a predetermined curriculum, the school is more likely to support homogeneous ability grouping. On the other hand, if the school is more concerned about the personal and social development of students and believes in diversity as a technique for stimulating educational experiences, it is more likely to favor a *heterogeneous* grouping practice. If homogeneous ability grouping is practiced, students may be grouped on the basis of intelligence tests, achievement tests, reading levels, grades, teacher evaluation—or any combination of these measures. All too often, however, ability grouping has usually been established only on the basis of intelligence and achievement test results. Because of the highly verbal nature of these tests, they tend not to be culture free and tend to place undue restrictions and labels on minority-group learners.

Despite the fact that the usual defense for ability grouping practices has been on the basis of providing for individual differences, school programs still tend to be group oriented, and individual differences are not given attention. Although ability grouping has been defended as a means to assist increased achievement levels of learners, this defense is only weakly substantiated by research findings. One of the major problems associated with the difficulty of establishing truly homogeneous groups can be found in the lack of precision of the measurement instruments used to establish groups. Another major constraint is the lack of flexible class and teaching assignments: it becomes almost impossible to select a completely homogeneous class when every class must have thirty students and when scheduling conflicts and student interests cause potentially valid diagnostic testing data to be discarded. If the school population of a school district is a sample of the total population, and if that sample is a mirror of some normal curve distribution, then all class sizes cannot be the same and still be classified as homogeneous for learning purposes.

The potential for problems generated by ability grouping far outweighs the scant benefits to be gained by rigid grouping practices. Some of the major problems associated with rigid homogeneous grouping practices are:

- Teachers tend to favor teaching average or above-average groups rather than low ability groups.
- Students who are given labels of low ability usually perform poorly because of the teacher's low expectation for the students.
- Problems associated with social-class and minority-group differences are usually increased with ability grouping.
- Ability grouping tends to reinforce unfavorable self-concept among children placed in low ability groups.
- Negative self-concept is most severe among minority-group learners when they are assigned to low ability groups.
- For the learners, ability grouping does not enhance the value and acceptance of differences within society.
- Academically talented students perform better in high ability groups; low achievers tend to perform poorly in low ability groups.

Despite the many negative aspects of ability grouping, the advantage of a limited and flexible grouping program is that it contributes to teaching effectiveness. There is little doubt that the task of instruction—and the general intent to provide individualized programs—is made somewhat easier if the range of abilities and interests is reduced through grouping. If grouping remains flexible and is based upon abilities, needs, interests, and social practices—and if students are not locked into fixed groups—the teacher can arrange instruction to achieve a set of appropriate objectives for a particular group.

The pressures for mainstreaming suggest that all grouping be on a heterogeneous basis; mainstreaming certainly requires the teacher to expect diversity in learners. As individualized programs are prepared for these learners, varied types of ability grouping will be employed. Where classroom atmospheres of cooperation and helping are intended, heterogeneous grouping will be warranted. On the other hand, formal learning activities employing peer learning, cluster arrangements, or individual study will suggest flexible grouping arrangements.

The current federal mandates for mainstreaming require an individualized program for all exceptional children. It is not surprising that since exceptional children are getting individualized programs, parents have begun to demand due process for their "nonexceptional" children. If successful, mainstreaming legislation may be helpful in providing individualized programs for all children—at which point, ability grouping, as we have known it, will pass from the scene of the public school.

Summary and Implications

The organization of the curriculum by any school district is dependent upon the manner in which the learner and knowledge are viewed. If the learner is viewed as passive in the learning process and if knowledge is viewed as absolute, the school district tends to favor a subject-centered curriculum. If, on the other hand, the learner is assumed to be active in the learning process and if knowledge is assumed to be changing and growing, the district tends to favor a student-centered curriculum. The teacher needs to have a thorough understanding of these extremes in curriculum organization in relation to the purposes and the role of the school in the community.

The future of rigid ability grouping, as has been practiced in the schools, is very bleak. Mainstreaming and the demand for individually tailored instructional programs compel the teacher to become better equipped as a diagnostician and a prescriber of a variety of learning activities. The teacher can no longer teach to some expected mean of ability but must employ flexible patterns of instruction that use a variety of materials. Curricular organization of the future will be more eclectic and will employ student- or subject-centered patterns of organization, depending upon the particular needs and interests of learners.

Discussion Questions

1. What are the unique features of the subject-centered curriculum?

2 What are the weaknesses of the student-centered curriculum?

3. Discuss the statement: "It makes good sense to organize the curriculum around the academic disciplines."

4. What educational and philosophical positions are associated with both the student-centered and subject-centered curricula?

5. Discuss the positive and negative effects of ability grouping on less able students, in general, and on minority children, in particular.

Supplemental Activities

1. Select two curriculum guides of different school districts and determine which pattern of curriculum organization each employs.

2. Write a brief paper explaining the relationship of educational philosophy to curriculum organization.

3. Obtain some classroom data on ability and performance levels of a group of learners and explain how they could be grouped for a particular learning objective.

4. Invite an elementary and secondary teacher to discuss how they employ grouping practices in the classroom.

5. Invite a special education consultant to discuss the effects of mainstreaming on grouping.

Bibliography

Doll, Ronald C. *Curriculum Improvement: Decision Making and Process.* 3rd ed. Boston: Allyn and Bacon, 1974.

Inlow, Gail M. *The Emergent in Curriculum.* 2nd ed. New York: John Wiley, 1973.

Krug, Mark M. *What Will Be Taught the Next Decade.* Itasca, Ill.: F. E. Peacock, 1972.

Rubin, Louis. *Curriculum Handbook.* Abr. ed. Boston: Allyn and Bacon, 1977.

Steeves, Frank L. *The Subjects in the Curriculum.* New York: Odyssey Press, 1968.

CHAPTER 22

Curriculum Innovation

ALTHOUGH THE TERM *INNOVATIVE* IS SUGGESTIVE OF NEW PRAC-
tices, it is not intended that the term *curriculum innovation* be applied
to only the most recently developed practices. Innovative practices have
been employed throughout the history of schooling. During the past
two decades, however, the ferment for educational change has
spawned a variety of practices aimed at improvement in the teaching-
learning process. Although too many school systems have opted to
hide in the traditions of educational practice, increasing numbers of
school districts have attempted a variety of different practices in an
effort to satisfy societal demands. Although innovation has assumed
various labels in recent times, this chapter will examine four broad areas
of innovation—organization, instruction, technology, and substance. Innovative practices in these areas do not occur separately but oftentimes are dependent upon one another. They can, however, be separated for closer analyses.

Organization   The major intent of organizational innovations is to change the structure or environment in which learners, teachers, and specialists reside.
Such structural innovations include team teaching, differentiated staffing, modular and flexible scheduling, nongraded schools, open space
facilities, and modular or minicourse programs. The major reason for
classifying these as organizational innovations is that they may occur
with no real difference in or alteration of instructional practice, little or
no change in substance or materials, and no increased use of technology. In other words, a secondary school may employ the use of a
modular scheduling program without any change in instructional practice. There may also be no change in the content selected for students
and no special way of employing technology to deliver instruction to

students. The same could be said of an elementary program introduced into an open space setting. More often than not, however, use of one type of innovative activity—in this case, organization—tends to incorporate other innovative practices.

Team Teaching   Although many have considered it a recent organizational innovation, *team teaching* is not an entirely new concept. It has been used for some time in athletics, where a team of coaches—each somewhat of a specialist in his own right—works together to develop the special talents of the team members. The team teaching approach also has been used successfully by the military services, when in a period of national crisis it became necessary to train masses of men in short periods of time. It is true, however, that only recently have the nation's schools begun to utilize team teaching on a larger scale.

The needs of students are more apt to be met when they are exposed to a variety of learning experiences. Learning can be maximized through a combination of large-group instruction (100 to 150 students), small-group instruction (8 to 15 students), and independent study. A teaching team, by subject or by a combination of subjects, can provide these three basic types of learning experiences. The distribution of time between the large group, small group, and independent study will vary according to the subject studied. As an average, it has been suggested that students should spend 40 percent of the time in large-group instruction, 30 percent of the time in small-group discussion, and 30 percent of the time in independent study.

Employed in both elementary and secondary schools, team teaching may take many different forms: size and composition of the team may vary, and the teams may teach one subject field or cross subject lines. Some of the specific advantages offered for team teaching include:

- The specialization of teaching whereby the particular talents of a teacher are used to the fullest.
- The improvement of supervisory arrangements whereby team teachers criticize one another's teaching performance.
- The use of nonprofessional aides for routine duties.
- The expanded and multiple uses of many of the new mechanical teaching devices that aid the teacher.

The teaching team may be organized in two general ways. The first is a more formal approach and is referred to as the *hierarchal team organization*. This is a type of line-staff organization wherein a team leader heads a team made up of regular teachers and teachers' aides. Usually there is a pay differential, with the team leader receiving a higher salary than the other teachers on the team. The aides may be noncertified personnel who handle many of the routine administrative and clerical duties formerly handled by the classroom teacher. Aides may also, under the careful supervision of the teaching team, be assigned some routine instructional tasks. The second type of organization is referred to as *collegial* or *equalitarian team*. There is no formal structure in this organization; leadership is shared or exchanged on a voluntary basis. This team differs from the hierarchal team in that all teachers receive the same pay and have equal responsibility and similar duties. The true team organization is binding, however, in that the teachers of the collegial team, while enjoying less formal organization, must work together in a common cause. It is important to distinguish the collegial team from the many types of cooperative or joint ventures that teachers may voluntarily join and from which they may withdraw whenever they wish.

Despite the many advantages of team teaching that have been presented, there are some potential difficulties that may prevent the beginning of team teaching movements or hinder the success of team teaching projects already under way. First, the preparation for team teaching is time-consuming; and in any planning for this type of instruction, adequate preparation time must be allotted. Second, the potential for personality clashes is ever present and should be avoided at all costs. If some teachers do not work well together, they should not be forced to do so. Third, there is the possibility of giving less attention to individual students if the team teaching should degenerate into nothing more than large-group instruction or "turn-teaching." Fourth, adequate physical facilities greatly enhance the success of team teaching. This is not to say that team teaching cannot be used in many existing school facilities. If team teaching is being anticipated and new facilities are needed, however, they should be built to accommodate this type of teaching. Fifth, team teaching cannot and should not be forced upon teachers by the administration. Teachers must possess the desire to participate, since team teaching takes maximum cooperation and effort if it is to be successful.

Differentiated Staffing

Differentiated staffing has added a new dimension to the organizational patterns for team teaching. In actuality, it may be viewed as a further refinement of the hierarchal teaching discussed earlier. More specifically, it does establish a particular kind of career-ladder approach that links the paraprofessional job with the superintendent's office, where a director of curriculum and instruction may be housed. Each particular instructional and research staff assignment carries with it specific prerequisites for training and special instructional changes. The essential elements for differentiated staffing consist of the following:

- A minimum of three differentiated staff teaching levels are suggested: paraprofessional, staff teacher, and senior teacher.
- Salary scales for each level should be different, but each should contain minimum and maximum ranges.

- Academic and professional preparation for each level should be different, with the senior teacher assuming the responsibility of staff leader.
- All levels are responsible for delivering instruction, but only the staff and senior teacher are responsible for curricular decision making.
- All positions may be tenured, but it is recommended that the senior teacher be on a yearly contract rather than tenured.

As has been the case with hierarchal team arrangements, one of the major deterrents to differentiated staffing has been the salary differences usually confused with a type of merit-pay system. There appears to be little doubt that some teachers are better than others at certain tasks, and vice versa. If the profession is concerned about accountability and quality education for its clientele, then it seems obvious that teachers should be placed in roles congruous with their abilities. In addition to using credentialing and advanced training, the profession is in desperate need of valid and reliable criteria that may be used to assign special roles and tasks for professional staff.

Modular and
Flexible
Scheduling

The two organizational terms, *modular* and *flexible scheduling*, actually imply two different concepts in scheduling and should not be considered as being one and the same. Modular scheduling has existed for quite some time in both elementary and secondary schools. At the elementary level, it has usually been associated with thirty-minute time blocks (modules), while at the secondary level it has usually been associated with forty- to sixty-minute time blocks (modules). The secondary school time blocks have been tied to the instructional time allocation of the Carnegie Unit. A modular schedule is just as rigid as the six- to eight-period schedule utilized for so many years in the secondary schools. On the other hand, a flexible schedule employs the use of smaller time blocks (*mods*), but the schedule changes on a regular basis during the school year as student needs and teaching objectives are altered for particular periods and types of instruction. A combination of these two organizational concepts, modular and flexible scheduling, implies that the traditional patterns of organization for instruction are altered to meet changing needs and concepts of learning as the student passes through the school.

The regimentation of the six- or eight-period day of the typical high school does not allow sufficient flexibility for maximum utilization of teacher and student resources and abilities. An increasing number of educators are questioning the practice of devoting the same amount of time to each subject. It appears that some subjects may be taught best in shorter blocks of time for fewer periods per week, while others may best be taught with longer blocks of time.

Modular and flexible schedules have unlimited possibilities that may be put into operation regardless of the pattern of curriculum organization—regardless of whether it is a subject-centered curriculum or student-centered curriculum. However, as one introduces flexibility into the pattern of organization for instruction, a theoretical shift begins to take place: the philosophical rationale adapted for flexibility tends to direct a program toward student-centered needs rather than subject-centered goals.

A potential deterrent to the adoption of modular and flexible scheduling at the secondary level has been and continues to be the Carnegie Unit. Despite this, some high schools have employed these newer types of scheduling and managed to fulfill the cumbersome Carnegie Unit requirements by counting independent study toward the time requirement. The fact that the Carnegie Unit seems destined to be discarded will probably lead to much further acceptance of the newer scheduling.

An example of a flexible schedule is one that calls for twenty- to thirty-minute modules for instruction. With this type of time allotment, the possibilities for flexibility are greatly increased. Instead of the typical school day having six to eight periods, it now has the potential for twelve to eighteen periods. Also modules may be used in various combinations; this flexibility begins to allow for maximum utilization of teacher and student talents. Some schools have combined modular and flexible scheduling and teaching teams for instruction so that the special talents of these professionals can be directed toward areas where they may be most effective. At the same time, students may be introduced to more teachers who are specialists in one type of instruction or another.

As students have needs and special abilities, so do the teachers who work with these students. We have continuously acknowledged the individual needs and talents of students but have ignored the individual needs of teachers. Teachers who are forced to fit into the traditional schedule must also come to grips with the frustrations experienced by their students. To operate effectively, teachers need:

1. A greater opportunity to use their professional skills. Typical classroom teachers, in addition to their twenty-five or thirty hours of classroom contact with pupils, spend many other hours in planning, grading, keeping records, collecting money, sponsoring student activities—and in multitudinous other duties. Such a heavy teacher load makes it increasingly difficult for the professional teacher to keep abreast of the new developments in the teaching field and of innovations in instruction and evaluation. The average teacher spends up to two-thirds of the day doing nonprofessional routine duties that could be done by others—or by a machine.

2. A suitable place in which they may perform their professional work. The schools of tomorrow need space facilities where teachers may

work together in developing instructional materials. The teacher needs an office and conference rooms for individual work with students and parents.

3. More appropriate salaries commensurate with the job they are performing. As the high school schedule is rigid, so is the salary schedule. Regardless of the level of performance, all teachers are paid equally. The superior teacher is seldom rewarded financially.

The teacher should not be bound to the rigid schedule of the typical high school. Time should be provided during the regular school day for planning and conferring with students, other teachers, and parents. Additional time should be allotted for professional activities that may aid the teacher in furthering his or her own professional growth. Students, on the other hand, still spend about thirty hours per week in planned school learning activities, but their time is arranged so as to provide them with the variety of learning experiences deemed appropriate for maximum learning. While the students' interests are being challenged through this multiple approach, the individual is still given the freedom to pursue subject areas in depth.

Nongraded Schools

The *nongraded school,* as now defined, involves a plan of school organization that allows each child to progress through the school system at his or her own rate of development. The lock-step grade level concept, with its set curriculum for each grade level, is abandoned in favor of an individual, flexible, and continuous educational program. Sometimes referred to as *continuous progress education,* this plan introduces the student to a series of stages of development geared to readiness for learning. Students are grouped flexibly on the basis of age, ability, maturity, achievement, and other developmental factors. Within this type of grouping, students are encouraged to move ahead through each subject at their own speed; their grouping arrangements vary with the progress made.

The nongraded curriculum makes the final move toward complete dissolution of the lock-step graded system. When an elementary school becomes nongraded, the kindergarten, grades one, two, three, and four are often simply designated the primary school. The upper elementary school, grades five, six, seven, and eight, becomes a new unit of organization labeled the intermediate or middle school; and the high school discards its strict traditional approach and graded pattern in favor of phases of learning and sequential development.

Whereas the traditional elementary school has been organized in blocks of time on a yearly basis, the nongraded school is organized in blocks of time suited for the development of basic skills preceding higher orders of learning. In the traditional school, the child progresses yearly from grade to grade, with advancement determined by minimum completion of set standards for that grade or, more often, the child is simply automatically passed to the next grade each year. Some students of this group fail to meet certain standards at each grade level and therefore are introduced to failure at a very early stage of their formal education. On the other hand, the student who learns at a rate significantly faster than the average child is slowed down and compelled to move along the graded plan with his peers. Frequently, for the above-average student, the most significant criterion for grade advancement is chronological age. Programs of double promotion, once somewhat popular for the above-average student, are rarely used today. The graded school fails to take fully into account one of the basic principles of child growth and development: *all students do not learn at the same rate.*

Many new audio-visual techniques are now utilized in the schools. (*Photograph by Talbot Lovering*)

The nongraded school attempts to minimize the many shortcomings of the graded system, and in so doing the conventional grade designations of the typical American school are discarded. With grade level designations gone, the more able student is permitted to advance at a rate commensurate with his ability. Whereas in the graded system, it would take five years to pass through the formal learning of skills expected for grades K–4, the child may now complete this block of learning in four or, in some cases, three years. On the other hand, in the nongraded school the slower student does not have to experience the psychological fear of failure or suffer the minimal learning associated with grade placement—and may take five or more years to master the necessary skills.

The vast majority of nongrading has appeared at the elementary level, although some high schools have begun to move in this direction. With the principle of nongrading applied to the total scheme of formal education, it is possible to envision the curriculum being divided into four areas—primary education, intermediate education, secondary education, and higher education—all of which could be nongraded and which would provide a continuous education organized around the individual progress of pupils.

Much of the criticism directed toward the nongraded school has come as a result of little or no empirical evidence showing its value over that of the graded school. If the nongraded school is to achieve any popular status, it must prove its worth in controlled studies. Some critics suggest that most of the desirable features of the nongraded school can be put into practice in a graded school; it appears fair to conclude that this eventuality would merely superimpose the nongraded organization onto an existing pattern of organization. If the theory were then truly practiced, grade level designations would tend to disappear eventually.

Open Space Facilities

The use of *open space facilities* does not imply the automatic implementation of an instructional program developed around the philosophy of open education. What an *open space facility* does imply, however, is another type of organizational innovation that alters the structure of a school plant. Instead of the single or double loaded corridors of small classrooms—plus or minus thirty students per room—a school plant is constructed with large open instructional spaces that may be kept completely open for all types of instruction or may be altered to obtain smaller areas by movable walls and furniture. This type of plant facility tends to be more conducive to a variety of instructional and grouping patterns. Its popularity for use in school construction has increased rapidly in the past ten years, but the open space facility is still found primarily at the elementary and middle school levels.

With declining school enrollments has come a decline in school building programs. If school districts are to attempt to provide open space facilities during a declining enrollment period, they must plan for the renovation of old buildings rather than for new construction. In the 1980s, enrollment reductions may be responsible for a cutback in the use of open space facilities.

Modular or Minicourse Programs

The use of *minicourses* as a pattern of organization provides expanded flexibility to the curriculum offerings. Instead of course offerings being built around one-semester or two-semester time modules, they are built into a variety of shorter time modules that award varying proportions of Carnegie Units. The minicourses may be of three-, six- or nine-week duration, but total time should be determined by the module objectives and by the time needed to accomplish those objectives. An example of a minicourse program is the one used in social studies at the Jersey Shore High School, Jersey Shore, Pennsylvania. All minicourses at this high school are of nine weeks or less duration, and a student is awarded one-quarter of a Carnegie Unit for each course that is completed satisfactorily. During the students' four-year program, they are required to complete, satisfactorily, four social studies Carnegie Units or sixteen courses; they may select from an offering of forty-seven minicourses grouped into five general areas: history, economics, cultural, social, and political science. There are particular advantages to a minicourse program:

1. A minicourse provides the opportunity for increased numbers of course offerings that may be elected by a student.
2. If a student fails a minicourse, he or she is not forced to repeat that short learning experience but may elect to participate in another course to meet the required Carnegie Unit.
3. During any one school year, teachers may teach a greater variety of course offerings and provide some specialization in their particular areas of competence.
4. During their school program, students may come in contact with a greater number of teachers.
5. Students may be grouped by grade level or not—as the school district desires.

Although minicourse programs have been operated successfully in English, social studies, science, and mathematics programs in many states across the nation, they have recently been cited as one of the "innovative ills" that have spawned the back-to-basics movement. The fact remains, however, that where data have been systematically gathered on minicourse programs, the basics have not been found to be wanting.

Instruction

Innovation in the area of instruction has focused on the development of particular strategies to bring about instructional objectives. There has been a deliberate attempt to define strategies as: instructional delivery systems that are particular to the intended learning outcomes expected by teachers as they develop curriculum. Instruction is viewed as having a direct relationship with the hierarchy of learning experiences encountered in the teaching-learning situation. As discussed earlier, the cognitive domain of learning, developed by Bloom and his associates, ranks learning from a low-order process (knowledge) to a high-order process (evaluation). As instructional objectives are developed to enhance learning processes, particular teaching strategies should also be developed that maximize the opportunity for a learner to meet the objective. This type of fit calls for a high degree of congruence between objectives and instructional behavior.

Lecture-recitation
The lecture or lecture-recitation instructional strategy is usually associated with a lower order of expected learning (knowledge and comprehension). The learner is not viewed as an active verbal participant in the learning situation but, instead, is expected to digest specific knowledge for recall. The learner is viewed as a receiver of knowledge, and the strategy for instruction is viewed as the delivery system. Employment of this strategy requires maximum verbal input on the part of the teacher. This may be accomplished by live teacher lecture, linear and/or branched programmed instruction, or use of special technology, television, dial access equipment, and computers.

Guided Discovery—Convergent Learning
Guided discovery as an instructional strategy is planned for those higher-order learning behaviors (application and analysis) that have as their objective a convergent learning behavior for the student. Verbal behavior on the part of the teacher is viewed as guiding learner responses; that is, as the teacher asks questions and students respond, the teacher's task is to use questioning techniques that are leading and "guide" the students to the desired responses. Rather than telling the "answers" as in the lecture-recitation strategy, the teacher, through a series of further questions, guides students through the necessary supportive knowledge to lead them to responses directed toward the correct answers. This type of convergent-thinking behavior is consistent with instructional objectives deemed appropriate for the application and analysis levels of learning.

Inquiry—Divergent Learning
As an instructional strategy, *inquiry* has as its goal the development of divergent thinking. This is considered to be the highest order of learning and is associated with synthesis and evaluation skills. The task of the teacher for this strategy is one of little teacher verbal input and increased learner verbal input. Through a series of questions and problem situations, the teacher seeks assertions or hypotheses from the learners. If, in a group situation, the teacher obtains two or more learner assertions, it is the teacher's task to help the students develop support (based on logic or data) for their assertions. In this type of

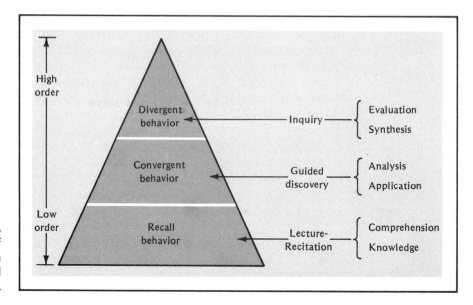

teaching-learning situation, the teacher must encourage and expect different "right" answers to students' assertions or hypotheses. Thus learning behavior planned for divergent learner responses is associated with the inquiry strategy. A graphical representation of the preceding discussion is shown in Figure 22–1. If instructional objectives are planned to achieve the knowledge and comprehensive levels of learning, then the lecture-recitation instructional strategy is an appropriate strategy. If analysis and application skills are sought for the learner, then the guided discovery strategy is an appropriate teaching strategy. Finally, if evaluation and synthesis skills are sought for the learner, then the inquiry strategy is the appropriate teacher-and-learner behavior. As expected learning for the student proceeds from low order to high order, the degree of teacher-and-student verbal output changes. At the low-order level, there is an abundance of teacher verbal output and a minimum of student verbal output. As expected learner behavior moves toward higher-order learning (divergent behavior), teacher verbal input decreases significantly and learner verbal input increases significantly. With increased development and use of systematic observation instruments, these strategies can be validated as to their degree of congruence with instructional objectives. The use of systematic observation instruments as evaluative tools is discussed later.

Simulation and
Gaming

Simulation and gaming techniques have received increased attention in recent years as appropriate instructional strategies if the objectives call for personal involvement of the learner. These particular strategies are particularly well suited to the social studies curriculum but also may be used in the industrial arts, home economics, business, science, and communications curricula of the elementary, junior, and senior high school. When employing this instructional strategy, the teacher places the students in preplanned situations with a multitude of data available to all students—and with some data available only to certain participants. The object of the strategy is to have the learners encounter lifelike situations that they must solve to the satisfaction of all participants. Games may be varied so that they have one best solution (convergent learner behavior) or many possible solutions (divergent learner behavior). The special task of the teacher is to see that all possible available data are used by the students in the problem they are attempting to solve. This strategy may be considered a type of learner role-playing; it meets a specific need for certain instructional objectives that are planned for analysis, synthesis, and evaluation levels of learning.

Programmed Instruction

Programmed instruction as a teaching strategy can be traced to the early work of Sidney Pressey during the 1920s. While Pressey was unable to promote any considerable acceptance of his ideas in the 1930s, B. F. Skinner presented them thirty years later, and since that time the concept of programmed instruction has gained significant acceptance. Although this strategy may be and has been used for application learning behaviors, it perhaps is best used for expected knowledge and comprehension behaviors.

Two major approaches to programmed instruction are used for teaching purposes. The first of these, *linear programming*, uses constructed-response frames for which the student must supply his or her own answer. The student may receive immediate feedback to a single response or may receive feedback after a planned series of responses. In the second method, *branch programming*, the student proceeds to additional frames for learning only after correct responses. If incorrect responses are recorded, the learner is directed along an alternate route for remedial or reinforcement activities. This branching technique is designed to help the student correct and understand his or her errors before moving on to an advanced series of frames. Programmed instruction is considered to have the following advantages:

1. Students are allowed the freedom to learn at a rate commensurate with their own ability. Programmed instruction permits individual study.
2. The basic facts of subject matter can be presented through a program; thereby the teacher obtains additional time to work with pupils on an individual basis.
3. The confirmation/correction feature of the program provides reinforcement of learning and builds student interest.
4. Programs can be designed to instruct in affective as well as cognitive areas of learning.

5. Programming assists the student in understanding a sequential development of complex materials and has the potential to accomplish this end in less time than formal classroom instruction.

The primary consideration that must be taken into account before using programmed materials is the student's basic level of reading. Since programmed learning relies on the printed word, there may be damaging effects on the poor reader. Another basic consideration is that, although programs can be designed for appreciation as well as skills, the latter area is dominant today.

Audiotutorial—IPI Audiotutorial and *individually perscribed instruction* (IPI) strategies have been designed to provide for individual pacing of learning activities for students. Direct student-teacher contact is at a minimum except when the teacher provides remedial, developmental, or enrichment services to the learner as a result of some diagnosis. One of the chief characteristics of these strategies is *test-teach-test*. On the basis of predetermined instructional objectives, curricular modules for individualized instruction are developed. For each module a diagnostic test is developed that measures before instruction starts how well the learner can reach the criterion for the module objectives. On the basis of this diagnosis, the learner proceeds through the instructional package and is retested at completion. If learners reach the expected criterion for the learning package, they proceed at their own individual rate. In a very real sense, the learning packages are individual tutors for the students. The task of the teacher is to monitor learner progress through diagnostic activities and testing.

The expression *audiotutorial* implies the use of audiotape recorders as an instructional delivery system, whereas IPI may utilize a whole host of instructional delivery systems ranging from paper materials to computers. Teachers using IPI generally follow these steps:

Step 1. Administer diagnostic test for learning module and establish entering learning behavior.

Step 2. Have learner encounter those elements of the learning module as diagnosed by entry level test.

Step 3. Test learner as he or she completes the module.

Step 4. If expected criterion for the module is attained by the student, move her or him to the next module and pretest.

Individually Guided Education (IGE) Originally sponsored by the Kettering Foundation's Institute for the Development of Educational Activities (IDEA), Individually Guided Education (IGE) has become an integral part of the University of Wisconsin Research and Development Center. Where IPI takes all learners through the same preplanned program with identical objectives, IGE promotes different specific objectives for individual learners and is heavily process-oriented. Objectives are preplanned by the teacher and student. IGE places a heavy emphasis on the process of both individualized and group learning.

Learning-Resource Centers

The use of learning-resource centers is an aid to any instructional strategy employed. This type of learning environment is not established to replace a school library but, rather, to enrich it. The typical verbal materials found in a library are supplemented with additional software and hardware instructional materials. With any teaching strategy that the teacher uses, the student now may be assigned to a center where he or she may pursue learning on an individual basis or in small-group activities. These learning-resource centers are equipped with books, programmed materials, closed-circuit television, and dial access audio or videotape banks; a variety of other materials provide auditory, visual, and audiovisual learning.

Although learning centers were used initially at the elementary level, they are found increasingly in newer junior and senior high schools. As school districts employ more varied patterns for organization and instructional strategies, the need for learning centers becomes more apparent. The learning center has become more than an administratively planned area. In a very real sense, it has become an adjunct classroom that the teacher plans for instructional use. The only limitation to the operational use of a learning center is the teacher's imagination as he or she develops objectives for learning experiences for children.

Technology

Proponents of the use of educational television (ETV) suggest it has the greatest educational potential of all instructional media, while many of the critics see it as a threat to active learning. It is interesting that the fears of a decade or so ago—that ETV would replace the classroom teacher—have been alleviated by an emerging consensus that the successful use of television is wholly dependent upon the classroom teacher. ETV is not the sole use of this innovation in technology: television may be utilized in at least three different ways.

Instructional Television (ITV)

As an aid to instruction, television may be used as an open- or closed-circuit medium. Examples of the use of closed-circuit television can be found in Hagerstown, Maryland, which began to use it in 1956, and the Midwest Program on Airborne Television Instruction (MPATI), which began in 1959. The latter program, because of financial and technical difficulties, ceased operations during the 1960s. The Communication Satellite System (COMSAT) has now opened new possibilities for mass education television transmission anywhere in the United States. With the use of closed-circuit television, school districts may create their own instructional materials as local needs dictate and provide all learners with access to the best teachers in the school system. As a method of formal class presentation, television has the capability of reaching extremely large groups of students.

If instructional television is to be used successfully, it should fit into the general scheme of teaching. Allowing it to assume a dominant role of instruction is a misuse of this medium. If the misuse is allowed, its instructional value becomes as questionable as the single textbook approach or overuse of the motion picture. Continuous evaluation of television instruction is all-important, since as a medium of large-group instruction its potential for misdirected learning or group indoctrination is ever-present. Its primary emphasis should always be directed toward the process of education—and not the television process itself.

Educational Television (ETV)

With the advent of statewide and national educational television channels or open-circuit television, ETV has yet to be realized as a powerful education medium. Two such examples of this type of use are "Sesame Street" on a national basis and the "Ripples Project" on a

The computer now acts as a tutor in the learning environment. (*Photograph by Talbot Lovering*)

statewide basis in Pennsylvania. There is little doubt of the positive impact that "Sesame Street" has had on the very young learner in American society, particularly the disadvantaged learner. Encouraged by the early research findings that "Sesame Street" had aided and abetted young learners in readiness for the formal education system, ETV began a second national program entitled the "Electric Company." Whereas "Sesame Street" was designed for younger learners, primarily preschool, the "Electric Company" has been designed for the primary and intermediate learner. The "Ripples Project," a central Pennsylvania project of the Allegheny Broadcasting Council, WPSX, is an example of statewide ETV efforts. Designed and operated with the cooperative efforts of university specialists, this project seeks to reach the young student and the parent-adult population responsible for the early learning development of young children. As the federal government continues to encourage the development of local educational television, it is safe to assert that the use of this medium for instruction has just begun. Recent Federal Communications Commission (FCC) regulations now allocate certain facilities of privately owned cable company stations for local educational uses. Where these cable companies provide quality commercial television viewing, they must also provide channel space for local school use.

Microteaching A third use of television is to help a teacher improve his or her instructional practices. Increasing numbers of teacher-training institutions have incorporated television or *microteaching* techniques. If the initial endeavors of teacher training are to be successful, school districts should provide television equipment and help for teachers who seek to improve their teaching skills. Through the use of videotapes, teachers can watch their classroom performance and thus identify and modify or eliminate teaching weaknesses. Further, television is a valuable tool for inservice training of teachers. With the use of videotapes, many outside consultants can be brought to the school district, where the grass roots approach to inservice training may be effected best.

Dial Access The use of dial access audio and video systems provides for increased
Systems attempts to individualize instruction. These systems may be used either as the sole method of instruction for some parts of the curriculum or as a supplement to regular classroom instruction. The use of dial access equipment on an experimental basis began in 1961 at the University of Michigan; since that time, its use has been primarily for language study. It is interesting to note that its use seems to be divided evenly between teacher-mediated instruction, that is, instruction that is part of the teacher's planned lessons, and enrichment.

The Coatesville Area Senior High School in Pennsylvania has been utilizing a dial access videotape system since 1968. Installed to help implement a philosophy of encouraging independent study and individualized learning, the system allows students to pursue a program by utilizing individual study carrels that provide automated information retrieval facilities. Videotapes are prepared as teaching aids for the teacher but are not intended to replace whole units of instruction. The tapes are of particular value for difficult and costly laboratory presentations or for specialists who otherwise could not be introduced to the learners. The dial access carrels are conveniently placed in many instructional areas of the school where a student may seek direct teacher assistance if needed. The curriculum has been built with instructional objectives, and students progress at individual rates based upon diagnostic test batteries. This particular use of technology creates time for small-group learning activities with live teachers, in that students may pursue the required common learnings through individualized dial access systems.

Other uses of dial access equipment may be found in listening laboratories that accommodate small groups of students. These laboratories may be used with records or audiotapes. A more expanded utilization of existing language laboratories in many schools could provide similar instructional services.

Computer-
Assisted
Instruction

Computer-assisted or computer-aided instruction has opened a whole new vista to individualized learning. In this type of instructional program, control of the learning environment on an individual basis is limited only by teacher input. The established techniques of linear and branch programming can be utilized in a variety of ways to accommodate individual or small-group learning sessions. In a very real sense, the computer now acts as a tutor in the learning environment. Through the use of computer-assisted instruction, it is now possible for a teacher to serve larger numbers of pupils and still have readily at hand instantaneous feedback and evaluation of pupil progress. The role of the teacher as instructor takes on new and needed dimensions: instead of being merely a dispenser of knowledge, the teacher can, with increased precision, serve as diagnostician, prescriber of learning materials, and devotee of increased teacher-learner interaction.

Computer-assisted instruction has also proved to be effective in gaming and simulation. Callahan and Clark report:

> In the multitude of cases where bona fide instructional practice is prohibitively expensive or excessively dangerous to life and limb, computer simulation of real life experiences has been found to be attractive as well as effective. One such example of simulation has been in medical schools where bodies have been fitted with sensors that feed signals to a computer program. The student's diagnosis and subsequent action upon the model result in the computer assessment of the success of such action, a rapid "recovery" or the untimely "death of the patient." Another example of long-standing use is the aircraft simulator, commencing with the Link Trainer of World War II fame and advancing to today's highly technical models that

are capable of simulating nearly any eventuality that could befall an air-craft. . . .[1]

The tutorial mode of instruction has been provided by both typewriter-type and cathode-ray typewriter computer systems. However, the new generation of computers has led to more limited use of computers in the schools: technological changes in computers make it costly for schools to purchase new computers continually. Control Data Corporation now offers the most advanced use of computers for educational instruction with its PLATO system.

Computer-Managed Instruction

Just as the computer may be used to deliver instruction, it may also be used to manage the whole instructional and record-keeping program of a school district. Records of student performances and accompanying reports, utilization of materials, management of scheduling, and storage capabilities of a learner's continuous progress are but a few of the possibilities of computer-managed instruction. Dupuis and Bell reported on the computer-management function developed for a vocational-technical school in Ebensburg, Pennsylvania:

> As the student proceeded through each task, module and unit, he was closely monitored by his instructor and his progress recorded and stored in a computer facility. Each teaching station in the new school was equipped with a computer terminal which could record the student's progress and direct him to modules and units as required to complete a total career area. . . . And computer storage of student progress provides prospective employers with data that are more meaningful than the usual letter grades that accompany a transcript.[2]

With this type of technology now available for use, it might appear that the teaching task has been greatly simplified. On the contrary, the teacher must now come face to face with curricular issues usually reserved for administrators and supervisors.

Substance

The continuous pressure for improvement of instruction has prompted the most significant overhaul of curriculum content or *substance* that this nation or any other nation has ever seen. Laypeople, educators, and academicians representing public and private interests have recently united to help bring organization and meaning to the curricula of the nation's schools. In addition to the National Defense Education Acts (NDEA) and the National Science Foundation, private philanthropic foundations have continued to support educational experimen-

1. Joseph F. Callahan and Leonard H. Clark, *Innovations and Issues in Education* (New York: Macmillan, 1977), pp. 92–93.
2. Victor L. Dupuis and Paul E. Bell, "A Modular Approach to Vocational Curriculum," *American Vocational Journal* 49 (April 1974): 35–36.

tation financially. In 1960, the Russell Sage Foundation in its *Foundation Directory* listed some 12,000 foundations with various assets; those that continue to support educational innovation include the Ford, Rockefeller, Carnegie, Kellogg, Sloan, Danforth, and Kettering foundations.

Alphabet Projects

Although other social motivating influences should not be discounted, the launching of sputnik helped to give direction to a more modern mathematics program for the more capable student. In 1958, the National Science Foundation helped to create the School Mathematics Study Group, which selected as its initial purpose the improvement of mathematics programs for junior and senior high schools. Under this program and many like it, students are introduced much earlier to more complex material, especially the structure of the discipline. Statistics and probability, formerly reserved for higher education, are now introduced and integrated into the regular high school program. It is not uncommon for high school graduates of today's large comprehensive high schools to have completed advanced algebra, analytic geometry, introduction to calculus, statistics, and computer mathematics. Other mathematics projects have gained considerable acceptance:

- University of Illinois Committee on School Mathematics. Directed by the late Max Beberman, this program has been developed for grades K–6. The emphasis of this program, as with others in mathematics and science, is teaching the pupil the principles of discovery.
- University of Maryland Mathematics Project. This project, begun in 1957, was piloted in the school systems of Montgomery County, Maryland, and Arlington County, Virginia. Designed for the junior high school grades 7 and 8, it focuses on deductive reasoning, number theory, and logic.
- Greater Cleveland Mathematics Project. Pioneered in the schools of Cleveland, Ohio, this project now has been revised and programmed by Science Research Associates. It currently has its greatest use in grades K–8.
- The Syracuse University-Webster College Madison Project. Another program designed to capitalize on student discovery, it is being used in grades 3–10.

Another discipline that has been extensively revised is science. Programs have been developed that place stress on theory rather than fact. The student is expected to experiment with discovery and inquiry rather than pursue that which is already known to science. Among the more notable courses developed are the Biological Science Curriculum Study (BSCS), Physical Sciences Study Committee, Chemical Education Material Study, Chemical Bond Approach, Earth Science Curriculum Project, and the Secondary School Science Project. The BSCS has developed three versions of its program: the Blue Version concerns itself with genetics and molecules; the Yellow Version covers cell development and its relation to evolutionary theory; and the Green Version—most successful with slow learners—focuses on ecological study.

In 1958, the Modern Language Association (MLA), supported by NDEA, began conducting research on the teaching of foreign language. Since then, much of this research has been centered on the audio-lingual or aural-oral methods of teaching. Additional influence of NDEA has been most noticeable through supportive funding for language laboratories, tape recording equipment, and the retraining of foreign language teachers. In addition, foreign language instruction has been introduced at an increasing rate into the elementary school. One of the problems associated with this foreign language instruction in the elementary school (FLES) is scope and sequence with the junior and senior high school.

Additional areas involving changes in substance include Project English, sponsored by the U.S. Office of Education (USOE) and centered in selected universities of this country. Project Social Studies has been the last discipline to undergo revision, under the sponsorship of the Cooperative Research Program of the USOE. This project has been centered at universities where historians, sociologists, economists, and other social scientists may interact collectively. Project Social Studies has built a social studies curriculum that offers depth in the understanding and analysis of present and past social issues. Rather than providing a survey look at social studies—so typical of traditional programs—this project stresses what the designers refer to as "post-holing." The students still survey—but also study selected issues in depth.

Another organization that has helped produce software products is the National Education Association with its Project on Instruction. In 1963, the project, directed by Ole Sand, printed "Schools for the Sixties," "Education in a Changing Society," "Deciding What to Teach," and "Planning and Organizing for Teaching." As an adjunct of the NEA, the Association for Supervision and Curriculum Development (ASCD) is responsible for numerous curriculum studies conducted at local and state levels.

Software— Teachers must make a continuous effort to keep themselves informed
Hardware of the newly available software and hardware media. Although the terms *software* and *hardware* seem to be appropriate in an age of "systems" and "systems development," they still refer to human resources, learning materials, and their uses. In the learning process, such products have greater significance today than ever before. The knowledge explosion has continued to accelerate and has had tremendous impact upon the curriculum. The American educational system continues to be faced with the enormous task of finding ways to incorporate

systematically this knowledge explosion into the planned program for all youth. The American inventive genius and advanced technology have produced a vast number of devices, programs, organizations for instruction, and materials to help the teacher do a better job. While layperson, educator, and academician have recognized and clarified the disciplines of knowledge, technological genius has produced a system of mechanical aids ranging from very simple recording equipment to complex computers. Many of these newer instructional media have become commonplace in the nation's schools and are being utilized in varying degrees by teachers. The teacher working in curriculum development should become part of the vast educational team that will continue to produce even newer hardware and software materials to facilitate learning.

Table 22–1 summarizes the four broad areas of curriculum innovation.

Learning Corporations
This nation has recently witnessed large-scale mergers of publishing companies, research bureaus, and manufacturers. Seeing a growing need for all kinds of educational software and hardware, plus an economy that promises to continue to allocate increasing funds for education, these corporations may have struck a bonanza. Capitalizing on a national concern for increased educational output, these corporations have the capacity to hypothesize, research, develop, produce, and market an endless variety of educational software and hardware for use in the learning process. The knowledge explosion, increasing rates of mobility, the quest for more knowledge in a shorter time, the complex pressures of providing individualized education for all, and the educational establishment's seeming inability to direct educational change effectively have all contributed to the birth of these corporations.

This type of industrial movement has placed an even greater responsibility on the teacher working in curriculum. Among the many splendid products on the market today, there also may be found hastily developed and poorly researched materials that purport to provide the teacher with "the answer" to learning problems. As a result, the teacher has the special task of discarding these inferior or worthless programs and adapting those that are useful to a particular situation. Of a far more critical nature, the teacher should, in addition to the culling of manufactured materials for use in the learning process, continue to develop his or her own new materials in light of personal experience with the learner.

Because of local and state control, the teacher generally uses materials for learning that are consistent with a philosophy acceptable to his or her own school district. Since such a philosophy is usually developed locally, the adaption and development of methods and materials should be an outgrowth of the needs of a particular school district.

Table 22–1. Areas of curriculum innovation.

Area	Examples
Organization	Team teaching
	Differentiated staffing
	Modular and flexible scheduling
	Nongraded schools
	Open space facilities
	Modular or minicourses
Instruction	Lecture-recitation
	Guided discovery
	Inquiry
	Simulation and gaming
	Linear or branch programming
	Audiotutorial—IPE—IGE
	Learning resource centers
Technology	Television:
	ETV, closed circuit,
	microteaching
	Dial access systems
	Computer-assisted instruction
	Computer-managed instruction
Substance	Mathematics projects
	Science curricula
	Project English
	MLA-NDEA programs
	Project Social Studies
	Arts Impact
	Industrial arts
	Career education clusters

Summary and Implications

Curriculum innovation is classified into four broad areas: organization, instruction, technology, and substance. Theoretically, any one of these may be incorporated into a school system by itself, but in practice most school districts use several forms of innovation when attempting a change of direction. In any implementation of innovative practices, it is imperative that the teacher not take an unconsidered approach and innovate for innovation's sake. Any change in the school program should have purpose and direction. When change does occur, it should be planned in such a way that solid data can be gathered when a necessary evaluation of the program takes place.

Despite the notion that curriculum innovation has resulted in poor treatment of the basics, tangible evidence for this assertion has not been forthcoming. Students in the so-called traditional schools have lagged in academic achievement as much as students in the so-called innovative schools. The important idea for the teacher to keep in mind is that innovative practices have evolved in the attempt to provide individualized learning for all students. This demand for individualization will continue in the foreseeable future, and the teacher must be knowledgeable about a variety of individual learning practices if the demand is to be met.

Discussion Questions

1. In what way does the nongraded plan of school organization provide for individual differences?

2. Discuss the advantages of computer-assisted instruction.

3. Which innovative practices do you feel hold the most promise for schools of the future?

4. Discuss the impact of team-teaching arrangements on teacher morale.

5. What are the major impacts that technology has had on instruction?

Supplemental Activities

1. Visit an IPI or IGE school and assess the learning atmosphere and how it affects students.

2. Invite a team teacher to explain his or her role as a member of a teaching team.

3. Prepare a one-lesson game or simulation exercise that could be delivered by computer.

4. Interview some students who are following a modular schedule and others who are in a regular schedule and compare their impressions of the learning environment.

5. Prepare an inquiry lesson based upon some high-level cognitive objective.

Bibliography

Aslin, Neil C., and DeArman, John W. "Adoption and Abandonment of Innovative Practices in High Schools." *Educational Leadership* 33 (May 1976).

Callahan, Joseph F., and Clark, Leonard H. *Innovations and Issues in Education*. New York: Macmillan, 1977.

DeCarlo, Marie. *Humanizing Alternatives: Education of Children in Our Society*. Washington, D.C.: American Association of Elementary-Kindergarten-Nursery Educators, 1976.

Glatthorn, Allan A. *Alternatives in Education: Schools and Programs*. New York: Dodd, Mead, 1975.

Kozol, Jonathan. *Free Schools*. Boston: Houghton Mifflin, 1972.

Lipham, James M., and Furth, Marvin J. *The Principal and Individually Guided Education*. Reading, Mass.: Addison-Wesley, 1976.

CHAPTER 23

Curriculum Evaluation

INCREASING EMPHASIS ON AMERICAN EDUCATION DURING THE past two decades has brought about a massive fluctuation in purpose, design, content, and methodology of curricula. Public and professional opinion has caused old programs to be dropped and new programs to be initiated. Many of the educational changes have come so rapidly that little concentrated effort has been given to the long-range evaluation of existing or potential educational programs. Partially because of many poorly planned "crash programs" in education, comprehensive guidelines have emerged by which curricula can be evaluated and continually improved. It is safe to assume that the teacher in today's and tomorrow's school will play a more vital and active role in evaluating and improving the curriculum. The following discussion is intended to help the beginning teacher become more familiar with the considerations and processes of curricular evaluation and improvement.

Horizontal Articulation
When evaluating a curriculum, the teacher becomes concerned with the *horizontal articulation* of the educational program. The most common cause of poor articulation is a lack of cooperative planning between teachers of the various academic disciplines. Too often teachers tend to teach their own subject area with little concern for what is taking place in the other subjects at that same grade level. So often teachers voice the complaint that there is little if any horizontal transfer of learning. A closer examination of this problem would point to a lack of cooperation on the part of teachers. Usually it is found that ninth-grade social studies teachers feel little obligation to correct a student's careless English usage in the social studies classroom. Emphasis in the class is placed upon the social sciences, and it becomes easy to ignore English. This same lack of horizontal articulation takes place between the mathe-

matics teacher and the science teacher; for the science teacher focuses concerns on scientific inquiry and tends to slight the importance of mathematical exactness.

Just as important as horizontal articulation between the various subject areas is the articulation within each subject area. In many of the larger schools, where more than one teacher instructs in the same subject at the same grade level, there is little or no articulation between these teachers. Course guides and outlines, which theoretically could greatly improve the articulation within courses, do not even exist in many schools. Under the guise of a given subject at the same level, teachers often tend to teach and emphasize whatever they desire. With little or no supervision, they tend to go their own separate ways under the cloak of academic freedom. This same lack of articulation exists in the larger elementary schools between self-contained classrooms. Rarely do these elementary teachers confer adequately with one another to correlate their educational programs. It seems that any constructive move toward horizontal articulation must begin within the narrower confines of the subject areas—before crossing over subject lines for complete articulation.

Vertical Articulation   *Continuity* within the schools' curricula refers to the problems of *vertical articulation*. In addition to horizontal articulation, the teacher must be concerned with the interrelationship of all grade levels of the school program in order to provide the student with continuous learning. Oliver has suggested the following as a means to improve continuity in a school program:

> More comprehensive is the trend to plan continuity from kindergarten through grade 12. In some systems supervisors are given a K–12 responsibility rather than elementary or secondary. In such a plan the director of curriculum is an overseer of the total range. More effective for communication is the establishing of committees representing all levels. Certainly schools that are being consolidated need to look at their total offerings. Related to this is the development of guides, for example, those for social studies, on a K–12 sequence, with a statement of overall objectives and philosophy. A high school that is working on its philosophy and objectives for the school as a whole should bring representatives from levels above and below in order to effect greater understanding and continuity.[1]

Figure 23–1 suggests one means for examining the vertical articulation problems of the total curriculum structure and applies whether the school district uses grade level division for its program or uses the nongraded organization. Concepts of a discipline may be identified for any curricular area. Every discipline has established concepts that make up

1. Albert I. Oliver, *Curricular Improvement,* 2nd ed. (New York: Harper & Row, 1977), p. 229.

Chronological Ages	4–8				8–12			12–15			15–18			Identified Curriculum Concepts
Grade Levels	K	1	2	3	4	5	6	7	8	9	10	11	12	
	I	I		I	E	E	Re	Re	E	DS	DS	DS	DS	Concept 1
			I	I	I	I	I	I	E	E	E	E	Re	Re	Concept 2
														Concept 3
	I	Re	I	I	Re	I	Re	I	I	I	DS	DS	DS	DS	Concept 4
														Concept K

Key:
I = Introduction to concept
E = Exploratory work in the concept
Re = Reinforcement
DS = Depth study of the concept

Figure 23–1. Chart for examination of vertical articulation in the curriculum.

that discipline. Because of degrees of difficulty among the concepts of a discipline, some concepts can be studied by learners at an early stage of development and other concepts by those at a later age of development. The teaching staff arrives at what concepts will be taught to whom and at what stage of learner development. Figure 23–1 offers one method of examining the vertical articulation of any set of discipline concepts used in the curriculum.

While problems of continuity demand the attention of all school personnel, it is the teacher in the classroom who is in the position to do the most to improve vertical articulation. The teacher improves continuity by planning lessons that take into account what the student has studied before and what he or she will study in the future. In planning for continuity, the teacher must remember that learning best proceeds from the simple to the complex, and from the concrete to the abstract. It must also be remembered that students need to review a certain amount of what they have learned before. The problem of continuity is a difficult one and requires constant attention from educators.

Balance   Another important feature of a curriculum is its *balance*. We have already discussed the positive and negative aspects of the subject-centered and student-centered curricula. As is often the case, the curriculum pendulum seems to swing from one extreme to the other—without being able to reach a sound combination of the positive features of both. Most certainly the school of the future must select the best of both if it is to accomplish its task. The Association for Supervision and Curriculum Development (ASCD) in its 1961 yearbook discussed balance in the curriculum:

> Balance to some seems a "good" word *per se*, suggesting structure and order in an enterprise leading to the realization of personal or group objectives. "Balanced diet" and "balanced economy," for example, are phrases which, in the former, connote desirable means and, in the latter, desirable ends. A balanced curriculum implies structure and order in its scope and sequence (means) leading to the achievement of educational objectives (end). . . .
>
> The problem of balance has two dimensions. First, and this is the dimension generally discussed, there is the balance sought in the curriculum provided by the school . . . subjects to be offered and required and programs of studies to be recommended . . . time allotments for various subjects and activities . . . the use of books and other educational aids . . . the respective amounts of general and specialized education to be provided.
>
> The second, and in many ways more significant, dimension of balance is that part of the curriculum actually selected by and/or experienced by each individual pupil. . . .
>
> Ideally, balance is attained in the individual's own curriculum as he or she develops an optimum level of competence in each of the areas for which provision is made in the curriculum.[2]

Problems in Balance

Society continually has called upon the schools to correct any existent ills of the time. The list of social problems seems to find its way to the front door of the school, and the school is expected to find a place within the curriculum to work toward correction. Increasingly, the school has discovered that what were formerly responsibilities of home and church have now become, at least in part, responsibilities of the school program. A question to be answered is to what extent might the inclusion of these societal responsibilities in the school program usurp the limited time that the learner now has for the acquisition of basic learnings.

Another problem of balance has developed because, in the recent past, the nation's schools have been bombarded by massive crash programs. The age of sputnik released a condemnation of the schools' curricula and created a demand for additional mathematics and science programs. The federal government stepped to the forefront and, through the National Defense Education Act, provided funds to improve and speed up the training of mathematicians and scientists to get the nation back into a commanding world role. Many educators believe

2. Paul M. Halverson, "The Meaning of Balance," *Balance in the Curriculum*, 1961 Yearbook (Washington, D.C.: Association for Supervision and Curriculum Development, 1961), pp. 4–7. Reprinted with permission of the Association for Supervision and Curriculum Development and Paul M. Halverson. Copyright © 1961 by the Association for Supervision and Curriculum Development.

that this was accomplished at the expense of the humanities and fine arts. More recently, educators in these latter areas have retaliated and have demanded equal representation within the curriculum. Seemingly, balance can be achieved at some point. Through all this restructuring, the length of the school day and school year has remained relatively constant.

The back-to-basics movement offers still another threat to balance in the school program. Declining SAT scores, increasing discipline problems, and general dissatisfaction with the school's inability to prepare learners for the work world and social change have all contributed to the strength of this movement. What basics will be taught has yet to be decided. The range of opinion extends from those who demand the three Rs alone to those who stress the three Rs plus generic life-coping skills—as found, for example, in the Adult Performance Level (APL) competencies developed in Texas or the ten goals for Educational Quality Assessment (EQA) developed in Pennsylvania. These and other potentially biased movements will continue to provide a threat to balance in the curriculum.

An additional concern of the teacher working to improve curriculum is the problem of the rapid explosion of knowledge. Students are in school for just so long, and there is only a certain amount of time in which to teach them. As the body of knowledge increases, the school must decide what to teach in the limited time available. Old theories

Testing allows the teacher to evaluate whether specific objectives have been achieved. (*Photograph by Talbot Lovering*)

and laws may have to be taught from a descriptive and factual viewpoint only in order to provide time for new concepts.

Because of the problems of balance in the curriculum, some people have made a plea for longer school days, increased length of school year, and an earlier introduction to formal learning. If proper curricular balance is to be achieved in the face of increased societal demands and the knowledge explosion, increased time for formal education may be the answer. A most serious question that creeps into the debate is: should this be done at the expense of the student's private time for just growing up. Should proper curriculum balance be achieved by taking more of the child's leisure time? If so, what effect may this have on the child's personal and emotional development?

Evaluation Procedures   An integral part of any curricular improvement is a continual process of evaluation. Curriculum appraisal involves an examination of all facets of the school, including the instructional program, physical facilities, methodology, and students. Appraisal of the school program involves such questions as what should be taught, to whom, and when. An examination of physical facilities includes analysis of space requirements, equipment, and materials. Curricular evaluation is further enhanced when a continuous assessment of the various methods of teaching is undertaken. Finally, the student becomes a significant factor in appraising ongoing efforts at curricular improvement. In terms of relative importance, the student stands at the forefront. The school seeks to bring about a change in behavior that is beneficial both to the student and to society. In any appraisal of change in student behavior, the school concerns itself not only with the tangible and cognitive aspects of learning but also with its intangible and affective aspects. Obviously it is the intangible area that is most difficult to assess. Ronald C. Doll defines curriculum evaluation as

> a broad and continuous effort to inquire into the effects of utilizing educational content and process according to clearly defined goals. In terms of this definition, evaluation may be expected to go beyond simple measurement and also beyond simple application of the evaluator's values and beliefs. If evaluation is to be a broad and continuous effort, it must rely upon a variety of instruments which are used according to carefully ascribed purposes.[3]

Formative Data   Evaluation in curriculum must be of two types—formative and summative—if it is to be meaningful for program development. *Formative* procedures are those that involve collection, processing, interpretation, and recycling of evaluation data while the program continues operation. The emphasis suggests continuous evaluation procedures that will yield

3. Ronald C. Doll, *Curriculum Improvement,* 3rd ed. (Boston: Allyn and Bacon, 1974), p. 361.

information about program effectiveness at any given point in time. It further suggests that if the program is not meeting desired objectives, there should be preplanned vehicles for adjustments that will not alter the original program intentions but will assist in how it functions. In addition, the student's personal welfare must be kept foremost in mind when curriculum programs are implemented and evaluated.

Summative Data   *Summative* evaluation procedures are employed at some predetermined terminal date for a curriculum project or for an innovative curriculum activity. To make this type of evaluation procedure as precise as possible, all previous formative evaluations have to be considered as having some positive or negative effect. All data that have been collected, considered together, should yield some conclusive answers to how successfully the original aims and objectives proposed for the program were met. Questions that formative and summative evaluation techniques should seek to answer include the following:

> In a general sense, curriculum evaluation is an attempt to throw light on two questions: (1) Do planned learning opportunities programs, courses, and activities as developed and organized actually produce desired results? (2) How can the curriculum offering best be improved? These general questions and the procedures for answering them translate a little differently at macro levels (for example, evaluating the citywide outcomes from several alternative reading programs) than at micro levels (evaluating the effect of a teacher's instructional plans for achieving objectives of a course). Classroom teachers often have an additional set of evaluation questions to guide them in making decisions about individuals:
>
> 1. *Placement.* At which level of learning opportunity should the learner be placed in order to challenge but not frustrate?
> 2. *Mastery.* Has the learner acquired enough competency to succeed in the next planned phase?
> 3. *Diagnosis.* What particular difficulty is this learner experiencing?[4]

Evaluation   Because of the comprehensiveness required in curricular appraisal, par-
Participants   ticipation by many groups is highly desirable. Various groups that should be involved with any curricular improvement include:

1. *Faculty and students.* Teachers should participate from the beginning in the formulation of all school practices, programs, policies, and procedures. Their active participation begins in the classroom with instruction, continues with participation on school or system-wide curriculum committees, and advances to the higher order of central planning. The students, on the other hand, act somewhat as planning partners to the teachers in that they are the recipients

4. John D. McNeil, *Curriculum: A Comprehensive Introduction* (Boston: Little, Brown, 1977), p. 134.

of classroom instruction. They become the products of any curriculum improvement initiated.

2. *School board and administrative staff.* Acting as a policy-making body, the school board strives to create the atmosphere for continuous curriculum improvement. The administrative staff sets in motion the wheels of curriculum improvement and acts as the coordinating agency for all the groups involved.

3. *Citizen advisory committees.* Parents and other lay groups of the community may serve on curriculum committees or may participate by responding to school questionnaires or interviews. As citizens of the community, they should be concerned with the improvement of the schools.

4. *Professional consultants.* The highly trained experts of the college or university play an important role in curriculum development. Their participating roles may take the form of inservice assistance for the other three groups, or they may use their expertise to help evaluate parts of the school program, or its totality.

Communication becomes the key to evaluation of a school's program. All people engaged in the educative process do not see things the same way. The student, teacher, administration, and public somehow must understand what each must do in order that the learning process will become productive and successful.

Criteria for Evaluation

Classroom Tests When appraising curriculum, the teacher has available a variety of techniques to aid him or her in obtaining a more comprehensive picture. By using classroom tests, the teacher may evaluate the achievement of specific objectives that were set forth for a certain subject. While test results are used primarily for teaching and for determining grades, they also can aid the teacher in planning for adjustments in methodology and course content. The use of standardized tests helps the school system see itself in perspective—in relation to the state, regional, or national picture. A few words of caution are offered, however, about the use of standardized tests: they should not be looked upon as effective methods of evaluating teachers, and they should not assume a position of such importance that they become the sole determiner of the curriculum.

Measurement Instruments To a certain extent, the teacher can evaluate progress toward educational objectives associated with the students' social development, educational and social interests, and values by using checklists, rating scales, inventories, and questionnaires. Teachers and guidance personnel can also gain insight into certain kinds of curricular changes by using observation techniques, interviews, anecdotal records, sociometrics, sociodrama, and autobiographies. The school system may make use of opinion polls, interviews with community employers, and follow-up studies of graduates to gain further insight into the effectiveness of the total school program.

Norm-referenced Data

Normative data—that is, data based upon local, state, or national norms—are easily obtained when the teacher uses standardized tests. In addition to those precautions mentioned in using standardized tests, there is the ever-present question of how effective a measure these tests are for a particular school's program. These tests should be used with some degree of caution for student placement. Unless caution is exercised with the identification and interpretation of student progress, these tests may be detrimental for use in evaluating the effect of a curriculum.

Criterion-referenced Data

Criterion-referenced data are gathered from specially constructed instruments designed to measure expected learning changes. These measuring instruments are constructed with stated operational learning objectives as guideposts. They do not yield test scores that indicate a percentage of achievement based upon some class standards or norms, but they do indicate how well a particular student has met the stated learning objectives of the teacher. If planned specifically for objectives that seek minimum levels of learner competence, these tests can be of considerable aid to the teacher, the student, and the parent. Not only will criterion-referenced tests yield total scores, but they will also indi-

Table 23–1. Norm-referenced and criterion-referenced data contrasts.

Norm-referenced Data	Criterion-referenced Data
1. Data gathered from instruments established from local, state, or national norms.	Data gathered from instruments established from a set of local instructional objectives.
2. Data that indicate how a learner or group of learners has performed in comparison with a like set of peers.	Data that indicate to what degree a learner has achieved a particular learning objective or set of objectives.
3. Data tend to be valid and reliable to some national expectations or norms.	Data have high degree of validity to a set of learner objectives. Reliability data, by usual measurement standards, are questionable.
4. Data indicate a student's overall performance, aptitude, or attitude on some broad continuum or domain. Usually data are used for some form of rank ordering.	Data indicate the specific level of competency or development as expected by previously stated objectives. Usually data are used for individual diagnosis and prescription.

Future educational programs will provide adults with courses both for job training and personal enrichment. (*Photograph by Eric Roth, The Picture Cube*)

cate how well each objective was reached. If certain objectives have not been reached, the student recycles his learning activity for those objectives only and does not repeat the activities for which he has met the desired achievement. Rather than assigning grades to achievement, the teacher assesses pupil progress on a pass/fail basis. When these kinds of measuring instruments are used along with norm-referenced instruments, the evaluation of curriculum, especially pupil evaluation, becomes considerably more precise. Table 23–1 shows the differences between norm-referenced and criterion-referenced data.

Accountability   We expect that accountability demands of the seventies will continue through the 1980s. During the past two decades, curriculum evaluation, although well intended and reasonably well supported, has failed to produce any significant outcomes. We still know too little about what actually goes on in classrooms. The effectiveness of costly materials, both hardware and software, has yet to be determined on a cost-effective or cost-benefit basis. The significant part of this problem may lie with the learner: because of individual differences in ability, needs, and interests, we have not found adequate ways to synthesize the teaching-learning process. The task remains formidable. It seems, however, that curriculum evaluation cannot be effective—that is, produce significant outcomes—until those who design, test, and evaluate the curriculum clarify, for measurement purposes, the intended goals for learners and teachers.

Summary and Implications   Curriculum evaluation is a sophisticated process requiring the cooperation of students, teachers, administrators, and groups. Accountability in education demands its continued practice. When preparing for curriculum evaluation, teachers must be cognizant of articulation and balance in the curriculum and must be knowledgeable about reliable instrumentation for both formative and summative evaluation schemes. Evaluation is a culminating activity that determines how well the preplanned objectives of schooling are being met. Teachers have a pressing need to become better prepared in measurement and evaluation techniques. With the greater flexibility in school programming now observed from kindergarten through high school, curriculum evaluation must provide significant data that determine the value of different programs for different kinds of learners.

Discussion Questions

1. Discuss some of the ways that classroom teachers can improve horizontal articulation.
2. Why should teachers be involved in curriculum evaluation?
3. Should teachers be held accountable for what learning takes place in the classroom?

4. To what degree should parents and other lay groups be involved in curriculum evaluation?
5. What effect do you think individualized programs will have on the collection and interpretation of normative data?

Supplemental Activities

1. Invite a curriculum coordinator and a teacher to discuss their roles in curriculum evaluation.
2. Compile a list of competencies that future teachers may need for adequate participation in curriculum evaluation.
3. Debate the statement: "All measurement

in schools should be criterion-referenced measurement."
4. Invite a group of local business people to discuss their views on accountability for the schools.
5. Visit a school and ask the students how much they participate in curriculum evaluation.

Bibliography

Beggs, Donald L., and Lewis, Ernest L. *Measurement and Evaluation in the Schools*. Boston: Houghton Miffiin, 1975.

Gronlund, Norman E. *Measurement and Evaluation in Teaching*. 3rd ed. New York: Macmillan, 1976.

Sax, Gilbert. *Principles of Educational Measurement and Evaluation*. Belmont, Calif.: Wadsworth, 1974.

Tanner, Daniel, and Tanner, Laurel. *Curriculum Development*. New York: Macmillan, 1975.

Wardrop, James L. *Standardized Testing in the Schools: Uses and Roles*. Monterey, Calif.: Brooks-Cole, 1976.

PART VII

American Education and the Future

Traditionally American education has been oriented to the past and to the present. One of the major purposes of American education has always been the transmission of knowledge and culture. A second purpose of the American school has been to respond to the needs of contemporary society. For example, schools today are viewed as one of the primary societal agencies to accomplish desegregation. In the past, some attempts were made to hold the schools responsible for the future improvements of society. In 1932, in *Dare the School Build a New Social Order?*, George S. Counts called for the schools to accept a role as the agent of change for society. In such a role, schools would not only prepare young people for the future but also prepare the future for young people. Chapters 24 and 25 are devoted to considerations of the future—and the potential role of American education in the future.

Historically people of all kinds and in all walks of life have expressed concern about the future. In recent years, deliberate and concerted attempts have been made to relate the past and present to possible future development. This new discipline has been referred to as *futuristics*, futures research, policies research, or futures studies. In general, the discipline deals with forecasting and, it is hoped, determining the future.

In Chapter 24, we will explore the concept of futuristics and illustrate the use of the concept in forecasting the future by a discussion of such social issues as population, urbanization, the quality of life, the nature of the family, and the status of women and minorities. Chapter 25 deals specifically with education in the future: the nature of the constituency likely to seek and to receive formal education; the types of education and educational services that might be appropriate for this constituency; and the nature of the prospective educators needed to provide such services. We will also explore the future of the teaching profession.

CHAPTER 24

Futurism and Future Society

Futuristics   HAROLD SHANE, USING THE TERM *FUTURES RESEARCH,* HAS WRITTEN: "It is a new discipline concerned with sharpening the data and improving the processes on the basis of which policy decisions are made in various fields of human endeavor such as business, government, or education. The purpose of the discipline is to help policy makers choose wisely—in terms of their purposes and values—among alternative courses of action that are open to leadership at a given time."[1] Toffler has stated: "Every society faces not merely a succession of *probable* futures, but an array of *possible* futures, and a conflict over *preferable* futures. The management of change is the effort to convert certain possibles into probables, in pursuit of agreed-on preferables. Determining the probable calls for a science of futurism. Delineating the possible calls for an art of futurism. Defining the preferable calls for a politics of futurism."[2] Futures research, therefore, includes not only studying and considering the knowledge of the past and present but also imagining and conjuring up alternative futures. It further involves valuing in the selection of a desired alternative and then planning and acting to create the preferred alternative.

Our ability to forecast the future is limited, as is our ability to generate potential and possible alternative futures. Furthermore, the selection of preferred alternatives from possible alternatives is likely to be more than difficult, and finally creating or bringing about the desired state of the future may be impossible. Yet a basic assumption is that

1. Harold G. Shane, *The Educational Significance of the Future* (Bloomington, Ind.: Phi Delta Kappa, 1973), p. 1.
2. Alvin Toffler, *Future Shock* (New York: Bantam, 1971), p. 460. Published by permission of Random House, Inc.

there *will be* a future and that it will be different from the past and the present. Can it be determined? Can the present human inhabitants of the world, with their finite wisdom and frailties, determine desirable living conditions for future inhabitants? Futures research, carried out on a global scale, deals with such questions.

Shane, after extensive interviews with futurists, concluded that futures research differed from conventional planning in the following ways:

1. Futures planning is deliberately directed by the planner's examined values and is action-oriented. It emphasizes alternative avenues rather than linear projections and concentrates on relationships among probabilities, their cross-impact upon one another, and the possible implications of such influences.
2. Futures planning is designed to point to more alternative courses of action than does conventional planning; to keep good ideas from being overlooked.
3. Traditional planning has tended to be utopian, to see tomorrow merely as an improved model of the present. Futures research recognizes the need to anticipate and to plan genuinely different concepts of the future.
4. It relies more heavily on the rational study of anticipated developments and their consequences and gives less heed to statistical analysis or projection *per se*.
5. In futures planning, the focus is not on the reform of the past. Rather, it concentrates on the creation of a "probabilistic environment" in which alternative consequences and possibilities are given careful study before choices are made.[3]

Futures planning, therefore, focuses "on conceptualizing and on creating a better human and physical environment as a result of considering alternatives and their consequences before they are translated into action."[4]

Change   One certainty of the future is change. From second to second, minute to minute, hour to hour, day to day, year to year, decade to decade, and century to century, change occurs. It occurs both imperceptibly and dramatically. It occurs slowly and rapidly. It is anticipated and unanticipated. It is, however, inevitable.

Change has been described as a roaring current, "a current so powerful today that it overturns institutions, shifts our values, and shrivels our roots."[5] Toffler, in 1965, coined the term *future shock* to describe the "dizzying disorientation brought on by the premature arrival of the future."[6] Change has at least two dimensions: direction and rate.

3. Shane, p. 2.
4. Ibid., p. 3.
5. Toffler, *Future Shock*, p. 1.
6. Alvin Toffler, "The Future as a Way of Life," *Horizons* (summer 1965): 109.

It is important to note that the rate of change has implications different from and sometimes more important than the directions of change.

An illustration representative of the rate of change deals with "the 800th lifetime." This concept divides the last 50,000 years of human existence into lifetimes of approximately 62 years each. Of the approximately 800 lifetimes, 650 were spent in caves.

> Only during the last seventy lifetimes has it been possible to communicate effectively from one lifetime to another—as writing made it possible to do. Only during the last six lifetimes did masses of men ever see a printed word. Only during the last four has it been possible to measure with any precision. Only in the last two has anyone anywhere used an electric motor. And the overwhelming majority of all the material goods we use in daily life today have been developed within the present, the 800th lifetime.[7]

Although change is inevitable, its direction and rate may be somewhat in the realm of human control; futurist researchers are attempting to forecast the direction and rate of change. They are also attempting to decide upon the types of changes that should occur, and the direction and rate at which these changes might or should occur.

Futurists vary in their opinions as to the desirability of planned intervention. It must be recognized, however, that intervention occurs whether it is planned or not. Actions of the present soon become history—but do in fact alter the future. Why do we suffer from pollution? Why is world famine a crisis? Why are we searching for new sources of energy? Daniel Bell clearly illustrates how present actions (interventions) influence the future:

> Time, said St. Augustine, is a three-fold present: the present as we experience it, the past as a present memory, and the future as a present expectation. By that criterion, the world of the year 2000 has already arrived, for in the decisions we make now, in the way we design our environment and thus sketch the lines of constraints, the future is committed. Just as the gridiron pattern of city streets in the nineteenth century shaped the linear growth of cities in the twentieth, so the new networks of radial highways, the locations of new towns, the reordering of graduate-school curricula, the decision to create or not create a computer utility as a single system, and the like will frame the tectonics of the twenty-first century. The future is not an overarching leap into the distance; it begins in the present.[8]

In summary, change is inevitable. It has two major interacting components: content or direction and rate. There is little question as to the desirability or need for intervention to control change in order to avert disaster. Yet there is considerable debate as to the soundness of

---

7. Toffler, *Future Shock*, p. 14.
8. Daniel Bell, "The Year 2000—The Trajectory of an Idea." In *Toward the Year 2000: Work in Progress* edited by Daniel Bell (Boston: Houghton Mifflin, 1968), p. 1.

the data upon which to forecast the future; and there is no firm consensus on the kind of future environment that should be created. Yet, as Daniel Bell points out, the importance of the relationship of present decisions to future events is clearly recognizable.

Alternative Futures

One of the goals of futures research is to generate possible alternative futures. There are *probable futures,* that is, future events that are likely to occur if there is no intervention in present trends; *possible futures,* that is, future events that could occur with intervention; and *preferable futures,* that is, future events that are valued as desirable and could occur with intervention. Many forecasts of probable futures are dismal and bleak; others based on interventions and on the premise that humans can, after a fashion, determine their own destiny are brighter and more palatable.

A number of present trends in society might have decided impacts on the future of society and, at the same time, on education in the future. A few of these trends have been selected for brief consideration. Although the trends are discussed separately, it must be recognized that they are, in fact, intricately interrelated.

Population

The total population of the world and its distribution are at the root of many current problems and therefore are related to the kind of life the future may hold. The population of the earth in 1950 was about 2.5 billion, reaching that level in approximately three million years. By 1975, the population had passed the four billion mark, and the rate of population increase had risen from 1.6 percent in 1950 to 1.8 percent in 1975. If the 1.8 annual rate of increase continues, the world's population will double to eight billion by the year 2015.[9] Forecasts for 2026 vary somewhat but cluster around seven billion.

One forecast based upon the projection of present trends indicates a crest of population at approximately ten billion occurring around the year 2000—then decreasing to a level of three billion around 2100.[10] The decline in population from ten billion in the year 2000 to three billion in 2100 will be accompanied by a steady decline in natural resources—a decline that had begun in the year 1900—and by a decline in industrial production and food supply, which will begin about the year 2000. In the same set of projections, a steady and exponential increase in pollution is projected. The assumptions upon which the forecasts are based are obviously crucial.

Another forecast indicates that world zero-population growth will become a reality as early as 1990 or 1995, on the assumptions that the explosive nature of the overpopulation problem will be recognized and

9. "World Population May Double by Year 2015," *The Futurist* 10 (October 1976): 289.
10. Shane, p. 51.

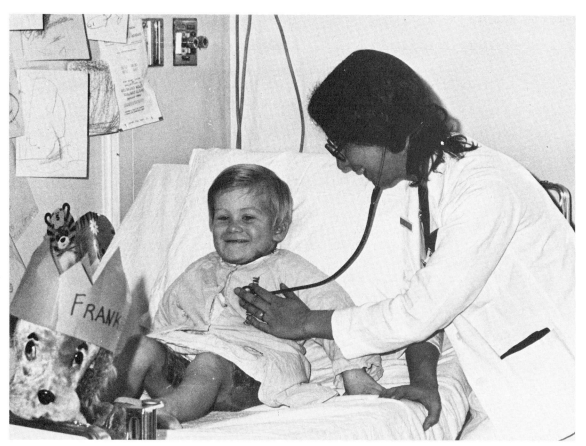

More and more women are seeking professional training in many fields. (*Photograph by Tania D'Avignon*)

will be dealt with; that equalization of opportunities for women will reduce the likelihood of large families; and that technoindustrial changes in underdeveloped countries will be a limiting factor.[11]

Highest rates of population growth in the world are now found in Latin America, Africa, and Asia. Latin America—with the exception of Argentina, Uruguay, and Chile—has had the highest growth rate of any major region in the world, rising from 2.6 percent in 1950 to 2.8 percent in 1975 and more than doubling its population in 25 years. Mexico has had an annual growth rate of 3.5 percent—its population doubling in only twenty years. Africa's annual growth rate rose from 2.1 percent in 1950 to 2.7 percent in 1975. Asia's growth rate of 2 percent is relatively low, but owing to its large population (approximately 2.3 billion) it contributes an additional 46 million people each year—about two-thirds of the world's yearly population increase. These

11. Ibid., p. 21.

rapidly growing areas are already overpopulated and are severely strain-
ing their food-producing facilities.[12]

In contrast, the more developed regions of northern America,
Europe, and the Soviet Union lowered their combined growth rate from
1.2 percent in 1950 to .8 percent in 1975. Doubling time for a growth
rate of .8 percent is eighty-seven years.[13]

Urbanization   Massive urbanization of the population is one of the most pronounced
trends of the twentieth century; industrialization and world trade have
led to the development of large cities. At the beginning of the century, only about 15 percent of the world's population lived in cities,
whereas by 1960 approximately one-third of the population lived in
cities. By the year 2000 it is anticipated that there will be more people
living in cities than in rural areas.

In 1900, there were 11 cities with a million or more inhabitants; by
1950, there were 75 cities; and by 1976, there were 191 cities with
more than a million inhabitants.[14] Barbara Ward, author of *The World
of Man*, speculates that the number of cities will have increased from
11 in 1900 to 273 in 1985—in less than a century; furthermore, 147
of them will be in the less developed countries. By 1985, there will be
17 cities with a population in excess of ten million—Tokyo at approximately twenty-five million, followed by New York close behind,
and Mexico City at nearly eighteen million.[15]

Kahn and Wiener have suggested that in the year 2000 there will
probably be at least three gargantuan megalopolises in the United
States.

> We have labeled these—only half-frivolously—"Boswash," "Chipitts," and
> "Sansan." Boswash identifies the megalopolis that will extend from Wash-
> ington to Boston and contain almost one-quarter of the American popula-
> tion (something under 80 million people). Chipitts, concentrated around
> the Great Lakes, may stretch from Chicago to Pittsburgh and north to Can-
> ada—thereby including Detroit, Toledo, Cleveland, Akron, Buffalo, and
> Rochester. This megalopolis seems likely to contain more than one-eighth of
> the United States population (perhaps 40 million people or more). Sansan, a
> Pacific megalopolis that will presumably stretch from Santa Barbara (or
> even San Francisco) to San Diego, should contain one-sixteenth of the
> population (perhaps 20 million people or more). These megalopolises will
> all be maritime. Boswash is on an extremely narrow strip of the North At-
> lantic Coast; Chipitts, on Lake Erie and the southern and western shores of
> Lake Michigan and Lake Ontario; Sansan, on an even more narrow strip on
> the West Coast. . . .

12.   "World Population May Double by Year 2015," pp. 289–290.
13.   Ibid.
14.   "The Explosive Growth of the World's Cities," *The Futurist* 10 (December 1976):
316.
15.   Ibid.

> The three megalopolises should contain roughly one-half of the total United States population, including the overwhelming majority of the most technologically and scientifically advanced, and prosperous intellectual and creative elements. Even Sansan will have a larger total income than all but five or six nations.[16]

The "Boswash" megalopolis, with a population of close to forty million, lagged behind the rest of the nation in growth from 1970 to 1974. While the population of the rest of the nation grew by about 5 percent, "Boswash" remained stable. The large cities (Boston, New York, Baltimore, Philadelphia, and Washington) actually lost population.

The fastest growing area in the United States is the "sunbelt," with gains of 10 to 15 percent in the Southeast and over 15 percent in the Southwest and West since 1970. Declining areas are in the Northeast and North Central portions of the country. Between 1970 and 1978, the Northeast will have increased in population by 2.3 percent; the North Central by 4.1 percent; the South by 15.3 percent; and the West by 15.9 percent. By 1980—on the basis of current trends—six of the ten largest cities in the United States will be in the Southwest: Los Angeles, Houston, Dallas, San Diego, San Antonio, and Phoenix.[17]

The world seems destined for increased population and for further urbanization. Recent trends in the United States indicate a slower growth in the established urban areas but new growth in other more recently developed urban areas. Increased population and urbanization generate other problems, including pollution, hunger, environmental illnesses, crowding, lack of energy and water, and lack of privacy. The population of the world may be ultimately limited by a lack of natural resources, as was indicated earlier. One of the most favorable signs for world population control has been the sharp increase in requests for assistance in family planning coming from developing countries. The principal agencies—United Nations Fund for Population Activities, International Planned Parenthood Federation, and U.S. Agency for International Development—are being overwhelmed with requests for assistance.[18]

Quality of Life   The *quality of life* is a difficult concept to predict for the future. In terms of the basic needs of people, it means at least freedom from hunger and adequate shelter. It may also mean freedom from fear,

16. Herman Kahn and Anthony J. Wiener, "A Framework for Speculation." Reprinted by permission of *Daedalus*, Journal of the American Academy of Arts and Sciences, Boston, Mass. (summer 1967). Also reprinted in *Toward the Year 2000: Work in Progress* edited by Daniel Bell (Boston: Houghton Mifflin, 1968), pp. 86–87.
17. From census data.
18. Lester R. Brown, Patricia L. McGrath, and Bruce Stokes, "The Population Problem in 22 Dimensions," *The Futurist* 10 (October 1976): 224.

freedom of speech, and the right to privacy. Quality of life is relative in nature: the current "haves" and "have nots" would undoubtedly have different definitions of freedom from hunger and of adequate housing. Freedom from fear, freedom of speech, and the right to privacy also undoubtedly have different meanings throughout the world. What lies ahead in respect to the quality of life?

Food and Shelter   With more people, accompanied by the depletion of many resources including energy, with the spoilage of existing resources through pollution, and with diminishing water suplies, the future in terms of adequate food and housing is not bright. Earlier in this chapter, we noted that one futurist predicted a cresting of world population at ten billion around the year 2000—decreasing to three billion by 2100. This projection was based, in part, on the diminution of natural resources, on a decline in food supply and industrial production, and on an exponential increase in pollution.

None of the basic resources required to expand food output—that is, land, water, energy, and fertilizer—can be considered abundant today.[19] Urban sprawl, soil erosion, and lack of water for irrigation have reduced the acreage under production in some countries. Food production has lagged behind demand in almost every geographic region except North America. If the population in North America had expanded as rapidly as that of South America, North America would be struggling for self-sufficiency rather than exporting agricultural products.[20]

It is well to remember that the energy that fuels the machinery to cultivate agricultural land is petroleum. The world's supply of oil is diminishing. The oceans, once considered a promising source of increased food production as populations increased, seem at present to be yielding at their full capacity. "From 1950 to 1970 the world fish catch more than tripled, from 21 to 70 million tons. But between 1970 and 1973 the long-standing trend was reversed and the fish catch declined by nearly five million tons."[21] Many marine biologists now feel that the global catch of table-grade fish is at or near the maximum sustainable level. Water pollution has obviously affected the fish production in both fresh water rivers and lakes and in the oceans.

It is obvious that, without some changes in existing trends, the projected population of the world in the year 2000 cannot be supported by the resources of the world. What hope is there? What positive signs are there? As we mentioned earlier, there is increased evidence of interest in population control in underdeveloped nations. Pollution controls are beginning to show their effectiveness in some nations.

19.   Ibid., p. 240.
20.   Ibid.
21.   Ibid., p. 238.

The new technology will undoubtedly affect the future. (*Photograph by Jonathan Goell, The Picture Cube*)

Scientists are exploring new sources of energy. Yet it may very well mean that an increased population will inevitably lead to a lower standard of living in some nations to permit survival in others. The standard of living in developed nations is likely to drop because of energy shortages.

Privacy Privacy will be difficult to preserve in future years. Concentrations of populations will make it increasingly difficult for a person to be alone, to commune with God, to meditate, to have a bit of private space. Sakharov has speculated on environmental alternatives to facilitate the individual's search for privacy:

> I imagine a gradual (completed long after 2024) growth of two types of territory out of the industrial world that is overcrowded and inhospitable to human life and nature. I will conditionally term them "Work Territory" (WT) and "Preserve Territory" (PT). The PT, larger in area, will be set aside for maintaining the earth's ecological balance, for leisure activities, and for man to actively re-establish his own natural balance. The smaller and more

densely populated WT will be the area where people will spend most of their time.

The WT will have intensive agriculture; nature will have been transformed completely to serve practical needs. All industry will be concentrated in giant automated and semi-automated factories. Almost all people will live in "super-cities," the centers of which will contain multi-storied apartment buildings with artificially controlled climate and lighting, with automated kitchens, landscaped walls, and so on.

But the man of the future will have the opportunity, I hope, to spend part, even though it will be the smaller part, of his time in the more natural surroundings of the PT. I predict that people will lead lives with a real social aim in the PT as well. They will not only rest but also work with their hands and their heads, read, and think. They will live in tents or in houses they have built themselves, the way their ancestors did. They will listen to the noise of a mountain stream or simply relish the silence, the wild beauty of the outdoors, the forests, the sky, and the clouds. Their basic work will be to preserve nature and themselves.[22]

Sakharov envisions WTs located in outer space: "flying cities—artificial earth satellites with important industrial functions." He also foresees a "widely developed system of subterranean cities for sleep and entertainment."[23] Perhaps such future developments would partially alleviate the individual's search and need for privacy.

The search for privacy will undoubtedly be made more difficult, however, because of improved technology—more specifically, the technology of eavesdropping. Privacy can today be invaded by remote control. Interested parties can now photograph from afar, conceal microphones in tiepins, observe by closed-circuit television, tap telephone lines, pick up conversations in another room by the use of electronic devices, and determine the content of mail without opening it.[24] There is little doubt that the technological capacity for surveillance will increase. Perhaps the solution to this dilemma lies in the individual's demand for privacy—that is, the individual's ability to control his or her right to privacy.

Emerging Life-styles Life-styles are affected by many variables including the interrelationships of culture, values, tradition, and environmental conditions, which, in turn, include population, economic circumstances, climate, and government. Life-styles vary widely throughout the world, based in part on the aforementioned variables. One's personal life-style might be influenced by living in a crowded apartment in a city, being extremely poor in a climate that is hot and humid, and living under a dictatorship. Our discussion is limited to forecasting and speculating on

22. Andrei D. Sakharov, "Tomorrow: The View from Red Square," *Saturday Review World*, 24 August 1974, pp. 13–14.
23. Ibid., p. 14.
24. Ibid., p. 108.

selected future life-styles in the United States, based in part on current trends.

Family The last decade has revealed an increase in the divorce rate, an increase in unmarried people between the ages of twenty and twenty-four, an increase in unmarried people who live with a person of the opposite sex, fewer live births, and an increase in the number of women working outside the home. The following quotation summarizes the past and speculates on the future of family life.

> The extended family, with several generations living under one roof, characterized American society early in this century, when it began to be replaced by the nuclear family comprised of a wife, husband, and their children. The nuclear family, considered the basic unit of American life, has become the firmly established norm in the past 20 years. Now some people such as the authors, are suggesting that the nuclear family may give way to the multi-adult living group or intentional extended family. Such groups would consist of networks of intimate friends who may or may not live together and for whom the possibility of sexual involvement with each other is open. Several such networks have lasted 30 or 40 years, which leads the Francoeurs to believe that this lifestyle may prove a good alternative to present marriage patterns.[25]

Housing The cost of housing will continue to increase, particularly the cost of single-family dwellings. Cost of labor, land, and materials will cause many young people to postpone buying homes; more people will opt for condominium living. New construction in the future will utilize solar heat where feasible. Since older homes tend to be large and expensive to heat and to maintain, they will not be suitable for those who desire to live as a nuclear family. These older homes may be suitable for the intentional extended family.

Work It has been forecast that the workweek will be reduced to thirty-four hours a week and that the percentage of people providing services will increase more rapidly than those producing goods. Carl H. Madden, former chief economist for the U.S. Chamber of Commerce, has stated that "today's 18 year olds, when they get to be 50, will be living in a society in which 1 out of 10 people will be able to produce all the things we need—from mining, manufacturing, and agriculture." He has forecast that 50 percent of the work force will be in service-oriented work.[26]

Status of Women Clare Boothe Luce has speculated about the future of women. In respect to the "establishment," Luce has stated: "It has sprouted a

25. Robert T. Francoeur and Anna K. Francoeur, "The Pleasure Bond: Reversing the Antisex Ethic," *The Futurist* 10 (August 1976): 180.
26. *U.S. News and World Report,* 27 December 1976, p. 84.

heavy thicket of female twigs at its base, and many of its middling branches are covered with feminine foliage. But out of a female population of about 107 million, there are not today 100 women perched in posts of high command or in high supervisory or policy-making positions in its upper branches."[27] Although Luce was not impressed with the progress of women up to the present, she did identify three breakthroughs that may alter the future:

1. The advance made by medical technology in giving women control over their own reproductive function.
2. The breakthrough favoring the goal of sex equality in the opening of doors of higher education to women.
3. The progress that has been made in the legal area, with women, in an organized way, taking advantage of civil rights legislation.[28]

She concludes:

I now reach somewhat reluctantly for my crystal ball. I am sorry to say that the picture I see there is *not* one of Woman sitting in the White House in 2024. I see her playing many more roles that were once considered masculine. I see her making a little more money than she is making now. But I see her still trying to make her way up—in a man's world—and not having much more success than she is having now. There may be, and probably will be, great political and technological changes in the world in the next half century. But I venture to suggest that none of them will greatly affect the relatively inferior status of the American woman.[29]

Luce sees, as the major inhibitor to women's upward mobility, an underlying reluctance in the American culture to allow women to have positions of authority over men.

Gloria Steinem, editor of *Ms.* magazine and women's activist, also speculated, in an interview dealing with the future, about the future for women. When asked "how will the lives of women change," she responded:

In every way. Autonomy—the ability to control our bodies and work identities and futures—is a revolution for women. We're only just beginning to understand what it might be like.

Many may go on for more education. Even now, women are going back to school after they've had kids. The campus is no longer an "age ghetto" of people from 17 to 22—and that makes it possible for men to go back, too. Education may become a lifelong process for all of us, not just an intense time of preparation.

Responsibility for children won't be exclusively the woman's any more, but shared equally by men—and shared by the community, too. That means

27. Clare Boothe Luce, "The 21st Century Woman—Free at Last?" *Saturday Review World,* 24 August 1974, p. 58.
28. Ibid., pp. 61–62.
29. Ibid., p. 62.

that work patterns will change for both women and men, and women can enter all fields just as men can.

It used to be that women couldn't succeed in work because they didn't have wives. In the future, men won't have "wives" either—not in the traditional, subservient sense.[30]

Asked if she thought there would be a woman president in the next one hundred years, Ms. Steinem responded:

I don't know. That may happen, but only after all the other male "outs" are elected—a Jewish president, a black president, a Spanish-speaking president.

If we can judge from history, sex-based prejudice is the most intimate and deep-rooted; the last to go. Even now in corporate board rooms, minority men are usually invited to join the board before women of any race. White men affirm their masculinity by having a minority man on the board —providing, of course, that there are only one or two and can't outvote them. But to have a woman enjoying the same position, especially at upper levels, just devalues the work. Why should a man be honored by a job that "even a woman" can do?[31]

Without doubt, the roles of women are changing. More women are working outside the home, and affirmative-action programs have been effective in helping women attain executive positions in business and in the professions. The implementation of the regulations of Title IX, mentioned earlier, will undoubtedly have some effects on enlarging the roles that women may assume in society.

Minorities   What of the present status of minorities? Documented evidence of the status of blacks in the United States over the last twenty years reveals that the percentage of blacks in professional and skilled work has increased, that the percentage of blacks with high school and college educations has increased, and that striking advances have been made in the numbers of blacks holding political offices. If this trend continues—and it seems likely that it will—the status of blacks and other minority groups will continue to improve gradually.

The percentage of persons of Hispanic origin has been increasing in the United States. Currently they number about 11.2 million and comprise about 5.2 percent of the population. Many school systems now offer bilingual classes for Spanish-speaking children. It is anticipated that the Spanish-speaking people will face a struggle similar to the blacks as they seek acceptance and upward mobility.

Man's inhumanity to his fellow man may be on the decline. Increasing tolerance for alternative life-styles has become more in evidence.

30. *U.S. News and World Report,* 7 July 1975, p. 47.
31. Ibid.

It is hoped that human beings will continue to value all other human beings and that the new-found humanism of equal opportunity for all—women, blacks, Hispanic minorities, American Indians—will continue to flourish.

World Governance

How shall the world be governed? Can the world achieve peace? These are haunting questions for the future.

Kurt Waldheim, fourth secretary general of the United Nations, has made the following observations:

> Our future on this earth will depend to a large degree on our ability to develop a new economic and social system which recognizes and balances the rights, interests, and aspirations of all peoples. This is a problem of such magnitude and complexity that it can only be dealt with by a degree of global cooperation far greater than anything we have hitherto achieved.
>
> The U.N. system, through its efforts to tackle such basic matters as poverty, population, food, and the law of the sea, international trade and development, the monetary system, the conservation and just apportionment of natural resources, and the preservation of the environment, has slowly begun to face up to this urgent challenge.[32]

Emmet Hughes has identified "three tolerable believable premises about global things to come":

> First, the thrust of nationalism, which so many sages thought had almost spent itself by the end of Wold War II, will continue to outrun all expert expectations, especially as it is reinforced by the fresh passions of the newly independent nations. Second, the force of ideology, as a guide to the conduct of nations, will continue to falter and become more feeble and irrelevant. As the dilemmas and distresses troubling the majority of peoples appear ever more insistently both practical and universal, they leave less and less place for the divisive role of the theoretical. The most inventive designs for reversing urban decay or slowing population growth—or curbing inflationary pressures or surviving energy crises—may be infinitely varied. But it will become increasingly implausible to label any of them as democratic, or communist, or fascist. Third, for these and related reasons, the line most seriously scarring the globe will be seen to run, not between East and West, but between North and South, between those societies that have perhaps enjoyed too much and those that still enjoy next to nothing, and between the most industrialized nations and the most industry-hungry nations, oddly blessed by the natural resources with which industry itself must be fed.[33]

32. Kurt Waldheim, "Toward Global Interdependence," *Saturday Review World*, 24 August 1974, p. 63.
33. Emmet John Hughes, "A World Atlas for 2024," *Saturday Review World*, 17 August 1974, p. 26.

It seems that the politics of the future will be increasingly influenced by economics, environments, energy, and the recognition of human rights—particularly the access of all people to a quality life.

Environment and Resources

There is little doubt that people have ravaged their natural environment:

> As far as humans are concerned, they have only very recently achieved the dominance of nature, and they suddenly realize that the long and difficult conquest of the planet and the enthusiasm of victory have spread worldwide devastation and ruin. As recently as seven or eight generations ago, Western civilization triggered various kinds of explosions: more children, more food, more tonnage of goods, more energy—which created an exhilarating climate of pride, of overconfidence. The rapture of growth. But after such a great wild party, we are just awakening with a painful hangover, and all around us our home is littered with the sad remains of the "morning after." While we are slowly and painfully attempting to clean the place and return to normal life, we realize that growth, at least in quantity, has limits, that our conventional resources can, and will soon, be exhausted, and that our very life depends on the quality of water.[34]

Advanced technology, population growth, exploitation of natural resources, urbanization, overconsumption, and innumerable other factors have contributed to our environmental problems. Toffler refers to the "industrial vomit that fills our skies and seas."[35] Shane has noted that "naive use has been made of technology to the point at which many ecologists and other scientists are deeply concerned lest—within the span of the next generation—irreparable damage be done to the environment."[36] He further noted:

> Just as misuse has created many present difficulties, so the *wise* use of technological developments is needed to extricate us from the pitfalls in which we find ourselves. In the process we must be wary that we do not demonize technology. The fault is not in our skills but in ourselves, and we need to find technically sound procedures to overcome technogenic crises.[37]

Many challenges must be faced in the future—just a few of which have been explored in this chapter. These challenges are clearly interrelated: perhaps one of the most serious deals with the world population and its relationship to resources and to environment. Clean water, clean air, and an abundant food supply are necessary to survival.

34. Jacques Cousteau, "The Perils and Potentials of a Watery Planet," *Saturday Review World*, 29 August 1974, p. 41.
35. Toffler, *Future Shock*, p. 429.
36. Shane, p. 47.
37. Ibid., p. 48.

It is hoped that the present inhabitants of the globe can learn from the past and will cooperatively solve the issues of the future. Education will certainly play a major part in determining that future.

Summary and Implications

This chapter introduced the concept of futurism and illustrated how it is applied by researchers. Futurism implies that humans should determine what is a desirable future and should plan to bring it about.

The students of today are the decision makers of tomorrow. Teachers, as they work with students, must make students aware of our communal need to determine and to plan for a desirable future. In many areas of the curriculum, particularly in the social studies and the sciences, the effects of a continuation of the harmful trends—for example, pollution and the depletion of natural resources—must be emphasized to students. The effects can be speculated upon in a quasi-scientific and in a creative way through class simulation of scenarios of life in the future. Students will need to examine their values carefully. What kind of life do they cherish? Is it possible to achieve such a life in the future if present deleterious trends continue—unless there is some sort of intervention? What kinds of interventions are possible? Without doubt, teachers can succeed in challenging students to think about the future and perhaps to begin to act in ways that will improve the possibilities for the future.

Discussion Questions

1. What does the concept of futuristics entail?
2. How does futures research differ from conventional planning?
3. How can humans begin today to determine the direction of the future?
4. How does the past influence the future? Provide illustrations.
5. What kind of world do you envision in the future?

Supplemental Activities

1. Write and enact a skit on life in future society.
2. Make a list of forecasts on future society. State the assumptions on which each forecast is based.
3. To which values would you prefer future societies to adhere? Compare your list with those of others.
4. Interview children and senior citizens about the future. Contrast their ideas.
5. Choose two or three aspects of the future—such as population, energy, or family life—and project two or three alternative futures based on these different premises:

Population
- Assume zero growth
- Assume increased growth
- Assume stability

Energy
- Assume total oil depletion
- Assume new energy resource

Family life
- Assume that marriage disappears completely
- Assume that single-family dwellings are no longer feasible

Bibliography

Bundy, Robert, ed. *Images of the Future: The Twenty-First Century and Beyond.* Buffalo, N.Y.: Prometheus, 1976.

Cornish, Edward. *The Study of the Future.* Washington, D.C.: World Future Society, 1977.

Counts, George S. *Dare the School Build a New Social Order?* New York: John Day, 1932.

The Futurist. Washington, D.C.: World Future Society. (A bimonthly journal of forecasts, trends, and ideas about the future.)

Harman, Willis W. *An Incomplete Guide to the Future.* San Francisco: San Francisco Book, 1976.

Hencley, Stephen P., and Yates, James R., eds. *Futurism in Education: Methodologies.* Berkeley, Calif.: McCutchan, 1974.

Kahn, Herman; Brown, William; and Martel, Leon. *The Next 200 Years: A Scenario for America and the World.* New York: Morrow, 1976.

Schaller, Lyle E. *Understanding Tomorrow.* Nashville, Tenn.: Abingdon, 1976.

Shane, Harold G. *The Educational Significance of the Future.* Bloomington, Ind.: Phi Delta Kappa, 1973.

Toffler, Alvin. *Future Shock.* New York: Random House, 1970.

Toffler, Alvin, ed. *The Futurists.* New York: Random House, 1972.

CHAPTER 25

Schools and the Future

THE CURRICULUM OF SCHOOLS HAS TRADITIONALLY BEEN ORI-
ented to the transmission of culture and knowledge. Changes in school
curriculums most often occur after changes in society. George S. Counts,
as long ago as 1932, in *Dare the School Build a New Social Order?*,
called for the schools to accept the role as the agent for change in society. The challenge issued by Counts has never been completely accepted by the schools or by society. Perhaps now is the time for schools
to attempt to change society, particularly to attempt to improve the
quality of life in the future. Changes in the schools to meet this potential
new role—while maintaining their traditional role—should be carefully
examined. This chapter speculates on some of the ways our schools may
change in the future.

Future Education
for Whom?
Schools are now being asked to provide formal education for an ever-
increasing proportion of the population. Whereas a few years ago children typically started school at age six, many children now start school
much earlier. The latest data available indicate that the *proportion* of
three- to five-year-old children enrolled in preprimary education rose
from 25 percent in 1964 to 45 percent in 1974. The steepest growth rate
was in the enrollment of three-year-olds where the percentage enrolled
was more than 4.5 times larger in 1974 than in 1964. The percentage of
four-year-olds in school increased 2.5 times during the decade. In 1974,
approximately 20 percent of the three-year-olds were enrolled in school,
as were 38 percent of the four-year-olds and 79 percent of the five-year-
olds.[1] It is anticipated that these percentages will continue to rise in the
future.

1. W. Vance Grant and C. George Lind, *Digest of Educational Statistics, 1976*
(Washington, D.C.: U.S. Government Printing Office, 1977).

A similar trend is occurring in adult education. The percentage of participants in adult education rose by 30.8 percent between 1969 and 1975. Adults, in this context, are defined as those age seventeen and older who are not full-time students in high school or college—and those over age thirty-five regardless of their enrollment status. There were approximately 17 million participants in adult education in 1975, as opposed to 13 million in 1969.[2] This trend is also expected to continue.

Participants in adult education enroll in programs sponsored by employers, two-year colleges, community organizations, trade and business schools, and union or professional organizations—in addition to regular high schools and colleges. The largest numbers of participants are in programs sponsored by union or professional organizations; the second largest numbers are enrolled in two-year colleges. These two types of programs also recorded the largest percentages of change between 1969 and 1975—increases of approximately 116 percent and 95 percent respectively. Occupational training represents the study area in which most participants enroll, yet the fastest growing area is the study of social life and recreation, followed by personal and family living.[3]

A recent study dealing with the future of education made four pertinent points—of interest to all educators: (1) a recognition of the need to make education a continuing lifelong process; (2) the need for continuing education on a worldwide basis that would serve both mature (past age thirty) and senior (past age sixty) learners; (3) the view that problem-preventing education begun in early childhood is distinctly superior to compensatory education provided at a later time; and (4) teaching and learning should not occur only in schools.[4]

In view of these findings, it seems logical to forecast that schools of the future will eventually be asked to provide various forms of continuous education for virtually all of the people—from the very young to the very old. How can our schools prepare for this expanded role?

Coping with Change   For millions of years, changes took place very slowly for humans—a fact documented earlier in this book. In recent history, however, change has accelerated to such a degree that it is one of the most discussed social phenomena. How often we hear that "we live in a changing world," and that "things aren't what they used to be." Planning for and coping with change is one of our most important social problems.

If we believe that changes will continue to take place rapidly—or perhaps even accelerate in the future—then surely we must reason

2. Ibid., p. 148.
3. Ibid.
4. Harold G. Shane, "The Views of 50 Distinguished World Citizens and Educators," *The Futurist* 10 (October 1976): 255–256.

Those who study futuristics attempt to control future outcomes. (*Photograph by Franklin Wing, Stock, Boston*)

that students should somehow learn to plan for and to cope with the changes that will occur during their lifetimes. The question for educators then becomes how can schools best prepare students for this task.

Students were interviewed as part of a National Education Association (NEA) study conducted by Harold Shane; ninety-five young respondents were asked what they thought might be done to improve their schools and their schooling.[5] Four points came through clearly in the study: "First, in a world that youth find frustrating, distressing, and sometimes frightening, the need for *coping* skills and techniques

5. Harold G. Shane, *Curriculum Change toward the 21st Century* (Washington, D.C.: National Education Association of the United States, 1977).

was expressed." Second, "young people wanted schools that cared about them," and third, students revealed loneliness and a desire for teachers who "radiated warmth and genuine interest in students."[6] Finally, the students sought help in communicating: rather than better language skills, they sought the "opportunity to have someone to talk with, someone to whom they could listen, someone to whom and with whom they could communicate and share their feelings, hopes and concerns."[7] The students' responses provide clues for the kind of curriculum, teachers, and instructional strategies needed now and for the future.

Cardinal Principles Reexamined

The original Seven Cardinal Principles of Education were formulated in 1918, arising out of an NEA study by the Commission on the Reorganization of Secondary Education. To review briefly, they were statements of educational goals that dealt with health, command of fundamental processes, worthy home membership, vocation, civic education, worthy use of leisure, and ethical character. In the Shane study, panelists were asked to respond to two related questions: Have the original 1918 cardinal principles retained their merit? If so, what are the new ways in which they now should be interpreted, amended, or applied in anticipation of changing social, economic, and political conditions in the world community? The members of the panel basically felt that the seven goals had retained their usefulness and importance. They did, however, seek to redefine, refine, and clarify the goals—for their applicability and appropriateness to the future.[8] The panel not only revised the principles for the future but provided an analysis of the existing principles. Their observations, which follow, provide insights into the reasoning behind the detailed changes that were suggested for each principle.[9]

1. The original cardinal principles did not distinguish between the general responsibilities for education and those that were best assumed by or shared with agencies such as the church, the community, and the family. Health, ethical character, worthy home membership, leisure activities, and civic skills often were influenced by or were influential in other arenas of life. The principles overpromised what the schools could do. We must now talk more sensibly about what schooling can actually accomplish.

2. The original principles did not anticipate how much learning we would require in the world of 1976. Now we must look at the total learning system. Except for literary, and possibly vocational efficiency, the cardinal principles are tasks for other educational agencies beyond the

6. Ibid., pp. 68–69.
7. Ibid.
8. Ibid., pp. 43–55.
9. Ibid., pp. 42–43.

school walls. These include the home, church, and peer groups as well as mass media.

3. The principles, quite understandably, did not allow for the increasing need for lifelong adult education.

4. The 1893 Committee on Ten report focused on *subjects;* the cardinal principles focused on *goals.* The commission that created these seven principles, despite its impressive contribution, erred in two ways: first, in failing to recognize the role of other agencies in achieving the principles; and second, in mixing command of fundamental processes (subjects) with the other six. This has created the sort of problem situation in which "one committee of teachers sits somewhere devising social goals for the school district and talks in terms of global concepts while another committee is selecting or reorganizing the subjects. The trouble in our time is that the two have failed to meet."

Curriculum for the Future: Cardinal Premises

The panel was also asked: "In anticipation of the 21st century, what premises should guide educational planning?" Premises are viewed as guides to action rather than as goals or principles. In discussing the premises, the report emphasized "that *education* needed to be seen in a much broader context than the setting in which formal schooling presently occurs."[10] Panelists further emphasized that "as we focus on the immediate social problems of the *next two decades,* we need to remember that *children now in school will not be decision-makers for nearly a generation.*"[11] Those who publish or produce books, television, and newspapers—and other potentially educational media— must assume more mature responsibility for continuing education of children and adults. Twenty-eight premises were generated and have been categorized into four groups: general premises, premises pertaining to process, premises related to educational structure, and premises bearing on content and instruction. The premises, listed below, project the opinion of one group of experts as to what the curriculum, teaching methodology, and the structure of education should be based on for the future.[12]

GENERAL PREMISES

I.   The need to develop a spirit of "global community" in an increasingly interdependent world has reaffirmed an important task for education: to recognize and to respect the concepts of multi-ethnic, polycultural, and multilingual education in pluralistic societies both in the United States and abroad.

II. Education has assumed new significance as a positive force for peace in a world capable of destroying itself.

III. Learning is a lifelong process, and education, therefore, should be seen as a seamless continuum of experiences from early childhood to old age.

IV. The value to the learners of their experiences obtained through educa-

10. Ibid., p. 57.
11. Ibid.
12. Ibid., pp. 58–70.

tion is more important than the routes they may follow in obtaining those experiences.

V.   There are standards that are essential to life on a planet sometimes imperiled by the less thoughtful of its human population.

PREMISES PERTAINING TO PROCESS

VI.   The aspirations and abilities of the student are best served when the student's learning experiences are at last partly self-directed rather than selected entirely by teachers.

VII.   Because of the impact of the attitudes, comments, and actions of teachers (the "hidden curriculum," reflecting what teachers really value) greater efforts should be made to insure that this latent curriculum becomes clear and provides wholesome input for the learner.

VIII.   Because the experiences of each learner are unique, teachers should expect a wide range of performance from children, youth, and adults.

IX.   Good instruction is personalized rather than individualized.

PREMISES RELATED TO EDUCATIONAL STRUCTURE, ORGANIZATION, OR POLICY

X.   The opportunity for universal early childhood education should be an integral part of the structure of education in a seamless learning continuum.

XI.   Adult education that exceeds mere literacy should receive worldwide emphasis.

XII.   Continuing educational opportunities should be designed to serve both mature (past 30) and senior (past 60) learners.

XIII.   Particularly at the transnational level, the application of instructional systems and technologies can make important contributions to education as ideas, knowledge, and know-how are shared with the illiterate and the semiliterate in order to further their education. However, the use of systems and of media must be consonant with carefully reasoned human values.

XIV.   Sharply delineated segments of education based on K–6–6 type grade levels ought to be eliminated as soon as feasible. Ability, motivation, and readiness rather than certificates or diplomas should serve as the learner's prime credentials.

XV.   When and where teaching and learning occur must not be bounded either by the school's walls or by our preconceived ideas as to what should be learned at the once-traditional age for learning it.

XVI.   Persons in the field of career or occupational education should develop their programs in ways which recognize even more fully that vocational activity—the jobs held and services performed—often is sequential and will require greater versatility from members of the work force in the years ahead.

XVII.   Traditional patterns of home-school relations need to be reconsidered and perhaps sharply modified in recognition of changes in the family which, in many instances today, is often an "affinity group" rather than the nuclear family consisting of mother, father, and children.

PREMISES WITH A BEARING ON CONTENT AND INSTRUCTION

XVIII.   Present social trends, which are characterized by accelerating change and increasing complexity, have enhanced the need for basic communication skills such as the ability to handle the written and spoken word and to deal with number concepts.

XIX. Valid methods of instruction vary from one learner to another, hence the goal of equitable educational opportunity can be approached only when schooling provides—at least in some respects—experiences that are different for each student.

XX. Traditional instructional methods should be expanded to include problem-solving approaches, and their emphasis on cognition and on valuing should be renewed.

XXI. Interdisciplinary learning should be stressed and the art of comprehending and anticipating complex relationships should be fostered.

XXII. Good vocational or occupational education should be more thoroughly permeated by the content of a general or "liberalizing" education; conversely, it should be recognized that a sound liberal education also will be inherently vocational in the years ahead.

XXIII. Because human differences and educational uniformity cannot be reconciled, the testing and measurement of content skills should be evaluated on an individual basis.

XXIV. There is a need to teach the concept of alternative futures since, lacking a desirable image of tomorrow's possible worlds, one lacks purpose, goals, and the motivating spirit of community that are needed to serve as guides to action.

XXV. Instruction in subject matter fields should develop a deepening understanding of contemporary threats to the biosphere, include socially useful service in its maintenance, and communicate to youth the need for achieving balance or equilibrium between humans and their environment.

XXVI. So that desirable alternative futures can be envisioned, work in the social studies should be redesigned so as to promote a grasp of human geography and of planetary cultures as they exist today.

XXVII. In studying possible futures, the natural and physical sciences, both in content and methodology, should serve as illustrations of truth-validating inquiry.

XXVIII. In the symbolic sciences—language arts, foreign language, mathematics, linguistics, and the like—more heed should be given both to basic communication skills as well as to the ability to recognize propaganda, shoddy advertising, and political doubletalk.

The twenty-eight premises appear to involve creating and strengthening five abilities or capacities in learners:

1. An in-depth knowledge of the world and its peoples; a knowledge of realities.
2. Awareness of *alternative* solutions to problems, a requisite in a world in which compromise and persuasion must replace force.
3. Sensitivity to the consequences of one's choices.
4. Insights and values that support wise *choices* among alternatives.
5. Skills, information, and motivation that are necessary for implementation of choices.[13]

13. Ibid., pp. 69–70.

In summary, Shane concluded: "A knowledge of realities, of alternative solutions and their consequences, the ability to choose wisely and to carry out ideas—these talents, acquired from warm and understanding teachers, seem to capture the spirit of the premises of both the adult and youth panelists."[14]

Tomorrow's Teacher

Just as future schools and curricula are destined to change, so tomorrow's teacher needs to change in many respects. Three roles of tomorrow's teacher—as a member of the teaching profession, as an instructional leader, and as a self-renewing professional—are presented.

As a Member of the Profession

Our American school system has become an extremely complex establishment. It is likely to become even more so in the future. By the year 2000, this educational establishment could well include:

2,100,000	public classroom teachers
750,000	faculty in higher education
300,000	paraprofessionals in public schools
224,000	nonpublic elementary and secondary teachers
150,000	miscellaneous (U.S. Office of Education, state departments of education, nonprofit educational organizations, etc.)
3,524,000	total educators

Futuristic questions that might be asked about the role of the teacher as a member of this large and complex profession include the following:

- Will teachers organize into a more unified and more powerful association or union in the future?
- What will a teacher's salary be in the future?
- What will tomorrow's teacher receive by way of fringe and retirement benefits?
- How much academic freedom will future teachers have?
- To what extent will teachers be held accountable in the future?
- What will employment prospects be for future teachers?
- Will teachers strike more or less often?
- What does the future hold in the areas of merit pay and tenure for teachers?
- What will be the length of the teacher's work day, week, and year in the future?
- What changes may be in store for future educational administrators and specialists (principals, superintendents, guidance counselors, supervisors, department chairpersons)?

The authors feel the following changes—among others—are likely to occur within the profession.

14. Ibid., p. 70.

- Teachers are likely to form better organized and more powerful associations or unions. This, in turn, will probably lead to better pay and improved working conditions for teachers.
- Employment prospects for teachers will probably remain poor for a long time—that is, supply will exceed demand for new teachers.
- Academic freedom, accountability, and tenure for tomorrow's teacher will probably not be radically different from what it is today.
- Professional organizations will become increasingly more political and activist.

As an Instructional Leader

In what ways will the day-by-day work of tomorrow's teacher change? In light of the expected changes in the school curriculum, the structure of the school, the nature of the learner, and teaching methodology already discussed, we anticipate that the role and behavior of teachers will change. More than in the past, teachers are apt to be developers of values, resource finders, learning diagnosticians, interdisciplinary specialists, human relations developers, career and leisure counselors, professional leaders, utilizers of futuristic processes, and teaching-learning specialists.[15] These expanded and creative roles will enhance the status of the teaching profession. As they prepare to become teachers for the future, those entering the teaching profession will be challenged.

As a Self-renewing Professional

The concept of self-renewal for teachers has received a good deal of attention during recent years. As the term implies, self-renewal deals with a teacher's continuous efforts to improve his or her professional skills and to keep abreast of the most recent developments in education. Self-renewal also suggests that a teacher must be able to constantly change as society and schools change.

Concerning the future self-renewal of teachers, one might ask:

- How can our teacher-training institutions best prepare teachers for tomorrow—teachers who will be capable of continuous self-renewal?
- How important will teacher-renewal be in the future? Will we be able to afford it?
- What conditions facilitate teacher self-renewal?
- What criteria will a future teacher be able to use in determining his or her need for self-renewal? What standards will guide the direction of a teacher's quest for renewal?

Although these are extremely difficult questions, answering them will provide exciting and challenging opportunities for future educators.

15. Joel L. Burdin, ''Futurism as a Focus in Instructional Planning,'' *Journal of Teacher Education* 25 (summer 1974): 146–147.

Who will control and finance the schools of the future? (*Photograph by Frank Siteman, Stock, Boston*)

The future is a paradox—frightening, yet exciting; predictable, yet unpredictable; inviting, yet foreboding; manageable, yet uncontrollable. How should educators approach the future? Perhaps we can take a cue from the unknown philosopher who suggests:

> You and I, since first we set out upon this strange, uncertain pilgrimage; we picked our way through the Slough of Despond and found that the bogs and quagmires were but figments of our imagination; we have visited the City of Despair and found it walled in only by its own fantasies of Space and Time; we have confronted the Lions of Automata and discovered them to be ephemera, the mirror image of our own minds; we have traversed the Valley of Paradise and eaten of its strange fruit, Leisure. Now, we have but a little further to go and our pilgrimage will be at an end. We must cross the Delectable Mountains. They may seem far away, shimmering there; but that

is an accident of our eyesight. They really are right here under our feet, if we will but look. Like the Chinese journey of a thousand miles, we shall approach them one step at a time. Shall we go? Now?

Summary and Implications

As society changes in the future, so will its means of educating its student population. The kinds of students pursuing education, the educators, the system of organization, the curriculum, and instructional methods all will change.

It is clear that more children below age five and more adults will be involved in public education. These new student populations will provide teaching positions that have not existed to any great extent in the past. The positions will become available both to beginning teachers specifically trained for them and to experienced teachers who may wish to prepare for them through inservice training. The role of the teacher for adult students will be modified not only because of the nature of these learners but also because of the nature of their attendance. Adults, in particular, are likely to be part-time students who are not available for instruction during traditional daytime hours when they are typically at work. It is also quite likely that the future location of the place of instruction will differ from the traditional school or classroom. Instruction will probably take place in business, factory, and community locations other than schools.

The system of education will become more individualized and personalized. Greater recognition will be given to differing abilities, achievements, and learning styles. Teachers will increasingly become learning diagnosticians, prescription specialists, and resource finders —as they guide their students in learning. The new curricula will be designed to prepare students to live in the future—and to help ensure that the future is livable. Tomorrow's teachers have significant work ahead—to encourage and challenge their students and to enhance their lives.

Discussion Questions

1. To what degree and in what ways do you feel teacher organizations, such as the NEA and the AFT, will change in the future?

2. What do you think future adult education programs will be like in America?

3. Do you believe that schools of the future should take the lead in helping to bring about social change or should simply serve society by transmitting the existing culture to our children? Defend your viewpoint.

4. Discuss what major functions you feel our elementary schools should perform in the next twenty years.

5. What are the major problems that you feel our public educational system will face in the year 2000?

Supplemental Activities

1. Make a list of forecasts about future schools. State several assumptions upon which each forecast is based.
2. Interview a retired teacher concerning the changes that have occurred in teaching during his or her career.
3. Discuss the future of teacher organizations with an educator who is a member of either the NEA or the AFT.
4. Compile a list of the ways in which future teachers might engage in self-renewal.
5. Interview a leader of a teacher organization to explore the role of his or her organization in encouraging teacher self-renewal in the future.

Bibliography

Clarke, S. C. T., and Coutts, H. T. "Toward Teacher Education in the Year 2000," *The Alberta Journal of Educational Research* 21 (December 1975): 221–240.

Galtung, Johan. "Schooling and the Future Society." *School Review* 83 (August 1975): 533–568.

Hipple, Theodore W. *The Future of Education 1975–2000*. Pacific Palisades, Calif.: Goodyear, 1974.

Howsam, Robert B; Corrigan, Dean C.; Denemark, George W.; and Nash, Robert J. *Educating a Profession*. Washington, D.C.: American Association of Colleges for Teacher Education, 1976.

Kauffman, Draper L. *Futurism and Future Studies*. Washington, D.C.: National Education Association, 1976.

Rubin, Louis, ed. *The Future of Education: Perspectives on Tomorrow's Schooling*. Boston: Allyn and Bacon, 1975.

Shane, Harold G. *Curriculum Change toward the 21st Century*. Washington, D.C.: National Education Association, 1977.

Shane, Harold G. *The Educational Significance of the Future*. Bloomington, Ind.: Phi Delta Kappa, 1973.

Shane, Harold G., and Weaver, Roy A. "Education as a Lifelong Process." *Vital Issues* 24 (June 1975): 1–4.

Toffler, Alvin, ed. *Learning for Tomorrow: The Role of the Future in Education*. New York: Vintage, 1974.

Index